GENESIS

THE MOVIE

GENESIS

THE MOVIE

Robert Farrar Capon

WILLIAM B. EERDMANS PUBLISHING COMPANY
GRAND RAPIDS, MICHIGAN / CAMBRIDGE, U.K.

Wm. B. Eerdmans Publishing Co.
255 Jefferson Ave. S.E., Grand Rapids, Michigan 49503 /
P.O. Box 163, Cambridge CB3 9PU U.K.
www.eerdmans.com

Printed in the United States of America

07 06 05 04 03   7 6 5 4 3 2 1

Library of Congress Cataloging-in-Publication Data

Capon, Robert Farrar.
Genesis: the movie / Robert Farrar Capon.
p.   cm.
ISBN 0-8028-6094-X (alk. paper)
1. Bible. O.T. Genesis I-III — Commentaries.   I. Title.

BS1235.53.C37   2003
222′.11077 — dc21

2003049064

Scripture quotations in this publication marked KJV are from the King James Version of the Bible.

Scripture quotations in this publication marked RSV are from the Revised Standard Version of the Bible, copyrighted 1946, 1952 © 1971, 1973 by the Division of Christian Education of the National Council of Churches of Christ in the U.S.A., and used by permission.

Scripture quotations in this publication marked NRSV are from the New Revised Standard Version of the Bible, copyright © 1989 by the Division of Christian Education of the National Council of Churches of Christ in the U.S.A., and used by permission.

For Valerie
My first reader
My best friend
My love

CONTENTS

INTERMISSION

CREATION FLOURISHING
ON ITS OWN GROUND
Genesis 2:4-25

Contents

A CHAT BEFORE WE BEGIN

I've titled this book *Genesis, the Movie* in the hope of giving you a new out-look on an old habit. Instead of urging you to *read* the Bible as a book of the-ology or a manual of ethics, I'm going to suggest that you *watch* it as a film. But since you'll need to change the way your mind approaches Scripture in order to make that switch, here's a little exercise in perception to help you. Look at this drawing and see what you come up with:

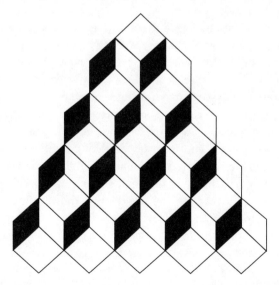

If you're like most people, your reaction to the diamond shapes in the pic-ture was to see them as a pyramid of *ten* blocks. But you came to that conclusion only because your mind's eye led you to make certain assumptions. At first glance, it told you that the drawing was to be read as a three-dimensional representation of white blocks with shadows on them. But at the same time, it also suggested that the shadows were being cast by a lamp located *above* and slightly *behind* the blocks, shining down on them from the upper left-hand corner of the frame. In short, you assumed that they were stacked on the *floor* of a room.

However (and here comes the switch), if you can now talk your eye into revising its assumption about the source of light, you'll get a dramatically different picture. If you put the lamp *below* and slightly *in front* of the blocks — and shining up at them from the lower right-hand corner of the frame — you'll suddenly see an upside-down pyramid of *fourteen* blocks hanging from the *ceiling* of a room. To be sure, this will be only a trick of perception. But since it makes a wonderful analogy to my suggestion that you *watch* the Bible as a movie, here are the parallels between the two.

First, just as the switch you made in your perception of the original drawing didn't change the contents of the drawing itself, so your switch to my cinematic view of the Bible will change nothing in the Bible. Unlike certain liberal approaches to Scripture, it won't require you to discount even a single line in the original text. If you didn't have to remove elements of my drawing that were "wrong" in order get the "right" view of it, you certainly won't have to get rid of "out-dated" or "unhistorical" parts of Scripture to see it as the greatest movie of history ever made.

Second, just as you managed to see both ten blocks and fourteen blocks in my original picture (and to realize that both counts were true), so you'll be able to find the contradictory facts in the Bible equally true. You'll discover that there's no single, literal sense in which every word of the Bible has to be read. As you were free to see in my drawing as many blocks as your right brain could tally up, so you'll be free (as some conservatives are not) to draw from the movie of Scripture as many senses as your believing mind can fairly find in it. Almost magically, then — simply by taking a different "slant" on the same thing — you'll be delivered from both the literalism of the left and the literalism of the right. Changing the angle of your approach to my drawing gave you four more blocks than you saw the first time around. Changing the angle of your approach to the Bible will give you at least two more reasons for not listening to people who insist on missing its point.

What this book provides you with, therefore, is precisely a new slant on Scripture. Here's just one example of how it works when you apply it to the question of the Bible's *historicity*. Ultra-conservatives may have told you that every scrap of biblical history must be taken as something that actually happened; and ultra-liberals may have warned you that large swatches of that history are just plain non-historical. But if you can find the new ground I'm suggesting, you'll take yourself right off their hopeless battlefield. Because when you're watching a movie, the only thing you need to accept about its historicity is that its events have been happening before your very eyes. No film (not even a documentary) can be judged on the basis of the "real facts" that might or might not lie behind it. A good film is a historical fact all by itself — and if it's a great film, as the Bible is, it can give you more historical truths than any mere list of events ever could.

For history is not just a sequential narration of occurrences. That would be only *chronicle*. And it would wear out your patience before it gave you even a shred of historical understanding. History isn't something *outside* yourself that you can dig up by shoveling your way through past events. Rather, it's something *inside* you, in your mind. You don't find it lying around in things that have happened; you create it by thinking, speaking, and writing about what's happened. And since history doesn't exist until you think it up, those happenings have no history of their own to give you. Above all, they have no history that can nullify the history you decide to give them. You can and will be judged, of course, by fellow historians; but only on the basis of the differences between their histories and yours, not on the grounds that theirs present factual events where yours have only fictional ones. Fact and fiction, you see, are not opposites in the history business; they're . . .

But whoa! I'm on the verge of reproducing the whole book instead of introducing it to you. Let me shift gears abruptly and give you a little background on the sources I've used in writing *Genesis, the Movie.*

*   *   *

My comments in this book are based on a careful study of every verse in six texts of the first three chapters of the book of Genesis — all of which you will find printed out as I take up the parts of the two creation stories those chapters contain. For the original Hebrew, I've used the *Biblia Hebraica Stuttgartensis* (abbreviated BHS). The Greek (LXX) is taken from the Rahlfs edition of the *LXX Septuaginta*, and the Latin comes from the *Biblia Sacra iuxta Vulgatam Versionem*, edited by R. Weber et al. (abbreviated VUL). For the English texts, I've used the King James Version (KJV), the Revised Standard Version (RSV), and the New Revised Standard Version (NRSV). When I quote Scripture, I generally follow either the KJV or the RSV — often giving key words in Hebrew, Greek, and Latin, and sometimes citing the NRSV for comparison. Frequently, though, I've taken the liberty of supplying my own translations (abbreviated RFC).

But I'll be giving you more than just the biblical texts and my comments on them. My principal source of inspiration will be Augustine, the Bishop of Hippo (354-430), whom I've been reading in Latin for over fifty years now. If you'll allow me a brief digression, I'll tell you how it all started. In my final year of seminary, I held the exalted rank of Senior Library Prefect. And at the end of that year, in the basement of the library, I discovered a damaged duplicate set of all of Augustine's works in the Migne edition of the Latin Patrology. I asked the head librarian how much he would charge me to take it off his hands. He said, "Name your price." I said, "Fifty cents a volume." He said, "Fine" — and ever since I've had all fifteen volumes on my shelves.

In preparing to write this book, I found my youthful infatuation with Augustine rekindled. In particular, I fell in love with two of his books that bear directly on my subject matter: his *Confessions* (Books XI through XIII of which contain his commentary on the first three verses of Genesis), and his *On Genesis to the Letter* (which covers the first three chapters of Genesis). I quote from these often; and when the passages I cite appear, you'll usually find them in both the original Latin and English. The Latin is from my bargain Patrology, the Benedictine edition of *Sancti Aurelii Augustini, Hipponensis Episcopi, Opera Omnia* (Paris, 1841). The passages from his *Confessionum Libri Tredecim* are from Volume I; and those from his *De Genesi ad Litteram* are from Volume III. All the English translations are my own.

But in addition to going back to Augustine, I've quoted from my old friend Thomas Aquinas (in his *Summa Theologica*, Rome, 1894) and from my favorite mother of the church, the Lady Julian of Norwich (in her *Revelations of Divine Love*, Methuen & Co. Ltd., 13th ed., 1949). But I've also borrowed from more recent writers — particularly poets. My source for the poems of Marianne Moore, Edna St. Vincent Millay, Gerard Manley Hopkins, Francis Thompson, and James Stephens is *A Little Treasury of Modern Poetry*, edited by Oscar Williams (Charles Scribner's Sons, 1946). The many quotations from T. S. Eliot are taken from *The Complete Poems and Plays* (Harcourt Brace Jovanovich, 1952); those from Joseph Addison's hymn "The Spacious Firmament on High" and from Henry Hart Milman's "Ride on, Ride on in Majesty" are from *The Hymnal* (The Church Hymnal Corporation, 1982); and the passage from John Donne's sermon delivered on Christmas Eve in 1624 is from *The Complete Poetry and Selected Prose of John Donne* (The Modern Library, 1946). Finally, the brief quotations from W. H. Auden's poems ("Compline" from *Horae Canonicae* and "Caliban to the Audience") are taken from *Selected Poetry of W. H. Auden* (The Modern Library, 1958).

Incidentally, I served with Auden on the committee of the Episcopal General Convention charged with revising the Psalms for the 1979 Book of

Common Prayer. He was on the committee because the Psalms, being poetry, called for the most significant poet we could find; I was there mostly to keep an eye on the Latin behind Myles Coverdale's 1540 English Psalter — which in 1549 became part of the First Prayer Book of Edward VI.

In any event, I got more from Auden than the committee got out of me. By the time he joined us, we'd been meeting three or four times a year for a week at a time, usually at a seminary. Our chairman, Canon Charles Guilbert, was a genial enough fellow; but he was also a martinet about our daily sched-ule. He kept our noses to the grindstone mornings, afternoons, and evenings — with time off only for meals and a glass of his (middling) scotch after ten P.M. We never rebelled, but the strain showed. At our morning sessions, we could get through as many as thirty verses; but in the afternoons, the bones of contention reduced our output to less than twenty. In the evenings, there was so much bickering that we could barely finish five.

I tell you this because Auden's best gift to me was his flat refusal, after just one evening session, to attend any more of them. The reason he gave had nothing to do with their minimal results: he simply said that he never worked after the cocktail hour. That liberating principle struck me like a bolt from the heavens — and it's been my watchword for three decades now. Ever since meeting him, I've begged off all invitations to give after-dinner speeches, or to attend evening meetings, or to do anything else that might require me to be creative at night. The hours of darkness, as I've come to see them, are less for creation than for recreation. Only God works well in the dark, so I no longer pretend to imitate that part of his *modus operandi.* If God can end his first week's work with a seventh day off, why can't I celebrate a mini-sabbath every evening of the week? Now and then, some odd group will catch me off guard and hook me into working after dusk; but in my inner freedom, I still refuse to like it. That liberty I owe to Auden.

*   *   *

But having done my duty as a responsible writer and given you my sources, let me tell you a bit about how I came to write this book. It began to take shape (or, better said, take over my mind) almost the minute I finished my previous work, *The Fingerprints of God* (Eerdmans, 2000). This book, there-fore, is a continuation of what I was doing there — namely, *watching* the Bible as a tissue of images woven together by the Holy Spirit, not reading it as a handbook of theological, moral, or religious information. If you like, you might even consider *Genesis, the Movie* a twin of that book, since it came out of the womb of my mind, as Jacob did, with its hand gripping the heel of the brother born before it. As you may know, the name *Jacob* means "he supplants"; and that's exactly what this book did to *Fingerprints*. For a year and a half after it was published, I would find myself lecturing not on the just-issued work I'd been invited to talk about but on the one that was getting ready to steal its birthright. I suppose authors do this all the time; but if my audiences noticed it, they were kind enough not to say so.

The eighteen months I spent on the road talking about this book were also the period during which I was soaking up what Augustine had to say about Genesis. His love affair with words — and, above all, his sparkling conciseness in using them — reaffirmed my conviction that the best theology is always a game of *playing* with language until it becomes an image of the Word beyond words. Augustine is full of surprises. He doesn't give you just one take on a scriptural passage; he gives you two, four, or six — and then he tells you (as I did with my drawing) that they're all acceptable. The more questions he could raise, the happier he was. He had a roomy mind.

In fact, he was a bit like a man in a delicatessen, relentlessly shopping for items that might please his palate. For example, when he explores the Zabar's of his mind for an understanding of a passage, he often begins his sentences with the Latin word *An* (meaning "or" or "whether"). It's a word that can be translated many ways. "Or possibly" might do the trick; but so would "Or it might be that," or even the lone word "Item." But however you render it, you must respect his conviction that however many senses you might assign to a text, you don't have to discard a single one, provided only that you can hear a ring of truth in it. As E. B. Pusey noted in his translation of Augustine's *Confessions*, "Such is the depth of Holy Scripture, that manifold senses may and ought to be extracted from it, and that whatever truth can be obtained from its words does in fact lie concealed in them."

Here then are three samples of how Augustine embodies this principle. The first is from *De Genesi ad Litteram*, III, 36, where he's writing about the sixth day of creation. Note if you will the compression of his style: it's almost as if he's jotting down shorthand lecture notes rather than writing a full-blown text:

> *An forte quia sexto die perficiuntur omnia, propterea de omnibus dicendum fuit, "Vidit Deus omnia quae fecit, et ecce valde bona"; non singillatim de iis quae ipso die facta sunt?*

> Or might it be, that when all things were perfected on the sixth day, the words "God saw everything he made, and behold, it was very good" were thus said of all the days, not just singularly of the things that were made on that day itself?

For the second sample, consider this passage from *De Genesi ad Litteram*, IV, 53, in which he manages to affirm both God's *sequential* creation of particular things during the six "days" and his creation of all things *simultaneously* on "day one":

> *Imo vero et prius et posterius per sex dies quae commemorata sunt facta sunt, et simul omnia facta sunt: quia et haec Scriptura quae per memoratos dies narrat opera Dei, et illa quae simul eum dicit fecisse omnia, verax est; et utraque una est, quia uno Spiritu veritatis inspirante conscripta est.*

Indeed, it's equally true that the things commemorated by the six days are made one after another, and that all things are made simultaneously. For this Scripture [Gen. 1:6-31], which relates the works of God by recording successive days, and that other [Gen. 1:1-5], which says he made all things at once, are both true; and both are one, because Scripture was composed by a single inspiration of the Spirit of truth.

Finally, here's a somewhat longer example of the inquiring subtlety of his mind, from *De Genesi ad Litteram*, V, 36:

> *Hujus universae Dei creaturae multa non novimus, sive quae in coelis sunt altius, quam ut noster sensus ea possit attingere; sive quae in regionibus terrarum fortassis inhabitabilibus; sive quae deorsum latent, vel in profundo abyssis, vel in occultis sinibus terrae. Haec igitur antequam fierent, utique non erant. Quomodo ergo Deo nota sunt quae non erant? Et rursus quomodo ea faceret quae sibi nota non erant? Non enim quidquam fecit ignorans. NOTA ERGO FECIT, NON FACTA COGNOVIT. Proinde, antequam fierent, et erant, et non erant: erant in Dei scientia, non erant in sua natura. Ac per hoc factus est dies ille cui utroque modo innotescerent, et in Deo et in seipsis: illa vero matutina sive diurna cognitione, hac vero velut vespertina. Ipsi autem Deo non audeo dicere alio modo innotuisse, cum ea fecisset, quam illo quo ea noverat ut faceret, apud quem non est commutatio, nec momenti obumbratio.*

There are many things we do not know about this universal creation of God. They might be things above us, such as our senses might reach, or things in the regions of lands that are perhaps uninhabitable, or things that lie concealed downwards, whether in the deep of the sea or in the hidden chasms of the earth. But it's also true that before these things came into being, they were altogether nonexistent. How then were things that did not exist known to God? And then again, how could he make things that were not known to him? For he made nothing in ignorance. HE MADE THINGS HE ALREADY KNEW; HE DIDN'T HAVE TO WAIT TILL THEY WERE MADE IN ORDER TO KNOW THEM. Therefore, before they came into being, they both were and were not. They were, in the knowledge of God; and they were not, in their own nature. And for this reason that day was made ["day one," Gen. 1:5] by which these truths might become known in a double way — namely, both in God and in things themselves: in the former, by a morning or daytime knowing, and in the latter, by an evening one. But with regard to God himself, I dare not say that when he makes those things, they become known to him in any other way than that in which he knows those things in order that he might make them — he, with whom there is no variableness, neither shadow of turning.

The whole of that passage bears so directly on this book that it could serve as an introduction all by itself. But I capitalized a single sentence of it so you might share my heart's astonishment at Augustine's writing. My translation is more or less adequate to its sense, but it took me twenty words to do what he did in six. As a cook myself, I can recognize a master chef when I see one. To me, those six words are the theological equivalent of *glace de viande*, the potent meat extract made by boiling down quarts and quarts of beef stock until they're reduced to a mere pint of thick syrup. After it's been refrigerated, it has the outward sheen of dark brown skin and the texture of a rubber sole. So too with Augustine's prose; only here he produces a concentrate that has the density of uranium. He may plod along for pages, but every now and then, he stuns you with something so elegantly condensed that it takes your breath away. He makes me think of lines from T. S. Eliot's *East Coker:*

> And what there is to conquer
> By strength and submission, has already been discovered
> Once or twice, or several times, by men whom one cannot hope
> To emulate — but there is no competition —
> There is only the fight to recover what has been lost
> And found and lost again and again: and now, under conditions
> That seem unpropitious. But perhaps neither gain nor loss.
> For us, there is only the trying. The rest is not our business.

But be all that as it may, you now have my book before you. I wish you Godspeed and good luck — or any other luck you may have with it. Just remember what Charles Williams once said: "All luck is holy."

THE FILM IN GOD'S MIND

ONE

The Director

In my new, cinematic image for the Bible, the film of Genesis begins in silence, with a black screen. First, the film's Hebrew title appears, scrolling up from the bottom. It holds for a few seconds in the center, then rolls up and off the screen. The credits follow in the same way:

בְּרֵאשִׁית

A TRINITY FILM

Produced by

GOD THE FATHER

Starring

THE FATHER'S ETERNAL WORD

and Directed by

THE HOLY SPIRIT

Then, with the screen still black, we hear various narrators' voices begin to speak the opening lines of Genesis:

[1]In the beginning God created the heavens and the earth.

[2]And the earth was without form and void, and darkness was upon the face of the deep; and the Spirit of God was moving upon the face of the waters. [3]And God said, "Let there be light"; and there was light. [4]And God saw that the light was good; and God separated the light from the darkness. [5]And God called the light Day, and the darkness he called Night. And there was evening and there was morning, one day.

Only then, as the narrators reach verse 6, do we see the screen begin slowly to lighten. Music (Vivaldi's *Four Seasons*) comes up underneath.

[6]And God said, "Let there be a firmament in the midst of the waters, and let it separate the waters from the waters."

Dimly at first, then more and more clearly, we begin to see the previously dark waters, and we watch as the firmament, like an expanding, translucent arch, lifts the waters above it from the waters below until there is a brilliant, clear space between them — and we hear the narrators again:

> ⁷And God made the firmament and separated the waters which were under the firmament from the waters which were above the firmament. And it was so. ⁸And God called the firmament Heaven. And there was evening and there was morning, a second day.

*   *   *

For the moment, that may be enough to give you a hint of what I have in mind. We're just eight verses into the book of Genesis, but it's obvious that the Director has her film-making well in hand. I've made her a woman not only because the Hebrew word for the *Spirit* she represents is feminine (*rûach*) but also because Liv Ullmann, whom I admire as an actress, has recently delighted me by directing her first film, *Faithless.* You and I, however, have some background work to do if we're to appreciate precisely what this movie's Spirit-Director is up to. Above all, she's a *poet.* Her filming of the scenes of Genesis isn't just a matter of cobbling together a whole whose parts continue to be what they were before she filmed them. She's making an entirely new whole that lifts its parts to another level of reality.

A chair manufacturer, for example, creates his product from wood, glue, stain, varnish, and cloth; but in the finished article, the wood is still wood, the glue is still glue, and the stain, varnish, and cloth remain what they were by nature. A poet, on the other hand, creates with nothing but language. But her words transcend themselves. They become *images* with powers that mere words can never have. Consider, for instance, Edna St. Vincent Millay's "Elegy Before Death":

> Oh, there will pass with your great passing
>   Little of beauty not your own, —
> Only the light from common water,
>   Only the grace from simple stone.

In those lines, *light* and *grace* have leapt up from the stage of physical and theological jargon and risen into images of grief over a love that cannot last. And the bare facts of *common water* and *simple stone* have danced themselves into icons of the same hard reality. The poet, you see, uses them as artistic *fictions* ("fiction" is from the Latin *fingo, finxi, fictum:* "to stroke, fashion, form; to arrange in order") — and she fashions them into signs that have a new significance. Indeed, she makes them into *sacraments,* into *real presences* of a hitherto unrecognized reality.

To help you see more clearly this device by which fictions can be as true as facts, I'm going to print out for you Marianne Moore's blank verse masterpiece entitled, fittingly enough, "Poetry." But if I may, I'll take two liberties with the original. Wherever the word *poetry* appears, I'll follow it with the word *Scripture* in square brackets; and wherever the word *poets* occurs, I'll do the same thing, following it with *preachers.* With that note tucked in your mind's pocket, I think you'll find her poem a splendid guide to the poetry of *Genesis, the Movie:*

> **Poetry [Scripture]**
>
> *I,* too, dislike it: there are things that are important beyond all this fiddle.
> Reading it, however, with a perfect contempt for it, one discovers in
> it after all, a place for the genuine.
> > Hands that can grasp, eyes
> > that can dilate, hair that can rise
> > > if it must, these things are important not because a
>
> high-sounding interpretation can be put upon them but because they are
> > useful. When they become so derivative as to become unintelligible,
> > the same thing may be said for all of us, that we
> > > do not admire what
> > > we cannot understand: the bat
> > > > holding on upside down or in quest of something to
>
> eat, elephants pushing, a wild horse taking a roll, a tireless wolf under
> > a tree, the immovable critic twitching his skin like a
> > > horse that feels a flea, the base-
> > ball fan, the statistician —
> > > nor is it valid
> > > > to discriminate against "business documents and
>
> school-books"; all these phenomena are important. One must make
> > > a distinction
> > however: when dragged into prominence by half-poets [preachers],
> the result is not poetry [Scripture],

nor till the poets [preachers] among us can be
  "literalists of
the imagination" — above
    insolence and triviality and can present

for inspection, imaginary gardens with real toads in them, shall we have
  it [Scripture]. In the meantime, if you demand on the one hand
  the raw material of poetry [Scripture] in
    all its rawness and that which is on the other hand
      genuine, then you are interested in poetry [Scripture].

*   *   *

On the very last page of my previous book, *The Fingerprints of God,* I quoted this poem's lines about "literalists of the imagination" and "imaginary gardens with real toads in them"; and I said that for me, they solved all the problems of biblical criticism. I stand by that here. In our Bible studies, we've spent far too much time worrying the bone of whether this or that passage of Scripture was factual or fictional — on the silly assumption that all facts are true and all fictions false. But that got us nowhere but into trouble. For example, when we dealt with the first chapter of Genesis, we found ourselves forced to conclude that because its literal details couldn't be squared with the theory of evolution or the cosmogony of modern astrophysics, we had to choose between the Bible and science. If we felt that the Bible was literally true, science had to be false. If we thought science was right, the Bible had to be wrong.

Since I'll be referring frequently to both cosmogony and cosmology, I think we should make friends with the etymologies and definitions of both words. *Cosmogony* is a compound of two Greek words: *kosmos* (the ordered world, the universe) and *gonos* (offspring, procreation, seed; generation, reproduction; the manner of a specified thing's coming into being). Webster's Unabridged defines it as follows:

> **Cosmogony 1:** the creation, origination, or manner of coming into being of the world or universe **2:** a theory or account of the origination of the universe <a primitive ~> **3:** a part of the science of astronomy that deals with the origin and development of the universe and its components.

Cosmology is another such compound, made up of *kosmos* (as above) and *-logy* (from *logos:* word, reason, speech, account; oral or written expression; doctrine, theory, science; discourse, treatise). The dictionary defines it thus:

Cosmology 1: a branch of systematic philosophy [or of systematic theology, I might add] that deals with the character of the universe as a cosmos by combining speculative metaphysics and scientific knowledge; . . . compare ONTOLOGY **2:** a particular theory or body of doctrine relating to the natural order.

To put the difference between the two in my own words, a cosmogony purports to be an account of *how creation happened*, while a cosmology tries to give the reason *why it exists* — or, in the case of a theological cosmology, *by whom it was made*. The thrust of cosmogony tends to be *physical*: it tries to describe the original conditions out of which the world of time and space arose. The thrust of cosmology, on the other hand, is mostly *metaphysical*. If it's a scientific cosmology, it seeks to investigate the philosophical roots of those beginning conditions; and if it's a theological one, it tries to get back to the Beginner who made all things out of nothing.

But since that *nothing*, that *nihil*, just isn't there at all, no one can investigate it. Not scientists, because the condition of the universe before the Big Bang is beyond the scope of their method; and not theologians, because the question of what God was doing "before" he made the heavens and the earth is a theological non-starter. In both instances, therefore, they're like the man who tried to reach a tree by going half the distance each time he started toward it. By definition, he never arrived at the tree. And by the same token, the closer they get to the original "nothing tree," the more clearly they'll see the unbridgeable gulf that stands between them and it.

Accordingly, cosmogony is the province of scientists, mythmakers, and poets (each of whom can often be skilled in the others' fields), while cosmology is the province of philosophers, theologians, and poets (ditto). As you can see, the only practitioners who are completely at home in both provinces are the poets.

But no poet like our Director would waste her talents on the lazy habit of seeing the first chapter of Genesis as literal cosmogony. The only literalism she will allow is Marianne Moore's *literalism of the imagination*. Any other kind is just a dead end — a road that can never open up the mystery of creation. Still, it's a road on which fundamentalism has often found itself trapped.

Historically, fundamentalism is a recent development, an early twentieth-century phenomenon that at least had the virtue of taking the Bible's words seriously. But the literalism that so often came hand in hand with it had no virtue whatsoever when it was made the only way to read the Bible. In fact, however, the literal approach to Scripture predates fundamentalism by some three hundred years. The thinkers who first set the stage for it were rationalists of the late seventeenth and eighteenth centuries who objected to the Bible's miracles because they couldn't see them as literal facts of history. But during the nineteenth century, the response of many believers to such skepticism was simply to stamp their feet and say, "They really *are* literal facts of history, and we're going to believe every one of them, no matter what you say. So there!"

Needless to say, that was the beginning of the much-touted war between science and religion, and it was a disaster for everybody. Literalists and anti-literalists alike went forth conquering and to conquer. "Truth itself is on the line," they said, "and we're willing to die for it!" But as it turned out, they didn't die for the truth of Scripture (which went grandly on being whatever kind of truth it pleased); they died in the trenches of their own narrowness — and they were buried in the common ditch of literalism. That's what happens when you let your enemy choose the field of battle: even if you think you're winning, you're losing.

Luckily, though, for the sixteen centuries before that war, almost no Christians let themselves fall into that ditch. If a "literal history" view of some portion of the Bible gave them problems, they felt quite free to assign other senses to it: a moral sense, perhaps; or a spiritual, mystical, or anagogical one. Still, since that approach too had its limitations and excesses, I feel just as free to urge my Bible-as-film approach upon you.

For a movie is always a historical experience quite on its own, even if it shows us only fictional events. While you're watching it on the screen — and in particular, when you're going over it in your mind after you've taken in all of its images — you're perfectly aware that what you see before you didn't necessarily have to happen on land or sea in order for you to enjoy the film as a historical experience. If it contains footage of a "perfect storm," for example, the fact that the actors weren't really exposed to such wild weather doesn't bother you in the least. The storm, as you watch it in the safety of your theater or living room, terrifies you almost as much as the real thing would.

In fact, even if the movie is a documentary, filmed strictly from scenes of real life, you're still being asked to accept its director's fictional juxtaposition of those scenes as factual history. While you're aware that what you're watching is "just a movie," the new configuration into which the director has put his materials gives them a life that's as real as the popcorn you're eating. The only caveat you must keep in mind is that this applies only to a documentary that's a brilliant piece of film-making. Take Ken Burns's series *The Civil War* as an instance. It consists only of still photographs taken on the battlefields of the time; but, fascinatingly, those non-moving pictures become a great motion picture by force of the director's art. Through his poetry, the stills acquire a *moving* life of their own on the screen.

And that's true of the biblical movie as well. In the Director's hands, its antique photos come alive despite their stilted poses. You may think, for example, that she shouldn't have included her scenes of vegetation sprouting up on the third day of creation before she brought on the sun to promote photosynthesis on the fourth. But she's making history here, not writing a seventh-grade science text. In fact, if you cast about in the film as it now exists in your mind, you'll find that she's pre-empted your objection. You'll notice that she's put the first creation of light on day one, thus anticipating your problem. And if that's not enough for you, think again. Light is actually electromagnetic radiation. It doesn't foster growth because it can be seen. (It can't be: it's invisible till it hits something other than empty space — and even then, you can see only a few of its frequencies.) Light makes plants grow just by being the radiant energy it is.

At the point we've reached in the film so far, of course, the physical world is just as invisible as the light. Throughout the first five verses of Genesis, darkness remains on the face of the deep — and on everything else. But even before the creation of the light in verse three, the Spirit has been warming the unseen creation. Like a mother hen, she's been *brooding* over the world since verse 2. (*Brooding* is a translation, based on the Syriac of *m'rachepheth,* meaning "moving, borne upon, borne over.") As a matter of fact, throughout day one, the earth is *invisible and unformed,* as the Greek Old Testament (the Septuagint) translates *tohû vabhohû,* "without form and void" (KJV). Nevertheless, although darkness reigns everywhere, the world as it exists in the Mind of God is still in the right place to absorb the invisible light he's already brought forth in his divine Intellect.

Better yet, though, you don't have to think that the Director is trying to give you any information, scientific or otherwise, about such matters. Her film is poetry: you don't have to reconcile it with anything outside itself. It's governed only by her unique talent, not by what you think she ought to be telling you. There's a line from a golf commercial put out by the PGA that may help here. After some scenes of Tiger Woods or Phil Mickelson making incredible drives and putts, the words "These guys are good" appear on the screen. That doesn't mean professional golfers are smart, or wise, or virtuous. It means only that they play the game better than almost anyone else — that they have a sixth sense for golf — and that no intellectual analysis of what they do is going to help you if you don't have that sense to begin with. So also with the Director of *Genesis, the Movie:* this gal is good too. Forget about trying to fathom her philosophy, improve her theology, or correct her science.

You don't have to understand or agree with anything she shows you. You have only to admire her game — and then *play,* as best you can, with the moves she's flashed before you.

*   *   *   **

It's the loss of that sense of play that's been our biggest hindrance since the advent of "higher" biblical criticism. Even today, many preachers are still stuck in the skepticism they picked up from that discipline. In their seminary days, they were more or less urged to shy away from the kind of exposition I've just been giving you. For one thing, having been taught that miracles must always be taken with many grains of salt, they let themselves be cajoled into writing them off as romantic fictions suitable only for less enlightened times. For another, they were led to think that because the six-day account of creation in Genesis 1 doesn't conform to our notion of science, it has to be dismissed as an outmoded cosmogony. But that flies in the face of the fact that most modern cosmogonists (and cosmologists too, I might add) have long since made friends with such poetic notions as indeterminacy, strangeness, charm, quarks, and broken symmetry when they hunt for the mysteries at the hidden recesses of matter.

But in ecclesiastical quarters, it was precisely our loss of that sense of poetry that most vitiated our preaching. Our seminary professors generally wrote off such image-play as mere allegorizing — as an imposition of alien interpretations on the text rather than a legitimate, if poetic, way of getting to its truth. But images are not allegories. They don't *mean* something other than what they are; they *are* something other than what they literally mean.

In the whole sweep of the biblical film, we can't properly grasp even the first image in Genesis, *b'reshith,* "in the beginning" (*en archēi* in the Septuagint; *in principio* in the Vulgate) until we've wrestled with all the repetitions of the word *beginning* in the Bible. First of all, we need to listen to the echo of that word as John puts it into the opening line of his Gospel: "In the beginning [*en archēi*] was the Word, and the Word was with God, and the Word was God. He was in the beginning [*en archēi*] with God. All things were made by him, and without him not a single thing was made" (John 1:1-3, RFC).

But we need to go further than that. We need to grapple with the cryptic words by which Jesus declares *himself* to be the Beginning in John 8:25. The context of this verse is important. John 8:12-30 contains a cantankerous dialogue that the Pharisees have with Jesus when they question his authority for claiming to be the light of the world. They first call him a liar because he has nothing but his own testimony to stand on (8:13). Jesus replies that he's not

11

alone: he and the Father are both testifying, and so he's not a liar because the Torah says that the testimony of two witnesses is true (8:14-18). But then he gives them another problem. He tells them he's going someplace they can't go (8:21). And when they wonder about this, he says "You are from below, I am from above; you are of this world, I am not of this world"(8:23, RFC).

Last of all, though (in 8:25), the Pharisees become completely confused: they ask him, "Who *are* you?" And Jesus, even though he's exasperated by their denseness, finally sees an opening for his punch line. But since there are almost as many translations of his reply as there are translators, let me give you the Greek of his reply first, and then the English in three versions:

GNT: *Tēn archēn ho ti kai lalō hymin.* [?]
KJV: "Even *the same* that I said to you from the beginning."
RSV: "Even what I have told you from the beginning."
NRSV: "Why do I speak to you at all?"

As you can see, some take this as a statement, some as a question. (The Greek has a question mark in some editions, the NRSV puts it in the text itself, and the RSV puts one in a footnote.) Furthermore, the word *beginning* here *(archēn)* is an accusative of time implying that the action of the verb covers the entire period — hence the KJV and RSV, "from the beginning." If I had to take a guess, the NRSV's theology-shy translation (avoiding *beginning* altogether) is relying on a usage for which it finds support in *koinē* Greek.

Taking it all in all, then, my own shot at the passage would be either "The Beginning, which is what I've been telling you all along," or "The Beginning, but why do I even bother talking to you?" (My capitalization of "Beginning" comes straight out of Augustine: that's how the Benedictine edition prints his Latin word: *Principium.* If you like, look over the whole passage in John 8 and decide for yourself.)

In the end, though, it's not until chapter 21 of Revelation that we clearly see the word *Beginning* in Genesis as an image of the Word of God himself whom the Director has had in mind all along. At the culmination of the movie, she has Jesus say, "Behold, I make all things new" (21:5). And then, in 21:6, she sums up her entire film by giving him these words: "I am the Alpha and the Omega [*to Alpha kai to Ō*], the Beginning and the Ending [*hē archē kai to telos*]." Unless we suspend judgment until that point in the picture, we'll never arrive at the *Word* whom the Director was showing us in the first place — and we certainly won't be of much use to her in the pulpit.

* * *

At this point (what with my complaints about literalism and my free-wheeling approach to the Bible), you may be wondering whether I'm a conservative or a liberal. In fact, I'm neither — just a conservator who wants to do justice to every word of Scripture without preconceptions. As I mentioned in our chat at the beginning of this book, there's a literalism of the left as well as the right. Conservatives may have made every word of the Bible a sacred original quite on its own. But liberals were just as guilty: the only difference in their case was that they arrived at a peculiarly unsacred original by culling out of Scripture whatever they thought couldn't be historical.

Here are just a few of the things they blithely excised. They discarded the creation of woman from Adam's rib because they thought it both sexist and non-factual. They edited out the image of the Red Sea waters piled up like walls because they thought it was fictional embroidery on history. And they took Jesus' feeding of the five thousand and turned it into a "miracle of sharing," by which people who'd been hiding their box lunches finally shared them after a little boy's generosity shamed them into it.

People who can do that sort of exegesis with a straight face are not just wrong — they're tone deaf to the musical comedy of Scripture. They do harm only when they become Bible professors and are able to persuade their students that they should be taken seriously. I once had a teacher whose view of John's Gospel was so dim that he suggested never preaching from it at all. Even at the time, I never paid any attention to him. But since then I've learned why that was a good idea. I think it was Jerry Seinfeld who said, "It's hard to explain bad taste to someone who actually has it." But I say, "If someone has no taste at all, don't argue with him, even in your own head. Just cut his course."

Seriously, though, the literalism of the left was very much a matter of no taste — or at least of no taste for what really matters. It was a retreat from the life-and-death battleground of the Bible to a safer but less interesting half-Bible where they wouldn't be endangered by the Spirit's friendly fire. And it was a capitulation to a host of safety-first admonitions that have plagued us ever since the seventeenth century. I've already mentioned the idea that "facts are true, fictions are false" as one of them. But there were others; and chief among them was the notion, borrowed from popular Darwinism but hardly supported by experience, that all new things are ipso facto advancements over what came before them — that tomorrow will always be an improvement on yesterday. But there's no such warranty in human life. We live exactly as we marry: "for better, for worse." For both, not either. Worse is just as much a part of the ecology of creation (and of the Bible) as better. Once again, *all* luck is holy.

Still, that "onward and upward" notion of evolution took its own toll on Scripture. For instance, the Babylonian creation stories that the ancient writers of Genesis used as a basis for their work were first labeled as primitive myths. Then, by extension, the Hebrew writers themselves were also marked down as primitive — despite the highly sophisticated job they did in ridding those myths of theological defects. They took a frankly polytheistic story about a god (Marduk) who made the world by conquering a monster of primeval chaos (Tiamat), and they turned it into a refined piece of theology in which nothing at all exists until the true God makes it. Those guys were good too. They may have been yesterday's experts, but today's professionals aren't necessarily better than they were. Your expertise at what you do isn't canceled out by someone else's later performance. Babe Ruth's stature isn't diminished by Hank Aaron; and it's surely not diminished by minor-league players, however numerous or loud.

If that applies to the work of the human authors who wrote the script for the film of Genesis, it does so in spades to the work of the divine Director herself. However good those writers may have been, she doesn't limit herself to merely reproducing their input. She grandly reserves her right to play fast and loose with their original materials. It doesn't bother her in the least that the blood of the Passover lamb in Exodus may originally have been just an explanation of how the Jews escaped an Egyptian disaster. When she's ready to have Paul identify the Paschal Lamb as the Christ, she'll gladly let him do so.

So if a Hollywood director who turns a novel into a motion picture can't be judged by the details of the book he uses, neither can the divine Director be judged by her original sources. Whatever her scriptwriters may have had in mind, the Director stands or falls only by the internal texture of the movie she's made from their contributions, not by how they (or anyone else) interpreted them. And when she's finished her film, she presents us with a totally new creation, not a remake of somebody else's picture. No matter where she got her first ideas, her end product sits only on its own bottom. If we're to admire it at all, we have to take the whole of what she makes us watch as her final word to us.

I've always subscribed to the *plenary inspiration* of Scripture — to the doctrine that every word of the Bible, where and as it is, is the Spirit's handiwork. The oath that I signed at my ordination some fifty years ago read, "I do believe the Holy Scriptures of the Old and New Testaments to be the Word of God and to contain all things necessary to salvation." I still believe that. And the nicest thing about my view of the Bible as film is that it enables me to go right on doing so. I can still take every scrap of it as the very thing the Director had in mind to show me, yet I'm mercifully delivered from the dangers of literalism, right or left. No matter where or how she got her materials, I'm able to see them all as transfigured by her direction into nothing less than the Word of God himself.

But enough of that for now. I think it's time to tell you how the title *Genesis, the Movie* came to me.

TWO

Flashback

A few years ago, when I was trying to take a nap in a hotel room after some lectures I'd given, my wife, Valerie, roused me with one of her quasi-imperative suggestions. "Why don't we buy a movie?" she asked. Groggily, I watched as she surfed through the TV menu until she came across *American Beauty* and said, "Oh, yes! This is the perfect time to watch it!" By then, of course, I was wide awake and had to agree: it was a film we'd both wanted to see but hadn't gotten around to yet. (I'd already read a couple of glowing reviews, but I was still in the dark as to why it had won so much praise.) In any case, we watched it straight through without comment. At the end, I think I said something like, "What a bunch of losers!" But we pretty much left it at that and slept on it because we had an early flight home in the morning.

It was only when we were killing time over Egg McMuffins at the airport that we began to discuss the film. What I'm about to give you here is an elaboration of the notes on our conversation that I made once we got on the plane. (If you haven't seen *American Beauty* and think I may spoil it for you, don't fret: it has so many subtleties that no review can harm it — or for that matter, do it justice.) First, then, a quick run-through of who's who.

The Characters

Everyone in the film is a bona fide loser: they're all trapped in dying lives. The *lead character* — Lester Burnham, played by Kevin Spacey — is as good as dead from the very beginning of the movie. Practically the first thing he says (in a voice-over) is, "I'll be dead in six months." For almost all the rest of the picture, his life is running relentlessly downhill despite his attempts to make something of it. And at the end, he's literally dead, shot in the back of the head: his eyes are open, there's a smile on his face, and (again in a voice-over) we hear him making an upbeat speech expressing satisfaction with the way things turned out.

The lead character's wife. Caroline Burnham is played by Annette Benning. Whatever kind of life she and her husband may once have had together has long since gone galley west. Like him, she's a married single, mirroring his mood swings between wistfulness and anger, but excluding him by her preoccupation with her own lifestyle. Her attempted career in real estate, however, gets her nowhere except into bed with her biggest competitor — a user who discards her at the first inconvenience. And just before the end of the film, we see her driving home with a pistol in her hand, swearing she won't be a victim anymore.

Their daughter. Initially, she's presented to us as a passive-aggressive piece of teenage work gasping for air in the vacuum of her parents' marriage. Eventually, though, she softens a bit when she falls in love with the boy next door; and at the end, the two of them are planning to go off to New York and support themselves by selling drugs.

The daughter's high school girlfriend (the "American Beauty" of the film). For most of the picture, we see her as a blonde bombshell, bragging endlessly about her sexual exploits with men. But just before the end (when Lester Burnham, having long fantasized about bedding her, finally makes a serious pass at it), we see her confess that her superslut identity has been a lie all along: she's still a virgin.

The boy next door. He's portrayed as a bright, independent type who nonetheless seems to knuckle under to his father's discipline. But when his father is out of sight, he goes his own way with a strange hobby of videotaping everything and everybody — and with a lucrative career of peddling drugs on the side.

The father of the boy next door. He's a gay-bashing, ex-Marine Corps colonel who rules his household with a rod of iron. But after the film is well along (and after he's been prying into the tapes in his son's room), we see him watching through the bedroom window as the boy apparently performs fellatio on Lester Burnham. Later, we see him walk over to the garage next door in pouring rain and make a homosexual advance of his own on Burnham. In a scene of masterfully mixed signals, Burnham rebuffs him in embarrassment, and we watch the colonel walk back home, destroyed. But next, we see an off-camera person with a gun steal up behind Burnham and fire a single shot into the back of his head. Only at the very end of the film (when we catch one last glimpse of the colonel wearing a bloody tee shirt) does it become clear that he, and not Burnham's wife, was the murderer.

The homosexual couple next door. With their obvious delight in each other's company and their innocent desire to please everyone they meet, these two are an exception to the pervading gloom of the rest of the picture. They are, in fact, a bit of comic relief that the director slips over on his viewers. He takes a pair of characters whom many people will perceive as flawed, and he makes them the movie's sole image of unflawed humanity: Adam and Eve in the garden before the Fall, perhaps, or even the redeemed and glorified saints at the marriage supper of the Lamb in Revelation. (They offer baked goods to their new neighbors.)

Finally, *the colonel's wife,* played by Allison Janney. Throughout the film, she's the most nearly dead of all the characters. We see her as a mere shell of a woman, drained of all signs of life by her husband's harshness — and, as we're left to surmise at the end, by the collapse of all sexual connection with him.

The Discussion between Valerie and Me

The first thing we agreed on was that the film was indeed depressing. But then, I suggested, so were many parts of the Bible. My point was that we can't grasp what any work of art is about if our only approach to it is to fasten on its details and ask what they mean or whether we like them. A movie is an integrated set of images that must be accepted into the mind on their own terms, not ours. If the images of *American Beauty* hadn't been integrated, it would have been only an uncommunicative mess, not an intriguing mystery — and certainly not the popular and critical success it plainly was.

Not only that, I said, but the communicative power of art functions on a level below that of the merely rational intellect. A good film doesn't speak to us by telling us things we already understand in words we can grasp literally; it installs its images in our minds and invites us to live with them — to overhear their conversation with each other in a language we can't understand at all. Even if a movie is in English, its deepest communications will always be foreign to us. This is especially true of our minds now, but it's been true for a long time.

As we sit here at the beginning of the third millennium, we're post-medieval, post-Reformation, post-Enlightenment, post-scientific, and even post-modern types who've all but lost the knack of thinking in images. For us, thought is a purely discursive process, a matter of drawing conclusions from previous conclusions. It's a closed system totally dependent on rational verifiability. We crave instant, logical understanding; but poetry, film, the Bible — precisely because they're infused with the logic of the imagination, not the intellect — utterly frustrate our desire for accessible meanings.

That wasn't always true, though. The Hebrew Bible, the New Testament, the early church fathers — and good poets ever since — have all known how to be patient with the foreign conversation between images. They knew they had first to hold those images, uninterpreted, in their minds, and then just listen, listen, listen until they picked up, without translation, the language of the images themselves. Only then could they be as free as they obviously were to search for mysteries by something more fundamental than the dim bulb of intelligibility.

I gave Valerie an illustration. If she didn't know a word of Italian, and if she were having dinner with an Italian family who spoke no English, *"Vino, per favore"* wouldn't mean a thing to her. But if, as he said it, her host caught her eye, touched the rim of his empty wineglass with his fingertip, and then pointed to the carafe next to her, the significance of his images would cancel out the incomprehensibility of his words. Images don't say things we can understand; images don't mean things we already know; images *point* — and they point to still other images as if they were trying to identify with them. Their communication is a silent direction of our attention. "There!" they say. "That's what I have in mind! That's the mystery I'm trying to get across to you!" Unlike words, they can never be dismissed with an "Oh, I get it." They do the work of words without the danger of words; they want us to exclaim, "Ah! I'm beginning to *see!*"

For example, if Valerie also saw a young man at the table tenderly kiss the girl next to him and say, *"Te amo,"* she would promptly read that image without translation. She'd instinctively hunt for still more images to figure it out: "Are they *lovers?* Are they *married?* Are they *engaged?* Is he her *long-lost brother?*" In short, she'd go straight to the mystery before her eyes, not to the phrase book in her purse.

At that point, as I remember, Valerie observed that I was fighting intelligibility by trying to be intelligible, so why didn't we just knock off the whole subject and start discussing the actual images of *American Beauty?* Stung, I agreed. Treading lightly, I asked her what she thought the principal image of the film was. That's easy, she said: it was *death.* It was about the lives of losers who were going nowhere except into nothing. And it was, if she might improve on my phrasing, an image so repeatedly presented in distasteful forms that only someone with a heart of stone could escape being depressed by it — and to despair of making any sense of the film at all.

Since Valerie was no stranger to my theological harping on death and resurrection — on life out of death as the underlying mystery not only of the Bible but of human life itself — I suggested we take a shot at that as a way of dealing with the film. She said, "Be my guest"; so, without deciding whether she was offering me encouragement or a dare, I just leapt in.

Taking the hardest image first, I fastened on the two voice-overs of Lester Burnham: the one at the beginning of the film, with him off-screen; and the one at the end, with only his corpse on-screen. True, they were both heard rather than seen images, but the last one obviously represented some kind of resurrection, and the first one was a flash-forward to that same reality. Still, in neither case were they to be taken as images of a resurrection that comes only *after* death. To read an "afterlife" into them would simply reduce their mystery to three discontinuous states of being: first, he was alive; then, he lost that life in death; but then, having gotten bravely over death, he got a different life as a reward. But that's not what the movie gave us. It gave us the image of life in the thick of death. It gave us resurrection *now*.

"That gives me an idea," Valerie said. "Remember what we used to do when we ran film-discussion groups at church? How we tried to pick out a character in the movie who represented the Christ figure — who depicted the image of life in the midst of death?"

"Yes," I said tentatively.

"Well, that's what I want to do right now. My first candidate for a Christ figure would be the colonel's son. For one thing, he even acts like Jesus. When his father physically abuses him, he never strikes back. And then there's his video camera. He lovingly preserves everything he sees with it: a paper bag dancing in the breeze with some leaves, children playing, a dead bird, mourners at a funeral. The camera, in fact, becomes an image of his having the whole world in his hands. And at the end, when he's about to leave for New York, he says to his mother, 'Take care of Dad,' which is a neat twist on Jesus' last word to his own mother, 'Woman, behold your son.'

"Don't interrupt," she warned me. "My next candidate is Lester Burnham himself. If you remember, after he overhears his daughter's girl-friend say she likes men who are in great physical shape, he goes into a middle-age frenzy of push-ups and weight training. But then, in the scene where the girl confesses she's still a virgin, his fantasy life instantly dematerializes, and without laying a hand on her, he gently smiles at her. As far as I'm concerned, that's an image of his restoration to the truth of his being. In that moment, the way forward to his becoming a caring father and loving husband opens up for him. For the first time in the movie, he's truly alive. And to drive that point home, the director had the brilliant idea of bringing that smile back in the shot of Burnham's face after he's dead. For me, it's the smile, not the words he says in the voice-over, that becomes the crowning image of the picture.

"And then there's the colonel. Of course, the movie doesn't show him literally dying or rising. But he does destroy his previous life of denial when he makes his homosexual advance on Burnham, and he ends his present life for all practical purposes when he kills Burnham. And when his wife silently promises to take care of him, there's at least a hint of resurrection. I do realize I'm making somebody who virtually committed suicide into a Christ figure. But that's okay. For all practical purposes, Jesus himself was a suicide. He said, 'No one takes my life from me; I lay it down of myself.' He set himself up to be crucified. If he'd stayed out of Jerusalem, at least he wouldn't have died at that particular Passover.

"But it's the colonel's wife who's my best candidate for a Christ figure. As you said, she's dead for the whole film, and she has no apparent resurrection. But if you're going to talk about life in the midst of death, why can't I take her ongoing death as at least an image of new life? Sure, most people would say it was just her way of coping. But so what? Corpses don't cope; only people who are alive do. And anyway, she's the only one who understands everything that's going on."

"Understands?" I asked. "How do you figure that?"

"She understands the way God understands. Like God, she just puts up with everything. She takes the messy lives of those around her into her death and lets them be, just as God takes all the sins of the world into his death on the cross and lets them be. Her son seems to have faith in her forgiveness when he commits his father to her care. But about her husband, we just don't know: the movie gives us no image of faith on his part. That doesn't matter, though. Whether he comes to faith or not, she still understands and forgives. All of which is made clear by her final scene in the movie. She's sitting at the foot of a staircase, head bowed and ears covered by her hands. And when the gunshot goes off, she doesn't even move a muscle! If that image doesn't point to 'Father, forgive them, for they know not what they do,' I don't know what does."

"Well!" I said to Valerie. "I can only congratulate you: you've out-imaged me by a country mile. If I had half your talent, I'd be twice the man I am. But I also have to thank you for giving me the thread that will tie the next book together. As you know, I was going to do it as a straight commentary on the first three chapters of Genesis. But thanks to you, it now occurs to me that I might take all three of them as a film — as the Holy Spirit's movie of creation and redemption by way of life in death. That way, I can take all the Bible's 'facts' seriously without having to take them literally — just as you did with the 'facts' of *American Beauty*. You never once tried to prove they happened 'objectively' because you knew that *the director had made them happen before your very eyes!* Terrific! You shot literalism in the heart. And I could do the same thing with all the other 'isms': fundamentalism, moralism, doctrinalism, and even deconstructionism. Our problem, as I suddenly see it, isn't only our general failure to hold the images of the Bible's movie in our minds. It's that even when we do manage to hold onto some of them, we insist on translating their language of mystery into the babble of logic-chopping. And therefore . . ."

"Stop!" Valerie shouted. "I've got it!"

"Got what?" I asked.

"The title for your book: *Genesis, the Movie.*"

"Ah!" I said. "A foreign film with no subtitles."

And that was that.

THREE

The Producer and Trinity Films

But, having considered the Director of *Genesis, the Movie,* it's time for you as the reader and me as the writer to resume our private screening of the picture. On then to the rest of the Principals behind its creation: the Producer, who is God the Father, and the Production Company, Trinity Films. (The Star will come later.)

The Father

Like the only-begotten Word by whom all things are made and the out-breathed Spirit who broods over (and under) the Word's speaking, the Father is just as much the Beginning of the movie of creation. God the Father has been called the *fons et origo Divinitatis,* the Fountain and Origin of Divinity — and for this film, that's exactly what he is. He's the Fountain of Creative Wherewithal for its production, the Original Backer of the project. Without his willingness to bankroll the film, it would never have existed: the whole enterprise was his *Idea* to begin with.

But beginnings are a mysterious category. They're always hidden in the beginner until they actually exist in themselves, and as I've already implied, no beginning is simply a matter of one thing coming before another. The origin of something, therefore, can never be discovered by rummaging through sequences in time or space. Take the case of the author of a novel. To say that the beginning of her book invariably comes to her "before" she writes the story, and that she thinks of the rest "after" it, doesn't advance your understanding of beginnings in any meaningful way. It may not even be true. The beginning you read in print may have been something she edited into the book only at the end of her labors, when the final shape of her story became clear to her.

That has been true of me as the author of this book, and it's certainly the case with the author(s) of the first book of the Bible. Genesis was not put into its present shape until the fifth century B.C.E., or even later — *after* most of the Old Testament was already written. So in both cases, the published beginning of any work can easily be the last thing its author thought of. It may well have been an *editorial* discovery of what the work had really been about all along, after the entire gestation of the book in the author's mind.

Accordingly, the "finished" opening of a literary work is always *in its author,* no matter how or when the author stumbles across it. In fact, even to speak of a story's opening scenes as if they came before or after the rest of the book is to sell the author short as a creative artist. A good limerick writer always has the last line in mind before tackling the first; Agatha Christie straightened up the beginnings of her mysteries only after she was sure of their endings. True, the categories of before and after might have been relevant to the characters within her stories. And because she was a creature of time and space, they might also have been relevant to the progress of her work — to the days, months, or years it took her to find the "right" beginning. But they're irrelevant to the creation of the story *in her.* In that "place," the story's beginning comes neither before nor after; it's just *there,* waiting for her to embrace it.

Admittedly, the story she creates has no being at all until it begins to exist in her mind. But once her story does exist there, it's simply present to her — and on two levels. On the one hand, it's a fact of her existence as she holds it in her creativity. But on the other hand, it's also a reality in its own right because what she's making is a self-contained world of temporal beings whose "freedom" she must respect every time she sits down to write. An artist, therefore, exists *simultaneously* with everything in her work; and all the "artifacts" in her work — all her characters, in all their time-bound fumbling and bumbling — exist simultaneously with her as she creates them.

So if I may take a giant leap from human authorship to the Author of all things, let me suggest that there was never a "point" in the Producer's eternity prior to which he "hadn't yet" decided to make the movie we see in Genesis. The Producer's act of creation is simultaneous with the universe at every moment of its existence; and every instant of the universe's being is simultaneous with God. God is the eternal contemporary of every event in time, and every event in time is held eternally in God. Once again, God's eternity doesn't precede our temporality, nor will our temporality someday be yanked back into his eternity. Eternity is the womb of time, and time is the fetus in that womb. In every present moment, from beginning to end, both mother and child are alive and well.

For another case in point, though, consider yourself. In those former days when you were "just a gleam in your father's eye," the only thing that existed then and there was his twinkle, not your being. But even when you finally began to be, the beginning of your being remained just as undiscoverable by you. It was never something you could work your way back to by retracing *chrono*logical steps of your life. (*Chronos*, in Greek, means "clocktime.") The only thing such a calendar search could lead you to is someone else in the same boat of *chronos* — to just one more clock-watcher whose true beginning is every bit as inaccessible as your own. Your beginning in God, therefore, and the beginning of all things in the Producer, always remains a mystery: an abrupt and paradoxical transition from nothing to something.

But once you've made that transition — now that you actually exist *extra nihil* and *extra causas,* outside nothing and outside your causes — you discover something more important still. You find that even in this seeming prison of temporal sequence, chronology isn't what calls the important shots of your life. You discover that clock time counts less for you than another, wholly different kind of time. What matters most to you is time in its deepest sense: not time as *chronos* (as in "*What time* is it?"), but time as *kairos* (as in "What is it *time for?*").

Kairos (the Greek word for "season") is time as the "high times" of your life; it's the time for your decisions about what to do with your existence. It's time as the "due seasons" of your being — time as it's summed up in Ecclesiastes 3: "To everything there is a season, and a time to every purpose under the heaven: a time to be born, and a time to die; a time to plant, and a time to pluck up that which is planted; a time to kill, and a time to heal; a time to break down, and a time to build up . . ." (KJV).

This is *kairos* as the times of your relationships and exchanges with other beings. *Kairos,* unlike *chronos,* is not an unwelcome, confining grid into which some incipient "you" was once slotted; it's the most liberating privilege of your existence. It's about your chances to solve the puzzles set before you by the seasons (glad or grim) that you've been graced with. And in that *kairos,* your beginning is not something behind you in an irretrievable past. Invisible though it may be, it's never not with you. There was once a season, of course, when you were not. But now that you are, your beginning in God is always here for you. Properly speaking, therefore, God never *made* you; he's *making* you right now. You're not sitting in your chair because you were there ten minutes ago. You're where you are because he's calling you by name — out of the nothing you're miles deep in at this very moment, and into a very present life that he'll keep you in eternally.

So each beginning is a mystery of both discontinuity and continuity. The discontinuity lies between your being no-thing and some-thing at the same time; but the continuity lies in the fact that both those states are held simultaneously in the Father who makes you. The discontinuity prevails between your way of holding your being and his way of holding his: he *is* being; you just *have* being. But the continuity prevails in the truth that your being is forever and inalienably your own: it's an irrevocable gift from your Producer to you. There was never a point in time when your being was "manufactured" (certainly not by you; and, equally certainly, not by God).

As I've said, even if the Big Bang theory of the universe's cosmogony is correct, there is no "point" before it that science can reach. The discontinuity is absolute. Prior to that grand fireworks display, there's only *nothing* — and that's a terrain beyond the explorations of scientists. The only Cause present in that nowhere is the God beyond time and place, who is by definition undiscoverable: "How unsearchable are his judgments, and his ways past finding out" (Rom. 11:33, KJV).

Even in the endless continuity of God, then, your existence (and the existence of the cosmos itself) is not the result of step-by-step craftsmanship. Rather, it's the outcome of a creative *presto!* forever uttered by a divine Magician — by the Father's Word through whom all things are made. But since the world originates in the love affair between the Father and his Significant Other, I want to give you another image for the Producer: he's not a CEO but a Lover. The Father is the Original Romantic.

Augustine called the three Persons of the Trinity the *Amans,* the *Amatus,* and the *Amor Mutuus* — the Lover, the Beloved, and the Mutual Love. That's always given me the perhaps risqué image of the Father making love to his Beloved Wisdom in the bed of the Spirit. Do you see what that does? It turns creation into the pillow talk of the Trinity. From the beginning, it makes the Father's loving the First Cause of everything. The world becomes not an artifact he sweated over but the apple of his eye. Unlike the popular but depressingly reductionist view of the universe as just so many hot (or cold) rocks drifting aimlessly in a great, black can, it gives us a universe we too can love. It provides us with a reassuring home where we can be participants in a romance rather than spectators of a mindless process. It gives us a *party* at which we can see ourselves as dancers instead of wallflowers.

Trinity Films

Since I've been encroaching on the territory of the Trinity in my comments on the Producer, let's turn directly to the Studio responsible for the whole picture: the Father, the Son, and the Holy Spirit, taken together as the holy and undivided Three-in-One.

Just to show you how easily the fathers of the church found the Trinity on the pages of the Old Testament, I want to begin this section with an excerpt from Augustine's *Confessions*. In Books XI to XIII of that work, he breaks off the previous story of his life and conversion and begins a commentary on the opening lines of Genesis. (He never gets much beyond the first two verses, though. Only in his *De Genesi ad Litteram* does he succeed in going through Genesis verse by verse — and even there, he gets no further than the coats of skins that God made for Adam and Eve on their way out of Eden.) Here then is the passage, from the *Confessions*, XII, 7. Aptly enough, the "Holy, Holy, Holy" at the beginning is not just from the *Sanctus* in the liturgy of the church; it's a direct quote from Isaiah 6:3.

> *Itaque tu Domine, qui non est alias aliud et alias aliter, sed idipsum et idipsum et idipsum, Sanctus, Sanctus, Sanctus, Dominus Deus omnipotens; in Principio quod est de te, in Sapientia tua quae nata est de substantia tua, fecisti aliquid et de nihilo. Fecisti enim coelum et terram; non de te: non esset aequale Unigenito tuo, ac per hoc et tibi; et nullo modo justum esset, ut aequale tibi esset, quod de te non esset. Et aliud praeter te non erat unde feceras ea, Deus una Trinitas, et trina Unitas. . . .*

> Therefore you, O Lord, who are not one thing to certain creatures and another to others, but the selfsame and the selfsame and the selfsame, Holy, Holy, Holy, Lord God omnipotent — you, O Lord, in that Beginning who is from you, in your Wisdom who was born of your substance — *in him,* you made something precisely out of nothing. For you made heaven and earth; but not from yourself, for no creature ought to be equal to your Only-Begotten, and thus also to you; and it would in no way be right that something not of yourself should be equal to you. Moreover, there was no thing besides you from which you might make those things — O God, one Trinity and triune Unity.

Needless to say, that identification of the second Person of the Trinity with the Beginning as it appears in Genesis is not the sort of exposition we've been (dis)graced with in recent centuries. What we've been given has been based on the assumption (I'd call it a prejudice) that identifying the Trinity with the God of the Hebrew Bible is both a non-historical overlay on the Bible and an insult to the Jews — and therefore dead wrong. But on my model of Genesis as a film, that's not necessarily so. True enough, the original authors of the book of Genesis may not have had a clue that the LORD God of Israel was one and the same God with the Father, the Son, and the Holy Spirit. Still, if you believe that the movie of Genesis confronts you with the only true God there is (whether under the name of Yahweh or the Holy Trinity), then my asking you to accept the Trinity Film Corporation as the outfit responsible for its production absolves you of such quibbles. My naming of the three Persons as Producer, Star, and Director frees you from having to stick at details like the "original intent" of the human authors.

But I've said all that more than once, so let it go. What I want to address here is another question that may be lurking in your mind. You're probably quite accustomed to the idea that you don't just read about God in the Bible, you meet him there. That's true enough; but it isn't the best way to put it. The truth is that God meets *you* in the Scriptures, whether you recognize him or not. This is the case, of course, with any great film: it's not until you've lived with the entire picture in your mind that you can decide whether you've met anybody worth meeting — let alone *who* it is you've met. But it's also the case with the church, the community of faith, that's been watching the biblical movie unfold ever since the Exodus. It may have taken God's people a long time (in both the Old and New Covenants) to pick up on the identity of the film-making Company, but that's no skin off Trinity Films' nose. It's skin off ours: it takes longer than we think to make friends with a really good motion picture.

As you probably know, the doctrine of the Trinity has been in the shade for most of the past three or four hundred years. The seventeenth-century philosophers and scientists (who were the first truly modern thinkers) pretty much dispensed with it in their writings. The eighteenth-century Deists of the Enlightenment followed suit, but they went them one better and got rid of the Trinity entirely. (Even many clergy of the time, not to mention a good number of America's founding fathers, were effectively Unitarians.) And as for the nineteenth-century biblical critics, most of them tended to write off the Three-in-One as unwarranted by Scripture. So after all that quibbling, it comes as no surprise that twentieth-century believers were left with a Hobson's choice: they either sat loose to the Trinity, or else left it completely out of account. Fortunately, though, the Trinity seems to be making a comeback now. This book is just one more effort to refocus the spotlight on it.

However, there's still a lurking error that I want to get off the board: the concept of God as Three-in-One is not opposed to the staunch monotheism of the Hebrew Bible. Actually, the "One" in that title supports it. In the Old Testament, the single sin most inveighed against isn't murder, adultery, or theft. It's *idolatry:* the worship of any god or gods who aren't the one and only true God. The Prophets berated Israel and Judah endlessly for this transgression; yet in spite of their warnings, the people of God fell into it again and again. To this day, it remains not just the sin of Adam and Eve at the tree of the knowledge of good and evil but also the principal sin of every last one of us as their heirs. We continually make new gods of our own devising. From money to marriage, from childhood to youth to maturity, from romance to religion to parenthood to accountability to guilt, there's probably nothing we haven't turned into a tin god. And the doctrine of the Trinity stands as firmly against all such idolatries as anything in the Old Testament. Jewish monotheism is alive and well.

Moreover, it continues to thrive in the New Testament. The earliest believers in Jesus were all of them observant Jews, and therefore strict monotheists. There's nothing in their proclamation of Jesus as Lord *(kyrios)* and Messiah *(Christos)* that contradicts the *sh'ma'* of God's first *church* (the *congregation* of God's ancient Jewish people): "*Hear,* O Israel, the LORD our God is *one* LORD."

Since it may surprise you to hear me speak of the "church" in the Old Testament, here's why I do it. When the "church" in the New Testament spoke of "the Scriptures," they were referring to the Hebrew Bible — which they quoted from the Septuagint. In Hebrew, one of the words for the "congregation" of Israel was *qahal.* The other one was *'edhah,* usually rendered as "assembly." *Qahal* appears in the Septuagint as *ekklēsia,* and *'edhah* as *synagōgē.* So when the fellowship of believers in Jesus as Lord and Messiah looked for a scriptural name to call themselves — a name that would show their *continuity* with Israel — they had two choices. But given the fact that *synagōgē* had already been used up as the name of an institution in first-century Judaism (the "synagogue"), only *ekklēsia* could fill the bill.

Back to the *sh'ma'* and its proclamation of the Oneness of the LORD. In John 10:30, when Jesus says, "I and the Father are one," he's practically reciting the *sh'ma'.* (In Mark 12:29, he literally quotes it.) And in John 14:16, when he says, "I will ask the Father, and he will give you another Comforter [*paraklētos,* "Advocate"]," he's saying the same thing (RFC). And finally, he's doing it again in John 16:13-15, where he says that this Advocate "will not speak of himself. . . . He will glorify me, because he will take of what is mine and proclaim it to you. Everything the Father has is mine; therefore I said that he will take of what is mine and proclaim it over you" (RFC). In all three instances, you see, John is having him assert the unity of the triune God. So in spite of all misunderstandings, the Trinity still stands forth as one God, pure and simple, not a committee of three gods.

But, more importantly, the doctrine of the Trinity doesn't so much tell us what God *is* as it warns us about what he *isn't*. It's full of statements like the one in the Athanasian Creed: "So the Father is God, the Son is God, and the Holy Ghost is God; and yet they are not three Gods but one God." Or consider the line in the Nicene Creed that says the Son is "begotten, not made." Those statements aren't solutions to a metaphysical puzzle or bits of information to increase our intellectual knowledge of God; they're outlines of the anatomy of a mystery that W. H. Auden described as "beyond all liking and happening."

To give that mystery its proper theological name, it's the *coinherence* of the three Persons — in all their acts and in every aspect of their essence — in the unity of their "Godness." But the most fascinating thing about this coinherence is that it rubs off on the world that the Trinity brings forth. When God creates man in his own image, for instance ("man," just to remind you, is the *'adham,* male and female), he makes us into beings totally in love with mutual indwelling, with walking into, with *dancing* into relationships at every turn of our lives. For one thing, he's made us positively wild about turning two people into "one flesh" in marriage. For another, he's made us just as driven to implicate ourselves in friendships, families, towns, cities, and states. He's made a *sociable* world. And when we (at our best) dance our way into that creation, it becomes a vast ballet of coinherences. But when (at our worst) we trample that world underfoot, it becomes precisely a failure of coinherence — a place where all our joinings go sour.

But it's not only human creatures who are made in the image of this dance. The whole natural order — from the nearest grain of sand to the farthest star — is just as much an image of the mutual indwelling of the Persons of the Trinity. Nothing in creation acts or exists by itself; everything interacts with everything else. Poetry invites us to fall in love with this dance. Science charms us with the intricacy and the elegance of it. And theology, at its best, lifts us to the true Reason for the dancing in the first place.

I often illustrate this coinherence with two examples, the first of which is from gardening. When you're breaking up the soil for planting, you sometimes come across a very large rock. This is especially true on Long Island, where I live. During the ice ages, the glaciers deposited half the boulders in New England in this terminal moraine. At any rate, the stone in your garden is often so heavy that it strikes you as the most immovable thing on earth. But as you dig down to free it, you reach a point where that immovable object finally has its chance to interact with the irresistible force of the earth's gravity. Suddenly, it drops down ever so slightly: it makes an *amorous advance* on the earth from which you're trying to extract it. Do you see my point? The rock was *always* dancing with the earth; but until you came along, it never had a chance to make its moves. You just freed it to do what comes naturally for something made in the image of the coinherence of the Trinity.

The second example is a *pas de deux* executed by a male and a female dancer on a stage. They're two distinct beings; but their moves are so perfectly matched that they seem to become one. When I use this illustration to talk about the dance of coinherence in marriage, I ask the couple I'm instructing how many dancers they visualize on that stage. Invariably, they say, "Two"; and just as invariably, I say, "No, there are three: the man, the woman, and the stage — or even four, if they include the entire mass of the earth itself, for which the stage is simply a front. Without the earth's gravity that pulls them down, they'd be in a weightless environment where they could only float aimlessly." And then I lead the couple to see that their marriage will be the sacrament of a ballet not only between the two of them but between all the partners in the dancing creation that God made in his image.

Indeed, sexuality (human, animal, or vegetable) is one of the choicest images of coinherence. The coming together of two people in intercourse, the mating of beasts, the pollination of plants — all these are steps in the dance of creation. The technical terms for *coinherence* in Greek and Latin theology are *perichōrēsis* and *circumincessio,* both connoting a "going around," a "rotation"; a "walking around," a "dancing around."

But whatever their etymology, those words stand for the eternal, interactive existence of one Person of the Trinity in the others without confusion of Person or Function. They sketch for us a mutual "entering into each other" of the three Persons by virtue of the oneness of their Godhead. I realize that's theological shoptalk; but perhaps you can see how nicely it lifts sexuality out of the quagmire of exploitation, reductionism, banality, porn, and guilt in which we've buried the subject. It enables us to see ourselves, under the image of a dance, as much more graceful than the clumsy characters we so often are.

But perichoresis does more than that. It lights up the death of Christ the Incarnate Word on the cross. It lets us see that death under the image of the good pleasure of all three Persons of the Trinity acting in concert. Jesus becomes not just an innocent man God picked on but the Father's Beloved in whom he delights. The Father, of course, doesn't suffer on the cross. (That's an old heresy that goes by the name of Patripassianism.) Only the Son suffers there — and he suffers only in his human nature, which nevertheless is inseparably one with him in his Person as the Father's Word. This is nicely portrayed in Albrecht Dürer's woodcut #264 (Kurth edition), which shows the Father and the Spirit hovering over the body of Jesus as it's taken down from the cross. Even in that death, you see, the Spirit, the *Amor Mutuus* who proceeds from the Father and the Son, is still brooding over the creation that all three of them have made. The crucifixion, when you see it under the image of coinherence, becomes neither an infliction nor an affliction but a reconciling step in the dancing of the Trinity with creation.

In particular, though, the perichoresis lights up Christ's burial in the tomb. Jesus, the Incarnate Word of the Father, died on the sixth day of the week, a Friday; and he was in the sepulcher for the whole of the seventh day, the Saturday of the Sabbath. Accordingly, on Good Friday that same Word recapitulated his creation of the *'adham* on the original sixth day of the world; and on Holy Saturday, he rested in the new creation as he rested on the original seventh day. But he finally revealed that he had "made all things new" on the first day of the week, the Sunday of his resurrection. Easter Day, then, is the Bible's second first day of the week. It's the vindication of the world in God's Mind as that world was first shown forth on day one. And at the end of Scripture, on a Sunday on the Isle of Patmos, Christ in glory recapitulates all of those days for John the Divine when he appears as the Bridegroom at the Marriage Supper of the Lamb. The perichoresis of the three Persons of the Trinity brings the whole creation to fruition in the New Jerusalem. It brings us back to the glory we had in our Beginning.

Sometimes, when I'm lying sleepless in bed at two in the morning, I fret my way through all sorts of horrors. I relive old insults, worry about the slow progress of my writing, think of loathsome diseases I might be contracting, or struggle to make mental lists of ideas that are flitting through my mind. (The only thing that last one does for me is keep me awake still longer.) But lately, I've developed a technique for getting through the nonsense of those night watches. When they torment me, I recite to myself the *Suscipe* of St. Ignatius of Loyola:

> Accept, O Lord, my entire liberty,
> my memory, my understanding, and my will.
> All that I am and have, you have given me,
> and I give all back to you to be governed by your will.
> Give me only the joy of your love and the comfort of your grace;
> with these I am rich enough, and I ask nothing more.

That prayer reminds me that I didn't get into bed with a right to eight hours' sleep, only with the privilege of being who I am, as I am, for as long as

I'm there. And I got that notion from Jesus in the tomb. In his death, by his coinherence in the Father, he just put up with being dead. Not usefully dead, or patiently dead, or creatively dead; just stone-cold *gone.* So if he, even in the grave, could just *be* what he was at that moment, why can't I? The Father who raises Jesus from the dead — and who, in him, raises me from the half-death of my fretful thoughts — has me just as much in the Sabbath rest of the perichoresis as he has Jesus.

FOUR

Creation in the Mind of God

To begin this new chapter about the "place" where creation first and foremost exists, let me go back to the passage that I quoted from Augustine's *De Genesi ad Litteram* in our chat at the beginning of this book. It was from Book V, 36; and in it, I want you to note the double question he asks.

> *Quomodo ergo Deo nota sunt quae non erant? Et rursus quomodo ea faceret quae sibi nota non erant? Non enim quidquam fecit ignorans.*

> How then were things that did not exist known to God? And on the other hand, how could he make things that were not known to him? For he did nothing in ignorance.

As you can see, Augustine is trying to take what his faith tells him about God's relationship with creation (namely, that the world exists in the Mind of God even before it exists in time and space), and to see if he can answer the questions it raises in his own mind. Indeed, he once defined the whole theological enterprise as *fides quaerens intellectum*, "faith seeking understanding." That was a wonderful formulation, and it put the first thing squarely in first place. Augustine, of course, constantly admits to himself and to God that no intellectual formulation can ever encompass the full mystery of the divine Mind. But, like a true lover, he finds himself so fascinated by the paradoxical truths about his Beloved that he can't stop himself from marveling at them.

Accordingly, his two questions here are not just the ruminations of a high-powered intellect; they're part and parcel of his enchantment with God. He totally believes that God *makes*, and he totally believes that God *knows* before he makes; but, like all the best theologians, he can't resist playing with the consequences of that faith. Theology for him is no deadpan enumeration of bright ideas; it's the fun he has with the pillow talk of the Trinity. And I myself had so much fun with his musings — such a sudden rush of hilarity at the words by which he distinguished between God's knowing and God's making — that I typed them in capitals: *NOTA ERGO FECIT, NON FACTA COGNOVIT.* (Literally, that reads, "known things he made, not made things he knew." If you're interested, go back and look at the somewhat different translation I gave you on page xviii.) In any case, here's the last part of the passage again, with yet another attempt at translation. Just remember, his answer to both questions isn't just straight talk about God; it's theology as solemn high larking around:

> *NOTA ERGO FECIT, NON FACTA COGNOVIT. Proinde, antequam fierent, et erant, et non erant: erant in Dei scientia, non erant in sua natura. Ac per hoc factus est dies ille cui utroque modo innotescerent, et in Deo et in seipsis: illa vero matutina sive diurna cognitione, hac vero velut vespertina. Ipsi autem Deo non audeo dicere alio modo innotuisse, cum ea fecisset, quam illo quo ea noverat ut faceret, apud quem non est commutatio, nec momenti obumbratio.*

> HE MADE THINGS HE ALREADY KNEW; HE DIDN'T WAIT FOR THEM TO BE FACTS TILL HE KNEW THEM. Accordingly, before things happened, they both were and were not: they were, in the knowledge of God; and they were not, in their own nature. And for this reason that day was made ["day one," Gen. 1:5] by which these things might become known in both modes: both as they are in God and as they are in themselves. In the former, by a morning or daytime knowledge; and in the latter, by an evening one. But with regard to God himself, I dare not say that when he makes things, they become known in any other way than that by which he knows them in order that he might make them — he, with whom there is no variation or shadow due to change.

This is such a marvelous object lesson in theology as wordplay — in creating theological image-gardens "with real toads in them" — that I can't resist taking you on a little excursion into the significance of the words *NOTA*, "things known," and *FACTA*, "things made."

Augustine is aiming at two truths here. The *NOTA* stand for God's universal, *intellectual* grip on creation as it exists in the endless Today of the Trinity's exchanges with each other. It's a knowing that holds all things, seen and unseen; and it holds them not only as they exist physically in their own natures but also as they exist *inchoately* in God as their Beginning. (*Inchoately* is from the Latin *inchoo*, "to begin, to commence.") This inchoate knowledge is God's *morning* knowing, his knowledge of creation in the "dawn" of the eternal Today. And as you're well aware by now, both Augustine and I take that "Dawn," that *Beginning*, to be God's eternal and only-begotten Son: the Word who is none other than the second Person of the Trinity — the Word who is Incarnate in our Lord and Savior Jesus Christ.

Consequently, even though the world that God knows in his beloved Son consists of nothing but creatures who come into being and pass away, God's knowledge of that world is just as beginningless and endless as the Word who is its Beginning. His knowing of it isn't a gradual thought-process *by which* God creates the world but an eternal grasp *in which* he holds it. And that grip on the world in the Beloved is the foundation, the rock on which the entire shooting-match rests. In fact, God's endless grip on it is the very Stone himself. That Stone is the Rock in the wilderness (Exod. 17:6) who is the Christ, and he is also the Savior who has "neither form nor comeliness" (Isa. 53:2), and who died for us on the cross. He is "the Stone whom the builders reject," but who becomes, by the mystery of his Incarnation, the *kephalēn gōnias,* the "head of the corner," the "chief cornerstone" of the created order. (This last passage is from Psalm 118:22 — as quoted by Jesus in Matthew 21:42, Mark 12:19, and Luke 20:17.)

The *FACTA,* on the other hand, stand for the world's *physical* grip on itself — which God also holds in his eternal knowing. This is God's *evening* knowledge of creation, which is just as beginningless and endless as his grasp of the *NOTA.* And it's just as universal. It includes everything that creation ever knew, knows, or will know about its own being (all its actions, all its thoughts, all its feelings, all its dreams, all its fears); and it includes every one of those, whether they were deliberate or accidental, facts or fancies, inexorable or avoidable. In short, it encompasses all the changes and chances of history as they are held in the evening of God's endless Today.

Note carefully, though, that Augustine doesn't posit two creations, one intellectual (the *NOTA*) and the other physical (the *FACTA*) — let alone two opposed creations, one "virtual" and one "real." Rather, he comes up with the startling formulation that "before things happened," all things "both were and were not." But, existent or non-existent in their own being, they're all fully known and fully real in the divine Mind. In other words, Augustine gives us one creation known by God in *two modes* — by a *matutina* knowledge and by a *vespertina* knowledge — but both are within the *simul et sempiterne,* the "at once and forever" knowing of God. The Trinity are just Know-It-Alls from the Beginning.

36

For me, this was an eye-opener — especially since while I was studying it, I came across a book called *The Bit and the Pendulum* (abbreviated here as *BP*) by Tom Siegfried, science editor of the *Dallas Morning News*. In this charming popularization of current scientific thought, Siegfried rings the changes on a model that some scientists are using to grasp the basic nature of reality. He calls it the "information" model; and it's based on what is probably the dominant machine of our day: the computer, our storehouse of *information*.

This borrowing of images from contemporary culture is nothing new. Previous scientific models were drawn in the same way. Siegfried points out that Heraclitus (500 B.C.E.) held that *fire* was the fundamental substance in nature. But then in the late Middle Ages, the invention of the mechanical clock paved the way for Newton's seventeenth-century physics, in which the world was seen as a mechanism governed by the interactions of *forces*. And then in the nineteenth century, the steam engine, run by heat, inspired the new science of *thermo*dynamics (*BP*, p. 7).

But in the twentieth century, Siegfried continues, Werner Heisenberg noted a curious coincidence. "Modern physics," Heisenberg said, "is in some ways extremely close to Heraclitus. If we replace the word *fire* with the word *energy*, we can almost repeat his statements word for word. . . . Energy is indeed the material of which all the elementary particles, all atoms, and therefore all things in general are made, and at the same time energy is also that which is moved. . . . Energy can be transformed into movement, heat, light, and tension. Energy can be regarded as the cause of all changes in the world" (quoted in *BP*, p. 8). Siegfried also notes that improvements on models of reality don't necessarily invalidate previous models. Each of the older ones remains an adequate explanation of reality — provided it's applied only to the grosser arrangements of nature that it originally contemplated. The Enlightenment's "billiard-ball" universe, for example, still explains planetary orbits; but if you try to make that model apply at the subatomic level, it just can't do the job.

Siegfried then goes into detail on the new computer model. "I think," he says, "that with just a little exaggeration, this view can be neatly expressed simply by paraphrasing Heisenberg's paraphrase of Heraclitus: *Information* (italics mine) is indeed the material of which all the elementary particles, all atoms, and therefore all things in general are made, and at the same time *information* is also that which is moved. . . . *Information* can be transformed into movement, heat, light, and tension. *Information* can be regarded as the *cause* of all changes in the world" (*BP*, p. 8).

To me, this insistence on information as the fundamental building block of the universe comes very close indeed to Augustine. A computer holds things by "bytes" — by strings of information in the form of "bits" — by combinations of ones and zeros (or by any other combination, as long as it uses only exclusive pairings like "on-off," "right-left," or "positive-negative"). Accordingly, I think that the computer offers a fair analogy to what Augustine calls God's eternal holding of creation in the *NOTA*, the "known things" that he hears in the speaking of his eternal Word. But, more than that, the world exists as an *ecology of opposites* in this "computer" of the divine Mind — in the Information that the Word gives to the Father. And the world, as it holds its own being in itself, exists in that same ecology.

However, while the being that creation has in the Mind of God is totally complete (containing not only things themselves but also all the "accidents" of their history), it's an existence that from the world's own point of view might as well be non-existence. We're so used to looking at words and pictures of the created order on the computer screens of our own history that the mysterious bits in which the divine Word relates them to his Father can strike us only as having no being at all. The *NOTA* and the *FACTA* may be held by him in one grand byte of "morning-evening" knowing — a single packet of divine Information in which even opposites like being/non-being, life/death, and good/evil are intrinsic parts of the ecology of creation. But ever since the tree of the knowledge of good and evil, we've fought against that ecology. What God has joined together, we've tried our best to put asunder. What he sees as a harmony to be cherished by "letting it be," we've heard as a discord to be abolished at all costs. Instead of accepting the ecology of good and evil as God does (barring the rare instances of his divine intervention), we've spent almost all of our history trying to improve the good — and trying to abolish the evil altogether.

And there you see the brilliance of Augustine's words. He saves the ecology by a paradoxical exaltation of the ultimate opposition: *being* and *non-being*. "Before things happened," he says, "they both were and were not. They were, in the knowledge of God; and they were not, in their own nature." Just like the information theorists, he gives you the paradox of a single, complete creation as God holds it in two modes: as the *intellectual Information* of creation held in his Word, and as the *physical embodiment* of that Information as the Word makes it appear on the screen of creation itself. He bypasses all our fuss over whether the "day one" of Genesis 1:5 is a physical or an intellectual act of creation, and he makes the whole of Genesis 1:1-5 cut both ways. God is eternally happy in his *matutina cognitio*, his morning knowing of the world as it exists in the divine Computer; and the world is just as happy in the physical existence it enjoys in his *vespertina cognitio*, his evening knowing as it works its wonders in time and space. All have won, you see, and all shall have prizes. And all shall be well, and all shall be well, and all manner of thing shall be well.

Just a few more observations now and we'll be ready to head for the barn in this chapter. Sooner or later, all analogies, all metaphors — and even all images — break down. And therefore, so does the computer analogy. The hard disk of a computer may hold the "program" for the letter "A," or for whatever it uses to represent "John Smith." But whether the computer itself can be said to "know" any of those things (as God knows them, or even as we know them) is another question entirely. In fact, it's an impossible one to answer. To be sure, we've gotten ourselves into the habit of bandying about phrases like "computer memory," "artificial intelligence," and "smart computers." But it seems to me that by endowing computers with "brains," we've made the two ends of the analogy (*person* and *machine*) line up by the shabby device of moving one of the ends. Either we've lowered the human brain to the status of a "computer made of meat" and then proclaimed it identical with something that's little more than a disk full of magnetic bits. Or we've raised the computer to the status of a person and said that it "knows" (or "will know" if we fiddle with it long enough) exactly as we do.

But when I say I "know" the letter "A" — and above all, when I say I "know" John Smith — I'm not talking about the information by which I hold an "A" or "John Smith." I'm saying that I know *what* an "A" is and *who* John Smith is. How I get the nerve to do that is something we don't know yet — and may never know. But it's certain that we'll never know unless we stop playing the reductionist game of forcing the higher end of the mystery down to the level of the lower. In any case, my knowledge of *what* I'm thinking of, or *whom* I'm dreaming about, shouldn't be reduced to mere information-retrieval. I'm talking about my unique possession of *memory*. And while my memory can be made roughly analogous to what is stored in a computer, a computer can be made analogous to my memory only at the unacceptable price of robbing me of 99 percent of what and whom I know. I meet entire histories when I think or dream, not just scraps of information. And I know I meet them: they please or displease me mightily. I'm not at all sure that a computer will ever have such a wide range of tastes.

Furthermore, when I speak of God's knowledge of me, I'm not talking about his knowledge of a *program* for me but about his personal acquaintance with *me*. And I think Augustine felt the same way. He might toy with analogies like morning and evening knowing; but when push came to shove, his *fides*, his faith, came before anything his *intellectus*, his understanding, might dredge up. For Augustine, all his mind needed to rest on was the fact that

God's Son died for him on the cross. His own cleverness at decoding biblical information never entered into the case.

So, in spite of my initial enthusiasm for the information model, I think it has to go the way of all analogies: into the dustbin of unserious theology. It's possible, of course, that everything Augustine and I think we know is just malarkey — that the reductionists are right, and that the world is nothing but whatever they say it's nothing but. But pardon us both if we don't cheer for such a dreary world — or for such a monochromatic God. It's so much more fascinating to embrace the paradoxes of "everything out of nothing," of "life out of death," and of "good and evil held simultaneously in God" than it is to put up with the grim cheerfulness of village atheists and the simplifications of tenth-grade science curricula. Paradox takes us on trips for which analogy can't even buy a ticket.

Which is why, I suppose, the Bible uses paradox when it needs a Sunday punch — and why good theology does the same. In Genesis 1:2, we read, "And the earth was without form and void." This is neither an analogy nor a metaphor nor an image. It doesn't tell us what the earth was like; it tells us what it was not like. It gives us, in short, the non-sense of paradox. And so do Paul's words in 1 Corinthians 1:18 and 1:25: "For the word of the cross is folly to those who are perishing, but to us who are being saved it is the power of God. . . . For the foolishness of God is wiser than men, and the weakness of God is stronger than men." And when we come to Jesus' parables (which we so often insist on seeing as analogies and then insultingly misrepresent by naming them after the human characters rather than the God-character), we find that what they really give us is not illustrative metaphor but mind-boggling paradox. His stories don't make lights go on in our heads; they put out all the lights we thought we had.

For example, the parable of the Lost Sheep in Luke 15:1-7 should be renamed The Shepherd Who Lost One Sheep, since the whole point of the story is the *foolishness* of a shepherd who leaves ninety-nine sheep to the jackals and runs after a single lost one. It's the *shepherd's losing* that's the driving force of the parable, not the sheep's lostness. For all practical purposes, therefore, he goes out of the sheep-ranching business — which is Jesus' way of preparing us for the fact that God, who is just as foolish, will go out of the "God business" on the cross. Or again, the parable of the Prodigal Son in Luke 15:11-32 should be renamed The Father Who Lost Two Sons, since it's his willingness to lose everything that leads him to drop dead legally at the very start of the parable by putting his will into effect while he's still alive. In effect, he goes out of the parenting business just as the Heavenly Father does when he paradoxically forsakes his only-begotten Son on Calvary. And in Luke 20:9-19, the parable of the Vineyard and the Tenants should be called the parable of the Absent Vineyard Owner: the man who plants a vineyard, lets it out to tenants, and then goes away on a long trip is just one more instance of the paradox of the Incarnate Word, whose implausible presence in Jesus will always strike our common-sensical minds as little more than an absence.

*   *   *

So if I had to grade Augustine on his performance in the passage we've been considering, I'd give him an A for his paradox that creation both *is and is not* as it exists in God, but only a B+ for his analogy of the *morning and evening knowing* of God. My reason for shaving a half-point off the second grade is that Augustine seems not to have taken all the advantage he might have from the Bible's odd listing of the days of creation. Contrary to our usual way of listing times of day, the mornings and evenings of the six days of creation in the first chapter of Genesis are mentioned in reverse order. At Genesis 1:5, a narrator says (in voice-over), "And there was evening and there was morning, day one." And at the end of all the other days, we hear the same thing: "And there was evening and there was morning, a second day [and a third, and so on]."

No doubt the film's departure from our custom can be attributed to the Hebrew habit of reckoning a day from the sundown of the day before. The Saturday of the Sabbath, for example, begins on Friday evening. But it seems to me that Augustine might have made some hay of his own with that reversal. Having spoken of the *nothing* out of which God made the heavens and the earth, he could easily have put the *evening* knowledge of God first and the *morning* knowledge second. That way, he could have put the "first" beginning of creation (the origin of the world in the mind of God) in the *nothing* of the darkness with which day one begins, and he could have assigned the "second" beginning of creation (the origin of the world in its own right) to the morning provided by the light created on that same day. Thus he might have made himself not only more Hebraic but perhaps even more Augustinian.

So if I may take Augustine where I think he was already going, I find another insight into his insistence on creation *ex nihilo*. It seems to me that all six days of *Genesis, the Movie's* opening sequence show us creation out of nothing. True enough, our modern "evolutionary" approach to creation leads us to think that God's creative act comes only at the start of the world's history; after that, we imagine that the world develops pretty much by its own intermediate devices. But the film of Genesis gives us *immediate* creative acts of God on each of those days. God just speaks, and things are: "And God said, 'Let there be light,' and there was light." And so on, with everything else.

I'm not the least bit interested in defending the "creation science" of fundamentalism here. All I'm saying is that, from the point of view of the Mind of God, the existence of every single thing is a leap out of nothing into being at every single instant of its history. I'm not sitting here at my computer, for example, because I was here ten minutes ago — or because once upon a time my parents gave me being. I'm here because *right now* God is bringing me out of nothing into being. And so it is with you, and your dog, and your shoes, and everything else in the universe. We're all hip-deep, up to our necks, and in over our heads in nothing at every moment. And yet at the same time, we're also marvelously and mysteriously outside nothing — and outside all other possible "causes" of our being. In short, no ancestors or antecedents of ours are sufficient to explain the alarming and glorious fact that we now *are*. Our present existence *extra nihil* and *extra causas* is a gift from God, not from them. And that birthday present — that "being-day" present — has always been ours, and will always be ours, in the endless Today of the exchanges of the Trinity. Even the resurrection of the dead is simply the Word's persistent speaking, over the nothing of our deaths, of the names he has always whispered into the Father's ear. Because he never forgets us, *nothing* is always the safest place for us to be.

*   *   *

Be that as it may, I want to end this chapter's peek into the Mind of God by giving you something else I've thought of on the subject of Augustine's *matutina* and *vespertina* knowledge. If you look at those two images in the context of the entire film of the Bible, you'll see that *morning* is the image that the Director, too, most wants to stress. Right at the beginning of the film, therefore, she takes its biblical position *after* evening as a place of honor. And why does she do that? Because she intends to bring up the image of *morning* over and over in her movie — and as Jesus said (in Matthew 19:30, KJV), "the last *shall be* first."

Consider some more of her repetitions — her *concordances,* if you will — of this exaltation of morning. When she gets around to filming the Gospels, she'll give you the Song of Zechariah in which (at Luke 1:78) the father of the infant John the Baptist sings of the promised Messiah as the *anatolē ex hypsous,* the *Rising Star* of the East, the *Morning Star,* the Incarnate Word who is the *Dayspring from on high.* Moreover, she's seen to it that this song, as a Canticle in the church's daily cycle of prayer, would appear in Matins, in Morning Prayer — in the Morning Office, where it goes by the name of the *Benedictus Dominus Deus Israel.* So when Augustine called God's knowledge of creation as it exists in himself a *matutina cognitio,* he wasn't just concocting an image out of his head; he was retrieving it from his heart, where it had long since taken up residence during all the prayerful attention he'd paid to Scripture since his conversion.

Furthermore, when Augustine gives us the image of a *vespertina cognitio,* we who've prayed the Office of daily Evening Prayer receive another illumination. (Evening Prayer, by the way, was created by the Reformers of the sixteenth century: they compiled it by putting together the monastic offices of Vespers and Compline.) In any case, as the Office now stands in the Book of Common Prayer, it contains the Canticle *Phōs hilaron,* which the 1979 Book borrowed from the Vespers of the Orthodox Church. In this song, as we sing of that *phōs hilaron,* we hear it referred to as the "gracious Light," the "gladsome Light," even the "hilarious Light." Vespers is prayed as the shadows fall at the close of the working day. But when we recite it, we look forward not only to the temporary end of our labors here but also to the perpetual Rest of all things in the Word, who is their End and their Beginning.

Therefore I'm now willing to give Augustine back his A on God's morning and evening knowledge, and even to give it a liturgical spin. Three insights have just become possible for me. The *Matins* of that day in the divine Intellect (Gen. 1:3) sing to me of the created but unseeable light, which God made in the image of his uncreated, invisible Light — of his only-begotten Word. The *Vespers* of that day sing to me from the blackness of the screen throughout the whole day. And the *Lauds* of that day — its *Night Office,* recited in the darkness just before the morning twilight of the second day — sing to me of the Dawning of the New Creation and the restoration of all things in the Morning Star from on high, by whom all things are made.

But even if you insist on seeing the whole movie of the Bible strictly as a picture of God's relationship with the physical creation, the images of God's morning and evening knowing can still serve you well. All you have to do is recognize that the world itself, in its very history, has its own Daily Office. Day One of its beginning in Genesis is its Matins. Its Last Day — the long, short day of the *parousia* of the Word in Revelation — is its Vespers. And its Lauds is recited as it rises from the dead in its Baptism, where its life in the endless Today of the Trinity is proclaimed over it.

Now, at last, it's time for the Star of the film.

THE FILM ITSELF

Genesis 1:1–2:3

FIVE

Day One: Genesis 1:1-5

THE HEAVENS, THE EARTH, THE DEEP, AND THE LIGHT

A Tour of the Star's House

So far in this book, my organizing principle (if that's not too charitable a description) has been to arrange my conversation with you as a dialogue on the credits of *Genesis, the Movie* that appeared on page 3. But if I may switch metaphors for two paragraphs, that conversation has been a bit like what the seller (myself) of a house (the first three chapters of Genesis) would say to a prospective buyer (you) before taking you inside the house itself. I've had you standing out in the yard all this time, giving you hints of what you'll see when we actually inspect the interior. But now, I finally begin our trip through all the rooms of the house as Augustine has shown them to me in his *De Genesi ad Litteram*: it will take us, verse by verse, through everything my promotional spiel thus far has been advertising.

First, though, I want to say something about the original Builder of the house, the Father's eternal Word. It's a commonplace among Christians to say that we believe the Bible to be the Word of God. But I want you to note precisely what that phrase signifies. It can't just mean that certain words spoken or inspired by God have been inserted here and there in a book. Rather, "the Word" must be taken in its most profound sense: not as a mere message from God but as the ultimate Messenger himself. He is the eternal Son of God, the second Person of the Trinity, the divine Wisdom who mightily and sweetly orders all things. In short, he's the Word by whom everything has been made and by whose Incarnation everything has been restored to its true nature. I know I've said all that many times now, but it's precisely the Word's mysterious presence in every room of the biblical house that enables us to meet him in all its nooks and crannies. Or, to return to my image of the Bible as a movie, that makes it possible for us to meet the Star of the film in every sequence of the picture, Old Testament or New, wherever and whenever we look for him.

You may be tempted to balk at that. Higher criticism has made cowards of us all. The critics have so often cautioned us against reading Old Testament passages as presences of Christ — and, I might add, have been so stuck in the notion that the Incarnation is God's late-afternoon foray into history — that we're positively terrified of seeing anything *before* Jesus as the Word Incarnate in person.

As I've said, the farthest we can go is to say that while certain Old Testament passages can be allegorized into suggestions of Christ, they themselves have nothing to do with the Incarnation. This comes, of course, from the critics' bad habit of looking at the scenes of the movie of Scripture in isolation rather than in the context of the whole film. They concentrate so much on the trees in the picture that they miss the forest in which they're standing. Yet that flies in the face of the church's long tradition of "finding Christ" in both Testaments — a tradition, unfortunately, that we've long since abandoned.

For example, we've lost our ability to see the Paschal Lamb in Exodus as an earlier appearance of Christ — as a *sacrament,* a *real presence* of the Word Incarnate. True enough, the Word's presence in the Jesus of the New Testament is the ultimate manifestation of the Incarnation. But since the Persons of the Trinity aren't bound by time and space, the Father's eternal Will to unite his Son with human nature can make anything in creation, human or non-human, into a sacrament of the Incarnation.

That's exactly what Paul makes of the Paschal Lamb (*pesach, pascha,* "Paschal Lamb/Passover") when he refers to chapter 12 of Exodus in 1 Corinthians 5:7. He writes, "Christ our Passover [*to pascha hēmōn etythē Christos*] is sacrificed for us" (KJV), thus equating the Paschal Lamb with Jesus. And he makes an equally sweeping identification when he comes to the water from the rock in Exodus 17. In 1 Corinthians 10:4, he says, "They drank of the spiritual rock that followed them; and the rock was the Christ [*epinon de ek pneumatikēs petras; hē petra de ēn ho Christos*]" (RFC). Sadly, we've lost our grip on that one as well. Bowing to the critics, we write it off as little more than a literary excursion from a text that can't support such a trip.

The same goes for Paul's reference to Abraham in Galatians 3:16: "To Abraham and his *seed* were the promises made." Paul's argument in this passage proceeds from a peculiarity in the text. He observes that it doesn't say "to his *seeds*," as if it were referring to a multitude of descendants, but as if it applied to just one: "to his *seed,* who is Christ" (RFC). In effect, then, he's asking us to envision the Word Incarnate as present in Abraham at the very moment God gave him the promises. And so Paul comes up with the remarkable if paradoxical statement that the promised Messiah, the Word Incarnate who is the Lord and Christ of faith, was already in the world before he manifested himself as Jesus of Nazareth.

If I may put this in terms of my film metaphor, the Incarnate Word who is the Star of the movie shows up as many different "characters" before he appears as Jesus in the climactic Gospel sequences. Fascinatingly, the author of the letter to the Hebrews does this same, flash-forward trick with Abraham's great-grandchild Levi, the progenitor of the priestly tribe of Israel. "And if I may say so," he suggests in Hebrews 7:9-10, "even Levi, who received tithes, paid tithes through Abraham, for he was still in the loins of his father when Melchizedek met him" (RFC).

Both Galatians and Hebrews, therefore, encourage us to revive the tradition of finding Christ in the Old Testament. Well before the church got itself hung up on the Incarnation as an insertion into history, those books were announcing a completely non-insertional Incarnation of the Word in the world. They were making it possible for us to see the Word's becoming flesh as something better than a house call made by a doctor who showed up long after the world really needed him. With their help, we can see the Incarnation as the age-long indwelling of the divine Physician from the beginning.

And there's much more along those same lines in the rest of Scripture. In Revelation 13:8, Christ is spoken of as the Lamb slain *from* the foundation of the world *(apo katabolēs kosmou)*. In John 1:1-4, he's the Word by whom all things have always been made — and who (as their Beginning) has always been present to them, start to finish, as the Life and the Light of the world. And he's been all of that not only from the foundation of the world but even before it. In Ephesians 1:4 we read, "He chose us in him *before* the foundation of the world [*pro katabolēs kosmou*], that we should be holy and blameless before him" (RSV). The Incarnation of the Word, accordingly, was never not in eternity — and it was never not in time and space.

But now for the opening sequence of *Genesis, the Movie* in all its glorious mystery.

The Text of Genesis 1:1-5

Now at last we come to the first installment of chapters 1 through 3 of the Bible. My plan is simple. At the beginning of each episode of the film, I'll print out for you the full biblical text that I'm about to deal with. And since you've bravely stayed with me despite all the Hebrew, Greek, and Latin I've thrown at you, I'll give you those texts in the three ancient languages as well as in three English versions. Here then, without further throat-clearing, is the passage.

LXX Gen. 1:1 ἐν ἀρχῇ ἐποίη-σεν ὁ θεὸς τὸν οὐρανὸν καὶ τὴν γῆν 2 ἡ δὲ γῆ ἦν ἀόρατος καὶ ἀκατασκεύα-στος καὶ σκότος ἐπάνω τῆς ἀβύσσου καὶ πνεῦμα θεοῦ ἐπεφέρετο ἐπάνω τοῦ ὕδατος 3 καὶ εἶπεν ὁ θεός γενηθήτω φῶς καὶ ἐγένετο φῶς 4 καὶ εἶδεν ὁ θεὸς τὸ φῶς ὅτι καλόν καὶ διεχώρισεν ὁ θεὸς ἀνὰ μέσον τοῦ φωτὸς καὶ ἀνὰ μέσον τοῦ σκότους 5 καὶ ἐκάλεσεν ὁ θεὸς τὸ φῶς ἡμέραν καὶ τὸ σκότος ἐκάλεσεν νύκτα καὶ ἐγένετο ἑσπέρα καὶ ἐγένετο πρωί ἡμέρα μία

BHS Gen. 1:1 בְּרֵאשִׁית בָּרָא אֱלֹהִים אֵת הַשָּׁמַיִם וְאֵת הָאָרֶץ: 2 וְהָאָרֶץ הָיְתָה תֹהוּ וָבֹהוּ וְחֹשֶׁךְ עַל־פְּנֵי תְהוֹם וְרוּחַ אֱלֹהִים מְרַחֶפֶת עַל־פְּנֵי הַמָּיִם: 3 וַיֹּאמֶר אֱלֹהִים יְהִי אוֹר וַיְהִי־אוֹר: 4 וַיַּרְא אֱלֹהִים אֶת־הָאוֹר כִּי־טוֹב וַיַּבְדֵּל אֱלֹהִים בֵּין הָאוֹר וּבֵין הַחֹשֶׁךְ: 5 וַיִּקְרָא אֱלֹהִים לָאוֹר יוֹם וְלַחֹשֶׁךְ קָרָא לָיְלָה וַיְהִי־עֶרֶב וַיְהִי־בֹקֶר יוֹם אֶחָד:

VUL Gen. 1:1 in principio creavit Deus caelum et terram 2 terra autem erat inanis et vacua et tenebrae super faciem abyssi et spiri-tus Dei ferebatur super aquas 3 dixitque Deus fiat lux et facta est lux 4 et vidit Deus lucem quod esset bona et divisit lucem ac tenebras 5 appellavitque lucem diem et tenebras noctem factumque est vespere et mane dies unus

KJV Gen. 1:1 In the begin-ning God created the heaven and the earth. 2 And the earth was without form, and void; and darkness *was* upon the face of the deep. And the Spirit of God moved upon the face of the waters. 3 And God said, Let there be light: and there was light. 4 And God saw the light, that *it was* good: and God divided the light from the darkness. 5 And God called the light Day, and the darkness he called Night. And the evening and the morning were the first day.

RSV Gen. 1:1 In the begin-ning God created the heav-ens and the earth. 2 The earth was without form and void, and darkness was upon the face of the deep; and the Spirit of God was moving over the face of the waters. 3 And God said, "Let there be light"; and there was light. 4 And God saw that the light was good; and God separated the light from the darkness. 5 God called the light Day, and the darkness he called Night. And there was evening and there was morning, one day.

NRSV Gen. 1:1 In the begin-ning when God created the heavens and the earth, 2 the earth was a formless void and darkness covered the face of the deep, while a wind from God swept over the face of the waters. 3 Then God said, "Let there be light"; and there was light. 4 And God saw that the light was good; and God separated the light from the darkness. 5 God called the light Day, and the darkness he called Night. And there was evening and there was morning, the first day.

Look first at the opening word of the Hebrew text. It's *b'reshith* ("In the Beginning"), and it's the very word I left untranslated and untransliterated as the title of the movie on page 3. My reason for doing that was my hope that the sight of a large-type, unpointed Hebrew word coming up in white letters on a black screen might serve as a sly intimation of the mystery of the Word of God himself. But the word is also the title of the book of Genesis in the Hebrew Bible. This custom of using "incipits" (first words) as book titles prevails in all five books of the Torah. Genesis is entitled *b'reshith,* "In the beginning"; Exodus goes by the name of *v'eleh sh'moth,* "And these are the names"; Leviticus has the title *v'yiqra',* "And he called"; Numbers, oddly, is called *b'midhbar,* "in the wilderness" (which is actually the fourth word); and Deuteronomy is named *eleh had'bharim,* "These are the words." (If you find this too minor for words, just move on.)

In any event, while I've still got you back at the beginning of this book, I should give you an explanation for the "various narrators" I alluded to on page 4. I made them plural for a reason I'm only now in a position to give you. Since the Persons of the Trinity as such were never going to be visible onscreen at any point in chapter 1 of Genesis (we see only the results of their creating, not the Persons themselves), I felt that the Director would need to supply just voices, not in-person actors, for those characters. So if you were wondering about my using more than one narrator, here's how I envisioned her casting of those voices. She would hire a single, male voice (a bass) for the Father; two voices, one male (a tenor) and one female (a soprano) for the Son; an exclusively female voice (an alto) for the Holy Spirit; and she would use all four voices in unison whenever she wanted us to hear the Holy Trinity speaking in concert.

If you're bothered by the two voices and two sexes for the Son, don't be. First of all, the Incarnate Word has two natures (divine and human) in one Person. But since divinity is to humanity (male *and* female) as lover is to beloved, as husband is to wife, as Adam is to Eve, why not give the divine Word a soprano as well as a tenor representation? After all, when the Word is portrayed at other places in the film as the divine Wisdom, the *Chokhmah,* the *Sophia,* the *Sapientia* of God (as he is, for instance, in Ecclus. 1:4ff.), the noun is feminine in all three ancient languages. But for a second point, when Jesus likens himself to a mother hen brooding over Jerusalem (Matt. 23:37 and Luke 13:34), that plaintive passage fairly cries out for a female voice.

Again, if you have trouble with an alto speaking for the Spirit, you can let go of that as well. While the Greek for Spirit *(Pneuma)* is neuter, and the Latin *(Spiritus)* is masculine, the original Hebrew word is *Rûach,* a feminine noun. Furthermore, the Spirit *broods* over the face of the deep: only a warm voice can fill that bill. (Listen to the lovely alto passages in Brahms's *Requiem.*) But finally, if my suggestion of four voices for the three Persons of the Trinity offends your numerical fastidiousness, remember that when you hear them in the film, they'll register as the *One* in God's Name of Three-in-One. Problems solved. On to the benefits of this casting.

To begin with, look at what this mixed chorus of God-voices does for the much-criticized "male chauvinism" of the Bible. Its inclusion of all the genders puts God beyond the limitations of any of them. The Persons of the Trinity, of course, are neither masculine, feminine, nor neuter in themselves. To be sure, the Trinity that makes sexual creatures holds all the sexualities of the world within its bosom; and we may freely use words of any gender when we try to speak of that triune God. But when we speak of the divine Essence, we ought to realize that everything, sex included, is transcended in the Deity. And what better way is there to convey that truth than by *not* making a "he," a "she," an "it," or a "them" the only way we refer to God?

One other note. You mustn't think I'm giving you a "shooting script" of my own for the movie of Genesis. The film I'm asking you to watch already exists on the pages of the Bible. All I'm doing here is suggesting a fresh way of watching it — of hearing what the divine Director has already put on the sound track for you. My talents don't extend to script-writing (though, Lord knows, I've often tried my hand at it). They're strictly limited to enthusiasm for the film-making of others. If you find them helpful, good. If you find them bothersome, good too: you may have creative talents of your own that will serve you better. But in either case, it's time for us to turn to the text of Genesis itself — and to my comments on it.

*   *   *

> Genesis 1, verses 1 and 2: *In the beginning God created the heavens and the earth. And the earth was without form and void, and darkness was upon the face of the deep; and the Spirit of God was moving over the face of the waters.* (RSV and KJV, conflated)

Let me begin with another passage from Augustine that corroborates his insistence that the word *Beginning* is a reference to the Father's Word himself. In his *Confessions,* XI, 9, he has this to say:

> *In hoc Principio, Deus, fecisti coelum et terram, in Verbo tuo, in Filio tuo, in Virtute tua, in Sapientia tua, in Veritate tua, miro modo dicens, et miro*

modo faciens. Quis comprehendit? quis enarrabit? Audiat te intus sermo-cinantem qui potest; ego fidenter ex oraculo tuo clamabo: "Quam magnificata sunt opera tua, Domine, omnia in Sapientia fecisti!" et illa Principium, et in eo Principio fecisti coelum et terram.

In this Beginning, O God, you made heaven and earth, in your Word, in your Son, in your Power, in your Wisdom, in your Truth, marvelously speaking and marvelously making. Who understands this; who shall declare it? Let him who is able to hear listen to you inwardly as you converse with him out of your scriptural oracle. I will confidently cry aloud, "How wonderful are your works, O Lord. In Wisdom you have made them all" [Psalm 104:24]. And she is the Beginning; and in that Beginning you made heaven and earth.

We, of course, are so used to seeing God's creation of the world as a "production," a "job" done to get things made, that we can hardly grasp what Augustine is saying here. We habitually think that the word *beginning* in Genesis refers to the *start-up* of things, and that thereafter they coast along quite nicely on their own. But that leads us to see the act of creation as a kind of divorce from God. It makes us, as it were, God's "exes" — creatures who, whatever our first connection to God may have been, are separated from him by a gulf that's now unbridgeable by us. In a word, it keeps us from hearing what Augustine is saying here.

He's talking about God's creating not as a once-upon-a-time production but as an act that has always been going on, an act that creates an abiding intimacy with God. And that act has been in progress forever in the exchanges between the Father, the Word, and the Spirit — and at every moment of the world's being. Anything said in the Trinity's Hotbed of Love stands fast in both eternity and time. Our divine Friends are continually creating us.

In other words, Augustine sees creation not as a single *event* back then but as an ongoing *mystery* right now — a mystery to be confidently confessed in every day of the world of time and space. Since the eternal Word is the Beginning in whom God creates all things, that Word, that Wisdom, is perpetually with us in every moment, bringing us out of nothing into being. God doesn't deal in yesterdays and tomorrows; he deals with us only in his endless Today. We mustn't look back into the past for God's making of us, or into the future for his remaking of us. Our choicest access to God will always be in our present — in every *today* that God so graciously gives us as a sacrament of his eternity.

This makes perfect sense, because the present is all we have. We've lost our grip on what has been, and what will be is always beyond our reach. It's his friendship with us *now* that's holding us outside nothing and outside our causes. He's creating us at every moment for the simple reason that his Word is intimate to us in every moment. Our being is an *immediate* — not a *deferred* — response to the speaking of God's Word. Each of us may have showed up at some point in the history of creation (mine came in 1925); but there was never a point in God's creating when the Word wasn't whispering my name in the Father's ear. We're all being brought out of nothing into being every day of our lives.

But since I've once again brought up the subject of God's creation of everything *ex nihilo,* I want to give you my reason for finding that "nothing" in these first two verses of Genesis. Admittedly, no such word appears anywhere in the text of these verses. This is partly due to the fact that Hebrew, unlike some other languages, isn't particularly fond of abstract nouns. *Beginning* is about the only word we might consider an abstraction, but I've pretty much ruled that out by following Augustine and reading it as a name for the Word Incarnate himself. The rest of the words, though, are indisputably concrete: *God, created, heavens, earth, darkness, face, deep, Spirit, waters.*

True enough, the words *tohû vabhohû,* "without form and void," have almost always been translated as an abstraction of sorts — as if they were an invitation to God's dance with the nothing sent to us in an envelope of negative words. But even that's forcing the text a bit, since the primeval chaos that those words represent in verse 2 is mentioned only *after* God has already created the heavens and the earth out of nothing in verse 1. Therefore, it's precisely the absence of any reference to a "raw material" for making everything that most clearly suggests God's creation *ex nihilo.* And if you add to this the fact that the authors of the first creation account in Genesis avoided the common pagan notion of pre-existing matter — of some *Urstoff* independent of God — you come up with a similar corroboration. Taken together, then, this double absence is what allows me (and Augustine) to claim that the paradoxical "stuff" out of which the world was made was precisely *nothing.*

Furthermore, Augustine was just as unwilling as I am to see *Beginning* as an abstraction. When he read the Fourth Gospel's recapitulation of the opening of Genesis, he found the word *beginning* in both books, and he identified it with the Father's Word Incarnate in each of them. Here's how I think he arrived at that insight.

He looked first at John 1:1-3, where he read, "In the beginning was the Word, and the Word was with God, and the Word was God. He was in the beginning with God; all things were made through him, and without him was not a single thing made." But then, Augustine headed straight for verse 14: "And the Word became flesh and dwelt among us" (RFC). After that, he had only to look back at Genesis in his mind's eye and exclaim, "By George, I know who that Beginning is. It's the same Person in both places!" His insight, you see, was not a matter of forcing a New Testament theological concept on an Old Testament text. It was a matter of remembering the biblical film's first presentation of *beginning* in the light of the *Beginning* that the Director shined on it later in the movie.

Indeed, I'd go so far as to say that for Augustine and the vast majority of interpreters before and after him (not counting the critics in the past three or four centuries), the best way to understand the Bible has always been to approach it *cinematically.* Even before the invention of motion pictures, the most useful commentators on Scripture have been those who wrote their reviews only after they'd watched the whole film of the Bible — who could see it as a single, harmonious garden of images, an "imaginary garden" in which they could find the "real toad" of the divine Frog himself in every part of the picture.

But it's even more fascinating to see how Augustine gets creation from the nothing, the *nihil,* the *nulla res* out of which God creates it in the Beginning to the lovely something it now is. In one of his comments on Genesis 1:2, "the earth was *invisible and without form,*" he comes up with a "three-step recipe" for God's act of creation. (The Latin version that Augustine was using translated those words as *invisibilis et informe,* following the Septuagint, which rendered the Hebrew *tohû vabhohû* as *aoratos kai akataskeuastos,* "invisible and unmade.") In any case, here's his recipe, from his *Confessions,* Book XII, 8:

> *Tu enim Domine, fecisti mundum de materia informi, quam fecisti de nulla re pene nullam rem, unde faceres magna quae miramur filii hominum.*

> For you, Lord, made the world from unformed matter; which you made out of *nothing* into an *almost-nothing,* from which you might then make the great *things* at which we children of men marvel.

As a cook, I can almost see the three divine Chefs at work in the heavenly Kitchen. It's practically as if Augustine has God the Father saying, "First, I shall take an infinite bowl of nothing. Then I shall have my Word knead that nothing into a next-to-nothing which, while it's no longer nothing, is not yet anything in its own right. But then, to complete the dish, I shall have my Spirit bake that almost-nothing in the oven of her brooding until it finally becomes something to behold. It will be delicious!" God's cooking show, you see, is the *Seinfeld* of eternity: he can make an entire series out of *nothing*.

In the light of this recipe, I'm tempted to improve on Augustine's notion of God's morning and evening Knowing of creation by turning it into a threefold distinction: a morning Knowing that would be God the Father's Knowledge of the nothing; a midday Knowing that would be the Word's Knowledge of the almost-nothing; and an evening Knowing that would be the Holy Spirit's Brooding over the world's physical existence. It strikes me that these distinctions might light up not only Genesis 1:2, where the earth is "without form and void," but also the grace of Christ's reconciling presence on the cross between noon and three — where even the Word himself is "without form or comeliness" (Isa. 53:2). As a matter of fact, *Between Noon and Three* happens to be the title of the book in which I wrote my way to the realization that it's grace alone which lies at the root of both the creation and the redemption of the world. Take a look at it if you like.

In any case, I have a better idea. Why not do a complete overhaul of the heavenly Kitchen and posit *four* modes of the divine Knowing, on the analogy of the four seasons? This would not only get us out of the prison of clock-time, in which creation now "serves time," and into time as the "high time" in which the Father holds all things in his Word and Spirit. It would also nicely echo the music of Vivaldi's *Four Seasons* that came up at the end of day one on page 4 of this book.

But now I have another thought. Why not apply those seasons both to God's *NOTA* (to the "things known" that God holds in Mind before they exist on their own), and to the *FACTA* (to the "things made" that God also holds in Mind), which creation is able to know in its own existence? Why not a *Winter* Knowing, a *Springtime* Knowing, a *Summer* Knowing, and an *Autumn* Knowing — all existing forever in the divine Mind? And why not a corresponding four-season knowing on the part of creation itself? Why not give the world a winter, spring, summer, and fall knowing as it contemplates its own history?

Finally, why not try to see all four of those seasons, in both God and the world, in the light of Tom Siegfried's *information* model of the act of creation? The seasons of the *NOTA* would then become God's complete "notes" for the created order (in whatever "code" the Trinity stores them); and the seasons of the *FACTA* would become that same code as it's spelled out in the being of creatures themselves. I realize, of course, that this may strike you as a bit high church, if not a downright reach. But for what it's worth, here goes.

In the beginning God created the heavens and the earth. This first verse becomes the Winter of the divine Knowing. All that exists here is the Trinity and the nothing out of which everything is to be made. The only thing we can see is a black screen. But as far as the winter knowing of the created world is concerned, it is the dead of winter indeed: we see nothing at all. Creation can't know God *as God* by its own devices; and it certainly can't know the nothing, because there's nothing there to know. None of the flowers and fruits of creation are visible. They're all hidden in the dark, impenetrable bud of the divine *NOTA*. (Even in the physical winters of the world, the buds of the next growth are present; but the things they will become are not present, except in a code suitable only for their existence in the bud.) So it is with the Winter Knowing of God: his *NOTA*, his "notes" for creation, are also in code. Perhaps not in a binary code but in a totally unreadable and immaterial code known only to the Father, the Word, and the Spirit.

But in God's Winter, everything is there in the *NOTA*, even if creation, in its winter, doesn't know a thing. In all their divinely created glory, the heavens, the earth, the primeval chaos, and the deep over which the Spirit broods have emerged from nothing into being in the Mind of God. In his *Confessions*, Augustine gives us another of his marvelous paradoxes. He calls everything at this point a "nothing-something" (a *nihil aliquid*), an "is, is not" (an *est non est*). Shades of his *et erant et non erant*: all things "both were and were not: they *were*, in the Knowledge of God; and they *were not*, in their own natures." Shades, too, of Lancelot Andrewes, the seventeenth-century Bishop of Winchester, as quoted by T. S. Eliot in his *Journey of the Magi*:

> "A cold coming we had of it,
> Just the worst time of the year. . . .
> The ways deep and the weather sharp,
> The very dead of winter."

In the deep chill of God's Winter Knowing at the beginning of Genesis, he has creation all together in himself. And "in the bleak midwinter" of our world of sad facts — after all the disasters of our history — the Incarnate Word by whom the Father makes all things will put it all together again. Everything comes full circle in him who is the Alpha and the Omega, the Beginning and the Ending.

But in the meanwhile, there is the Springtime of God's Knowing in verse 2: *And the earth was without form and void, and darkness was upon the face of the deep; and the Spirit of God was moving over the face of the waters.*

The Spirit is the first breath of the divine Spring. The Trinity have already known the Winter of the nothing out of which they intend to bring the creation. But now the Spirit turns it into an almost-nothing, into the *pene nulla res* from which God will ultimately cause the world to exist in itself. This preliminary step, if you will, is the greening of the black bud of God's Winter Knowing just before it bursts into leaf under the Spirit's brooding. Or, possibly, we might see it as the beginning of the Spirit's conversion of the code of God's "notes" for creation into what will eventually be the "facts" of creation. (Nevertheless, it's still not springtime for creation.) Or, for a third possibility, we might take God's Springtime Knowing as the Spirit's "rebooting" of the divine Computer after she's installed the new software needed to run the final program. In that case, creation's springtime would be just around the corner, waiting for the world to trip over it when the light is created in verse 3. Pay your money and take your choice.

At any rate, it's the Spirit's brooding — her hovering over the *NOTA* in the divine Mind — that's the key to the rest of the seasons. To the full burgeoning of the divine Springtime under the light created in verse 3 (and to the world's first whiff of its own spring); to God's Summer Knowing of the emerging world; and to the day and night by whose lengthening and shortening creation will eventually know its own summer as it follows in verse 4 and in the rest of the six days of creation. And finally, there will be the bountiful Autumn of God's Knowing on the sixth and seventh days, and the world's autumn as it reaps the harvest of its being. But at this point, creation still exists only in God's code, not in its own realization of it. On to the next part of this chapter's text.

> Genesis 1, verse 3: *And God said, "Let there be light"; and there was light.*

This verse gives us the late Spring of God's Knowing and the first sign of creation's own springtime. And in both of those springs, all things are preparing to bear fruit under a Light beyond all created lights. Let me give you a few scriptural references to support that.

Everything that comes out of the nothing now greets the rising of the Morningstar, the Dayspring from on high that has visited us (Luke 1:78). Everything now feels the heat of the Sun of righteousness, who rises with healing in his wings (Mal. 4:2). And everything is now basking in the radiance of the Word who is the Life and Light of the world (John 1:1-4). Even though there's as yet no sun in the heavens of the physical world, perhaps those scriptural references can stand as witnesses to the eternal Spring (and the spring of time and space) in God's Mind as he beholds it in the Light of his Incarnate Word.

But this verse is also the bridge to the high Summer of the divine

Knowing — to the exuberance of the code in which the Trinity spell out creation to themselves. God may know all things in his Word as their Beginning; but he knows none of them in a merely *incipient* way — as if he would have to wait and see how things turned out. His code is so complete that it anticipates, and makes provision for, every possible action of creation. All its accidents, all its free choices, even all its sins. But it's so mysterious a code that it in no way predetermines what creation will do with its freedom. And therefore the divine Summer is the perfect analogy to illuminate the mystery of the divine *Tolerance* that God extends to absolutely everything.

Summers are a grand ecology of accepted opposites, a concert of relished differences. Too hot in one place, too cool in others; torrential rains and relentless droughts; thunderstorms and clear skies — all of them are gladly allowed within the providence of the divine code. But none of them is a matter of divine manipulation. God creates by *letting things be,* not by shoving them around. He gets his way by not getting in anything's way. Which brings us at last to the all-inclusiveness of the divine Autumn.

> Genesis 1, verse 4: *And God saw that the light was good; and*
> *God separated the light from the darkness.*

Let me begin here by quoting from the sermon John Donne delivered on Christmas Day in the evening, 1624. It's a perfect introduction not only to the glories of God's Autumn but also to the dismal seasons that the world has brought on itself in its fall from grace — and to the happy ending to which God brings it when he restores creation in his beloved Son:

> God made sun and moon to distinguish seasons, and day and night, and we cannot have the fruits of the earth but in their seasons: But God hath made no decree to distinguish the seasons of his mercies; in paradise, the fruits were ripe, the first minute, and in heaven it is alwaies Autumne, his mercies are ever in their maturity. We ask *panem quotidianam,* our daily bread, and God never sayes you should have come yesterday, he never sayes you must againe to morrow, but *to day if you will heare his voice,* to day he will heare you. If some King of the earth have so large an extent of dominion, in North, and South, as that he hath Winter and Summer together in his Dominions; so large an extent East and West as that he hath day and night together in his Dominions, much more hath God mercy and judgement together: He brought light out of darknesse, not out of a lesser light; he can bring thy Summer out of Winter, though thou have no Spring; though in the wayes of fortune, or understanding, or conscience,

thou have been benighted till now, wintred and frozen, clouded and eclypsed, damped and benummed, smothered and stupefied till now, now God comes to thee, not as in the dawning of the day, not as in the bud of the spring, but as the Sun at noon to illustrate all shadowes, as the sheaves in harvest, to fill all penuries, all occasions invite his mercies, and all times are his seasons.

The first word of the verse we now have in hand is "And God *saw*." Under the influence of Augustine's preoccupation with God's knowing, I've given a lot of space thus far to his concept of the *NOTA* of creation as they're held in the divine Mind. But despite my enthusiasm for that "intellectual" approach to the mystery of creation, it strikes me that this verse makes a major improvement on it. The trouble with talking about what God *knows* is that it inevitably stirs up the subject of *foreknowledge* in our minds. And that in turn suggests predetermination, or even predestination. Strictly speaking, of course, those words can't apply to God at all. In his endless and beginningless Today, there is no before or after — and consequently no "pre-" or "post-." As I've said, God is simply the eternal Contemporary of every event in time.

Of course when I say, "I know the sun will rise at 5:45 tomorrow morning," there's always a hint of predetermination. In the back of my mind, I'm convinced that the sun *has to rise* at that time. But this verse takes me light years away from such a conclusion. It doesn't say that God *knew* the light was good; it says he *saw* it was good. G. K. Chesterton, with his flair for making light shine in darkness, once said that the sun doesn't rise because it has to; it rises because, as God watches it set each evening, he says, "That was nice; do it again." God, therefore, is the eternal Beholder of creation. He is the Watcher and the Holy One of the book of Daniel, viewing the film of creation right along with the rest of us. He is the divine Spectator of the world he's created. God looks at everything in admiration; and whatever he admires, he simply *lets be*.

The world is to God as wine and chocolate are to us. Creation isn't something God needs; it's something he likes. He doesn't say, "I need the world." That's a statement that would get him off the train of delight many stops short of "I love the world." Therefore, the world is not something God has to have; it's the *overflow* of the totally unnecessary love of the Trinity as they tell each other how delicious they find things. And it's precisely that deliciousness of things in the sight of God that's the taproot of our existence. We're all fine wines in God's cellar. He has all of eternity to give us the aging we deserve.

So here God simply looks at the very first thing he's made — the created light that is the image of his only-begotten, uncreated Light — and the final thing he chooses to say about it is simply, "Delicious! *Tôbh! Kalon! Bona!* Good!" He runs the world, you see, not by a plan that makes it behave but out of his heart's desire to see it do its own thing. No matter what creation does with its freedom, he sees in that freedom only the goodness that it has in the Word who is its Beginning — and the goodness to which that Word restores it as its Ending.

The word *good* is repeated seven times in chapter 1 of Genesis (eight times, if you follow the Septuagint), and those repetitions are what make it the principal theme of *Genesis, the Movie.* Unfortunately, though, we find goodness entertaining only until our favorite subject, naughtiness, comes along. Once we've seen chapter 3 — with its portrayal of Adam and Eve, and the serpent, and the tree of the knowledge of good and evil — our fascination with moral turpitude drives the original deliciousness of the world right out of our minds. Even Augustine fell into that trap. Indeed, it was he who almost single-handedly gave Western Christianity its preoccupation with sin. In *De Genesi ad Litteram,* he often swamps his usual brilliance in the quagmire of guilt and blame. And he compounds the felony by his insistence that sin goes clean against the grain of God's Mind.

To be sure, when he looked at chapter 2 of Genesis, he decided that everything was still coming up roses. He described our condition there as a *posse non peccare,* a possibility of pleasing God by not sinning. But when he looked at chapter 3, with its picture of our first parents' disobedience and their expulsion from the Garden, he called the resulting condition of the entire human race a *non posse non peccare,* an impossibility of *not* sinning. True, when he finally looked at our ultimate condition as risen and glorified in Christ, he did manage to get goodness back into the picture. In our redeemed state, he said, we'll have a *non posse peccare,* an inability to sin. Still, the net effect of his harping on sin was to convince fifteen hundred years' worth of Christians that their sins went utterly against the grain of God's Mind.

But in the verse we're considering here ("And God *saw* that the light was good"), I think I see something better than that. It suggests to me that while God may find that our sins rub him the wrong way, his delight in our goodness (as he sees us in the uncreated Light of his only-begotten Son) is such that he will put up with our sins rather than set himself against us because of them. And that, as it turns out, is precisely what God does throughout the movie of Scripture.

In the Noah story, for example, he first proposes to destroy the world because of sin; but at the end, he takes it all back and sets up the rainbow as a promise that he'll never do any such thing again (Gen. 6–9). With Abraham, he first commands the sacrifice of Isaac but then provides a ram as a substitute (Gen. 22). He berates Israel for its unfaithfulness but he himself remains faithful to Israel (Hosea). And in the Incarnation of his Son, he "makes him who knew no sin *become sin* for our sakes, that we might become the righteousness of God in him" (2 Cor. 5:21, RFC).

Theologians can talk all they like about the unchangeableness of God and his unswerving antipathy to sin. But the God who appears in the film of the Bible apparently never read the etiquette manuals they wrote for him. It makes no difference to the God of Scripture when (or even whether) we change for the better: "*While we were still sinners,* Christ died for us" (Rom. 5:8). God's longing to see us as "Good!" is the only thing that counts. In Christ, therefore, he has no problems with sin — which is exactly what the Lady Julian said back in the fourteenth century: "Sin is behovely; and all shall be well, and all shall be well, and all manner of thing shall be well." From the beginning, the Best News has always been that the world is good in his eyes. So Adam, Noah, Abraham, Hosea, you, and me (sin to the contrary notwithstanding) are all "first" proclamations of the Gospel. The Beginning himself simply insists on a happy ending from the start.

That brings me to the third and last consideration in this verse: "And God *divided* [*separated*] the light from the darkness." Having said that God is willing to go against his own grain to vindicate the goodness of the world, I want to insist now that the goodness he sees in creation lies precisely in the *graininess* of things — in the *granularity,* the *cellularity* of the world.

The universe as God creates it is not a piece of molded plastic. It isn't a "model world" made from a kit in which all the pieces have the same substance. Rather, it's a world that revels in differences of structure and texture, in the varieties of its parts and parcels. As I've said many times (and will say many times more), it's an *ecology of opposites. Wood,* for example, has a grain built into it: you can split it with a wedge if you go at it with the grain, but you need a saw if you want to cut it across the grain. For another illustration, think of a *tree.* It consists of roots, trunk, bark, branches, and leaves — and each of those elements functions in a way the others do not. Every natural whole is made up of parts that are different from one another. The entire world that God creates, therefore, is a *body,* not a blob. It's made up of members; and each member, despite its differences, dances with all the others.

Some theologians have gone so far as to say that in God himself there is a *coincidentia oppositorum* — a coinciding of opposites. We've already seen some of those opposites in the verses we've covered so far. There is God, who *is* being; and there is the nothing, which has no being at all. There is the *nothing* and the *almost-nothing* he creates from it. In this verse, there is the *light* that he divides from the *darkness*. And to give you just two more that we'll see soon enough, there will be *life* dancing with *death* as the engine of creation (on the third, fifth, and sixth days), and there will even be *good* and *evil* dancing with each other at the tree of the knowledge of good and evil — which I think God put in the Garden of Eden to show how far he will go to make his ecology of diversities a success.

As a matter of fact, in the creation of the angels (which the fathers put at the very start of day one), we find an even more splendid diversity. Although each one of them is supposedly a single, simple substance — an immaterial intelligence which, like a kind of spiritual plastic, is the same for all of them — God gets variety in their cases (according to Aquinas) by making only one of each kind. The differences that God achieves in the material orders of creation come about because creatures *reproduce*. Each species gives rise to many individuals; but each individual within a species has the same basic "substance" as all the others. But angels don't beget little angels. In the angelic orders, each individual angel is a species unto itself.

The archangel Michael, if you will, is a whole species on his own. Gabriel is another, and the Cherubim, Seraphim, and Thrones, the Dominions, Principalities, and Powers are all, every one of them, yet more species. The Wisdom of God achieves the variety of the angelic orders (again, according to Aquinas) not by extrapolating "sameness" but by making so many unique angels that they outnumber all the material individuals the world has ever held. The "heavenly host" is the biggest army God ever assembled.

In any case, I want to end my remarks on this verse by finally giving you a comment on the passage from John Donne with which I began. The unhappy changes and chances that result from the differences in the world may plague the human race in its fallen condition. But "though in the wayes of fortune, or understanding, or conscience, thou have been benighted till now, wintred and frozen, clouded and eclypsed, damped and benummed, smothered and stupefied till now," those painful differences of condition have always been held reconciled in God, who is the *coincidentia oppositorum*. And in that reconciliation, "now God comes to thee, not as in the dawning of the day, not as in the bud of the spring, but as the Sun at noon to illustrate all shadowes, as the sheaves in harvest, to fill all penuries, all occasions invite his mercies, and all times are his seasons." "In heaven it is alwaies Autumne." On to the final verse.

> Genesis 1, verse 5: *And God called the light Day, and the darkness he called Night. And there was evening and there was morning, one day.*

First, consider the introduction of morning and evening at this point in the movie. Setting aside my elaborate variations on Augustine's theme of God's *matutina* and *vespertina* knowing, perhaps the simplest explanation for the presence of these words here is that the Director of the film, having decided to use a six-day format for her creation scenario, now wants to tie all six days together by putting the same coda at the end of each. But I also think it's possible to see this verse as her bridge from the endless Today of God — from the "one day" of the Trinity to the successive "days" of the world of time and space. Even before she gets to the fourth day (when God makes the sun, moon, and stars by which we reckon physical days and years), she's leading us to see time itself not simply as a parameter of things that exist in the physical realm but as a treasure held forever in the bosom of God. She's pointing us to a vision of time as something *inside* God — time as somehow co-eternal with God, not as a lesser piece of business opposed to his eternity or disconnected from his Mind.

But I still owe you a word about the Director's unique, *cardinal* numbering of the opening day of creation. The Hebrew text calls it *yôm echadh*, "day *one*"; but when it comes to the other days, it gives them *ordinal* numbers (a *second* day, a *third* day, and so on). Augustine takes note of this oddity at many places in his *De Genesi ad Litteram*; but among his remarks on it, there are three in particular that leap out at me. The first is from Book I, 33:

> *An hic dies totius temporis nomen est, et omnia volumina saeculorum hoc vocabulo includit; ideoque non dictus est primus, sed unus dies?*

> Or possibly, can "day" here be a name for the whole of time, with all the scrolls of the ages included in it? Can that be why it's not called "a first day," but "one day"?

I give you this quote because it dramatically shows the freedom with which Augustine approaches Scripture — and the almost experimental way he investigates its possibilities. As many commentators have done, he takes note of this "one day," but he doesn't just skip over it or explain it away. Instead, he lets himself play with possible interpretations of it, and he comes up with the remarkable notion that it might refer to the entire course of the world's history — to "all the volumes of the ages." In other words, even though he's talking about time, he can still see it *sub specie aeternitatis*, from the viewpoint of God's eternity, where every moment of time is stored as one of his favorite playthings. All the world's nows and thens are simply delights to him in his eternal *Now*.

Shades of John Donne's "*to day* if you will heare his voice, *to day* he will heare you"; of his "*now* God comes to thee"; and of his "*all times are his seasons.*" And shades, once again, of my own notion that our choicest access to God's "volumes of the ages" lies in every present moment — in each second of every minute that finds us penciling into those scrolls what God finally recopies in ink. For Augustine, the short days of our times are just one long day in the presence of God, and everything we write in them God writes as well. He may indeed make corrections of his own, but he never erases the pencil marks of our sins. He leaves them written forever on the Body of his beloved Son. Jesus sits at the right hand of the Father with the Glorious Scars of our sins in his hands, feet, and side.

The second passage is from *De Genesi ad Litteram*, IV, 37, where Augustine suggests that the seventh day, on which God rested, is a repetition of that same "one day":

> *Quomodo ergo requievit in die quem non creavit? Aut quomodo eum post sex dies continuo creavit, cum sexto die consummaverit omnia quae creavit, nec aliquid septimo die creaverit, sed in eo potius ab omnibus quae creaverat, requieverit? An unum tantummodo diem creavit Deus, ut eius repetitione multi, qui dicuntur dies, praeterirent atque transcurrent; nec opus erat ut septimum diem crearet, quia illius quem creaverat, septima repetitio hunc itaque faciebat? Lucem quippe de qua scriptum est, "Et dixit Deus 'Fiat lux,' et facta est lux, discrevit a tenebris, eamque vocavit diem, et tenebras vocavit noctem."*

How then did he [God] rest on a day in which he didn't create? Or how did he go on creating in it after the six days, when on the sixth day he would have finished everything that he created? Nor would he have created anything on the seventh day, but rather he would have rested from everything he had created. Or is it possible that God created on one day only, so that by the repetition of the word "day," the many "days" that are spoken of might pass quickly by, and there would be no need for him to create on the seventh day, because what he might have made on this day would thus be the seventh repetition of that same "one day" on which he created [the heavens and the earth]? For indeed the light — of which it is written, "And God said, 'Let there be light,' and there was light" — that light, he separated from the darkness, and he called it day, and the darkness he called night.

That was more of Augustine's sometimes wordy playfulness with Scripture. First, he wonders whether God created on one day only (on "day one" alone, or on the five succeeding "days" considered as "repetitions" or extensions of that day). But then he suggests that the seventh day too is a repetition of "day one," and he reasons that God had no need to create in the seventh day because all his work was done as soon as he said "Let there be light" on "day one."

All I have to add to Augustine's theological wordplay here is one observation of my own. His scrunching together of all the "days" in the opening of *Genesis, the Movie* will be supported by the rest of the film when we come to it. In Genesis 2:4, we'll find, "These are the generations of the heavens and of the earth when they were created, *in the day* that the LORD God made the earth and the heavens" (KJV, italics mine). Enough said. Once again, we have never been anywhere but in the light of that Dayspring without morning or evening, and in the presence of his heavenly Father, who invites us to sit back and rejoice that all manner of thing shall be well.

The third passage is from Augustine's *Confessions,* XI, 9, where he goes even further. He turns the creation of the world into an all-at-once, eternal act. He not only counteracts the apparent "successiveness" of the biblical accounts; he roots them all in the *eternity* of the Father's Word:

> *Non ergo quidquam Verbi tui cedit atque succedit quoniam vere immortale atque aeternum est. Et ideo Verbo tibi coaeterno, simul et sempiterne dicis omnia quae dicis; et fit quidquam dicis ut fiat.*

> Nothing then of your Word either gives place or is replaced because he is truly immortal and eternal. And therefore, in the Word who is co-eternal with you, at once and forever you say all that you say; and whatever you say comes into being.

What this last passage brings up once more is the question of whether God made the world by successive acts of creation in time or whether he made it all at once in his eternity. There's no doubt in my mind that most people think that creation (on the analogy of physical evolution) was a one-thing-after-another proposition. But here, Augustine opts for the Word's speaking all things into being *simul et sempiterne,* "at once and forever," as the cause of their being. Obviously, I'm inordinately fond of that phrase. But better minds than yours or mine have wrestled with the question, and they've come up with answers that at least keep it open. Augustine, for one, seems to opt for at least the possibility that the world may in some sense have existed from all eternity.

As you already know, he reads "in the beginning" as "in the *Beginning,*" that is, as "in the eternal Word himself" — which is exactly what he just said above: "Therefore, in the Word who is co-eternal with you, at once and forever you say all that you say; and whatever you say comes into being." On the other hand, his distinction between God's *NOTA* and God's *FACTA* seems to point both ways. What *God knows* about things is certainly eternal because it's in the Mind of the eternal God. He can't possibly be said to have decided to create at some point in eternity, because eternity has no "points." But insofar as creation *knows itself*, God's act of creation would not seem to be eternal at all. Everything in the world begins and ends at some point in time; therefore, it would seem at least likely that the world as a whole has a beginning and an end. So Augustine ends this part of his cosmology-cosmogony game with a tie score: yes, the world is eternal in God; no, the world is not eternal in itself.

And that's where the question was left until Augustine's greatest disciple, Thomas Aquinas, had his innings. Following the newly discovered Aristotle (courtesy of the Arabic scholars who translated him into Latin), Aquinas made some further distinctions. Aristotle had argued for the existence of God by holding that a world of causes and effects could not be the cause of itself because we can't find a real reason for its existence just by positing an "infinite regress" — that is, an endless going back — in the chain of efficient causes *within* the system of the world. Accordingly, he felt it necessary to posit a "first cause" that would lie totally outside the system.

Aquinas used this same line of reasoning to come up with still more "proofs" of the existence of God: an *unnecessary* world needed to rest on a *necessary* Being; a world of *movers* and *things moved* had to have an Unmoved Mover if it was to exist at all. But the most fascinating thing about those "arguments" was that Aristotle arrived at them despite the fact that he thought the world was *just as eternal as God.* For him, even an everlasting creation needed more than itself to explain itself.

Which is where Aquinas comes into the picture. In Question XLVI, Article II of his *Summa Theologica*, entitled "Whether it is an article of faith that the world began," he adduces arguments, as he always does, both against and for a "yes" to that inquiry. Here's a fair excerpt from that passage, at the place where he shifts from the negative to the positive:

> Articles of faith cannot be proved demonstratively, because as it's said in Hebrews 11:1, faith is not about things seen ["Now faith is the substance of things hoped for, the evidence of things not seen"]. But that God is the creator of the world in such a way that the world began to be is indeed an article of faith. And the reason for this is that the "origination" [the "newness," the *novitas*] of the world cannot be demonstrated on the basis of the world itself. Because the basis of any demonstration is what something is here and now. But when we speak of the intellectual concept of a thing, we abstract from the here and now — which is why it's said that the

"universals" [the abstract intellectual concepts that we form of things] exist everywhere and always. And because of that, it's impossible to demonstrate that "man" or "heaven" or "stone" have *not* always been.

Similarly, the "origination" of the world cannot be investigated by arguing from the agent who caused it, because an agent works by will. But the will of God can't be investigated by reason, except in the case of things that it's absolutely necessary for God to will [such as the Father's begetting of the Son]. Such, however, is not the case with creatures made by God.

But it is possible for the will of God to be manifested by revelation to someone who leans on faith. Therefore, the truth that the world began is believable but not demonstrable or knowable. And this is useful to consider lest someone who has faith, presuming that he can demonstrate his faith intellectually, might adduce reasons that have no necessity to them, and so might give unbelievers material for ridicule, thinking that it's for reasons of this sort that we believe things that can only be of faith.

To sum up that rather free translation in my own words, Aquinas is saying that any rational solution to the problem of whether the world has existed eternally in its own right must be based on conclusions drawn from the facts of the world's history. For him, of course, revelation was just such a fact: it simply sat there in the historical Scriptures of God's people. And if we have faith in Scripture, it will take us to truths that cannot be demonstrated on the basis of the world itself. But note something important here. Aquinas also gets us out of the bind of literalism. He makes it a matter of indifference whether we think the "facts" of the film of Scripture are correct or incorrect. In either case, they're enough to get us to where the Director wants us to be.

Our simple watching of them on the biblical screen is as much a part of our history as lions or unicorns, Philadelphia or Camelot, the internal combustion engine or the warp drive of the Starship Enterprise. God's *FACTA* in the Bible don't have to be "factual" to be real. To quote Marianne Moore one more time, "imaginary gardens with real toads in them" will be quite sufficient to show us the deepest realities of our historical existence.

Still, it might well be that certain other "facts" of history, unavailable to Aquinas but now available to us, may help us corroborate the Bible's suggestion that the world, in itself, is *not* eternal. I have in mind, of course, the Big Bang hypothesis for the origin of the universe — which looks for all the world like the beginning of creation's career. At the very least, it seems to point to a "once," to a "time" when everything was new — to a "borderline," if you will, between nothing and something for which Aquinas had no evidence other than Scripture.

To be sure, all the votes are not yet in on that question. Not every astrophysicist buys the Big Bang. Some have already come up with the notion that while *this* universe may have begun with a bang, there may be *other* universes that existed before it or outside it. But for me, that just muddies the waters of the subject. For one thing, "plural universes" is an oxymoron. (The "uni-" in *universe* demands only *one* such creation.) Besides, the actual existence of other universes is a matter of conjecture at the present time. But, for another thing, even if they were to find that those universes had no comparable big bang, all they would have done is land themselves right back in the eternal world that Aristotle took for granted. With any luck, they might even join him in discovering at least the philosophical necessity of an uncaused first cause to get their universes going to begin with.

But on the other hand, there's also the concept of *entropy* (the notion that the universe will eventually run down to absolute zero), which suggests that if we explore the universe forward in time, it will indeed turn out to have an end, or at least a "state" in which it will just stop cold. Anything left hanging around after that less-than-happy denouement might possibly go on forever; but since it would have neither *chronos* nor *kairos* (no clocks running to tell us what time it isn't, no high times anywhere, no motion of any kind), it certainly wouldn't be as much fun as the unique universe that got us into the cosmological ball game in the first place. If it wouldn't be *nothing*, it would be pretty close to Augustine's *almost-nothing*, which was fun only for God.

Therefore, the best mark I can put down in my record book about all the scientific pitchers in the game so far is "no decision." I do, however, have two hunches. One is that maybe Aquinas is still right. The origination of the world can't be demonstrated from the world itself — and, by extension, neither can its non-origination. The other is that in any case, I think I'll go with Augustine and say the whole discussion matters less than we think. The deepest truth about the doctrine of creation is that the world is not so much a collection of facts caused by a metaphysical God as it is the *relationship* of those facts to their Creator — to the Father as he sees the world in his beloved Son and Spirit. The answer to whether my being began or didn't begin hardly amounts to a puff of hot air compared with the truth that, either way, I ultimately exist inside that divine Love Affair. I may know that out of my already small number of days, I have only a still smaller number left. But I also trust that every one of those days, up to and including the hour of my death, is in the Today of the Trinity.

I rest my case in their endless Rest.

SIX

A Second Day: Genesis 1:6-8

THE FIRMAMENT

Let's begin this chapter by going straight to the text without ceremony.

LXX Gen. 1:6 καὶ εἶπεν ὁ θεός γενηθήτω στερέωμα ἐν μέσῳ τοῦ ὕδατος καὶ ἔστω διαχωρίζον ἀνὰ μέσον ὕδατος καὶ ὕδατος καὶ ἐγένετο οὕτως 7 καὶ ἐποίησεν ὁ θεὸς τὸ στερέωμα καὶ διεχώρισεν ὁ θεὸς ἀνὰ μέσον τοῦ ὕδατος ὃ ἦν ὑποκάτω τοῦ στερεώματος καὶ ἀνὰ μέσον τοῦ ὕδατος τοῦ ἐπάνω τοῦ στερεώματος 8 καὶ ἐκάλεσεν ὁ θεὸς τὸ στερέωμα οὐρανόν καὶ εἶδεν ὁ θεὸς ὅτι καλόν καὶ ἐγένετο ἑσπέρα καὶ ἐγένετο πρωί ἡμέρα δευτέρα

BHS Gen. 1:6 וַיֹּאמֶר אֱלֹהִים יְהִי רָקִיעַ בְּתוֹךְ הַמָּיִם וִיהִי מַבְדִּיל בֵּין מַיִם לָמָיִם: 7 וַיַּעַשׂ אֱלֹהִים אֶת־הָרָקִיעַ וַיַּבְדֵּל בֵּין הַמַּיִם אֲשֶׁר מִתַּחַת לָרָקִיעַ וּבֵין הַמַּיִם אֲשֶׁר מֵעַל לָרָקִיעַ וַיְהִי־כֵן: 8 וַיִּקְרָא אֱלֹהִים לָרָקִיעַ שָׁמָיִם וַיְהִי־עֶרֶב וַיְהִי־בֹקֶר יוֹם שֵׁנִי:

VUL Gen. 1:6 dixit quoque Deus fiat firmamentum in medio aquarum et dividat aquas ab aquis 7 et fecit Deus firmamentum divisitque aquas quae erant sub firmamento ab his quae erant super firmamentum et factum est ita 8 vocavitque Deus firmamentum caelum et factum est vespere et mane dies secundus

KJV Gen. 1:6 And God said, Let there be a firmament in the midst of the waters, and let it divide the waters from the waters. 7 And God

RSV Gen. 1:6 And God said, "Let there be a firmament in the midst of the waters, and let it separate the waters from the waters." 7 And God

NRSV Gen. 1:6 And God said, "Let there be a dome in the midst of the waters, and let it separate the waters from the waters." 7 So

made the firmament, and dividedt he waters which *were* under the firmament from the waters which *were* above the firmament: and it was so. 8 And God called the firmament Heaven. And the evening and the morning were the second day.	made the firmament and separated the waters which were under the firmament from the waters which were above the firmament. And it was so. 8 And God called the firmament Heaven. And there was evening and there was morning, a second day.	God made the dome and separated the waters that were under the dome from the waters that were above the dome. And it was so. 8 God called the dome Sky. And there was evening and there was morning, the second day.

Since the script for this second day in the film of Genesis is a single, run-on sentence in the ancient languages, I'm going to give you my comments on it by topics rather than by verses. As you may know, the verse numbers in the Bible were put in well after the text was written — and as you might have noticed, they sometimes make little sense. In fact, some wag once suggested they were inserted by a tipsy scholar riding a blind mule over a rocky hillside: his pencil was often jolted away from the spot he had in mind.

Be that as it may, here's my outline of the topics for this chapter. I'll start by revisiting the distinction I've already made between the "one" day in Genesis 1:1-5 and the "second" through "sixth" days that follow it, and then I'll give you a new image for their relationship. But from that point on, my agenda will be as straightforward as I can make it. I'll comment first on the main image of this passage, the firmament itself; then I'll take up its relationship to history; and finally I'll visit some of the other images that have been used to interpret the firmament. (Having already given you an overdose of my reflections on "evening" and "morning," I'll try not to administer any further doses here.) I can't promise that I'll stick slavishly to this outline: my freely associating mind reserves its right to flit back and forth between items as the spirit moves me. But perhaps even my wanderings will serve the Holy Spirit's purpose.

First, then, the new image — which I'll approach by reviewing the train of thought that brought me to it. In the previous chapter, I raised the question of whether this second day is to be seen as inside the "one day" of God's eternity or outside it as an actual day in time. And as you've seen, my answer was that we can take it either way — or even both ways. So I made my choice and decided to get on the train that took this second day to eternity rather than time. In other words, I did what Augustine did in the quotation I gave you back on p. 65. I interpreted that day (and all the succeeding days) not as a reference to the physical creation but as repetitions, under the guise of successive days, of the "one day" on which God creates a world that exists entirely in his Mind. When I did that, my train of thought began to move.

Its first stop was chapter 2 of Genesis. I got off for a moment, and I saw the unquestionably physical world there not as an inferior piece of business that God made "down here" but as the temporal expression of a world that God eternally holds "up there" in the exchanges of the Trinity. But then I recognized that even a time-bound world could be seen as a sacrament, a real presence, of the eternally playful world that God already enjoys in the conversation between the three Persons. So I got back on and took the train to its final stop. As it rolled on, the world no longer appeared to me as a chore that God once did and got bravely past. Instead, I saw the physical world as a delightful embodiment of the divine Whimsy — as a *fillip*, an *effervescence* of the endless joy of the God who has *always* been creating every minute of both worlds. In a word, it became for me what Scripture says it is: the apple of God's eye.

And there at last was the station my train of thought pulled into: the image of *the apple of an eye*. Let me unpack for you some of the parcels it delivered to me. On the platform (in Deuteronomy 32, the "Song of Moses"), I found this at verses 9-10 (KJV): "For the LORD's portion is his people; Jacob is the lot of his inheritance. He found him in a desert land, and in the waste howling wilderness; he led him about, he instructed him, he kept him as *the apple of his eye*" (italics mine). And in Psalm 17:8, I found this (KJV): "Keep me as *the apple of the eye*, hide me under the shadow of thy wings" (italics mine).

But on closer examination, I found still more imagery. In the Hebrew of Deuteronomy, the words of that phrase are *'ishôn 'enô*, meaning "a little man of his eye"; in the Hebrew of the Psalm, they're *k"ishôn bath-'ayin*, which means "as a little man, the daughter of an eye"; in the Greek, the words are *koran ophthalmou*, a "maiden," a "damsel," the "young wife" of an eye; and in the Latin, they're *pupillam oculi*, the "little doll" of an eye. In the simplest sense, of course, all those images were poetic ways of referring to the pupil of the eye. But the most fascinating thing about them was the human experience that led to their being seen that way in the first place. Watch, and I'll illustrate it for you.

When I stand in broad daylight and look into my wife's dark pupils, I see two minuscule reflections of myself — two tiny Roberts. And I see them dancing like puppets in the slight movements of her eyes. But then, remembering that her eyes are entrances to her mind, I see something more. I begin to understand them as an image of the way she holds me in her love. In other words, my being now appears to me not as it exists in my mind but as it is in her mind. In my own memory, of course, I still possess my being in myself — but there, the glory of my goodness and the shame of my sins are hopelessly entangled. In her reflections of me, however, I see the glory vindicated and the shame forgiven. In short, I see myself reconciled as the sweet apple of her eye.

If I go one step further and apply that image to the reflections of the whole world in God's eyes — where what stands before him is his beloved Son by whom all things are made — I see that in God's sight it has never been anything less than a *redeemed* creation. From the first "Good!" he says over the light at the beginning of chapter 1, to the last "Very Good!" he says over everything at the end, that world has always been the apple of God's eye. It doesn't need to find its own way home; it has been *at home* all along. And in the eyes of the Trinity, that apple has always been "Delicious!"

But there's another advantage I gain by taking all six days of creation as repetitions of day one — as *unum tantummodo diem,* as only one day. When I do that, I find myself completely off the hook of having to reconcile anything in those days with scientific or historical "facts." Everything in them, as it's held in the pupil of the divine Eye, has a reality (and even a history) that puts it beyond prosecutorial cross-examination. There's no need to ask whether it was or was not in the tavern of the physical creation on the evening and morning in question. For me, creation was *all there* in that Eye, even before it got to be *here* in itself. At one stroke, my interpretations of chapter 1 are delivered from the clammy grip of any literalism, conservative or liberal.

*   *   *

Nevertheless, if you prefer not to interpret the six days as repetitions of "day one," you're free to read all of them the other way around. You may take everything that God creates on them as physically existing. In fact, that's what I did back on page 4 of this book where I had the screen begin to lighten when the narrators reached the words of Genesis 1:6. But even more convincingly, it's what Psalm 19:1 does when it speaks of the world we can see: "The heavens are telling the glory of God; and the *firmament* proclaims his *handiwork*" (RSV, italics mine). Or alternatively, you may have it both ways. Following Augustine's example, you may on one occasion take them as acts of creation in the divine Intellect alone, and on another as acts of creation in time and space. Still, if it's all right with you, I'll land on the physical side of those options for awhile and consider what this "firmament" might mean if it's read as the first of the *visible facts* of creation in its own right — which certainly seems to be what all the renderings of the word in the various texts suggest.

Take a look at them. In the original Hebrew, *raqiaʿ* meant something like the "vault" of the heavens (or the skies, if you like); and that vault was thought of as a solid dome set over the earth. In the Greek of the Septuagint, the word *stereōma* signified a solid, three-dimensional body set over the earth. (The root *stere-* appears in our words *stereopticon, stereophonic,* and *steroids.*) In the Latin of the Vulgate, *firmamentum* (with *firmus* as its root) meant much the same thing. And in the English renderings, *firmament* (KJV and RSV) and *dome* (NRSV) have an identical force. Needless to say, these images came out of a historical context in which the earth was seen as a flat body resting comfortably at the center of the universe.

There was nothing particularly philosophical or theological about such images in that view. They simply represented a part of the physical creation that was "up there" or "out there." So the initial reason for introducing a "firmament" at this point in the film was most likely the one given in the text, namely, to "divide the waters from the waters" — that is, to explain why some waters come up out of the ground while others come down from the sky. Accordingly, the firmament had to be "solid" enough to keep those waters separate from each other (hence the "vault"), but still sufficiently permeable to allow rain, sleet, and snow to get through.

At this place in the script, however, there's yet another image for God's action with regard to the firmament. It's an image that now does go to philosophy and theology — to the question of whether God made the firmament out of nothing or out of something with a previous existence, however tenuous. So far in the narration, God has "created" *(bara')* the heavens and the earth, and he has said "let there be" *(y'hî)* to bring the light into being. Both of those have at least a hint of creation *ex nihilo.*

But now a new word appears: "and God *made* [*'asah*] the firmament." "Making," however, is quite different from "creating." With its implication of things produced not out of nothing but out of some prior "matter," it definitely leans in the direction of Augustine's second step in his "creation recipe," namely, the *almost-nothing* that lies between no-thing and thing. And therefore it supports my decision to dwell momentarily on the firmament in these verses as the first of the things God made out of that *pene nulla res* — the first physical *thing.*

Still, it's interesting to note that while the word *made* appears many times after this in chapter 1, the word *created* doesn't reappear in the narrative until human beings show up near the end of the sixth day. But since *the 'adham* at that point are created *in the image of God,* that also supports my earlier decision to see creation as existing in the Mind of God even before we show up with minds to hold our own being. At the very least, it's another reason for me to follow Augustine and keep my options open.

Nevertheless, if we take the words about the firmament we've considered so far in all their solidity, they do seem to be giving us an actual fact in the history of the world. But even at that, there's more to be said about them. For a vault is also an arch; and an arch (as embodied in the proscenium of a theater) is something under which a play is acted out. And that gives us one more way of imaging the firmament: it turns it into the proscenium set up over the drama of the world's history. It makes the firmament into the "setting" of history — into something that serves as the context of all the plot developments of our story as it's played out in time and space.

This will become clearer when we come to the fourth day, with its "lights in the firmament" that divide day and night, and are "for signs, and for seasons, and for days, and for years." I mention it here only because one of the principles of seeing the Bible as a movie is that we must watch the earlier appearances of an image in the light of its later occurrences. It's far too fast a shuffle to decide what a scene means before we've watched the rest of the film.

Admittedly, this penchant of mine for interpreting Scripture by browsing through its images may annoy some people. They'd like me to keep worrying the question of whether the firmament was a real thing in the history of the world or just a mythological fancy of primitive minds. But I won't, because their very question belies their failure to grasp the relationship between images and history. The two are not opposites; they're complementaries. Images don't preclude history; as a matter of fact, history written without images can't be valid history at all. Once again, facts proclaim only themselves, not their connections to other facts. You may see me, and you may see the little boy standing next to me; but until you invent the images of grandfather and grandson (and many more besides), you'll never be able to grasp the history by which the two of us arrived in front of you. So at last I'm ready to take up the second of the items in the outline I gave you: the Bible's presentation of the firmament, and all the other "facts" in this part of the movie of creation, as images of history.

*   *   *

The question now becomes, "How, in our own very different day, can these images help us do what the Bible does with them, namely, weave the phenomena of the world into a history that will make both divine and human sense of them?" For history is more an art than a science. It isn't just the keeping of a logbook in which we set down the bare facts of past events in the order in which they occurred. (If history were simply that, the firmament, as an "event" that never happened, wouldn't make it into the record.) But since history is above all the enterprise by which our image-making minds rummage through the past in *memory*, no mere logging of verifiable facts can do the job. History, you see, is precisely a *remembering*. Or, better said, it's a *re-membering*, a reassembling of the disjointed fragments of the past by means of a narrative that will hold them together as *members* in the *body* of that narrative.

Let me stop right here for a moment and give you three illustrations of this "members–body" image. The first is Paul's use of it in 1 Corinthians 12. In that passage, he's trying to get the members of the church at Corinth past the carping differences that are dividing them. And he does this by telling them that while the members of a human body are many, they're nevertheless one body. An eye can't say it has no use for a foot, or an ear for a nose. All the members are necessary for the well-being of the body, but each of them can be alive only as long as it continues to be a member of that body. As individuals, he admits, they may have distinctive gifts; but those gifts are distributed to the members as the spirit of the body sees fit. Finally, he wraps up his argument by saying (on his way to chapter 13, with its hymn to the love that governs the body), "Now you are the body of Christ and individually members of it."

My second illustration is from the hobby of vegetable gardening I pursued for eleven years. It leads me straight to the connection between the image of the body and history itself. When I planted lima beans, for example, I already held each successive event of their future history *simultaneously* within me, even before the plants themselves germinated. In my mind, I could see the individual members of that history (seeds, roots, shoots, stems, leaves, blossoms, pods, and finally beans) as a unified body. I knew, in a word, what was coming for them. At any given point, of course, the plants themselves had no inkling of that — and in no way did I specifically know all the changes and chances that might affect the individual courses of their histories. But even with that limitation, my all-at-once, intellectual grasp of their history-before-it-happened was not just a true image of their development. It was also the first cause of the actual history they enjoyed in their own times and spaces. In all modesty, I was as good as God for them.

But my third example is perhaps the most telling. When I was in college, a professor suggested that I read Carl Becker's *The Spirit of '76*. That essay, he told me, would teach me more about what was really going on in revolutionary times than almost any textbook. Obediently, I read it — with some mystification at first, because it turned out to be an imaginary conversation between a New York merchant of the time and an adult son who was his business partner. How, I wondered, could a fiction be a reliable guide through the real events in the past?

But after I finished it, I saw the professor's point. To give you just one insight, I appreciated for the first time not only the profound differences between the New York business community and the supporters of Samuel Adams in Boston but also the deep misgivings that those differences called forth. In other words, I finally grasped, by means of fictional images, the forces that were driving real people in real time.

The reason Carl Becker's essay could do that for me was that he was a superb historian. He re-membered all the events of revolutionary history so clearly in his mind that he could communicate the body of that history even by images that weren't facts. But I also realized that the writers of the Bible (and especially the Holy Spirit as its presiding editor) were doing the same thing. The events recorded in Scripture, as they existed in themselves, had no clue to where they were going. But once they were imaged into a story with a significant beginning, a confusing (or even confused) middle, and a triumphantly happy ending, the Bible *made history* out of things that, in their own time, made no historical sense at all. Scripture, you see, is not about a history that made itself. The poets who wrote it were the makers of it — just as we, in our time, are the poets of our own history. We are the only ones who can create the imaginary gardens in which the real toads of the past can come to life.

Furthermore, when film critics write their reviews of a movie, they don't address themselves simply to the bits and pieces in which its "events" are presented. They don't confine their comments, for example, to the "facts" of the celluloid frames on which the picture physically exists (nor, if they watch it on a videotape, do they try to interpret the magnetic impulses by which it's recorded). Instead, they watch the picture as they hold it *in their minds* — and they pronounce it good, bad, or indifferent to the degree that they can or cannot see it as *one story*. Even archaeologists, whose work consists chiefly of looking for evidences of the past, still have little to say until they *think* about their findings.

Indeed, the only place on earth where the events of the *past* currently exist is in the human mind. Properly speaking, then, even the events recorded in the Bible don't exist on the pages of a book. Just as a film actually exists only in the minds of its viewers, so the movie of Scripture exists only in the minds of those who have sat through the whole picture. So while the *raqia'*, the firmament as it's presented in these verses, may never have existed anywhere on land or sea or in the air, the various images it conjures up co-exist in our re-membering imaginations. And as we reckon with them there, they can still be images powerful enough to *make history*. So back to the text — and to just a little more about the meaning of its images.

Admittedly, as I've reviewed the movie of Genesis so far, I've spoken of the firmament both as the first of the visible *FACTA* in the physical creation and as one of the invisible *NOTA* of creation as those "mental notes" exist eternally in God's Mind. And so far in this chapter, I've landed pretty much on the physical side of that duality. But it's worth noting here that when God decides to translate the codes by which he holds those notes in himself, he's free to write them out any way he likes.

On the one hand, he can have the Director of the film translate them into literal facts in the history of the world (as he does in Luke 3:1, for example, where he has her put John the Baptist in the reign of Tiberius Caesar). But on the other hand, God can also have the Director translate those codes into an imaged history of the world (as he does in Galatians 4:21-31, where he has his Director inspire Paul to identify the bondwoman Hagar and her son Ishmael with the law from Mt. Sinai, and the freewoman Sarah and her son Isaac with the promise fulfilled in Christ). God, you see, can eat his cake of history as facts and he can have it, too, as images. But in either case, the images as well as the facts will be nothing less than faithful translations of his *NOTA* — and thus in both cases they'll be quite true enough for God's government work in history. And they'll also be historical enough for us to give yet another goodnight kiss to literalism, whether from the right or the left.

But even on the old, earth-centered view of the physical creation, there was still more to be said than that. We may know now that the sky waters originate in the atmosphere, which is presumably *under* the firmament. But in ancient times, that firmament of the heavens was often thought of not just as a single vault but as a series of vaults stacked one over the other. They were rather like transparent domes (a succession of huge glass colanders, as it were), one for each of the heavenly bodies. The first of these was the heaven in which the moon ran its monthly course. The next was the heaven in which the sun made its daily circuit of the earth. Then there were the heavens of the planets (in which those celestial "wanderers" made their ways against the background of the stars). Then there was the heaven in which the stars themselves danced their courses year after year and, by their dancing, influenced all things below them. And finally, above and beyond all else, there was the heaven of the heavens — the *empyrean,* the heaven of God himself — which was also the home of the angelic orders.

Even on the old view, therefore, these many firmaments served two historical purposes. They provided employment for the divine Cosmologist, who holds all of history in his "things known" (his *NOTA*), and they did the same for the divine Cosmogonist, who holds that same history in his "things made" (his *FACTA*). As I said, those assorted firmaments are now passé; but as I also said, they had a certain charm about them. They offered us a more hospitable universe than our current view does, with its spectacle of hot rocks rattling around in an oversized can. At least they gave us a history worth a long evening's watching.

This is more than you can say for the unencouraging cosmos the modern world has now constructed for itself. Its promoters inform us that we live on a minor planet, orbiting an insignificant star, whose entire solar system is only a drop in the bucket of one of the lesser galaxies. They tell us that our Milky Way itself is only a drifter among innumerable other systems, all of which are moving away from each other at alarming speeds. And for a final bit of non-reassurance, they regale us with the grim news that the entire universe is headed for the end of all motion in the ultimate deep-freeze. Don't get me wrong, though. Even if all of that turns out to be as true as trees, I'll have no objections to it as a theologian. If my death can be as much a part of God's ecology of opposites as my life, then a dead universe can be as pleasing to him as a live one. After all, he started out by being crazy about *nothing*. A second helping of it would be just one more cup of his favorite tea.

I'll admit that I've been something of a wanderer myself so far in this chapter, what with all the imagery I've been shopping my way through. But if you'll let me meander a little longer, I want to introduce you to another poet who was able to reinterpret the image of the firmament by creating still more images along the same lines. I have in mind Teilhard de Chardin's more "science-friendly" imagery in his book *The Divine Milieu*. Instead of conceiving the firmament as a vault or a dome over a flat earth, he begins with the spherical earth that scientists now insist on, and he moves outward from its core, positing a *succession* of spheres. As I recall them, there is first the *lithosphere*, the rocky crust of our terrestrial ball; next, there is the *atmosphere*, the spherical envelope of the lower air; and then there is the *stratosphere*, the globe of the upper air.

But finally and most fascinatingly, Teilhard comes up with his greatest poetic invention of all, the *noösphere*: the vast, all-encompassing sphere of *mind*. In the first instance, this is the envelope that the human mind creates in order to understand the thrust of the world's history toward some kind of destination — a sphere that in a very real way enables our minds to surround, contain, interpret, and even shape the world. But, more than that, it's also the sphere that the divine Reason creates when he does those same things. And that Reason is the *Logos* himself. He's the eternal Word by whom everything is made for the Father's glory; and he (she) is the divine Wisdom who reaches from one end to the other and mightily and sweetly orders all things.

It was those images of creating and governing, I think, that led Teilhard to call that Word and Wisdom the *Omega Point* of creation. He (she) is the

79

Beginning who is also the Ending and the First who is also the Last. But above all, he (she) is the Alpha who is the Original Reason for history and the Omega who is its Final Prize. As you can see, Teilhard was not a person of leisurely mental growth. He was a scientist, a philosopher, and a theologian. But by his poetic imagination, he outgrew all the temptations to compartmentalize those talents — and he came up with the stunning image of a creation whose history is always going home to the land of the Trinity.

*   *   *

It's Teilhard, in fact, who leads me to the third item on my agenda: some of the other images that have been applied to the firmament. And as I've been doing all along, I'll let Augustine show them to you. The first of them comes in his *Confessions*, XIII, 16, where he uses the firmament as an image of the Bible itself. As he does throughout that book, he addresses his thoughts here to God; but his reflections give us another proof of his ability to browse through the Scriptures as he held them in his mind.

Just one note. When you read Augustine, or any of the early fathers, you should always recall that they lived long before the days of printed concordances. They were not looking up passages in books of "Bible helps"; they found them in the "concordances" they had in their heads. Only when you remember that can you appreciate the brilliance of their work. Here then is Augustine re-membering some images of the firmament in Scripture:

> 16. *Aut quis, nisi tu, Deus noster, fecisti nobis firmamentum auctoritatis super nos in Scriptura tua divina? "Coelum enim plicabitur ut liber," et nunc "sicut pellem extenditur" super nos. Sublimioris enim auctoritatis est tua divina Scriptura, cum jam obierunt istam mortem illi mortales, per quos eam dispensasti nobis. Et tu scis, Domine, tu scis quemadmodum pellibus indueris homines cum peccato mortales fierent. Unde sicut pellem extendisti firmamentum Libri tui, concordes utique sermones tuos, quos per mortalium ministerium superposuisti nobis. Namque ipsa eorum morte, solidamentum auctoritatis in eloquiis tuis per eos editis sublimiter extenditur super omnia quae subter sunt: quod cum hic viverent, non ita sublimiter extentum erat. Nondum sicut pellem coelum extenderas, nondum eorum famam usquequaque dilataveras.*

Or who except you, our God, has made for us a firmament of authority above us in your divine Scripture? For "heaven will be rolled together as a scroll" [Isa. 34:4], and now it is "stretched out like a skin" over us [Ps.

104:2]. But your divine Scripture is of an even more sublime authority now that those mortals by whom you dispensed it to us have died. And you know, Lord, you know how you clothed human beings with skins when they became mortal by sin [Gen. 3:21]. And that was the reason you stretched out the firmament of your Book, those harmonizing words of yours, which by the ministry of mortals you set above us. For by their very death, that solid vault of authority in your utterances put forth by them is sublimely stretched out over all things that are under it. But while they were alive here, that firmament was not so sublimely extended. You were not yet stretching out that heaven like a skin, you were not yet spreading their renown far and wide.

This is Augustine *playing* with Scripture. He takes the image of a "skin" (a vellum, a parchment, a scroll, a book) as an image of the firmament, and he makes the firmament an image of the Bible itself. He says that while the material Bible will pass away (be rolled up like a scroll), the words of God contained in it will go on forever. But then, recalling that skins are also used as tents and curtains, he takes that skin of God's words as a sublime tent of authority spread over the whole world, combines it with the deaths of the Bible's writers, and thus manages to put eternity and time into a single tent. Not bad for just one paragraph.

My second quotation is from the *Confessions,* XIII, 18, and it shows how Augustine's playfulness with Scripture can lead him to a more sublime image not only for the waters above the firmament but also for the romantic inclinations of the human race:

18. *Sunt aliae aquae super hoc firmamentum, credo, immortales, et a terrena corruptione secretae. Laudent nomen tuum, laudent te supercoelestes populi Angelorum tuorum, qui non opus habent suspicere firmamentum hoc, et legendo cognoscere verbum tuum. Vident enim faciem tuam semper et ibi legunt sine syllabis temporum, quid velit aeterna voluntas tua. Legunt, eligunt, et diligunt; semper legunt, et nunquam praeterit quod legunt.... Sed et coelum et terra transibunt; sermones autem tui non transibunt: quoniam et pellis plicabitur, et fenum super quod extendabatur, cum claritate sua praeteriet; verbum autem tuum manet in aeternum; quod nunc in aenigmate nubium et per speculum coeli, non sicuti est apparet nobis; quia et nos quamvis Filio tuo dilecti simus, nondum apparuit quod erimus. Attendit per retia carnis, et blanditus est et inflammavit, et cucurrimus post odorem ejus. Sed cum apparuerit, similes ei erimus, quoniam videbimus eum sicuti est: sicuti est, Domine, videre nostrum, quod nondum est nobis.*

But I believe there are other waters above this firmament [of Scripture], waters that are immortal and kept apart from earthly corruption. They praise your name, the supercelestial folk of your Angels praise you, and they have no need to look upwards at this firmament and know your Word by reading it there. For they "always see your face" [Matt. 18:10], and there they read, without any syllables of time, what your eternal will decrees. They read, they choose, they love; and what they read never passes away. . . . Both heaven and earth will pass away; but your words will not pass away [Matt. 24:35]: because the skin of this firmament will be folded up [Isa. 34:4], and the glory of the grass over which it was spread will fade [Ps. 90:5-6], but your Word remains forever [Isa. 40:6-8]. And that Word now appears to us not as he is but in an enigma of clouds and through the looking glass of the heavens [1 Cor. 13:12]; because however much we might be the beloved in your Son, it does not yet appear what we shall be [1 John 3:2]. He has looked at us through the lattice of his flesh, and he has romanced and enflamed us, and we have run after the fragrance of his ointments [Song of Songs, *passim:* see my comments below]. But when he shall appear, we shall be like him [1 John 3:2], for we shall see him as he is — *as he is,* Lord — so we might see what is already ours, though not yet visible to us.

In this passage, Augustine begins by taking the firmament as a kind of borderline between time and eternity. He sees time under the image of the waters below the firmament, and eternity under the image of the waters above the firmament. And so he makes the waters above the firmament become the heaven of heavens in which God and his angelic creatures dwell. But note well: Augustine isn't talking about that heaven as a space "up there." To be sure, the physical creation "down here" below the firmament is entirely spatial and temporal. But the realm of God himself, and the realm of his entire spiritual creation, is beyond any such limitations. Accordingly, while the "supercelestial folk" of his angels do indeed read the words of Scripture, they read them not from books but as they see them (and all the rest of creation) in the Face of God. They read them, as Augustine says, without any syllables of time or space. But then he goes on to move their reading to an even higher plane.

"They read, they choose, they love," he says: *legunt, eligunt, diligunt.* Augustine is famous for such choice turns of phrase. Some of his commentators have even called them his *florilegia,* the flowers of his prose — the bouquets with which he romances his readers. And in this present instance, it's the last of those three words that's not only the climax of the phrase but the key to the rest of the passage we're dealing with. *Love* will become the final significance of all his images.

However, I want to look back now at both of the passages I've given you and show you how he worked his way to that destination. He went first from the firmament to a "skin" or a "tent." Next, he moved from the tent to the waters above the tent and made them into the realm of the angels. And then he told us that the angels read, choose, and love the words of Scripture as they read them there in God's Face. But now, beginning at the second sentence from the end of the last quotation, he makes a dramatic leap. He goes from the words of Scripture to the Word of God in Person; and having thus arrived at the eternal Father's Beloved Son, he goes straight to the greatest love poem in the Bible, The Song of Songs — and he speaks of the Love in which that Word holds the entire creation.

So when he arrives at that point, it seems to me he does something that extemporaneous preachers often do. Rather than write out his allusions to the Song of Songs in full, he summarizes them in a "purple passage," a *florilegium*, a nosegay of words plucked from the book — and he puts that passage into his notes as a "flag," a reminder to himself to let them out ad lib for the benefit of his listeners. But even if I'm wrong about Augustine's intentions, I've made it a rule that whenever I come across one of these *florilegia*, I stop in my tracks, go right to the book in question, and hunt for the passages that inspired him.

To help you do the same, I'm going to print out for you the allusions to the Word as Lover and Beloved that I found in my search through the Song of Songs (KJV). As a matter of fact, even while I was translating this last passage, I observed my rule. Following the KJV, I chose to render *retia carnis*, "the netting of flesh," as the "*lattice* [KJV] of his flesh"; and in the same vein, I translated *post odorem ejus* as "after the fragrance of his ointments" (also KJV). In any case, here's my sampler from the Bible's only epithalamium — the love poem composed as an ode on the wedding of King Solomon (who, if you remember, was the Lord's Anointed, the *mashiach*, the Messiah, the Christ of God, even before Jesus' time):

> 1:2 Let him kiss me with the kisses of his mouth: for thy love *is* better than wine. 3 Because of the savor of thy good ointments thy name *is as* ointment poured forth, therefore do the virgins love thee. 4 Draw me, we will run after thee; the king hath brought me into his chambers: we will be glad and rejoice in thee, we will remember thy love more than wine: the upright love thee.

> 2:4 He brought me to the banqueting house, and his banner over me *was* love. 5 Stay me with flagons, comfort me with apples: for I *am* sick of love.

6 His left hand *is* under my head, and his right hand doth embrace me. 7 I charge you, O ye daughters of Jerusalem, by the roes, and by the hinds of the field, that ye stir not up, nor awake *my* love, till he please. 8 The voice of my beloved! behold, he cometh leaping upon the mountains, skipping upon the hills. 9 My beloved is like a roe or a young hart: behold, he standeth behind our wall, he looketh forth at the windows, shewing himself through the lattice.

2:10 My beloved spake, and said unto me, Rise up, my love, my fair one, and come away. 11 For, lo, the winter is past, the rain is over *and* gone; 12 The flowers appear on the earth; the time of the singing *of birds* is come, and the voice of the turtle is heard in our land; 13 The fig tree putteth forth her green figs, and the vines *with* the tender grape give a *good* smell. Arise, my love, my fair one, and come away.

As you can see, Augustine — and the author of the Song of Songs, and the Director, who included it in the film of Scripture — were all romantics long before the invention of Romance in the thirteenth century. Unfortunately, though, their romanticism has been put in the shade by the bad rap Augustine has gotten on the subject of sexuality. True enough, he did say over and over that the physical passions of the fallen human race are desperately out of kilter. But his heavy-handed distrust of our sexual desires went hand in hand with a skepticism of all our faculties — physical, mental, and spiritual.

In this, he was faithfully adhering to Paul, who, when he spoke of "the flesh," was referring to the fallenness of *all* our faculties, not just our physical ones. (See Paul's comments in Romans 8:6-7, where he includes the "mind," the "wisdom [*phronēma*] of the flesh" in the general shipwreck of human nature.) Augustine is also echoing John, who in 1 John 2:16 says, "For all that *is* in the world, the lust of the flesh, and the lust of the eyes [the eyes are the doorway to the mind], and the pride of life [pride as the evidence of the fall of our spiritual capacities], is not of the Father, but is of the world" (KJV). For Augustine, then, the "warfare" between flesh and spirit was a battle not between lower and higher parts of his nature but between all his "parts" and the Holy Spirit, who is sent to show us ourselves as we are held in Christ. "All that the Father has is mine; therefore I said that he will take what is mine and declare it to you" (John 16:15, RSV).

It's true, of course, that when Augustine speaks of his sexual adventures before his conversion, he roundly condemns them. But I think his later interpreters carried his self-criticisms too far. Calvin, for example, used them to bolster his view that our present human condition is simply a *massa damnationis,* an unrelieved lump of damnation. Worse yet, modern readers have done still more damage to Augustine's reputation. Failing to do justice to the "romanticism" in the *Confessions* (their brand of liberalism was not quite liberated enough to recognize it), they've blamed him for almost every sexual hang-up in the history of Western civilization — medieval, reformed, or present-day.

There's a grain of plausibility in that, but it needs to be taken with a grain of salt. If Augustine could lift even the waters above the firmament to the sublime level of the angelic orders, why can't we hear the equally sublime lift he gives to our physical passions? Don't misunderstand me. I'm not talking about the dreadful subject of "sublimation" here. The way we use that word now is simply derogatory. It implies a running away from sexuality to something else entirely — it suggests a substitution of "spirituality" for sex. What I'm saying is that Augustine made no substitution whatsoever. Instead, the incurable romantic in him raised our sexual longings to the great Original of all desire, namely, the *Word of God* who is incarnate in human nature — to the Light who is the light of humankind.

In lumine tuo videbimus lumen: "in your Light we shall see light" (Ps. 36:9). Those words are the motto of my alma mater, Columbia University — and they're also the inscription over its chapel. As the former chaplain of Columbia, the late Stephen Bayne, once pointed out to me, they express a thoroughly Augustinian sentiment. Therefore, I think that however fallen our sexuality might be, its beauty also exists in the Light himself — in the Word who holds it risen and glorified now. He is the Light in which our sexuality has always been bathed. He is the Beginning and the End to whom all our longings are inexorably drawn, because he is the Alpha and the Omega who is the ultimate *Point* of everything he made, sexual desire included. Our sexual natures may be in exile here; but as he has them there, they've gone home in triumph, *now.*

*   *   *

On to the third day.

SEVEN

A Third Day: Genesis 1:9-13

THE ECOLOGY OF GOOD AND EVIL:
SEAS, DRY LAND, AND VEGETATION

The Text

LXX Gen. 1:9 καὶ εἶπεν ὁ θεός συναχθήτω τὸ ὕδωρ τὸ ὑποκάτω τοῦ οὐρανοῦ εἰς συναγωγὴν μίαν καὶ ὀφθήτω ἡ ξηρά καὶ ἐγένετο οὕτως καὶ συνήχθη τὸ ὕδωρ τὸ ὑποκάτω τοῦ οὐρανοῦ εἰς τὰς συναγωγὰς αὐτῶν καὶ ὤφθη ἡ ξηρά 10 καὶ ἐκάλεσεν ὁ θεὸς τὴν ξηρὰν γῆν καὶ τὰ συστήματα τῶν ὑδάτων ἐκάλεσεν θαλάσσας καὶ εἶδεν ὁ θεὸς ὅτι καλόν 11 καὶ εἶπεν ὁ θεός βλαστησάτω ἡ γῆ βοτάνην χόρτου σπεῖρον σπέρμα κατὰ γένος καὶ καθ' ὁμοιότητα καὶ ξύλον κάρπιμον ποιοῦν καρπόν οὗ τὸ σπέρμα αὐτοῦ ἐν αὐτῷ κατὰ γένος ἐπὶ τῆς γῆς καὶ ἐγένετο οὕτως 12 καὶ ἐξήνεγκεν ἡ γῆ βοτάνην

BHS Gen. 1:9 וַיֹּאמֶר אֱלֹהִים יִקָּווּ הַמַּיִם מִתַּחַת הַשָּׁמַיִם אֶל־מָקוֹם אֶחָד וְתֵרָאֶה הַיַּבָּשָׁה וַיְהִי־כֵן: 10 וַיִּקְרָא אֱלֹהִים לַיַּבָּשָׁה אֶרֶץ וּלְמִקְוֵה הַמַּיִם קָרָא יַמִּים וַיַּרְא אֱלֹהִים כִּי־טוֹב: 11 וַיֹּאמֶר אֱלֹהִים תַּדְשֵׁא הָאָרֶץ דֶּשֶׁא עֵשֶׂב מַזְרִיעַ זֶרַע עֵץ פְּרִי עֹשֶׂה פְּרִי לְמִינוֹ אֲשֶׁר זַרְעוֹ־בוֹ עַל־הָאָרֶץ וַיְהִי־כֵן: 12 וַתּוֹצֵא הָאָרֶץ דֶּשֶׁא עֵשֶׂב מַזְרִיעַ זֶרַע לְמִינֵהוּ וְעֵץ עֹשֶׂה־פְּרִי אֲשֶׁר זַרְעוֹ־בוֹ לְמִינֵהוּ וַיַּרְא אֱלֹהִים כִּי־טוֹב: 13 וַיְהִי־עֶרֶב וַיְהִי־בֹקֶר יוֹם שְׁלִישִׁי:

VUL Gen. 1:9 dixit vero Deus congregentur aquae quae sub caelo sunt in locum unum et appareat arida factumque est ita 10 et vocavit Deus aridam terram congregationesque aquarum appellavit maria et vidit Deus quod esset bonum 11 et ait germinet terra herbam virentem et facientem semen et lignum pomiferum faciens fructum iuxta genus suum cuius semen in semet ipso sit super terram et factum est ita 12 et protulit terra herbam virentem et adferentem semen iuxta genus suum lignumque faciens fructum et habens unumquodque sementem secundum speciem suam et vidit Deus quod

χόρτου σπεῖρον σπέρμα
κατὰ γένος καὶ καθ᾽
ὁμοιότητα καὶ ξύλον
κάρπιμον ποιοῦν καρπόν οὗ
τὸ σπέρμα αὐτοῦ ἐν αὐτῷ
κατὰ γένος ἐπὶ τῆς γῆς καὶ
εἶδεν ὁ θεὸς ὅτι καλόν
13 καὶ ἐγένετο ἑσπέρα καὶ
ἐγένετο πρωί ἡμέρα τρίτη

esset bonum 13 factumque
est vespere et mane dies
tertius

KJV Gen. 1:9 And God said, Let the waters under the heaven be gathered together unto one place, and let the dry *land* appear: and it was so. 10 And God called the dry *land* Earth; and the gathering together of the waters called he Seas: and God saw that *it was* good. 11 And God said, Let the earth bring forth grass, the herb yielding seed, *and* the fruit tree yielding fruit after his kind, whose seed *is* in itself, upon the earth: and it was so. 12 And the earth brought forth grass, *and* herb yielding seed after his kind, and the tree yielding fruit, whose seed *was* in itself, after his kind: and God saw that *it was* good. 13 And the evening and the morning were the third day.

RSV Gen. 1:9 And God said, "Let the waters under the heavens be gathered together into one place, and let the dry land appear." And it was so. 10 God called the dry land Earth, and the waters that were gathered together he called Seas. And God saw that it was good. 11 And God said, "Let the earth put forth vegetation, plants yielding seed, and fruit trees bearing fruit in which is their seed, each according to its kind, upon the earth." And it was so. 12 The earth brought forth vegetation, plants yielding seed according to their own kinds, and trees bearing fruit in which is their seed, each according to its kind. And God saw that it was good. 13 And there was evening and there was morning, a third day.

NRSV Gen. 1:9 And God said, "Let the waters under the heavens be gathered together into one place, and let the dry land appear." And it was so. 10 God called the dry land Earth, and the waters that were gathered together he called Seas. And God saw that it was good. 11 And God said, "Let the earth put forth vegetation, plants yielding seed, and fruit trees bearing fruit in which is their seed, each according to its kind, upon the earth." And it was so. 12 The earth brought forth vegetation, plants yielding seed according to their own kinds, and trees bearing fruit in which is their seed, each according to its kind. And God saw that it was good. 13 And there was evening and there was morning, a third day.

From this point on (and without further apology or explanation), I'm going to take all the rest of the "days" in Part One of *Genesis, the Movie* as Augustine did in the passages I've already quoted for you. That is, I'll be reading each one of them as a *repetition,* under the guise of successive "days," of the *one day* with which the film begins. As you'll remember, in the light of this interpretation, the being that the world has on its opening day is strictly in the Mind of God, not an existence that it possesses in its own right. In other words, the "things" God makes in his Beginning have an intellectual rather than a physical reality. They do indeed exist fully in God's *NOTA* as things he knows, but they do not yet exist as *FACTA* that he causes to be in their own right. Accordingly, I won't be returning seriously to the creation as a fact of history until we come to chapter 2 of Genesis, where we'll see it standing unquestionably in time and space.

With that bit of housekeeping out of the way, let me begin by offering you my own translation of the script for this third day. As I've promised, I'll try to show you the creation as it exists first and foremost in the divine Conversation between the three Persons of the Trinity. But to underscore the present reality of that Conversation in the endless Today of God, I shall take the liberty of converting all the past-tense verbs in the text to the present tense, and I'll put them in italics. Here it is:

V. 9: And God *says*, "Let the waters below the firmament be gathered together into one place, and let the dry land appear"; and it *is* so.

V. 10: And God *calls* the dry land earth, and he *calls* the gathering together of the waters seas; and God *sees* that it *is* good.

V. 11: And God *says*, "Let the earth bring forth vegetation producing seed and the fruit tree bearing fruit after its kind upon the earth"; and it *is* so.

V. 12: And the earth *brings* forth the herb, green and bearing seed, and the tree bearing fruit with seed in it after its kind; and God *sees* that it *is* good.

V. 13: And there *is* evening and there *is* morning, a third day.

By way of commentary on this day, here are a few notes on my translation.

V. 9: The words "into one place" appear in the Hebrew and in the versions I've quoted as follows. The Hebrew reads *'el-maqôm 'echadh;* the Septuagint, *eis synagōgēn mian;* the Vulgate, *in locum unum;* and the KJV, RSV, and NRSV all read "into one place." This is the first mention of *place* in the text; and along with the firmament on the second day, it constitutes the *invention of space* in the Mind of God. Even in the divine Colloquy, therefore, the world is not a metaphysical abstraction but a *sitting down together* — a "session," a "meeting" of the things God has in Mind. So this entire passage gives us still more "convocations" at which things (in this verse, the waters and the dry land) acquire new names in God. In the Hebrew, the "waters" are *dammim;* and in the other versions they are *to hydōr,* which is singular in the Septuagint; *aquae* — plural — in the Vulgate; and "waters" — plural — in the KJV, RSV, and NRSV. And "the dry land" is *hayyabbashah, hē xēra, arida,* "dry land." Which brings us to the next verse.

V. 10: God now recognizes the gatherings of the previously undifferentiated waters as "seas" (*yammim, thalassas, maria,* and "seas"); and he calls the so far hidden land "earth" (*'erets, gēn, terram,* "earth"). And once again, in the Conversation between the three Persons, God declares the creation "good." This is the second time that word appears in the script — or if you count the Septuagint (which includes a "good" in the second day), it's the third manifestation of the Trinity's delight in its works.

V. 11: This verse, with its seed-producing vegetation, brings us directly into the *ecology of opposites* as it exists in the divine Intellect — and specifically, it leads us into the ecology of *life and death.* The words for "vegetation" are *deshe' 'esebh, botanēn chortou, herbam virentem,* "green herbs"; and the words for "producing seeds" are *mazria' zera', speiron sperma, facientem semen,* "sowing" or "making seed." And since seeds produce new plants by dying to their previous existence, this verse becomes the first manifestation of *death* in God's biblical film of creation.

V. 12: Here we have an expansion in the Mind of God of what's already been said in verse 11. Having made plants that scatter their seeds more or less directly over the earth, he now mentions yet another design he has in Mind for the propagation of the vegetable order. He includes the trees that bear fruit with the seed in it: *'ets p'ri, xylon karpimon, lignum pomiferum,* "the fruit tree." And he pronounces this arrangement "good" as well. (This is the second "good" on this day — and the fourth so far, all told. If you'll promise to keep track of them on your own, I'll promise to stop bothering you with the count until we get to the sixth day.)

V. 13: Finally, with yet another declaration of evening and morning, God recognizes a third day within the eternity of his *one day.* (For the record, "evening" is *'erebh, hespera, vespere;* and "morning" is *boqer, prōï, mane.*) Time now for a more careful look at all of these ecologies.

*　　　*　　　*

Needless to say, the ecologies have been going swimmingly ever since the beginning of the film of Genesis. But just so you won't forget the opposites that have so far surfaced in the Trinity's Conversation, let me give you a résumé of the ones we've already seen. In the Beginning, there is *God* and *nothing.* Next, there is the *nothing* and the *almost-nothing,* and after that there is *nothing* and *something.* Then there is *darkness* and *light,* the separation of the waters *below* and *above* the firmament, the naming of the light *day* and the darkness *night,* and the *evening* and the *morning* of day one. Finally, when God calls the firmament "heavens," there is the implicit ecology of the *heavens* and the *earth,* and yet another *evening* and *morning* at the end of the second day. But however contrary to each other those opposites may be in themselves, they all co-exist, simultaneously and harmoniously, in the eternal Today of God.

Now, though, at the beginning of the third day, the Three-in-One give us a further manifestation of the creation's ecology. They speak to each other not only of a world that embodies abstractions like the *nothing* — and rarefied creatures like the *energy* of light and the *transparency* of the firmament, and mineral creatures like the *waters* below the firmament; they also speak of a whole new class of creatures, namely, the *vegetable* orders of the world. (The *animal* orders and the *human* order will appear on the fifth and sixth days — after a brief interruption to include some additional mineral creatures on the fourth day: the sun, the moon, and the stars.)

Therefore, what's being introduced here is the "ladder of creation," the *scala creationis,* by which the Trinity builds a "staircase," an "escalator" that will lead not only the Mind of the Word and the Mind of the Spirit but also other minds and beings (human and angelic) to their home in the Intellect of the eternal Father. In short, creation becomes not a puzzle to be worked out but a mystery to be enjoyed. It isn't a contraption we have to understand before we can hitch a ride on it. It isn't even a vehicle we have to choose in order to escape our "exile" from God. Rather, it's an *escalator* we've been standing on all along — a moving staircase that's always been taking us straight to the heart of God.

Still, with the advent of the vegetable creation we see for the first time the ecology of *good* and *evil,* of *life* and *death.* Understandably, this may strike you as far-fetched. For a very long time, biblical interpreters have imagined that good and evil are implacable enemies, and that death (at least human death) came into the world only as a punishment for sin. (Despite my enthusiasm for Augustine, there's no doubt in my mind that he was as responsible for such views as anybody.)

But right on the face of this third day — with its invention of plants bearing seeds — something more complex is being said. The "evil" of the seeds' corruption and the new life that comes out of their deaths point to God as the party responsible for the introduction of death into a world *which has not yet fallen.* As I've said many times already, death has been the engine of the world's life from the beginning. It's never been absent from the creation

God loves. And thus when the Beginning himself appears as the Incarnate Word in the death and resurrection of Jesus, he's not doing something new; he's just reiterating the same old story he's told from the start. Every death in the world has always been a sacrament, a real presence, of the rising from the dead that the Word has had in mind all along.

So death as it appears here is not a curse but a blessing. True enough, we human beings may see it as a robbery of life, a fatal abolition of our being. But that's only because we rejected God's *hands-off* management of the ecology of life and death at the tree of the knowledge of good and evil. Refusing to see our mortality as a boon, we decided to use our own *hands-on* mismanagement and fight it as an enemy. I'm not saying, of course, that we're meant to rush to our deaths at the first opportunity. (By God's Design, no living creature with its wits about it does that.) Still, by God's eternal Purpose, every living creature does die sooner or later — and its death becomes an instrument of life for other creatures.

Think about that last point. You are alive at this moment because innumerable other creatures have fed you by their deaths. Fish, chickens, cows, deer, and pigs — and, more to the point here, all the seeds on all the bagels you've ever eaten, and all the oils you've ever cooked with after the cottonseeds, sunflower seeds, soybeans, and olives had the living daylights crushed out of them — all of these have died for you. Their deaths were gifts to you. Moreover, you rise up every morning because God wills your resurrection from the death of sleep — and because you wisely decided (in spite of Adam and Eve's mistake at the tree) to accept God's boon of death in the vegetable and animal orders, and to avoid a strictly mineral diet of salt and pebbles.

Furthermore, in the general wisdom of the human race (again, the disaster at the tree notwithstanding), we've always been able to see even certain human deaths as blessings. We praise the martyr who dies for the good of a cause. We celebrate the firefighter who gives her life to save a child from a collapsing building. We commemorate the soldier who falls on a live grenade, sacrificing himself for his comrades. All these become heroes of the ecology of life and death — and so does the terminally suffering ninety-year-old whose final breath we pronounce a mercy. We may have fallen from the acceptance of death as part of life, but we've never been entirely out of touch with the ecology those two mysteries proclaim.

Every now and then, God's sovereign gift of death still "speaks through our muffling banks of artificial flowers and unflinchingly delivers its authentic molar pardon" (as Auden says in "Caliban to the Audience"). Lost though we may be in the tawdry obsequies we give our dead, death itself remains the Good Shepherd's ultimate finding of us. True enough, in my death I lose my grip on everything. But since that everything includes my sins, my death becomes my final *absolution* in the power of the Word's Resurrection.

But let me go back and delve a little more deeply into the ecology of good and evil as it exists in God. The Old Testament is of two minds on the subject of God and evil. On the one hand, you can find statements like the one in Habakkuk 1:13: "*Thou art* of purer eyes than to behold evil" (KJV). But then you can also come up with Isaiah 45:7: "I form the light, and create darkness: I make peace, and create evil; *I the* LORD *do all these things*" (KJV, italics mine). However, God does more than speak with a forked tongue. The Bible sometimes takes his ambivalence about good and evil still further and portrays it by using two different characters to represent the one God. But for that statement, I owe you a bit of explanation.

In Greek syntax (and in other languages as well), there's a figure of speech called *hendiadys*. (*Hen* means "one," *dia* means "by means of," and *dys* means "two.") It's the linguistic trick of using two things to signify one thing. For example, when you hear an ancient author say, "They dined with *cups and gold,*" all you're meant to understand is that they had *gold cups* on the table.

The best illustration, however, is in Jesus' parable of the Talents (Matt. 25:21, 23). In those verses, he has the master say to each of the two slaves who trusted his gift of the talents, "Well done, *good and faithful* servant; you have been *faithful* over a few things, I will make you ruler over many things: enter into the joy of your lord." If you listen carefully to that, you'll see that the master isn't praising two different qualities (*goodness* on the one hand and *faithfulness* on the other). Rather, by repeating only the word *faithful* later on, he makes it clear that faithfulness (and *not* goodness) is the only thing that enters into his judgment. "Good and faithful," therefore, simply means "very faithful."

And we ourselves do this all the time. If I tell you I'm good and tired, you don't conclude that I'm first bragging about my virtue and then complaining about my exhaustion. You realize instantly that all I have in mind is the single truth that I'm ready for bed. (Try this for yourself with "sick and tired," or "good and hungry." In both cases, the first word simply intensifies the second. *Hendiadys* — saying one thing by means of two — is as natural to us as sneezing.)

But it's in the Old Testament that hendiadys has its most fascinating innings. In the book of Job, Satan is right up there in the heavenly council chamber of God himself. But more than that, I think he actually represents the "other side" of God's Mind. After all, it's God who lets him destroy Job's flocks, herds, and children; and it's God who allows him to give Job a near-terminal case of boils. In the book of Exodus (32:1-14), it's Moses who gets to play God's alter ego. While Moses is up on Mt. Sinai with the LORD, Aaron and the people make a golden calf and worship it. And the LORD says to Moses, "Now therefore let me alone, that my wrath may wax hot against them, and that I may consume them: and I will make of thee a great nation." But then Moses, in a daring speech, reminds the LORD of the damage he's about to do to his divine Reputation: "Wherefore should the Egyptians speak, and say, For mischief did he bring them out, to slay them in the mountains, and to consume them from the face of the earth?. . . Remember Abraham, Isaac, and Israel, thy servants, to whom thou swarest by thine own self, and saidst unto them, I will multiply your seed as the stars of heaven." But then comes the punch line, which I think proves that this dialogue was *internal* to God: "And the LORD repented of the evil which he thought to do unto his people" (all quotes, KJV).

I also happen to think that the serpent who tests Adam and Eve at the tree in the third chapter of Genesis can be seen as another instance of divine Hendiadys. What God allows the snake to do there is for all practical purposes what God accepts as his own Will. And he gives that permission just to make clear that it's only "left-handed" management of good and evil, and not "right-handed" mis-management of it, that can successfully bring off God's ecology of good and evil. The same goes for Jesus' meeting with the devil at the beginning of his public ministry (Matt. 4:1-11). In that strange encounter — presented as a conversation between two persons at cross-purposes with each other — we see a "testing" (and a hendiadys) that was already present in Jesus' human mind as a result of his familiarity with Scripture. The devil quotes "messianic" passages from the Old Testament, and Jesus replies with simple, "commandment" passages from the same source. The *test,* therefore, was for Jesus to decide which of those two options (conquering hero or suffering servant faithful unto death) would best suit the Messiahship he would eventually manifest in his own death and resurrection.

And if God can thus use hendiadys to show that good and evil are mysteriously compatible with each other in himself, I think it's quite clear that God is just as responsible for evil as he is for good. There's no doubt, of course, that some of the evils in the world are attributable to human agents; but *all* of them, in the last analysis, are also God's fault. Earthquakes happen because he made the earth out of hot slop and set it to cool in frigid space. The dinosaurs went out of business because he let an asteroid kick up so much dust that it put them through a winter they couldn't survive. But even human sins like rape, cruelty, and murder are ultimately God's responsibility as well. He may advise sinners not to sin; but on the whole, he does a poor job of stopping them once they decide to go ahead with their unfortunate plans for the season. Sin too, then, happens under the aegis of his hands-off management of creation.

And therefore *theodicy* — which is our minds' attempt to get God off the hook of responsibility for evil — is a fool's errand. It's barking up a tree that doesn't exist. The attempt, for example, to save God's face by distinguishing between "natural" evils and "moral" evils (thus making God responsible for tidal waves but never for adulteries) falls flat on its face. If God has the whole world in his hands, his hands hold both the glory of its goods and the grime of its evils, whether they're natural or moral. He invented the ecology of good and evil when he made free creatures. He sustains the ecology of good and evil by letting them do whatever they want with their freedom. And in the end, he takes even the sins which violate that ecology into himself in the death and resurrection of his Incarnate Word: "He made him who knew no sin to *become sin* for our sakes, that we might become the righteousness of God in him" (2 Cor. 5:21, RFC). Once again, good and evil are not problems to be solved; they're mysteries to be embraced by us — just as God has embraced them both from the foundation of the world in his beloved Son.

*   *   *

But since no moral evils have yet appeared in the film of Genesis (everything will continue to be guiltless until chapter three of the script), we're getting ahead of the story. On to the main subject for the rest of this chapter, the *seeds* and their ecology of life and death. For the first time, that ecology now appears as a *dance* in which many dancers interact with each other. The film begins to move beyond mere pairs of opposites into a ballet that displays not only the various roles the seeds play but also the manifold and multiform talents each of them possesses. Let me take up the roles first.

Seeds are designed by God to die; and his Purpose in their deaths is nothing less than the reproduction of life. At this point, let me touch on the current debates over the question of deliberate "cloning" of human beings. If reproduction already happens by devices *within* the natural order (which it does), it's only a matter of time before some bright type or other will be able to replicate those devices. As a matter of fact, when and if that happens, I think it will put us right back at the tree of the knowledge of good and evil — with the same old temptation to mismanage God's Ecology of them by assuming hands-on control rather than by following his hands-off policy of letting them be. In any case, what we have in God's creation of seeds at this point is a glimpse into the *variety* of reproductive devices that the Trinity permits itself when it lets creation be.

As you know, reproduction can occur either asexually or sexually. But since asexual reproduction isn't a major factor in the careers of seeds, I'll confine my remarks here to the subject of sexuality as it appears in the vegetable creation. The flowers of plants are actually *ovaries* containing unfertilized female germ cells. When a male germ cell in the all-pervading pollen combines with one of those female cells, it produces a fruit, which is a *ripened ovary* that produces the seeds of new life. But when those seeds are released by the bursting of the ovary (as in the rose hips that eventually yield up their seeds), or by the rotting of the fallen fruit (as in the apple that decays and lets its seeds enter the soil), the reproductive process takes off in earnest.

The tough husks of the seeds, which can last above ground for years or even centuries, are first softened by the moisture of the earth, which then activates the seeds' power to bring life out of death. So if you ask the old "chicken or the egg" question in the light of the sexual creation as it exists in the divine Conversation, you get not a conundrum but an intelligible reply. "Which came first, the flower or the fruit, the seed or the plant that springs from it?" ceases to be a riddle and becomes a home truth. In the light of the at once and forever *NOTA* of God, the answer is this: *Both* came first, because both are with him simultaneously in the Beginning — in the Word by whom he creates all things.

Still, there's an even deeper mystery than sexuality here. In the natural order as it exists in the Mind of God, this process of reproduction by life out of death works by a *random distribution* of seeds. The seeds of plants fall where they fall by an elaborate pattern of changes and chances. Some fall where they grow. Dill reseeds the bed in which it's planted, and cilantro (coriander) manages to do it so quickly that you can get two crops in the same summer. As a gardener, I loved that. The second crop, coming in the short days of late fall, was much slower to bolt to flower, thus giving me a longer time to pick the leaves I was after in the first place. Parsley was also a pleasure. It too reseeds itself in place; but being a biennial, it makes neither flowers nor seeds until the next spring. And apples? Well, the apple may not fall far from the tree; but that doesn't stop a small girl or boy from picking one up, eating it, and throwing away the core (with its seeds) a hundred yards down the road.

This brings me to other factors than gravity in the random distribution of seeds. First of all, there's the wind. Some seeds are tailor-made (or Tailor-made, if you see them in God's Mind) to take advantage of the motion of air currents. Dandelions equip their seeds with parachutes for riding the winds; maples provide theirs with propellers; milkweed fairly explodes with fuzz; and tumbleweed can roll for miles in a stiff breeze. But the kid with the apple is still a favorite of mine — and his brother and sister creatures in the non-human orders please me even more, with their careless distribution of seeds.

Take birds, for instance. They're so attracted to seeds — and still more to the fruits that contain the seeds — that they'll pick your blueberry bushes bare unless you cover them with netting as soon as the berries start to ripen. And while our feathered friends can digest some of the seeds, many pass through them scot-free. In a marvelous manifestation of God's willingness to co-opt creatures into his hands-off way with the natural order, he has managed to have those seeds deposited in distant locations purely by chance. Birds have no anal sphincters: they just let go of the seeds without thinking about it — and with a gratuitous dollop of fertilizer to help them on their way. Or, as the German take-off on the proverb has it, *Der Apfel fällt nicht weit vom Pferd*: the apple doesn't fall far from the horse.

In any case, what I see in all this randomness is *romance*. The Trinity has filled its internal Movie with a cast of free creatures who are moved strictly by their *attractions* to other creatures. It may be love that makes the world go round, but it's by the *likings* of his creatures that God produces this world "beyond all liking and happening." God makes the world not out of necessity but by a divine Whim, and the world he makes is a whimsically romantic place. We're all crazy for each other because we're made in the image of Someone who's always been crazy about us. I don't love cilantro, or wine, or my wife because they're good for me. (Sometimes they are; sometimes they're just too much.) I love them because they're too attractive to resist. I love them, in short, because I'm no less nuts than God is — and if I'm as wise as the birds of the sky, I'll never stop being that way. When I was in my seventy-sixth year, someone asked me to give him my program, as he put it, for looking younger every time he saw me. My reply was, "A genteel sufficiency of alcohol and tobacco; but never firearms." God (and my liver) willing, may I always be able to give the same answer.

*   *   *

But having given you creation as an ecology of opposites and their attractions to each other, I want to move on now to the sheer profusion of seeds in the world — to what I shall call the ecology of large numbers. As I've said, the way God gets his druthers with creation is by *chance*. He uses the permutations and combinations of a vast assortment of different *species* to produce the variety of the world; and then, by an almost senseless proliferation of *individuals* within those species, he multiplies that variety exponentially. In a word, he runs the world by the *luck of the divine Draw* that he deals out to his creation. I realize that my parking of chance in the bosom of God may irk you. But that doesn't surprise me because I've gotten that reaction before. Many people have insisted that I'm wrong about this. Chance, they've assured me, is the enemy of design, and it's nothing less than blasphemy to attribute anything like it to God. (Even Einstein, when he objected to Heisenberg's "principle of uncertainty" at the sub-atomic level, felt obliged to say, "God doesn't roll dice with the universe.")

But in the world's exuberant production of seeds — and even more, in the profligate excess of sperm cells and blastocysts that are first brought into being and then discarded (only one in hundreds or thousands ever makes the procreative cut) — I would even go so far as to say that *chance is the design.* For me, chance isn't chaos, like the *nothing* out of which God made the heavens and the earth. Nor is it even impure chaos, like the *almost-nothing,* the *tohû vabhohû* of the "earth without form and void." Rather, it's not chaos at all but the very instrument by which design is achieved. It's simply the planned dis-order out of which God brings order.

If I had to justify this, I would say that God "operates" the world just as an honest casino-owner runs his gambling palace. God doesn't need to stack the cards in his divine Blackjack Shoe, and he has no reason to rig the Roulette Wheels of his stars and galaxies. All he needs is to know the odds of their free behavior and to reap his profits from the certainty of their probabilities. He can be sure of the "take" he's after simply by *letting everything be.* So in the last analysis, God's ecology of large numbers is not a forced harmonization of opposites, let alone an abolition of their opposition. Instead, it's a reconciliation of those opposites in the very thick of their unaltered contrariety. He's been reconciling them from the start.

And at the end of his movie of creation, the Word of God Incarnate (who makes the opposites of life and death for his Father's delight) will sit at the right hand of the Father with his own death perpetually present in the risen and glorified scars of his Passion. In the silent witness of those Sacred Wounds, even our sins will be at the Father's side. Eternally present in his beloved Son, and eternally unmentioned by his beloved Son, they will not stand against us because in him they never did stand against us. With his hands up on the cross, he took his chances with an unfettered and often hostile creation. And having played the game to the end, he still wins, hands down.

Chance and chaos, therefore, are not the opposite of order; they're the luck-impregnated soil out of which order sprouts. From beginning to end, God runs the world by Holy Luck. But now I'm going to take a giant leap and suggest to you that Luck is the Little Sister of the divine Wisdom — she's the Young Girl who runs after the Word of God and follows his every move. And to prove that, I'm going to give you a marvelous statement from the Song of Solomon. At 8:8, there's this: "We have a little sister, and she hath no breasts; what shall we do for our sister in the day when she shall be spoken for? If she *be* a wall, we will build upon her a palace of silver: and if she *be* a door, we will inclose her with boards of cedar" (KJV).

It isn't considered good form anymore to take the Song of Songs as a revelation of the love of Christ for creation — as a description of the love affair between the divine Word and the world who becomes his bride. I don't care, though. The parallels between Christ and Solomon are just too tempting to resist. To begin with, both of them were the "LORD's Anointed," the *Mashiach,* the *Christos.* Moreover, when you see the Word as the feminine Wisdom of God, the *little sister* in the verse I've quoted is a dead ringer for Wisdom's Kid Sister. The young girl Luck is the foundation on which all the silver palaces of this gorgeous world are built; and she becomes a doorway paneled with fragrant woodwork: a pleasant entrance through which the Door himself takes us home.

To be sure, Solomon may never have been the king his biblical ad-men tried so hard to make him. He rode to the throne on his mother's apron strings; he took it by bumping off all his father's generals; he dallied with pagan gods; and as soon as he died, his kingdom went to wrack and ruin. But none of that matters to the Director of the biblical film. In her finished movie, *the hype becomes him!* In the Song of Songs, then, Solomon becomes the sacrament of the Incarnate Word; and the little sister who has no breasts grows up to be the bountiful Lady Luck.

Let me run with that and show you what it can do for our view of the Bible's attitude toward women. The first thing I think it suggests is that the Blessed Virgin Mary is the supreme manifestation of Wisdom's Little Sister. She accepts her pregnancy by the Holy Spirit as her luck of the draw: "I have no idea how any of this is possible," she says to the angel of the Annunciation; "be it unto me according to thy word." She lives the next thirty-three years of her life with the words of crazy old Simeon in her heart: "This *child* is set for the fall and rising again of many in Israel; and for a sign which shall be spoken against; (Yea, a sword shall pierce through thy own soul also,) that the thoughts of many hearts may be revealed" (Luke 2:34-35, KJV). Not only that, but she loses her son twice: once in Jerusalem (Luke 2:41-52), when he is twelve; and once outside the same city at his crucifixion (Luke 23). And through all that luck, good and bad, she remains steadfast, finally becoming (in the words that the old Latin litany borrowed from the Song of Solomon) the *turns eburnea,* the "Ivory Tower" (Song of Sol. 7:4) who rises above all the silver palaces that the world has built on the walls of her Holy, Inconvenient Luck.

But, just like Mary, all other women have the same luck. By the very nature of their menstrual cycles, women are more at home with chance than men are in their presumption of control. Every woman knows what it is to be the little sister with no breasts, and by the age of twelve, every woman knows firsthand the challenging luck of a life over which she has less-than-perfect control. From the onset of "the curse" or "my friend" (wisely, she can see her luck both ways) — and all the way to the unpredictable relief of menopause — she lives a life manifestly at odds with her will. Men may think that life is what they make happen; women are at home with the inexorable "happenings" of their lives.

Finally, though, the feminine earth itself (the *gē*, the *terra*) lives under the aegis of Lady Luck. From its beginning in a series of "happenings" over which it has no control, to its consummation in the arms of the eternal Bridegroom — from its first status as a figment of God's Mind to its last as the Bride of the Lamb — it's always the beloved of the divine Lover. In Hebrew, the "ground" is *'adhamah,* the feminine form of the *'adham,* male and female, who are charged with replenishing the earth. (The Hebrew for "earth," *'erets,* may sometimes be masculine, but "the ground," our "mother earth," is always feminine.) The little goddess Gaia (from *gē*, earth) may begin her career as a gawky, self-conscious girl; but she finishes it as the wife of the King of kings — as the mistress of a household with silver palaces, whose doors are inclosed with boards of cedar.

I know. These last excursions of mine through the gallery of biblical images are probably sending you up the wall. But all I'm asking you to do is look at what's on the wall, not climb it. Such pictures! Such liberations from the barren literalism that stands between you and your freedom to enjoy the gallery! They draw you to the wall, not drive you up it. And if you'll just look long and long at them, you'll be so overcome by their gorgeousness that your problems will vanish. With your final glimpse of Wisdom's Sister Luck in the Song of Songs, I think you'll see what I've been trying to show you. In verse 10 of chapter 8, the mature Queen of Chance has her last say as the bride of the Lord's Anointed. She speaks for herself and says, "I *am* a wall, and my breasts like towers: then was I in his eyes as one that found favor" (KJV).

*   *   *

And with that lover's exaltation of Holy Luck, we're finally ready for the fourth day.

EIGHT

A Fourth Day: Genesis 1:14-19

GOD'S INVENTION OF TIME: SUN, MOON, AND STARS

The Text

LXX Gen. 1:14 καὶ εἶπεν ὁ θεός γενηθήτωσαν φωστῆρες ἐν τῷ στερεώματι τοῦ οὐρανοῦ εἰς φαῦσιν τῆς γῆς τοῦ διαχωρίζειν ἀνὰ μέσον τῆς ἡμέρας καὶ ἀνὰ μέσον τῆς νυκτὸς καὶ ἔστωσαν εἰς σημεῖα καὶ εἰς καιροὺς καὶ εἰς ἡμέρας καὶ εἰς ἐνιαυτοὺς 15 καὶ ἔστωσαν εἰς φαῦσιν ἐν τῷ στερεώματι τοῦ οὐρανοῦ ὥστε φαίνειν ἐπὶ τῆς γῆς καὶ ἐγένετο οὕτως 16 καὶ ἐποίησεν ὁ θεὸς τοὺς δύο φωστῆρας τοὺς μεγάλους τὸν φωστῆρα τὸν μέγαν εἰς ἀρχὰς τῆς ἡμέρας καὶ τὸν φωστῆρα τὸν ἐλάσσω εἰς ἀρχὰς τῆς νυκτός καὶ τοὺς ἀστέρας 17 καὶ ἔθετο αὐτοὺς ὁ θεὸς ἐν τῷ στερεώματι τοῦ οὐρανοῦ ὥστε φαίνειν ἐπὶ τῆς γῆς 18 καὶ ἄρχειν τῆς ἡμέρας καὶ τῆς νυκτὸς καὶ

BHS Gen. 1:14 וַיֹּאמֶר אֱלֹהִים יְהִי מְאֹרֹת בִּרְקִיעַ הַשָּׁמַיִם לְהַבְדִּיל בֵּין הַיּוֹם וּבֵין הַלָּיְלָה וְהָיוּ לְאֹתֹת וּלְמוֹעֲדִים וּלְיָמִים וְשָׁנִים: 15 וְהָיוּ לִמְאוֹרֹת בִּרְקִיעַ הַשָּׁמַיִם לְהָאִיר עַל־הָאָרֶץ וַיְהִי־כֵן: 16 וַיַּעַשׂ אֱלֹהִים אֶת־שְׁנֵי הַמְּאֹרֹת הַגְּדֹלִים אֶת־הַמָּאוֹר הַגָּדֹל לְמֶמְשֶׁלֶת הַיּוֹם וְאֶת־הַמָּאוֹר הַקָּטֹן לְמֶמְשֶׁלֶת הַלַּיְלָה וְאֵת הַכּוֹכָבִים: 17 וַיִּתֵּן אֹתָם אֱלֹהִים בִּרְקִיעַ הַשָּׁמָיִם לְהָאִיר עַל־הָאָרֶץ: 18 וְלִמְשֹׁל בַּיּוֹם וּבַלַּיְלָה וּלֲהַבְדִּיל בֵּין הָאוֹר וּבֵין הַחֹשֶׁךְ וַיַּרְא אֱלֹהִים כִּי־טוֹב: 19 וַיְהִי־עֶרֶב וַיְהִי־בֹקֶר יוֹם רְבִיעִי:

VUL Gen. 1:14 dixit autem Deus fiant luminaria in firmamento caeli ut dividant diem ac noctem et sint in signa et tempora et dies et annos 15 ut luceant in firmamento caeli et inluminent terram et factum est ita 16 fecitque Deus duo magna luminaria luminare maius ut praeesset diei et luminare minus ut praeesset nocti et stellas 17 et posuit eas in firmamento caeli ut lucerent super terram 18 et praeessent diei ac nocti et dividerent lucem ac tenebras et vidit Deus quod esset bonum 19 et factum est vespere et mane dies quartus

100

διαχωρίζειν ἀνὰ μέσον τοῦ
φωτὸς καὶ ἀνὰ μέσον τοῦ
σκότους καὶ εἶδεν ὁ θεὸς ὅτι
καλόν 19 καὶ ἐγένετο
ἑσπέρα καὶ ἐγένετο πρωί
ἡμέρα τετάρτη

KJV Gen. 1:14 And God said, Let there be lights in the firmament of the heaven to divide the day from the night; and let them be for signs, and for seasons, and for days, and years: 15 And let them be for lights in the firmament of the heaven to give light upon the earth: and it was so. 16 And God made two great lights; the greater light to rule the day, and the lesser light to rule the night: *he made* the stars also. 17 And God set them in the firmament of the heaven to give light upon the earth, 18 And to rule over the day and over the night, and to divide the light from the darkness: and God saw that *it was* good. 19 And the evening and the morning were the fourth day.

RSV Gen. 1:14 And God said, "Let there be lights in the firmament of the heavens to separate the day from the night; and let them be for signs and for seasons and for days and years, 15 and let them be lights in the firmament of the heavens to give light upon the earth." And it was so. 16 And God made the two great lights, the greater light to rule the day, and the lesser light to rule the night; he made the stars also. 17 And God set them in the firmament of the heavens to give light upon the earth, 18 to rule over the day and over the night, and to separate the light from the darkness. And God saw that it was good. 19 And there was evening and there was morning, a fourth day.

NRSV Gen. 1:14 And God said, "Let there be lights in the dome of the sky to separate the day from the night; and let them be for signs and for seasons and for days and years, 15 and let them be lights in the dome of the sky to give light upon the earth." And it was so. 16 God made the two great lights — the greater light to rule the day and the lesser light to rule the night — and the stars. 17 God set them in the dome of the sky to give light upon the earth, 18 to rule over the day and over the night, and to separate the light from the darkness. And God saw that it was good. 19 And there was evening and there was morning, the fourth day.

For this chapter, my own translation of the script will appear in three installments, with comments as I go along. As before, the verbs that refer to God's action will be in italics and in the present tense. I'll also continue to follow the Hebrew and translate "the heavens" as plural.

Incidentally, if you've ever wondered why the KJV has so many italicized words sprinkled through it, here's the explanation. They're not inserted for *emphasis* (as italics usually are), nor are they put in to make a *theological* point (as I've been using them). Rather, the KJV's reason is *linguistic*. When the translators of that version came across Hebrew passages that couldn't be "Englished" without the addition of words that weren't in the original, they put the words they supplied in italics. Perhaps this strikes you as a bit fussy on their part — as excessive literalism, or even a failure to recognize that translation from one language into another sometimes requires help-words in the second tongue if it's to communicate the sense of the first. On the whole, though, I think you'll find the KJV's italicizations helpful once you understand them.

As a case in point, take the end of verse 18 in the KJV translation I've just given you: "and God saw that *it was* good." Now that I've clued you in, you realize (without knowing a word of Hebrew) that the original text (lacking the words in italics) reads "and God saw 'that good' [*ki-tôbh*]." Indeed, it's this attempt to render passages as *literally* as possible (in the best sense of the word) that's one of the charms of the KJV. It gives you the actual flavor of the original, which is more than you can say for certain recent translations. They sometimes leave you with little more than the sour taste of over-explanation — and to my palate, the NRSV is the worst offender.

That doesn't apply in the NRSV's translation of verse 18, but take a look at its use of *sky* instead of *heavens* throughout this passage. (See verses 14, 15, and 17.) To be sure, *hashshamayim* can indeed mean "the skies"; but so for that matter can "the heavens." I see no reason to obscure the fact that the Hebrew is content to use the word in several senses. Why deprive the English reader of the wordplay? Especially when preserving the double meaning of *heavens* keeps your theological options open.

My taste in versions to one side, though, here's the first part of my translation:

> V. 14: And God *says,* "Let there be lights in the firmament of the heavens to separate the day from the night; and let them be for signs, and for seasons, and for days, and for years . . ."

First, some word-study and a bit of commentary on this verse. The word for "lights" is *m"oroth* in Hebrew, *phōstēres* in Greek, and *luminaria* in Latin. In all three ancient languages, it's a plural derived from the word for "light." And while I've toyed with the notion that the invisible light created on day one begins to illuminate the firmament on the second day, I want to add now that these "lights" in the firmament are the first indisputably visible luminaries that the Mind of God thinks up. Forget about the problem you had with vegetation sprouting up on the third day before the sun shows up on the fourth. That may have been an unresolvable conflict when you were seeing it as a succession of events in the physical world. But now that you can see the world as it's held in God's Intellect, there's no problem at all. God knows all the days of time *simul et sempiterne,* at once and forever. Consequently, he can run his film of them past his eyes any way he likes. If he chooses, he can hit his rewind button and watch them backwards. Or he can zip through them in fast-forward. Or if he wants, he can examine later days before earlier ones and see them as the "causes" of what subsequently happened.

This last trick of the divine Knowing may strike you as bizarre. But if you think about it, you'll realize that your own mind can do something quite like it. You have a hint of God's knowledge of all time in your own knowledge of the past as you hold it in memory. For example, you can think of last week's Monday, Tuesday, and Wednesday in the sequence in which they occurred, or you can review them backwards, starting with Wednesday — or you can even see Wednesday's events as a "magnet" that was drawing Monday and Tuesday forward.

Thus the wonderful thing about your knowledge of past events in memory is that the nasty notions of *foreknowledge* and *predetermination* don't bother you in the least. When you're beholding Tuesday in your memory, you don't *foreknow* what you did on Wednesday, you just *know* it, right along with what you did on Tuesday. God, of course, can go you one million better than that; but at least it gives you a clue as to how he does it. And if you follow that lead, you'll realize that since God knows all time as we know the past, the only way you can do justice to both God's knowing and your own is to say, "God *knows* [*present* tense] what I *did* [*past* tense] tomorrow [*future*]." That keeps your freedom intact when tomorrow becomes today. But if you say, "God knows what I'm *going to do* tomorrow," you've blown it. You've trapped yourself in a future that's been completely spelled out before you get a chance to try your hand at it. You're in a world that doesn't give a fig for your choices.

It's at the end of verse 14, though, that we catch our first glimpse of God's invention of time. The "lights" in the firmament are put there to *separate* the day from the night. The words *to separate* are *l'habh'del, tou diachōrizein,* and *ut dividant.* They tell you that in the forward movement of the now separated days and nights as God holds them in his Mind, *history* becomes a possibility for the first time. The rhythm of their successions becomes the beat to which creation dances. Even though the physical world of time and space is still waiting in the womb of the divine Intellect, we now hear the prenatal heartbeat of its history.

In God, the pulse of its daily lying down and rising up is already established. And like the beloved in the Song of Songs, the feminine creation sings of him as the Lover who holds her in his heart: "I sleep, but my heart waketh: *it is* the voice of my beloved that knocketh"; and the Lover answers her, "*say-*

ing, 'Open to me, my sister, my love, my dove, my undefiled: for my head is filled with dew, *and* my locks with the drops of the night'" (Song of Sol. 5:2, KJV). In the spirit of the ancient commentators, I'll offer you a short exegesis of that verse to mull over. The dew that fills the Lover's head is the bloody sweat that falls from the brow of Christ in Gethsemane — and the night in which it drops is the darkness of his death on the cross. Call that eisegesis if you like; I still think it's right on the mark.

However, it's in the concluding words of this verse that God's invention of time finally shines forth in all its glory. God says of the lights in the firmament, "and let them be for *signs* and for *seasons* and for *days* and for *years.*" The words in this nosegay of temporalities are *l"othoth ûl'mô'adîm ûl'yamîm v'shanîm, eis sēmeia kai eis kairous kai eis hēmeras kai eis eniautous, in signa et tempora et dies et annos.*

Signs is the first of these time-flowers, and it was picked by the Director from the gardens of ancient astrologers who thought that the motions of the heavenly bodies could be seen as portents of the events in the world below. Astrology, of course, is now frowned on by people with reductionist minds. (Even Augustine, who was no reductionist, had some unkind words to say about it in his *De Genesi ad Litteram* — but only because of the "fatalism" he detected in so many of its purveyors.) But none of that deters people of other dispositions from consuming astrological advice columns as if they were hotcakes. I myself keep an open mind. I may have some questions about the mechanisms by which the motions of heavenly bodies might influence earthly events — and even more about what astrologers say those motions might be signs of. But I do find the *vocabulary* of astrology a useful — indeed, even a venerable — tool for analyzing human personality.

Why? Well, if people can find enlightenment about themselves by using the eight descriptive categories of the Myers-Briggs Personality Index (Introvert/Extrovert, iNtuitive/Sensate, Thinking/Feeling, Judging/Perceiving), why should they be afraid of using the more numerous and subtle categories of astrology for the same purpose? According to Myers-Briggs, I'm an ENTJ — not an ISFP, or any other combination of characteristics. But in the vocabulary of astrology, my personality gets a much richer analysis. According to my astrological chart, my natal Sun is in Libra (which is both a cardinal sign and an air sign), and my Moon is in Capricorn (a cardinal sign and an earth sign). Mercury in my chart is in Libra (cardinal, air); Venus is in Scorpio (fixed, water); Mars is in Virgo (mutable, earth); Saturn is in Libra (cardinal, air); Jupiter is in Sagittarius (mutable, fire); Uranus is in Aquarius (fixed, air); Neptune is in Leo (fixed, fire); Pluto is in Gemini (mutable, air); and the Ascendant is Cancer (cardinal, water).

As briefly as possible, let me offer you some comments on this richness. There are *twelve signs* of the zodiac among the "fixed" stars: *Aries,* the Ram; *Taurus,* the Bull; *Gemini,* the Twins; *Cancer,* the Crab; *Leo,* the Lion; *Virgo,* the Virgin; *Libra,* the Scales; *Scorpio,* the Scorpion; *Sagittarius,* the Archer; *Capricorn,* the Goat; *Aquarius,* the Water Bearer; and *Pisces,* the Fishes. What's noteworthy about these signs, though, is that they're imaged not as abstract notions like "sensate" or "perceiving" but as star performers dancing to the music of the spheres.

Next, there are the *four elements* assigned to the twelve signs: *fire, earth, air,* and *water.* And these are distributed among the signs in order, Aries being assigned *fire;* Taurus, *earth;* Gemini, *air;* and Cancer, *water* — with each of the remaining signs being given an element in the same order, for a total of *three* trips through the list of twelve. Then there are the *three modes of action* that the signs embody (*cardinal* behavior, *fixed* behavior, and *mutable* behavior), and these again are distributed in order, starting with Aries as the first *cardinal* sign and making *four* trips through the zodiac. Finally, there are the *eight planets* that dance their way through the signs to the beat of their own drums. So if you calculate the permutations and combinations of all those possibilities — which I can't, because I slept through my college course on probability — the odds against your being told that you're astrologically just like the next fellow get a lot longer and happier — which is just fine by me, because I don't think I'm like him, either.

But even if you balk at such astrological shoptalk, the "signs" in the firmament have a significance far beyond anything you might "read" from them. Even if you can't understand a sign, you still see it. And if you can recognize it as a beautiful sign, perhaps that's enough. Maybe you've stumbled onto the Creator's ultimate reason for putting up these signs in the first place. "The heavens declare the glory of God, and the firmament showeth his handiwork" (Ps. 19:1, KJV). I can't resist quoting for you Joseph Addison's eighteenth-century paraphrase of that Psalm:

> The spacious firmament on high,
> With all the blue ethereal sky,
> And spangled heav'ns, a shining frame,
> Their great Original proclaim.
> The unwearied sun from day to day
> Does his Creator's power display;
> And publishes to ev'ry land
> The work of an almighty hand.

Soon as the evening shades prevail,
The moon takes up the wondrous tale,
And nightly to the list'ning earth
Repeats the story of her birth:
Whilst all the stars that round her burn,
And all the planets, in their turn,
Confirm the tidings, as they roll
And spread the truth from pole to pole.

What though in solemn silence all
Move round the dark terrestrial ball?
What though no real voice nor sound
Amid their radiant orbs be found?
In reason's ear they all rejoice,
And utter forth a glorious voice;
Forever singing as they shine,
"The hand that made us is divine."

Do you see? The signs in the heavens don't just have meanings for you to read; they point to Someone you need to meet. So no matter what you think about them, they make their own confession of God's majesty simply by flaunting their beauty before your eyes. Whether you "get" them or not, they're *sacraments,* real presences, of the Sign-Maker himself. As I've said many times, sacraments *are* what they represent. The waters of Baptism and the bread and wine of the Eucharist are the Incarnate Word present to us in Person. And the sun, moon, and stars are nothing less. At the depths of their being, they *are* the presence of God to his creation. Not that they're God *qua* God, of course. That would make them into idols — and an idol points only to itself. But the signs in the firmament *are* God's intimate Presence in his works. So through all the days and nights in which those works are present to the world, their Author unfailingly communicates with you. If he can be in, with, and under them, he can be in, with, and under you.

On to the second word, *seasons.* In the Hebrew, it's *mô'adhîm;* in the Septuagint, it's *kairous,* "seasons"; and in the Vulgate, it's *tempora,* "times." While the Latin hedges a bit on the "seasonality" of the word, tempting you to see it as clock time rather than as the "due seasons" of God's relationship with his creatures, both the Hebrew *(mô'adhîm)* and the Greek *(kairous)* opt for the appropriate reading. The Hebrew word comes from the verb to "appoint" a time or place of meeting; and the Greek — well, I think I've done enough with *kairos* as opposed to *chronos,* so I'll spare you anything more here. Suffice it to say that when the heavenly bodies show us seasons, they serve as both the *clock* and the *calendar* of creation — and they were doing that long before we invented either.

The sun taught us to tell time by its position at the meridian every day at noon, thus enabling us to divide our days as A.M. and P.M. The earth, by orbiting the sun once every three hundred sixty-five days, taught us to speak of years. And the stars taught us even better when they returned year after year to their appointed places — in the same number of days, *plus six hours,* thus teaching us to correct terrestrial time with sidereal time by making every fourth year a leap year. But more than that, the "times" of the heavens also taught us to see time itself as the recurring seasons *(kairous)* of our ongoing appointment with the Author of all things. They enabled us to see our world as a place where there's always another meeting just around the corner — and where there's always the best possible Someone waiting to greet us.

The world is not a boring cog in a tiresome piece of mechanical clockwork. It's a place of assignation — a romantic rendezvous with a Lover who never fails to show up. In fact, it's such a lovely, un-boring place that I've sometimes gotten carried away with it. I used to tell my children that boredom should be made a federal crime. They always thought I was being silly and went right back to being bored. So then I told them it was already a *cosmic* crime, and that its punishment was their boredom itself. That got me nowhere, too; but it did make me feel better.

The remaining words, *days (yamîm, hēmeras, dies)* and *years (shanîm, eniautous, annos),* need less comment since they have the same significance in the ancient languages as in ours. But because I've nearly worn you out with my remarks on day one and the other days, I'll give you a rest here. Still, it's worth noting that "the day" is the Bible's favorite shorthand for the arrival of an appointed time. Take the classic Easter text from Psalm 118:24 as it's applied to the day of Jesus' resurrection: "This *is* the day *which* the LORD hath made; we will rejoice and be glad in it" (this and subsequent references, KJV). Or if you'd like a less cheerful text, take Joel 2:1-2: "Blow ye the trumpet in Zion, and sound an alarm in my holy mountain: let all the inhabitants of the land tremble: for the day of the LORD cometh, for *it is* nigh at hand; a day of darkness and of gloominess, a day of clouds and of thick darkness, as the morning spread upon the mountains: a great people and a strong; there hath not been ever the like, neither shall be any more after it, *even* to the years of many generations." Or for something less gloomy, take Zephaniah 1:7: "Hold thy peace at the presence of the Lord GOD: for the day of the LORD *is* at hand: for the LORD hath prepared a sacrifice, he hath bid his guests."

Therefore, from the "one day" of the beginning to the "last day" of the end — and for all the years in between — the world's life is a succession of *present days* that God gives us as signs of his constant presence to us. If I may borrow a notion from science fiction, every *now* of your life is a *wormhole* between the two dimensions of time and eternity. It's the toll-free tunnel that invites you to travel freely between the two, and it stands open to you in every passing moment. Past moments can't do that for you because they're not in front of you anymore (except in your shaky memory); and future moments can't do it because they're not in front of you yet (except by unreliable speculation).

But *today* — and in particular, this very second of this very day — is the chosen point at which God's eternity stands right over your time and calls you to a daily commutation between the two realms. In your mornings, you go from his eternal One Day into the busyness of time; and in your evenings, you go from the weariness of time back into his everlasting Sabbath Rest. Time may be *nunc volans* ("now flying" from the future into the past), and eternity may be *nunc stans* ("now standing still"). But it's always the *now* that's our common ground with God: "Behold, *now* is the acceptable time; behold, *now* is the day of salvation" (2 Cor. 6:2, RFC).

To quote John Donne one more time: "*To day,* if you will heare his voice, *to day* he will heare you.*" That was true of Jesus at his Baptism when the Father said, "*This* [the time-bound son of Mary] *is my beloved Son* [my eternal Word]." It's true of you and me no matter how perfunctory our daily prayers may be. And it's true of all human beings, even if they never pray at all. We cannot be closer to God than we now are under his signs and in his seasons, and he will never be nearer to us than in this day of this year. His gift of time is the sacrament of that closeness — and it's a sacrament that will cease only when time itself comes to its fulfillment in the ultimate *Now* of God's Eternity.

*   *   *

Let's you and I, then, make a pause here and spend a bit more time on time itself. Having given you the entire previous chapter without a single quotation from my current favorite among the fathers of the church, I find myself in need of a fix. In Book XI of his *Confessions,* Augustine sets out to answer a person who asks, "What was God doing *before* he created the heaven and the earth?" — as if a long stretch of God's endlessness had gone by before he got around to thinking up the world. But Augustine points out that the way most people apply "before" and "after" to God simply makes a hash of time and eternity. And in his colloquy with God in the *Confessions,* XI, 17, he tries to set such people straight:

> *Nullo ergo tempore non feceras aliquid, quia ipsum tempus tu feceras. Et nulla tempora tibi coaeterna sunt, quia tu permanes; at illa si permanerent, non essent tempora.*

> *At no time,* therefore, had you not made something, because it was you who had made time itself. And no times are co-eternal with you, because you continue forever; but if those [times] were to continue forever, they would not be times.

Let me expand on that a little. In the opening sentence of that quotation, Augustine is saying that there's no time (in our sense of the word) at which God isn't creating things because he's always been making everything, time itself included, *within* his eternity. For God, time doesn't lie outside his eternity like a welcome mat, inviting him to come in and get busy. So there's no use trying to figure out "when" God's eternal act of creation began, or what he was doing "before" he got around to it. No "time-specific" question can apply to God as God.

But despite the negative tone of his second sentence, I don't think you can read Augustine as saying that the *events* of time will somehow disappear from eternity after the world passes away. All of those events are in God's eternity from the start. Admittedly, the temporal existence they eventually acquire in themselves may be radically different from their eternal existence in God; but in both "places," their existence is totally real. And therefore, even if we can't foist our rules on God, he will always know them and respect them in himself.

Time, then, is not a condition of estrangement from eternity; it's simply the only way eternity can appear to us when we're sitting in the thick of past, present, and future. Our times are a series of anniversary cards that God is perpetually sending the world; and the Post Office from which he mails them is precisely the endless Today of the Trinity. To repeat myself, God is the eternal contemporary of every event in time. Nevertheless, time as such is still not "co-eternal" with God. In itself, it has a beginning, it runs its course, and then it runs out. (If our times lasted forever in their own right, Augustine points out, they just wouldn't be times for us.)

But in the God who neither begins nor ends, his fascinating invention of time stands forever. For him, therefore, and for us in him, all our times are sacred. Last year, this week, next Monday, or a week from some Tuesday — at the hour of our death or in the day of judgment — all of those times that precede or follow one another make a difference to him because all of them make a difference for us. All our times are in his hand (Ps. 31:15); and all of them, quite simply, are always *today* in him.

Now, though, I want to go a little more specifically into how things can be said to *precede* one another by quoting a further passage from Augustine on the subject. In Book XII of his *Confessions,* he's been trying his subtle best to improve the thinking of someone who thinks that "In the beginning God made the heavens and the earth" means simply "*at first* God made" the world. He suggests that such a person should think again, because the heavens and the earth that God made are nothing other than the entire physical universe. He says that the fellow should be asked, "If God made the universe first, what did he make afterward?" — and he points out that after the universe, the man will find nothing. And so Augustine proposes another question for him: "How did God make this first if he made nothing after it?"

But then he gives this fellow some distinctions to help him out of the quandary he's put himself in. First, he distinguishes between the *nothing* and the *almost-nothing* that I've spent so much time on; and he tells his friend that if only he would say, "God made matter *first formless, then formed,*" he'd be free of such absurdities and be able to use a *before-and-after* formulation like "First. . . . Then . . ." with impunity.

Augustine, however, goes the second mile and gives the fellow still more help. He tells him that he may legitimately use "before" or "at first" when talking about God — *provided* he's willing to make some distinctions about precedence itself. (I used to make a similar point when I was teaching theology to beginners: "If you won't distinguish," I told them, "you can't theologize.") In any case, here's his *proviso* as he lays it out in his *Confessions,* XII, 40. His interlocutor will be on safe ground, he says,

> . . . *si modo est idoneus discernere, quid praecedat aeternitate, quid tempore, quid electione, quid origine. Aeternitate, sicut Deus omnia; tempore, sicut flos fructum; electione, sicut fructus fructum; origine, sicut sonus cantum. In his quattuor primum et ultimum quae commemoravi, dificillime intelliguntur; duo media facillime.*

I've given you only the Latin for openers because this is another instance of Augustine as a master chef. He's boiling down his theological stock to a very small quantity of literary syrup. And while it's delicious in Latin, putting it into English calls for the addition of some linguistic water to make it accessible. Here then is my more fulsome translation:

... if only he be qualified to distinguish between what precedes by *eternity,* what precedes by *time,* what precedes by *choice,* and what precedes by being a *principle of origination.* If he considers precedence by *eternity,* he will see that God is *before* all things; if by *time,* he will find that the flower comes *before* the fruit; if by *choice,* he will discover that the fruit rather than the flower is our *first* choice; and if he considers precedence by *principle of origination,* he will see that the sound is metaphysically *prior* to the song. Of these four, the first and the last that I mentioned can be understood only with extreme difficulty; the middle two, very easily.

But Augustine, without forsaking his intellectual acrobatics, continues to press his point by addressing God himself. I apologize for the length of this next quotation (it continues from the previous one, at XII, 41 of the *Confessions*), but I think you'll find his distinctions as entertaining as they are helpful:

Namque rara visio est et nimis ardua conspicere, Domine, aeternitatem tuam incommutabiliter mutabilia facientem, ac per hoc priorem. Quis deinde sic acutum cernat animo, ut sine labore magno dignoscere valeat, quomodo sit prior sonus quam cantus, ideo quia cantus est formatus sonus, et esse utique aliquid non formatum potest, formari autem quod non est, non potest? Sic est prior materies, quam id quod ex ea fit: non ideo prior quia ipsa efficit, cum potius fiat; nec prior intervallo temporis. Neque enim priore tempore sonos edimus informes sine cantu, et eos posteriore tempore in formam cantici coaptamus aut fingimus, sicut ligna quibus arca, vel argentum quo vasculum fabricatur. Tales quippe materiae tempore etiam praecedunt formas rerum quae fiunt ex eis: at in cantu non ita est. Cum enim cantatur, auditur sonus ejus; non prius informiter sonat, et deinde formatur in cantum. Quod enim primo utcumque sonuerit, praeterit; nec ex eo quidquam reperies quod resumptum arte componas: et ideo cantus in sono suo vertitur; qui sonus ejus, materia ejus est. Idem quippe formatur ut cantus sit: et ideo, sicut dicebam, prior materies sonandi quam forma cantandi: non per faciendi potentiam prior; neque enim sonus est artifex, sed cantanti animae subjacet ex corpore, de quo cantum faciat. Nec tempore prior; simul enim cum cantu editur. Nec prior electione; non enim potior sonus quam cantus, quandoquidem cantus est non tantum sonus, verum etiam sonus speciosus. Sed prior est origine: quia non cantus formatur ut sonus sit, sed sonus formatur ut cantus sit. Hoc exemplo qui potest intelligat materiam rerum primo factam, et appellatam coelum et terram, quia inde facta sunt coelum et terra: nec tempore primo factam; quia formae rerum exserunt illa autem erat informis; jamque in temporibus simul animad-

vertitur, nec tamen de illa narrari aliquid potest, nisi velut tempore prior sit; cum pendatur extremior, quia profecto meliora sunt formata quam informata, et praecedatur aeternitate creatoris, ut esset de nihilo, unde aliquid fieret.

For it is a rare and a difficult vision, O Lord, to behold your eternity un-changeably making changeable things, and therefore existing before them. And again, who is of such sharp-sighted understanding as to be able, without tremendous effort, to distinguish how the sound might be prior to the tune, since the tune is a formed sound? And while something can certainly be unformed, it is not possible for something that does not exist to be formed.

Thus the matter of something is prior to that which comes into being out of it — not indeed prior because it makes it, since it itself is made; nor is it prior by an interval of time, for we do not in some prior time utter unformed sounds, and then in some later time adapt or fashion them into the form of a song (as when wood is fashioned into a box, or silver into a vase). For such materials do indeed precede the forms of the things made from them, but in singing that is not so.

For when something is sung, its sound is heard. It doesn't first sound as unformed and after that as formed into a tune. For whenever something sounds first, it passes away, and you will not find any of it to pick up again and compose into a tune by art. So then the tune depends on its sound, and that sound is its matter. And this matter is indeed formed so that it might be a tune.

And therefore, as I was saying, the matter of the sounding is prior to the form of the singing. But it's not prior by any potential of making it a tune, for the sound is not the artisan of the tune. Rather the sound, as something corporeal, is subjected to the soul of the singer — and out of it, he makes the song. The sound is not prior by *time;* for it is put forth simultaneously with the tune. Nor is it prior by *choice;* for the sound is not better than the tune, since a tune is not just a sound but a beautiful sound.

But it is prior as a *principle of origination:* because a tune is not formed so it might be a sound, but a sound is formed so it might be a tune. By this example, let anyone who is able understand that the matter of created things was first made, and called heaven and earth, because heaven and earth were made of it. It was not made first in point of time, for it is the forms of things that actually lay bare that unformed matter. But now, in time, it is an object of sense together with its form. Nor can anything be said about that matter except in terms of priority by *time.* However, when

112

the question is weighed as a whole, it is indeed true that formed things are better than unformed things, and that both are surpassed by the eternity of the Creator, so that it might be out of nothing that something comes into being.

Let me see if I can paraphrase the nub of Augustine's argument here. He's saying that his two "most difficult" examples of *precedence* (the way that God's *eternity* precedes *time* and the way that a *sound* precedes a *melody*) can in fact provide an illustration of how something in our experience can help us understand God's eternal "experience." He suggests that just as a melody "originates" in its sound, so all things originate in God. This is a particularly apt comparison because while the sound may be the "matter" of the melody, it doesn't come before the melody at some earlier point in time. Since it's the matter that the singer forms into a melody, it simply comes *with* the melody. But for all that, the sound does indeed precede the melody as its *principle of origination*.

So also with God. His eternity doesn't precede time by any clock or calendar, nor does the "formless matter" (the *nulla res*) he first makes in his Mind precede the "formed matter" that we see. Still, his eternity does precede all things as their principle of origination. Without it, they simply wouldn't *be* at all.

I realize that my paraphrase may strike you as hardly less obscure than Augustine's Latin. But your patience in slogging through both our efforts has been admirable, so as a reward I'll give you something personal about Augustine. From his words here and elsewhere in his writings, it's obvious that he was more than a good theological cook. In fact, he was also a gifted singer. (In one place, he even entertains doubts about his vocal talents: he wonders whether his delight in singing might be a form of vanity.) But here he puts that gift to the service of metaphysical analysis, and he comes up with a stunning performance: technically brilliant, yet charmingly warm. To me, it's just grand — and my hope is that you'll see it the same way. In any event, on now to the next two verses in my own translation of the script.

*　　*　　*

V. 15: "and let them be for lights in the firmament of the heavens to give light upon the earth." And it *is* so.

V. 16: And God *makes* two great lights, the greater light to rule the day and the lesser light to rule the night, and the stars also.

I think I've already said enough about the sun and the moon (here referred to as the "greater" and "lesser" lights). But I'd like to give you a little diagram that I've sometimes passed around during lectures to illustrate the history of the world over which those lights rule. (For the record, the words for "to rule" are *l'memsheleth/v'limshol, eis archas/archein,* and *ut praeessent/ut praeesset.*) My diagram takes the form of a time line from the beginning of the world to the last day. I'll comment on it after you've had a chance to digest it.

THE HISTORY OF THE WORLD FROM ETERNITY TO THE END OF TIME

NOTHING

! _____

(Billions and Billions of Years)

_____ !

Explanation of the Diagram
1. The blackness represents God's creation of the world *in himself, outside of time,* and *ex nihilo.*
2. The exclamation point at the beginning of the time line represents the Big Bang, or anything else you may choose as the start of the universe in time and space.
3. The line that runs for billions and billions of years represents all the time from the Big Bang to the emergence of the human species.
4. The exclamation point at the end of the line represents the entire history of the human race, give or take 50,000 years.
5. Finally, the two exclamation points taken together represent the *parousia,* the *presence,* the "coming" of the Incarnate Word to the world at the two key points of its history. The initial one stands for his presence as the Word by whom all things are made at the beginning; and the final one stands for his presence at the last day of the world as the Word by whom all things are restored.

As I see it, this can do wonders not only for your theology of creation but also for your appreciation of the world's history. First of all, it gives you a theologically sound *cosmology.* The black and timeless *nothing* at the top of the diagram displays the Trinity eternally creating the world *ex nihilo* within its own exchanges — which is right where I've put it by saying that the opening scenes of *Genesis, the Movie* show us a world that has a genuine intellectual existence in the Mind of God before it acquires a physical existence in itself.

Just remember that in the film of the Bible, it's the *movie itself* that's the revelation, not the script alone, or the ideas alone — or, God forbid, the "historical" parts of it alone. The whole film, as the Holy Spirit has been showing it to the people of God for eons, is the "Director's cut" of the picture. Don't let anyone try to sell you a pared-down version of it — and above all, don't forget the "imaginary gardens with real toads in them."

Second, this diagram gives you a flexible *cosmogony*. The exclamation point at the beginning of the world's physical history puts the Big Bang, or any other starting point you prefer, squarely within time. And the "!" at the end (which stands for all of human history) gives you a place to put everything else in the biblical film, from Adam and Eve all the way to the new heavens and the new earth that become the bride of the Christ at the Marriage Supper of the Lamb.

Third and fourth, both the time line that represents the physical existence of the world and the exclamation point that stands at its end emphasize the *continuous presence* (the *parousia*) of the Incarnate Word in every moment of time. Just as an "!" at the end of a sentence is present to all the words that precede it, so the *parousia* of Christ at the last day presides over every part of the run-on sentence that comprises the world's history.

So, fifth and last, if you take the line and the two exclamation points together, you get a more liberating view of the "second coming" of Christ. Whatever else that *parousia* may involve, it's not the return of someone who's been on an extended vacation during the course of history. Rather, it's the final revelation of the mystery by which the Incarnate Word has been present to all of history from start to finish. The "!" at both ends of the time line displays the Incarnate Word as the Beginning and the Ending of creation, thus making his words on the last day — "Behold, I am making all things new" (Rev. 21:5) — a recapitulation of his speaking the heavens and the earth into being on day one.

But more than that, the very narrowness of the final exclamation point opens up the possibility of compressing all 50,000 years of human history into "the last day," enabling you to see the Word's *parousia* as something better than an event that *will* happen in a distant future. It makes it into a single, ongoing mystery that's present to you and every other child of Adam and Eve all the days of our lives. Theologians have called this transposing of the *parousia* into all times and seasons *realized eschatology*. That does the job well enough, if you can stand theological abstractions; but I think my less arcane diagram does it better.

Therefore, the only important thing you need to note about all the days of the world (first, middle, or last) is that they make no difference as far as Christ's *parousia* is concerned. They're all his *presence:* he's always been "coming" to the world. As Jesus said to his disciples when he scared them out of their wits by walking on the water in a storm, so he says to us on every day of the world's existence: "Cheer up — it's just me!"

Scripture does say, of course, that there will be a last day of history at which the Son of Man *will* come to judge the living and the dead. But my diagram enables you to see that *parousia* too in a better light. True enough, his presence "back then" at the beginning is mysterious and creating, and his presence "out there" at the end is open and reconciling. But wherever or whenever you contemplate it, it's nothing other than the creating Word himself, intimately and immediately present to every day of history. The Incarnation is not a late-afternoon visit from the divine Carpenter; it's a revelation of the divine Architect who's never left the job site.

Time now for the final installment of my translation — and for the end of this chapter.

V. 17: And God *sets* them in the firmament of the heavens to give light upon the earth,

V. 18: to rule over the day and over the night, and to separate the light from the darkness. And God *sees* that it *is* good.

V. 19: And there *is* evening and there *is* morning, a fourth day.

These verses are a summary of what's gone before in the script, and they contain no words you haven't seen before. But if you remember to look at the movie of Scripture as a whole, you'll find that they point you to the end of the picture. In Revelation 21:23, where the New Jerusalem is portrayed in its splendor, you'll hear, "And the City has no need for the sun or the moon to shine upon it, for the glory of God has shined on it and its lamp is the Lamb" (RFC). In the end, you see, the created lights pass to their fulfillment in the great Original himself — in the Light who, coming into the world, lightens every human being (John 1:9).

And in Revelation 22:5, you'll hear the ultimate consolation: "And there will no longer be night, and they have no need of lamplight or sunlight, because the Lord God will shine on them and they will reign for ever and ever" (RFC). The lights in the firmament that taught us when to sleep and wake, and the lamps of the heavens that gave us signs and seasons and days and years have been transfigured by the uncreated Light who is the Father's Word. After all our efforts to grasp the fleeting now of our existence, the Now himself, who is the "still point of the turning world" (T. S. Eliot, *Burnt Norton*), finally clasps us in his everlasting arms and takes us home. Or, as Eliot envisions that homecoming at the end of his *Little Gidding:*

> We shall not cease from exploration
> And the end of all our exploring
> Will be to arrive where we started
> And know the place for the first time.

It's a home we've never left, because he has never left us. On to the fifth day of the Word's *parousia* as the Beginning of creation.

NINE

A Fifth Day: Genesis 1:20-23

THE ECOLOGY OF LIFE AND DEATH:
SEA CREATURES, BIRDS, AND SEX

Even though you may think I've already given you enough about God's ecology of opposites, I'll begin this chapter with a more detailed look at the dance of life and death as it appears in the creatures of the fifth day. That dance was evident in the vegetable orders as they appeared in the Mind of God on the third day, but now it comes closer to the bone of our existence as human beings. Seeds and fruits may oblige us by dying quietly for our life, but fishes and birds put up a fight. When a trout gasps for oxygen after being reeled in, or when an inexpertly shot pheasant writhes on the ground in its death throes, we see in them something of our own struggle to hold on to our lives. Worse yet, we realize that we're not just spectators of their agonies; we're often the perpetrators of their deaths.

That realization, of course, comes to few of us now. Shrimp arrive in our kitchens after being mined from ten-pound blocks in a butcher's freezer, and chickens pay us visits as legs and breasts tricked out in plastic wrap. The day of cutting up whole birds at home is rapidly drawing to a close, and the times of plucking and gutting them ourselves are long since gone. Dinner has become something we buy at the checkout counter.

For most of our history as a race, however, the festivity of eating was always preceded by the necessity of killing. The first sharp tool that the woman of the house applied to poultry was usually a hatchet, and the prelude to pork chops was her husband's pig-sticker. Obligingly or not so obligingly, therefore, the food on our tables had to die to be of service to us. Even vegetarianism, as a universal recipe for obviating the deaths of other creatures, is not an option. Stir-frying bok choy in a wok cooks the life out of it just as surely as slitting the throat of a bird.

But this fifth day comes on the scene before any human creatures are on hand to be glad or glum about the mayhem of supper at six. In the depths of the seas, there are only creatures who at all hours eat or are eaten by others. Big fish devour little fish, who in turn feast on still smaller fish. Whales cruise through the waters like giant vacuum cleaners, taking hordes of plankton to their deaths; and when they themselves meet the grim reaper, the scavengers of the ocean's bottom make short work of their remains. But even though we've named that murderous dance "the food chain," it's in fact a happier and more liberating spectacle: a command performance ordered by the God who loves the theater of it all.

That mysterious dance of life and death appears most clearly in the birds of the air. I live on a small island between the two easternmost forks of Long Island. You live elsewhere, of course, and you've no doubt seen birds I've never watched. But if I may, I'll speak only from my own experience.

In the spring I've seen an osprey (which is actually a fish hawk) swoop down talons-first from the sky and come up with a fish, still resisting its fate, to carry home to his nest. And all year long I've watched seagulls (those lucky birds whom few other creatures find palatable) eat almost anything under the sun. *Almost.* One day, at a wedding reception in an ocean-front restaurant, I did see a gull walk away from a plate of limp-fried shrimp that a bridesmaid had abandoned on the railing. Obviously, she thought they were for the birds; but after watching the seagull, I realized there was at least one bird who thought otherwise.

But above all I've watched crows. One morning I was sitting with my wife on our back deck after I'd thrown a potful of soup bones on a leaf pile in the woods. First, a single crow flew in, landed on the pile, and examined the bones. But then, without touching a scrap, he flew to the top of a nearby tree and began to caw. Other crows came and repeated his performance; but still, none of them ate. Finally, the emperor crow appeared, made a royal inspection, and had himself a leisurely meal. Only after he finished did the rest come down from the trees and feast on his leavings.

For me, that was proof of the intelligence and advanced social behavior of those royal courtiers. To be sure, the denizens of the deep also display those qualities. (Porpoises, for instance, are just as smart and gregarious.) But mostly they exercise them beyond the range of our admiration. The creatures of the skies, however, are continually before our eyes; and of them all, crows are my favorites.

To begin with, they're birds of carrion, eating only what has already died. They're the groundskeepers of the earth, cleaning up after the wild party of life and death. Or, better said, they're the black-suited undertakers of the world, generously providing free funerals for even the most wretched of the dead. And what enables them to find such derelicts is their incredible eyesight. They can spot a squashed squirrel from a great distance; and while they're down on the road conducting their ceremonies, they can also spot a speeding car long before it reaches them. Robins and wood doves in such a situation don't see the danger till it's almost on top of them: they always fly off in panic, and some of the robins fly off too late.

Crows, on the other hand, just walk gravely to the side of the road and wait for a suitable time to return to their duties. Everybody has seen dead robins on the pavement; but when was the last time you saw a dead crow? To be sure, they die as inevitably as all other living creatures. But I doubt that one ever died at the hands of anyone (except somebody who was forced to "eat crow"). Indeed, I think that the motto on the crows' coat of arms should read *Nemo me impune vescitur:* "No one eats me with impunity." As a proud clan, they disdain being anybody's dinner — and they keep their deaths a family secret.

This brings me to the next mystery revealed by the animals of the fifth day: the mystery of *free choice.* It's not just the human race that has *liberum arbitrium,* free will. All of God's creatures have one degree of liberty or another. After all, he makes the world by *letting it be,* and it would be odd if some traces of that divine Permissiveness didn't show up in everything he makes. Go back to the vegetable orders for a moment. A sunflower chooses sunlight with such liberty that it turns toward it not just gradually, over weeks or months, but at every hour of the day. Mushrooms decide to seek air so freely that they'll break through even asphalt to reach it. And seeds? Seeds are famous not only for the spontaneity of their travels but also for their freedom to choose any carrier that will take them aboard as standbys.

But of all the creatures so far, its the animals of sea and air who most deserve the freedom prize. The common eel, I've been told, is spawned in the Sargasso Sea. Nevertheless, it migrates far from that North Atlantic weed patch (having picked up its wanderlust, I imagine, from the example of the Sea's own drifting life). Salmon return to the rivers of their birth to procreate and die. The blue crab (wonderfully named *callinectes sapidus,* "the beautiful swimmer who is also a tasty treat") goes to great lengths to flaunt both of those attributes. And the whales, the tuna, and the swordfish travel north and south with the seasons as if they were politicians or wealthy garment manufacturers commuting between New York and Florida.

And as for the birds and the butterflies, the freedom of their migrations, not to mention the skill of their navigation, is at least as wonderful. Most of them choose to go south for the winter, but there are some who just as freely decide against it. I have in mind Canada geese, who in my lifetime seem to have decided to spend their winters using our local golf courses as a public accommodation. Naturally, almost everyone here resents the liberty they've taken. But the geese and God find it admirable — and I, if I may put a mere theologian in such exalted company, find it instructive.

It reminds me that the indignation of human beings is not a reliable guide when we're dealing with the inconvenience of other creatures' freedom. Whenever possible, we would do better to manage our own behavior more prudently. If the jellyfish in the bay are stinging, for instance, I can always stay out of the water. And if mosquitoes cross my path, I can wear trousers and long sleeves and only swat the ones that land on my hands and face. But until I and the rest of our chronically inconvenienced race understand the ecological dance better than we now do, it's probably a bad idea to put out contracts on our fellow dancers just because their freedom interferes with ours.

There's a fate worse than death lurking in that mania. It's the eventual demise of the ecology itself under the aegis of our refusal to accept death as the engine of life. One of the biggest red herrings ever dragged across the path of Christian theology was the notion that human beings were created by God to live forever in this world — and that death as we know it came into our lives only as a result of sin. I'll have much more to say about this when we get to chapter 3 of Genesis. All I want to note here is that while there's a large truth in the Bible's linking of sin and death, there's also a lie lurking in it if we read it wrong. What the sin of the human race introduced into the world was not the fact of our mortality. (That was a truth about us, and all other creatures, right from the beginning.) Rather, the falsehood lay in the way we began to look at death as the enemy of life — as a curse instead of a gift.

I know. You want to remind me that it was God who uttered the curse. Of course he did — but if you insist on taking every word God says in Scripture as his final truth, you've missed one of the Bible's most important literary devices. It often puts into God's mouth statements that he intends to take back. Think of the destruction of the world by the flood and his subsequent rejection of the idea in his promise to Noah. Or consider once again the dialogue between God and Moses in Exodus 32, with which I've already dealt. Or, best of all, look at God's draconian punishments for sin in the Old Testament and the universal forgiveness he bestows on the sins of the whole world when he draws *all* to himself in the death of his only-begotten Son. Literalism in such cases will give you nothing but a headache.

At any rate, the lie we've told ourselves about death is particularly evident in our quest for a kind of bogus immortality to call our own — a pursuit that I for one have never understood. It's not at all clear to me why we should want an interminable life in a world we've made a mess of when God has already given us a glorious life in the world he holds reconciled in himself. Still, we go right on acting as if it were a good idea. We feel fully justified in complaining that this baby died too soon or that Aunt Tillie went on too long. These deaths may be sad in the extreme. But the assumption that each of us is metaphysically entitled to some specific number of days or years is — pardon the expression — hogwash. God didn't give any such promise to the plants and their seeds or to the fishes and the birds — or to any other creature, us included. As John Donne once observed, there are no long leases here. There aren't even short ones: we're all squatters, subject to eviction on no notice whatsoever.

So to say of death, "This shouldn't happen to me" — or of the hour of my removal, "It's not time for me to go" — is to speak without a shred of empirical evidence. Sooner or later, we all go; and in the way of all flesh, many of us go badly. There's no point in objecting to the rhythms of life and death. As Auden said in his poem *Compline,* we can only "join the dance/As it moves in perichoresis,/Turns about the abiding tree." And when all is said and done, that Tree is none other than the Word of God in Person.

He is the Wisdom who in the beginning wills the deaths of the creatures of the third, fifth, and sixth days. He is the Word who in the humanity of Jesus endures the death of the cross. He is the Lord who ascends to his Father's right hand with the glorious scars of his Passion in his hands, feet, and side. And he is the Alpha and the Omega who at the end reveals himself as the Tree of Life, bearing fruits for all times and seasons, and whose leaves are for the healing of the nations (Rev. 22:2). My death, therefore, is my ultimate safety. I couldn't ask for a better outcome.

*   *   *

But since I began this chapter with my own ramblings on the creatures of the fifth day, let me get back to business and give you the words of the script itself.

LXX Gen. 1:20 καὶ εἶπεν ὁ θεός ἐξαγαγέτω τὰ ὕδατα ἑρπετὰ ψυχῶν ζωσῶν καὶ πετεινὰ πετόμενα ἐπὶ τῆς γῆς κατὰ τὸ στερέωμα τοῦ οὐρανοῦ καὶ ἐγένετο οὕτως	BHS Gen. 1:20 וַיֹּאמֶר אֱלֹהִים יִשְׁרְצוּ הַמַּיִם שֶׁרֶץ נֶפֶשׁ חַיָּה וְעוֹף יְעוֹפֵף עַל־הָאָרֶץ עַל־פְּנֵי רְקִיעַ הַשָּׁמָיִם: 21 וַיִּבְרָא אֱלֹהִים אֶת־הַתַּנִּינִם הַגְּדֹלִים וְאֵת כָּל־נֶפֶשׁ הַחַיָּה הָרֹמֶשֶׂת	VUL Gen. 1:20 dixit etiam Deus producant aquae reptile animae viventis et volatile super terram sub firmamento caeli 21 creavitque Deus cete grandia et

21 καὶ ἐποίησεν ὁ θεὸς τὰ κήτη τὰ μεγάλα καὶ πᾶσαν ψυχὴν ζῴων ἑρπετῶν ἃ ἐξήγαγεν τὰ ὕδατα κατὰ γένη αὐτῶν καὶ πᾶν πετεινὸν πτερωτὸν κατὰ γένος καὶ εἶδεν ὁ θεὸς ὅτι καλά 22 καὶ ηὐλόγησεν αὐτὰ ὁ θεὸς λέγων αὐξάνεσθε καὶ πληθύνεσθε καὶ πληρώσατε τὰ ὕδατα ἐν ταῖς θαλάσσαις καὶ τὰ πετεινὰ πληθυνέσθωσαν ἐπὶ τῆς γῆς 23 καὶ ἐγένετο ἑσπέρα καὶ ἐγένετο πρωί ἡμέρα πέμπτη

אֲשֶׁר שָׁרְצוּ הַמַּיִם לְמִינֵהֶם וְאֵת כָּל־עוֹף כָּנָף לְמִינֵהוּ וַיַּרְא אֱלֹהִים כִּי־טוֹב׃ 22 וַיְבָרֶךְ אֹתָם אֱלֹהִים לֵאמֹר פְּרוּ וּרְבוּ וּמִלְאוּ אֶת־הַמַּיִם בַּיַּמִּים וְהָעוֹף יִרֶב בָּאָרֶץ׃ 23 וַיְהִי־עֶרֶב וַיְהִי־בֹקֶר יוֹם חֲמִישִׁי׃

omnem animam viventem atque motabilem quam produxerant aquae in species suas et omne volatile secundum genus suum et vidit Deus quod esset bonum 22 benedixitque eis dicens crescite et multiplicamini et replete aquas maris avesque multiplicentur super terram 23 et factum est vespere et mane dies quintus

KJV Gen. 1:20 And God said, Let the waters bring forth abundantly the moving creature that hath life, and fowl *that* may fly above the earth in the open firmament of heaven. 21 And God created great whales, and every living creature that moveth, which the waters brought forth abundantly, after their kind, and every winged fowl after his kind: and God saw that *it was* good. 22 And God blessed them, saying, Be fruitful, and multiply, and fill the waters in the seas, and let fowl multiply in the earth. 23 And the evening and the morning were the fifth day.

RSV Gen. 1:20 And God said, "Let the waters bring forth swarms of living creatures, and let birds fly above the earth across the firmament of the heavens." 21 So God created the great sea monsters and every living creature that moves, with which the waters swarm, according to their kinds, and every winged bird according to its kind. And God saw that it was good. 22 And God blessed them, saying, "Be fruitful and multiply and fill the waters in the seas, and let birds multiply on the earth." 23 And there was evening and there was morning, a fifth day.

NRSV Gen. 1:20 And God said, "Let the waters bring forth swarms of living creatures, and let birds fly above the earth across the dome of the sky." 21 So God created the great sea monsters and every living creature that moves, of every kind, with which the waters swarm, and every winged bird of every kind. And God saw that it was good. 22 God blessed them, saying, "Be fruitful and multiply and fill the waters in the seas, and let birds multiply on the earth." 23 And there was evening and there was morning, the fifth day.

Once again, let me give you my own translation:

V. 20 And God *says,* "Let the waters bring forth swarms of living creatures and the birds that fly above the earth across the firmament of the heavens."

V. 21 And God *creates* the great whales, and every living creature that
moves, with which the waters swarm, according to their kinds,
and every winged bird according to its kind. And God *sees* that it
is good.

V. 22 And God *blesses* them, saying, "Be fruitful and multiply, and fill
the waters in the seas, and let the birds multiply on the earth."

V. 23 And there *is* evening and there *is* morning, a fifth day.

The new words that appear here deserve a few remarks before I continue with my comments. First, from verse 20, there's "Let the waters swarm
with living creatures." The Hebrew reads, *yishr'tsû hammayim sherets nephesh
chayyah* (literally, "Let the waters swarm with swarms of ensouled living
things" — or something like that). And the Greek and Latin read, *exagagetō*
[let bring forth] *ta hydata herpeta psychōn zōsōn,* and *producant* [let produce]
aquae reptile animae viventis. It's from those last two versions that we inherited the tradition of avoiding "double swarming" in our English translations;
and it's also from them that we got "living creatures." Incidentally, the words
herpeta psychōn zōsōn and *reptile animae viventis* (strictly, "creeping things"
or "snakes" with souls) can also be used to denote animals that move on the
earth as opposed to those that fly above it. And at the end of verse 20, the
birds themselves finally come into the picture. In the Hebrew, they're *'ôph
y"'ôpheph,* "flying birds"; and in the Septuagint and the Vulgate, they're the
same thing: *peteina petomena* and *volatile.*

Verse 21 rounds out the list of creatures made on this day. First, it includes the "great whales," or "sea monsters" *(hattannînim hag'dholîm; ta kētē
ta megala; cete grandia).* It then repeats the words "according to their kinds"
over all the creatures of sea and air, and God once again sees that they're *good.*
In verse 22, we hear the words "God blessed them": *vay'bharekh 'otham
Elohim; ēulogisen auta ho theos; benedixitque eis.* The word *blessed* is used only
three times in the opening sequence of *Genesis, the Movie:* once on this day;
once on the sixth day over *the 'adham* as they're created male and female; and
once over the seventh day itself, on which God rested. Here, though, it's followed by the first command to "be fruitful and multiply": *p'rû ûrbhû;
auxanesthe kai plēthynesthe; crescite et multiplicamini.* Oddly, this phrase is
applied only to the fishes and the birds and not to the land animals that appear on the sixth day. Most significantly, though, it is spoken over *the 'adham,*
whom God creates on that same day.

*   *   *

Back now to my general commentary, beginning with the *airs* of the skies that surround the earth, and the *waters* that are the matrix of all its life.

One of the most pleasant surprises in the photographs of earth taken from the moon was the discovery that we live on a blue planet. After eons of looking at the busier colors of the rest of the heavens (the white of the stars, the yellow of the sun, the redness of Mars), we finally saw that the place of our birth had all along been painted as a nursery. Distance lends enchantment. For all the problems of our fallen race, the long-range picture of the earth is as charming to us as it is to God when he calls it "good" from start to finish. Strictly speaking, of course, the blue doesn't come from the waters that cover so much of the earth. We may speak of the deep blue sea, but that's accurate only on clear days. When clouds overshadow them, the waters can look gray, or green — or even, in the words of Homer, wine-dark. So actually it's the deep blue sky of our home that makes it such a restful-looking place.

Still, it's the sea from which all life comes, and the paradox of the ocean's effects on our lives deserves some recognition. (I'm indebted to the 1966 *Encyclopedia Britannica*, Vol. 16, for some of what follows here.) On the one hand, the ocean stores the heat and water that influence our weather for good. But on the other hand, a castaway on the open sea may die of cold or thirst. Where I live, the Atlantic gives us warm Octobers but frigid Aprils; and in the Pacific, *el niño* and his sister *la niña* take turns playing tricks (some nice, some nasty) on climates all over the map. The seas serve nations as barriers to invasion, but they're also corridors of commerce. They bring us necessities like oil, and they offer us luxuries like pearls and French Camembert. But the waters are also a major source of our food as well as a much put-upon recipient of our pollution. In sum, the ocean is our jack-of-all-trades and our knave of hearts. We can hardly live without it, but we have an equally hard time living with it.

The water of the seas, however, does have one indisputable virtue without which this planet would be out of luck. To our great good fortune, water becomes ice when it freezes — and the ice thus formed rises to the top of the water from which it was made. This is such an obvious fact that most of us have never given it a moment's thought; but it's water's most important contribution to life on earth. Almost all substances contract when cooled. And almost all liquids, as they pass through their freezing point to become solids, continue to shrink. Water, though, is an exception: it's one of only two substances on earth (gallium is the other) that *expand*, and become *lighter*, upon freezing.

Do you see? With the ice floating on the surface of the seas, the waters are insulated against the ravages of the cold: the danger of the ocean's freezing solid is practically nil. But if the ice sank to the bottom, it would build and build. The earth could easily become (like some other planets) a frozen, lifeless place. I can't give you an estimate of how much extra time that has provided for the evolution of life here, but we both know it's been more than sufficient. So, as it turns out, God's command to "Let the waters bring forth abundantly" is a repetition in words of the implicit instruction he gives to the formless world of Genesis 1:2, when he first thinks of making the *deep,* the *abyss* over which darkness hovers, and then has his Spirit brood upon the *face of the waters* to keep them warm.

The word *abyss,* though, brings me to something else. Just as the heavens declare the glory of God and the firmament shows his handiwork, so the deep sea speaks to us of its Maker. *Abyssus abyssum invocat in voce cataractarum tuarum; omnia excelsa tua et fluctus tui super me transierunt:* "One deep calls to another at the voice of your waterfloods; all your waves and your storms have gone over me." That passage is from Psalm 41:8 in the Vulgate — which turns out to be Psalm 42:8 in the Hebrew, Psalm 41:8 in the Septuagint, and Psalm 42:7 in the KJV. As you can see, the book of Psalms is numbered differently in the different languages. This is due in part to the fact that the Hebrew text as we now have it is not identical with the text used by the translators of the Septuagint and the Vulgate. The Septuagint came into being in the third and second centuries B.C.E. It was based on unpointed Hebrew — that is, on a text of consonants only. (The vowels were later supplied by the Masoretic editors, who labored from the seventh to the tenth centuries C.E.) The Vulgate was produced in the fifth century C.E. by St. Jerome — who was also working from the consonantal text.

In any case, what we have here in the words *abyssus Abyssum invocat* is another instance of the Bible's insistence that the world is a "conversation partner" with God. It not only speaks *of* him, declaring his marvelous works; it speaks *to* him in wonder and adoration. And through it, God speaks to us. So we can capitalize the words of our translations any way we like (or not at all) and still be on target. We can read it as "deep calls to deep" if we want to listen to creation's gossip with itself about itself. Or we can set it up as "Deep calls to deep" if we choose to hear God's speaking to the world. Or we can print it as "deep calls to Deep" if we long to relish the mystery by which even speechless things call out to God himself. But no matter how we do it, all of those dialogues take place *in voce cataractarum tuarum:* "in the voice of God's mighty waters."

That voice, therefore, proclaims the harmony between creation and creation's Lord. It's the heavenly music to which the words of the universe have been set. And that harmony has been expressed from the beginning in both sound and silence. On *day one,* the supercelestial choirs of the angelic orders (whom Augustine called the *waters above the heavens*) sing a song beyond the range of our hearing: "Holy, Holy, Holy is the LORD of hosts," they chant (Isa. 6:3). In Ezekiel 1:24, they speak "with the voice of many waters"; and in Revelation 1:8, they "worship him who is, and who was, and who is to come" (translation, RFC). But on that same *day one,* the Trinity sings the first song of the material creation when it utters the words "Let there be light!" This *recitatif,* if you will, is first heard in the sounds of silence as the Son and the Spirit hum the tune of the heavens and the earth into the ear of the Father. But soon enough, in the Big Bang, it will become the fortissimo chorus of God's cataracts, and their waves and their storms will pass over us in all the splendor of his light-splashed universe.

But even on the second day, we continue to hear no sound. In silence, the Word sings, "Let there be a firmament in the midst of the waters." The physical universe of the heavenly bodies has as yet no voice, but the empty heavens still sing the wordless song of creation. Permit me a bit of whimsy here on *silence.* Years ago, I owned a 72 rpm record of *The Hoffnung Interplanetary Music Festival.* Gerard Hoffnung was the first tuba of the London Philharmonic, and he was also a cartoonist for the magazine *Punch.* His *Music Festival* was another evidence of his humor. It was a spoof of epic proportions, featuring such delights as the *Sonata for String Orchestra and Floorwaxer in E-flat,* and his presentation of the *1812 Overture* played by a recorder consort using cap pistols for cannons: *poot poot poot poot poot poot poot poot, poot poot, blap blap!*

As I now go over the record in my mind, however, it reinforces what I've been saying about sound and silence — though far more hilariously than any efforts of mine so far. In addition to its other takeoffs, it contained a lecture by two German musicologists about a composition by a putative twelve-tone composer named Bruno Heinz Jaja. In the course of their remarks, they noted that in the middle of the piece, there were three measures of silence. The first measure, they said, was marked ⅞, and the last measure was marked ⅞; but (and I shall now quote them with at least a hint of their accents), "Ze central measure of silence iss marked ¾, giving ze entire piece a qvasi-Viennese flavor." They went on to say, "In zis measure there is a bottom B-flat in *die Bratschen* (or, as you vould call zem, *zee violen*), and zis note iss marked *tremulando ma qvasi pensato.* Zey must not play zis note; zey must only *tzink* it. As a matter of fact, zey can only tzink it, because zis note iss not on ze instrument."

The longest way 'round, especially if it's fun, is often the shortest way home — so I hope you see what I'm getting at: silence is every bit as necessary as sound to a song. The spacious firmament, even when it's a solemn silence devoid of stars, still rejoices in the ear of the divine Reason. There is no music without pauses, and there are no songs of revelation that don't have the silence of God as their pedal point. God loves a still, small voice as much as he does the noise of his waterspouts. And he comes to us most of all in our own silences. "In returning and rest shall ye be saved; in quietness and in confidence shall be your strength" (Isa. 30:15, KJV). "The Egyptians shall help in vain, and to no purpose: therefore have I cried concerning this, Their strength *is* to sit still" (Isa. 30:7, KJV). We are never more sung to than when we sit out our three measures of silence.

Back on the third day, it was the vegetable creation that took up the music — at that point, with the bawdy songs of sexuality. Andrew Marvell begins his poem "To His Coy Mistress" with the words, "Had we but world enough, and time/This coyness, Lady, were no crime." But world enough and time are precisely what the plants and their seeds now have. Each of them, as Marvell went on to do, sings, "My vegetable love should grow/Vaster than empires, and more slow." You and I, unfortunately, seldom hear the note of desire in the intercourse of pollen with plants; but that's not the plants' fault, it's ours. We hear only the din of abstractions like asexual and sexual reproduction. But the vegetable orders sing a song of colors and odors to the bees, and the bees run after the fragrance of their ointments. And on our better days, their buzzing can be music to our ears as well.

Moreover, the fourth day, with its sun, moon, planets, and stars, takes up the song of desire in full throat. The motions of the heavenly bodies are *courting* dances set to the music of the spheres, not mindless responses to blind laws. The force of gravity isn't what makes the universe go 'round; it's just the instrument on which the melody of its attractions is played. If the sunflower can desire the sun, how much more can Mercury, Venus, Earth, and Mars delight in actually dancing their way around it? To be sure, there are those who write off such an assessment as mere anthropomorphism — as the foisting of human longings for romance on beings that are as dumb as a bag of rocks.

You may dally with such reductionists if you like. But the bland world they offer you is gray and passionless compared to God's world as it dances under the banner of desire. If sex is only the way the gene pool defends itself against extinction, or if it's nothing more than a moment of warmth before an eternity of cold, we've excited ourselves over not much at all. But if it has anything to do with love, then no matter how badly we've damaged the subject, the subject itself, as God invented it, lies close to the bone of the universe. Our sexuality may be only a microcosm of reality, but the macrocosm is sexier still.

It's on the fifth day, however, that the general sexuality of creation finally comes into something like our own. Gone into the shade now is the quiet sexiness of plants. And on to the scene bursts a sexuality that can resonate with ours. Think of the anadromous fishes — the ones that fight their way up the rivers to spawn. I suppose that for most of us, the depositing of eggs by a female salmon and the squirting of sperm over them by a male doesn't look much like passionate lovemaking. But that's because we've never wondered why they do it in the first place. Is it because they've read the salmon sex manual and are just following instructions? Of course not. The reason has to be that they *feel* like doing it. On any sane view, they mate in response to physical longings much like ours — and in all likelihood, they even have orgasms to match. In the spring, the young (and even the old) creation's fancy lightly turns to thoughts of love.

Let me tell you about springtime from the perspective of an old East Coast cook. April is the month when the shad and the mackerel are bursting with roe and milt — all prepackaged in neat sacs. The shad is the largest member of the herring family, and the roe of the female is a rosy red, while the milt of the male is white as snow — and both are on hand in staggering quantities. God is prodigal with his sexual presents in the mating season. The fishes, of course, have their own plans and will swim their hearts out to bring them off. But I also have plans, and they include a host of presentations for shad roe. The simplest and best, perhaps, is broiled shad roe with bacon and a squeeze of lemon. But for variety, I sometimes wrap the roe sac in a thin vestment of prosciutto (or partially cooked bacon), sprinkle it with some lemon juice, wrap it in layers of buttered phyllo pastry, and then bake it for five minutes or so in a 500-degree oven. The shad may have their orgasms far up the Connecticut River; but I come close in my own kitchen — and guests sing the praises of my *œufs d'alose en croûte* in the same spirit.

Unfortunately, shad roe is pricey unless you fish the rivers for it yourself. But mackerel roe, while not quite as splendid, is dirt cheap by comparison. Better yet, fishmongers will practically pay you to take the milt off their hands. So just as I've taken advantage of God's April largesse in other respects, I've been equally resourceful with the glut of milt he provides. If I may speak plainly to you as a cook, calf's brains are the closest comparison I can think of for the taste and texture of milt. It's not fishy at all, just delicate. My preferred way of dealing with it is to treat it as if I were preparing *cervelles au beurre noir,* brains with black butter. First, I blanch the milt sacs for a few minutes in barely simmering salted water with a bit of lemon juice or dry white wine. Then I drain them and let them cool thoroughly. After that it's only a matter of heating some oil in a skillet over a high flame, frying the milt briefly till they take on a nice color, and removing them to a warmed serving dish. Finally, I make the "black butter" sauce in the same pan by pouring off the oil, adding fresh butter, heating it to a good shade of hazelnut, and then sprinkling in some lemon juice or white wine to stop the browning. Finally, I pour the sauce over the milt and serve it. To those with open minds and palates, it's simply delicious — a bit less than orgasmic, perhaps, but still sexy in its understated way.

*   *   *

Let me close this chapter with a coda to the song of sexuality on this fifth day. Not only is it unqualifiedly passionate; one of its parts in particular stands out as a virtuoso example of divine Overachievement. I have in mind the sexual activities of the great whales. That God should make the waters swarm with copulating fish, that he should make their gametes almost as numberless as the sand on the seashore and their fertilizations as fruitful as those of rutting bucks — all that is small compared to the sheer hugeness of sex among the whales.

You may know little or nothing about the couplings of these sea monsters; but you don't need much imagination to see that they hold sexual congresses far more fascinating than the dull, quasi-Viennese meetings through which you and I have so sweatily bumbled our way. This is our kind of sex taken to an almost eschatological *O Altitudo!* It's as if God, having decided on a sexual creation in his divine Mind, now feels the urge to show us the vastness of his enthusiasm for it. The lovemaking of whales is a bigger accomplishment than anything I've presented you with thus far. The vast weight of bull whales is fully supported by the waters, and far from pressing heavily on their partners, they can be as gentle with them as bees caressing a flower.

So don't tell me that the intercourses of whales are nothing but sex, or that they're of no more consequence than the matings of moles. Such reductionism is dead wrong — and I'll give you an example to prove it. The gray whale of the Pacific breeds in the lagoons of Mexico's Baja California peninsula; and over the last decade conservationists, movie stars, and just plain folks have made pilgrimages there to watch their sporting. I got that bit of information from a piece that ran in the *New York Times Book Review* (12 August 2001) in which Nathaniel Philbrick was reviewing Dick Russell's *The Eye of the Whale.* Here's the rest of the passage verbatim: "The whales, which have grown increasingly benign and playful over the years, are said to look into the eyes of these water-borne tourists as if imparting some ancient, transcendental wisdom. If all goes according to plan, a person leaves the lagoon

130

changed, wise in the ways of whales, the cosmos, and if he or she is lucky, whale sex (it's not uncommon for an aroused male to turn on its back and display what is euphemistically referred to as a Pink Floyd)."

That, my friend, is sex writ large — and with a mighty pen. If you keep on with your nothing-butting in the face of such overwhelming evidence, you'll write off every love story ever told. And all because you lost sight of the greatest, grandest copulation God ever thought of. No other sexual creature of land, sea, or air can hold a candle to the whale. Not the giraffe, who admittedly has to aim higher than any other animal. Not the elephant, who has fearsome tusks but lifts them clear when he mounts his beloved. And certainly not we ourselves, who might have had the most enlightened sex of all, but who have freighted it with so much solemnity and guilt that it's all but collapsed under the baggage. Still, God has given us the whales to assure us that while we may foolishly make sex smaller than it is, we can't possibly make it larger than he already knows it to be. Like him, we will never make too much of his good thing.

*   *   *

But with that happy issue out of all my ramblings through the creatures of the fifth day, it's time to close this chapter and move on to the sixth and climactic day of the world as it exists in the Mind of God.

TEN

A Sixth Day: Genesis 1:24-31

THE CROWNING OF THE ECOLOGY:
LAND ANIMALS AND THE HUMAN RACE

This is the final day of the creation of all things in the Trinity. Appropriately enough, I'll deal with it in three parts. I'll first take up the land animals that God conceives in his Mind (Gen. 1:24-25). Then I'll spend more time on the creation (again in God's Intellect) of the *'adham*, male and female, because the Director of *Genesis, the Movie* has made the creation of man the crowning touch of her opening treatment of the world's ecology (in Gen. 1:26-30). And lastly, I'll consider the final "Very Good!" (Gen. 1:31) that the Three-in-One pronounce over everything they make.

I suppose you'd like an apology for all the masculine pronouns I've thrown at God in this book so far — and I'm certain you'll want a still bigger one for the political incorrectness I'm about to display in this chapter by using the words *man, mankind,* and the *'adham* rather than circumlocutions like *humankind* or *humanity*. Instead, though, I'll just give you an explanation. Having immersed myself for so long in the biblical texts and the fathers of the church (and mothers too: Dame Julian is never far from my mind), I see no reason for slavishly following a mid-twentieth-century fad. After all, even before 1950, modern writers understood perfectly well that "man" *included* woman.

Archbishop Temple, for instance, with no loss of clarity and with admirable concision, entitled one of his best books *Nature, Man, and God*. If we now have to edit all such usages out of works written before the Second World War, we're in a bad way. Nobody in his or her right mind has ever tackled that job; indeed, the only alternative to such folly is to refuse to read them at all, which is still more foolish. But I'm also convinced that in the case of the biblical text, the acrobatics of number and gender performed by those who try to expunge its "masculinisms" are more than a waste of time. Even though I do try to accommodate such people from time to time (as I just did with "his or her"), I still think that translating every "he" as "he or she," or every "man" as "person" — or, worst of all, falling into the inelegant redundancy of phrases like "God sits upon God's holy seat" just to avoid using "his" — serves only to obscure, if not to obliterate, the Bible's concordances to itself.

Anyway, if you watch Scripture as a movie, such tin-eared improvements amount to little more than balking at the work of a competent Director. If the Holy Spirit was content to make a film for all time by using scenes or vocabulary or moral strictures from less enlightened times, who's to say her nay? Take *The Godfather,* for example, which won the Academy Award for best motion picture in 1972. To be sure, it contains many "period" references to "the mob" — not to mention a great deal of violence and a good many other ethical lapses you wouldn't want your children to take as models for their behavior. But the reruns of it remain, with no censoring whatsoever, every bit as gripping and watchable as the Bible.

Or take the episode in *The Godfather II,* in which Michael Corleone's executions of his Mafia enemies are cross-cut with a scene of the Baptism of his sister's child, at which he's acting as a godfather. On the surface, it comes across as nothing but blasphemy; but in the context of the whole film, it stands as a master image of the conflict in Michael's own soul — which is in fact the theme of the entire story.

Someone once asked me how I as a priest could be so enthusiastic about the HBO series *The Sopranos,* with all its murderous, North-Jersey Mafia carryings-on. I answered that maybe it was because I'd spent so many years reading the Old Testament. Since that shocked him even more, I pressed my advantage and said that no doubt he would have the same objection to the *Godfather* films — and that I'd give him the same reply. "Michael Corleone," I said, "strikes me as a dead ringer for Solomon in the first two chapters of 1 Kings. When Solomon is consolidating his power as the new king by putting out contracts on all the old retainers who'd dishonored the legacy of his dying father, David, he brings off a string of rub-outs worthy of The Family. And he wraps them up with the ultimate blasphemy of telling his new commanding general — Benaiah, the son of Jehoiada — to murder Joab, the old commander-in-chief, while Joab is holding onto the horns of the altar in the tabernacle of the LORD."

As I recall that conversation now, I might have added that he should also take a look at *Brideshead Revisited,* which I've recently been re-watching in all its decadent splendor. It's a brilliant adaptation, by John Mortimer, of

Evelyn Waugh's novel of the same name. It tells the complicated and often morally perplexing story of a titled British family as seen through the eyes of a narrator, Charles Ryder (superbly played by Jeremy Irons), who is actually the central character of the film.

At any rate, I'm sure I would have confronted my critic with the character of Sebastian Flyte, Ryder's great and good friend. If ethical scruples led him to edit out Sebastian's vague sexuality and unshakable childishness, or the grim inexorability of Sebastian's alcoholism, the true moral point of the picture would be lost. He'd have nothing but *It's a Wonderful Life* as an incomprehensible tragedy — with the pivotal role played by a Jimmy Stewart who, for no discernible reason, starts out rich but ends up a wreck. He'd miss entirely the significance of Charles Ryder's tears at the end of the film where Ryder, the lifelong agnostic, finally grasps the torment of all the characters he's known. Kneeling before a crucifix in the mansion's abandoned chapel, he sees both their sufferings and their sins as Christ saw his beloved, pitiful city when he wept over it before his Passion: "Jerusalem, Jerusalem, . . . how often I have longed to gather your children together as a hen gathers her chicks under her wings, and you would not!" (Matt. 23:37, RFC).

On the other hand, I might also have called my critic's attention to the film's most bizarre character, Anthony Blanche. If he chose to edit out Anthony's flaming gayness, he'd have deprived himself of one of the best portraits ever drawn of British university life in the 1920s. Worse yet, if he refused to watch *Brideshead* because its female characters (Lady Marchmain, for instance, or her daughter, Julia) were insufficiently "liberated," he'd lose sight of how the grandmothers of today's women struggled to find freedom *within* the strictures of their religion — or their irreligion, as the case might be.

Didn't he see? I would have asked him. If we have to revise old cinematic depictions of history to suit our current agendas, we run the risk of forfeiting their "literalism of the imagination" — their imaginary gardens of the past in which they offer us a real, if frog-ugly, understanding of our present. Better to leave both the original movies (not to mention the original Scriptures) as unaltered as possible. If we feel we must "improve" them, we should do so only with new analyses and appreciations. At least that way, we'll still be dealing with the originals themselves in all their complexity. But best of all, each of us will have the same set of images in our minds — which, alas, is more than I can say for our current confusion of Bible versions. If a colorized *Gaslight* simply takes away the captivating strangeness of that master film, how much more do remakes of Scripture deprive us of its matchless mystery?

*   *   *

You may be tempted, after all that film-reviewing, to congratulate me on what you see as my newfound conservatism. Don't bother. As I said, I'm not a conservative, just a conservator. Still, with my apologia for not apologizing off my chest, it's time for me to give you the first installment of this chapter's text, Genesis 1:24-25.

LXX Gen. 1:24 καὶ εἶπεν ὁ θεὸς ἐξαγαγέτω ἡ γῆ ψυχὴν ζῶσαν κατὰ γένος τετράποδα καὶ ἑρπετὰ καὶ θηρία τῆς γῆς κατὰ γένος καὶ ἐγένετο οὕτως 25 καὶ ἐποίησεν ὁ θεὸς τὰ θηρία τῆς γῆς κατὰ γένος καὶ τὰ κτήνη κατὰ γένος καὶ πάντα τὰ ἑρπετὰ τῆς γῆς κατὰ γένος αὐτῶν καὶ εἶδεν ὁ θεὸς ὅτι καλά

BHS Gen. 1:24 וַיֹּאמֶר אֱלֹהִים תּוֹצֵא הָאָרֶץ נֶפֶשׁ חַיָּה לְמִינָהּ בְּהֵמָה וָרֶמֶשׂ וְחַיְתוֹ־אֶרֶץ לְמִינָהּ וַיְהִי־כֵן: 25 וַיַּעַשׂ אֱלֹהִים אֶת־חַיַּת הָאָרֶץ לְמִינָהּ וְאֶת־הַבְּהֵמָה לְמִינָהּ וְאֵת כָּל־רֶמֶשׂ הָאֲדָמָה לְמִינֵהוּ וַיַּרְא אֱלֹהִים כִּי־טוֹב:

VUL Gen. 1:24 dixit quoque Deus producat terra animam viventem in genere suo iumenta et reptilia et bestias terrae secundum species suas factumque est ita 25 et fecit Deus bestias terrae iuxta species suas et iumenta et omne reptile terrae in genere suo et vidit Deus quod esset bonum

KJV Gen. 1:24 And God said, Let the earth bring forth the living creature after his kind, cattle, and creeping thing, and beast of the earth after his kind: and it was so. 25 And God made the beast of the earth after his kind, and cattle after their kind, and every thing that creepeth upon the earth after his kind: and God saw that *it was* good.

RSV Gen. 1:24 And God said, "Let the earth bring forth living creatures according to their kinds: cattle and creeping things and beasts of the earth according to their kinds." And it was so. 25 And God made the beasts of the earth according to their kinds and the cattle according to their kinds, and everything that creeps upon the ground according to its kind. And God saw that it was good.

NRSV Gen. 1:24 And God said, "Let the earth bring forth living creatures of every kind: cattle and creeping things and wild animals of the earth of every kind." And it was so. 25 God made the wild animals of the earth of every kind, and the cattle of every kind, and everything that creeps upon the ground of every kind. And God saw that it was good.

Since there are few words in this passage that I haven't already commented on, I'll spend my time in this chapter by giving you some deeper background. The first phrase I want to look at is *nephesh chayyah, psychēn zōsan, animam viventem,* "a soul of life." While almost everybody now thinks of "soul" as the defining property of human beings, it's important to note two things about it. First, Genesis has already given that attribute to the creatures of the sea on the fifth day. And second, there's a long tradition, in both Christian and non-

Christian philosophy (all the way back to Plato, Aristotle, and the Neo-platonists), for assigning a "soul" — an *anima* — to *anything* that has life.

That last assertion has a lot of history lurking in it, but let me see if I can make short work of the subject. To start with, there are the early Greek fathers, of whom Origen was the most notable. He took Plato's doctrine of the soul as something existing in a realm of pure ideas and ran energetically with it. Later on, Augustine joined the race and put the immortality of the human soul in the forefront of the Western church's thinking — where it stayed for almost a thousand years. (Augustine had been a Neoplatonist before his conversion, but he went on to be the greatest Christian Platonist of all time.) But then, in the thirteenth century, Thomas Aquinas joined the running. To be sure, he continued in the Augustinian tradition. (Augustine, in fact, was far and away his favorite theologian.)

By Thomas's day, however, Latin translations of Aristotle (by Arabic scholars) had become available, and Aquinas fell in love with that more down-to-earth philosopher — so much so that he "christianized" Aristotle's doctrine of the soul. In Thomism, there are three different classes of souls: an *anima vegetiva,* a "vegetive" soul for the plants and the trees; an *anima sensitiva,* a "sensitive" soul for the animal orders (indeed, the word *animal* contains the very word *anima*); and an *anima rationalis,* a "rational" soul, in the case of man.

For Aquinas (as for Aristotle), those souls differed considerably in their capacities. Plant souls had the lowest degree of knowledge and awareness; but minuscule though it might be, it was sufficient for their purposes. Animal souls were higher, knowing the world by "sensible species" — that is, by an intellect that worked mostly by "pictures," by the *"species"* they formed in their minds. But rational souls were the highest of all, knowing the world by means of "rational species" — in other words, by means of the abstract mental pictures we call "concepts." (The difference between these last two classes can be put this way: a doe may realize her fawn has stopped breathing, or a wolf may know that his prey has eluded him; but neither of them seems able to abstract from those experiences anything like our strictly human concepts of *death* or *nothing.*)

In all cases, however, Aquinas held that the soul is the "form," the "informing principle," of the body in question. For him (as for Augustine), every physical thing is *formed matter.* But matter without form is invisible and infinite (very much as the earth at the beginning was "invisible and unformed"); and form without matter (as, for example, a soul without a body) is totally immaterial. Accordingly, Thomas concluded that the souls of turnips or tigers perished when the bodies they informed perished. But when he came to the rational soul of man, he made what I consider to be an unnecessary move. Following the tradition of Augustine and almost all the theologians who preceded him, he made an exception for the human soul: he said it was by nature immortal, and so survived the death of the body.

Why do I think that was unnecessary? First of all, because it's totally unsupported by the Old Testament. Nowhere on the pages of the Hebrew Bible is an ongoing life attributed to a "departed" soul. Aside from a few passages where people who have died are mysteriously summoned back from Sheol, the dead (soul and body alike) are just out of the picture as far as present reality is concerned. So much so, in fact, that to this day Judaism has no doctrine of the immortality of the soul: the departed live on only in the remembrance of the community of Israel, not in some independent, continuing existence of their own. And second, the Gospel of Christ in no way requires an immortal soul for its authentic proclamation. It proclaims the resurrection of the dead, not the rejoining of dead bodies to souls that floated up to God by virtue of their unique spirituality.

Moreover, the New Testament proclaims that this Resurrection is not an event that will someday happen to us but rather a Person who has known and held us all along. "I am the Resurrection and the Life," Jesus tells Martha in John 11:25. He doesn't *do* resurrections as a service for cooperative souls; he *is* the resurrection for everybody. And to underscore that cosmic fact, he says, in John 12:32, "I, if I be lifted up from the earth, will draw *all* to myself"(RFC). Still, after two thousand years of "immortal soul" talk, we're probably stuck with the notion that after the death of the body, the soul continues to hang around forlornly, waiting for Jesus to do a resurrection-of-the-body number on it.

Even in the church's revised funeral rites, we lose Gospel ground. In the old days, we used to bury a *corpse*, which is the right word for a body without a soul. (The old word for a soul without a body was *ghost*.) But now we bury a *body*, which suggests that Uncle Harry is somehow still in the coffin — and when we talk about his soul, we imagine that it's the old boy himself waiting for us to catch up with him. For those of us who preach (as I do) that Jesus *is* the Resurrection, it's enough to drive us up the nearest tree. When I remind the mourners at a funeral that both they and Uncle Harry were once and for all declared risen from the dead in their Baptism, they look at me as if they'd never heard of such a thing. They still go on thinking that Jesus their Resurrection hasn't yet gotten around to them. But then I remind myself that maybe that's only a tree they've climbed up themselves — and that maybe even there, like Zacchaeus, they'll catch a glimpse of Jesus, and hear him invite himself to stay at their house (Luke 19:5).

But enough already of the soul. The other word I want to comment on is the Hebrew *l'minah*, "after its kind," which appears four times in this passage. The Septuagint translates it throughout as *kata genos*, "according to its kind"; in the Vulgate, however, Jerome indulges in elegant variation and renders it twice as *in genere suo*, once as *secundum species suas*, and once as *iuxta species suas*. (In the English, only the KJV preserves the singular of the original Hebrew.) In any case, what's important here is that this much-repeated phrase is finally being used for the last time. (It will occur once more in the Vulgate, but that's probably because Jerome's Hebrew text had it in verse 29, whereas our Masoretic text doesn't.)

My point, which I shall enlarge upon in the next section, is that while the sea and land creatures are made "after their kinds" because they comprise many species, God makes man as a *single species*. The unity of the human race is not something to be achieved by raising "lesser breeds" of people to human privileges. There are no lesser breeds of man. We're all one in the Mind of God, not only from the beginning but also in his only-begotten Beginning and Ending. From start to finish, man (the *'adham*, Jew and Greek, bond and free, male and female) "are all one in Christ Jesus" (Gal. 3:28).

*   *   *

And having thus arrived at the arrival of the *'adham* — at the creation on this sixth day of the human race, male and female, as it exists in the divine Intellect — we're now ready for the longest passage in the script so far: Genesis 1:26-30.

LXX Gen. 1:26	BHS Gen. 1:26	VUL Gen. 1:26 et ait
LXX Gen. 1:26 καὶ εἶπεν ὁ θεός ποιήσωμεν ἄνθρωπον κατ᾽ εἰκόνα ἡμετέραν καὶ καθ᾽ ὁμοίωσιν καὶ ἀρχέτωσαν τῶν ἰχθύων τῆς θαλάσσης καὶ τῶν πετεινῶν τοῦ οὐρανοῦ καὶ τῶν κτηνῶν καὶ πάσης τῆς γῆς καὶ πάντων τῶν ἑρπετῶν τῶν ἑρπόντων ἐπὶ τῆς γῆς 27 καὶ ἐποίησεν ὁ θεὸς τὸν ἄνθρωπον κατ᾽ εἰκόνα θεοῦ ἐποίησεν αὐτὸν ἄρσεν καὶ θῆλυ ἐποίησεν αὐτούς 28 καὶ ηὐλόγησεν αὐτοὺς ὁ θεὸς	וַיֹּאמֶר אֱלֹהִים נַעֲשֶׂה אָדָם בְּצַלְמֵנוּ כִּדְמוּתֵנוּ וְיִרְדּוּ בִדְגַת הַיָּם וּבְעוֹף הַשָּׁמַיִם וּבַבְּהֵמָה וּבְכָל־הָאָרֶץ וּבְכָל־הָרֶמֶשׂ הָרֹמֵשׂ עַל־הָאָרֶץ: 27 וַיִּבְרָא אֱלֹהִים אֶת־הָאָדָם בְּצַלְמוֹ בְּצֶלֶם אֱלֹהִים בָּרָא אֹתוֹ זָכָר וּנְקֵבָה בָּרָא אֹתָם: 28 וַיְבָרֶךְ אֹתָם אֱלֹהִים וַיֹּאמֶר לָהֶם אֱלֹהִים פְּרוּ וּרְבוּ וּמִלְאוּ אֶת־הָאָרֶץ וְכִבְשֻׁהָ וּרְדוּ בִּדְגַת הַיָּם וּבְעוֹף הַשָּׁמַיִם וּבְכָל־חַיָּה הָרֹמֶשֶׂת עַל־הָאָרֶץ: 29 וַיֹּאמֶר אֱלֹהִים הִנֵּה נָתַתִּי לָכֶם	faciamus hominem ad imaginem et similitudinem nostram et praesit piscibus maris et volatilibus caeli et bestiis universaeque terrae omnique reptili quod movetur in terra 27 et creavit Deus hominem ad imaginem suam ad imaginem Dei creavit illum masculum et feminam creavit eos 28 benedixitque illis Deus et ait crescite et multiplicamini et replete

λέγων αὐξάνεσθε καὶ
πληθύνεσθε καὶ πληρώσατε
τὴν γῆν καὶ κατακυριεύσατε
αὐτῆς καὶ ἄρχετε τῶν
ἰχθύων τῆς θαλάσσης καὶ
τῶν πετεινῶν τοῦ οὐρανοῦ
καὶ πάντων τῶν κτηνῶν καὶ
πάσης τῆς γῆς καὶ πάντων
τῶν ἑρπετῶν τῶν ἑρπόντων
ἐπὶ τῆς γῆς 29 καὶ εἶπεν ὁ
θεός ἰδοὺ δέδωκα ὑμῖν πᾶν
χόρτον σπόριμον σπεῖρον
σπέρμα ὅ ἐστιν ἐπάνω
πάσης τῆς γῆς καὶ πᾶν
ξύλον ὃ ἔχει ἐν ἑαυτῷ
καρπὸν σπέρματος
σπορίμου ὑμῖν ἔσται εἰς
βρῶσιν 30 καὶ πᾶσι τοῖς
θηρίοις τῆς γῆς καὶ πᾶσι
τοῖς πετεινοῖς τοῦ οὐρανοῦ
καὶ παντὶ ἑρπετῷ τῷ
ἕρποντι ἐπὶ τῆς γῆς ὃ ἔχει
ἐν ἑαυτῷ ψυχὴν ζωῆς πάντα
χόρτον χλωρὸν εἰς βρῶσιν
καὶ ἐγένετο οὕτως

אֶת־כָּל־עֵשֶׂב זֹרֵעַ זֶרַע
אֲשֶׁר עַל־פְּנֵי כָל־הָאָרֶץ
וְאֶת־כָּל־הָעֵץ אֲשֶׁר־בּוֹ
פְרִי־עֵץ זֹרֵעַ זָרַע לָכֶם יִהְיֶה
לְאָכְלָה: 30 וּלְכָל־חַיַּת הָאָרֶץ
וּלְכָל־עוֹף הַשָּׁמַיִם וּלְכֹל
רוֹמֵשׂ עַל־הָאָרֶץ אֲשֶׁר־בּוֹ
נֶפֶשׁ חַיָּה אֶת־כָּל־יֶרֶק עֵשֶׂב
לְאָכְלָה וַיְהִי־כֵן:

terram et subicite eam et
dominamini piscibus maris
et volatilibus caeli et
universis animantibus quae
moventur super terram
29 dixitque Deus ecce dedi
vobis omnem herbam
adferentem semen super
terram et universa ligna
quae habent in semet ipsis
sementem generis sui ut
sint vobis in escam 30 et
cunctis animantibus terrae
omnique volucri caeli et
universis quae moventur in
terra et in quibus est anima
vivens ut habeant ad
vescendum et factum est ita

KJV Gen. 1:26 And God said, Let us make man in our image, after our likeness: and let them have dominion over the fish of the sea, and over the fowl of the air, and over the cattle, and over all the earth, and over every creeping thing that creepeth upon the earth. 27 So God created man in his *own* image, in the image of God created he him; male and female created he them. 28 And God blessed them, and God said unto them, Be fruitful, and mul-

RSV Gen. 1:26 Then God said, "Let us make man in our image, after our likeness; and let them have dominion over the fish of the sea, and over the birds of the air, and over the cattle, and over all the earth, and over every creeping thing that creeps upon the earth." 27 So God created man in his own image, in the image of God he created him; male and female he created them. 28 And God blessed them, and God said to them, "Be fruitful and multiply, and fill

NRSV Gen. 1:26 Then God said, "Let us make humankind in our image, according to our likeness; and let them have dominion over the fish of the sea, and over the birds of the air, and over the cattle, and over all the wild animals of the earth, and over every creeping thing that creeps upon the earth." 27 So God created humankind in his image, in the image of God he created them; male and female he created them. 28 God blessed them, and

tiply, and replenish the earth, and subdue it: and have dominion over the fish of the sea, and over the fowl of the air, and over every living thing that moveth upon the earth. 29 And God said, Behold, I have given you every herb bearing seed, which *is* upon the face of all the earth, and every tree, in the which *is* the fruit of a tree yielding seed; to you it shall be for meat. 30 And to every beast of the earth, and to every fowl of the air, and to every thing that creepeth upon the earth, wherein *there is* life, *I have given* every green herb for meat: and it was so.

the earth and subdue it; and have dominion over the fish of the sea and over the birds of the air and over every living thing that moves upon the earth." 29 And God said, "Behold, I have given you every plant yielding seed which is upon the face of all the earth, and every tree with seed in its fruit; you shall have them for food. 30 And to every beast of the earth, and to every bird of the air, and to everything that creeps on the earth, everything that has the breath of life, I have given every green plant for food." And it was so.

God said to them, "Be fruitful and multiply, and fill theearth and subdue it; and have dominion over the fish of the sea and over the birds of the air and over every living thing that moves upon the earth." 29 God said, "See, I have given you every plant yielding seed that is upon the face of all the earth, and every tree with seed in its fruit; you shall have them for food. 30 And to every beast of the earth, and to every bird of the air, and to everything that creeps on the earth, everything that has the breath of life, I have given every green plant for food." And it was so.

The first thing I want to note about this passage is that it comes on the same sixth day in which the beasts of the earth are made. It's almost as if God makes the land animals and, while he's at it, makes man as a kind of superanimal. The creation of man, therefore, points two ways: in the direction of man's solidarity *with* the animal kingdom, and in the direction of his exaltation *over* it. Sadly, of course, the human race has chosen to act on the latter far more often than the former — to the detriment of both man and beast, and to the destruction of the ecology that God clearly seems to have in mind for the whole shooting match. But if I may harp once more on my notion of theological hendiadys, it seems to me that what we have here is yet another instance of God's saying one thing by means of two. We're animal and we're human at the same time. Our commonality with our "lesser brethren" is just as much a God-given fact as our superiority over them. Therefore, the only way we can truly be better than they is to make ourselves the best possible friends they can have.

If we do that, we won't look down on their knowledge, or their feelings, or their freedom, or their sexuality. Instead of sitting over them in solitary splendor, we'll use our exalted status to appreciate how much companionship we have in this lovely world. The account of the "fall" of man (which we'll come to later in this book) is the story of how we lost what the animals still retain — namely, the ability to accept the world in all its lovely roughness, and to love it as it is. Chapter 3 of Genesis will be the story of our history-destroying refusal to leave God's well-enough alone, and of our insistence — as little tin gods trying to redesign the world — on turning creation into a debacle rather than a dance.

After that disaster, we've never again been as happy as they are in their acceptance of God's invitation to the ecological ball. They roll with the punches of creation; we fight its changes and chances — and lose our composure in the bargain. They do indeed die, you see; but all in the course of a day's play. We, however, spending our lifetimes in a struggle against death, do nothing but fill the world with deaths that would never have happened if we'd kept our controlling hands off creation. It was not the animals who invented world wars, genocide, or capital punishment.

*   *   *

Now, though, for the text itself. Often enough so far, I've made the observation that the early fathers of the church took the "Let *us* make" in this passage as the first mention of the Trinity in Scripture. But I've also noted that in recent times, biblical scholars have been squeamish about following their example. But just to give you an instance of how easily (and how meticulously) the fathers discovered the Three-in-One in Genesis, I'm going to give you another illustration from Augustine. In Book III, 29 of his *De Genesi ad Litteram*, he's laid out the text as it appeared in his Latin version — much as I've done here with the original and the five versions I've been using all along. Here is how he goes about arguing the case that the Trinity appears in the first creation account:

Etiam atque etiam de natura hominis post erit uberior considerandi et diligentius disserandi locus. Nunc tamen, ut opera sex dierum nostra inquisitio pertractioque concludat, hoc primum breviter dicimus, non indifferenter accipiendum quod in aliis operibus dicitur, "Dixit Deus 'Fiat'"; hic autem, "Dixit Deus, 'Faciamus hominem ad imaginem et similitudinem nostram'": ad insinuandam, ut ita dicam, pluralitatem personarum propter Patrem, et Filium, et Spiritum sanctum. Quam tamen deitatis unitatem intelligendam statim admonet, dicens, "Et fecit Deus hominem ad imaginem Dei"; non quasi Pater ad imaginem Filii, aut Filius ad imaginem Patris; alioquin non vere dictum est, "ad imaginem nostram," si ad Patris solius, aut Filii solius imaginem factus est homo: sed ita dictum est, "fecit Deus ad imaginem Dei": tanquam diceretur, fecit Deus ad imaginem suam. Cum autem nunc dicitur, "ad imaginem Dei," cum superius dictum sit, "ad imaginem nostram"; significatur quod non id agat illa pluralitas personarum, ut plures deos, vel dicamus, vel credamus, vel intelligimus; sed Patrem et Filium, et Spiritum sanctum, propter quam Trinitatem dictum est "ad imaginem nostram," unum Deum accipiamus, propter quod dictum est, "ad imaginem Dei."

Later on, there will again and again be room to consider the nature of man more fruitfully and to expound it more diligently. Now, though, in order that our inquiry and study might bring the works of the six days to a conclusion, we first briefly say this: There is indeed a difference between what is said in the other works, namely, "God said, Let it be" and what is said here: "God said, Let *us* make man in *our* image and likeness" — because if I may say so, this insinuation of a plurality of persons is made on account of the Father, and the Son, and the Holy Spirit. However, the text immediately admonishes us to understand that plurality as the unity of the deity, saying, "God made man in the image of God." It's not as if the Father made man in the image of the Son, or the Son made man in the image of the Father. Otherwise, the words "in *our* image" are not truly spoken if man was made in the image of the Father alone or of the Son alone. But what has been said is this: "God made in the image of God," as if it were saying, "God made in his own image."

But when "in the *image* of God" is now said, after "in *our* image" has already been mentioned, it shows that the first-person plural was introduced not so that we might speak of, or believe in, or think about many gods, but so that we might understand the Father, and the Son, and the Holy Spirit as the *Trinity* on whose account "in *our* image" was spoken, and as the *one* God on whose account "in the *image* of God" was spoken.

This is Augustine speaking not as a Platonist philosopher but as an expositor of Scripture who holds the catholic faith of the church. But instead of muddying his observations with comments of my own, I shall use them as an introduction to the remarkable new words that now appear for the first time. The first and obviously the most important of them are in verse 26: "Let us make man in our image, after our likeness." In the Hebrew, this reads as *na'aseh 'adham b'tsalmenû kidhmûthenû*. The Septuagint has *poiēsōmen anthrōpon kat' eikona hēmeteran kai kath' homoiōsin*, and the Vulgate has *faciamus hominem ad imaginem et similitudinem nostram*. Now for my remarks.

The phrase "in our image, after our likeness" as it appears in this verse clearly brings up both the *imago Dei* and the *similitudo Dei* which have so long fascinated Christian theologians. Aquinas, for example, took this double reference as an opportunity to make a distinction. For him, the "image" represented an unlosable participation of man in the divine Will. Even after the Fall, he said, we remain in that happy condition. But after our disobedience at the tree of the knowledge of good and evil, we lost our "likeness" to God. Our entire history since then has been ungodly in the extreme. No doubt this was a perfectly decent way of making sense of the duplication, but there are two reasons why I think there's a better way.

First of all, it's a bit un-Hebraic: Hebrew uses repetition not to invite the discovery of differences between two expressions but to reinforce our appreciation of the first with a second that puts the same thing in other words. (The Psalms — and all Hebrew poetry, for that matter — have this device as their most characteristic feature.) But second, because verse 1:27 drops the "likeness" and mentions only the "image," it seems to me that this is one more invitation to take *imago* and *similitudo* as a hendiadys — which is what I shall now proceed to do.

Since the "our" attached to "image and likeness" so plainly signifies the Trinity — and specifically, the mutual exchanges of the three Persons as they coinhere in action and essence — I'll begin by saying that the *'adham,* male and female, are created by God as the great, earthly sacrament of this coinherence. And our possession of that image and likeness makes all our exchanges with each other light up. Our daily work, our leisure pursuits, our love affairs, our marriages — all of these, even when contaminated by sin, are our share in the divine Work, Play, Romance, and Longing by which the Three-in-One draw the world home to the family life of God. Therefore, the homesickness we so often complain of is actually God's gift to us. We're not sick because we're exiles here but because, like the bride in the Song of Solomon, we are "sick of love" (5:8) — fainting with desire to return to the Love that made us in the image and likeness of God. But even in our faintness, that Love beyond all liking and happening will always be the home we cannot lose.

But there's more than that to the notion of man in the image and likeness of the Trinity. We're also created (despite Augustine) in the image of each of the divine Persons. To begin with, the Father's overarching care for everything he chooses to make is reflected, when we're at our best, in our own responses to the creatures of the world. Our delight in the heavens, our love of the beauties of earth and ocean, our affection for the fish of the sea and the animals of the earth — all are real presences of the Fatherhood of God in our nature. And our fondness for our children is nothing less than a likeness of the Father's divine Fondness for us all.

Then there's the creation of the *'adham* in the image of the Son, the divine Word, which is seen in the fact that we too shape the world by means of *words*. Animals, for example, may recognize *salt* when they come across it; but only we have managed to recognize it as *sodium chloride*. We've named our way into an entirely new universe called physical chemistry. And we've done the same in all our other activities. I'll give you just one more illustration here, from the kitchen so dear to my heart. The cooking of our food — not to mention the upper reaches of *haute cuisine* — would never have been possible had we not invented the concepts of *boiling, steaming, frying,* and *roasting.* And the creation of desserts would never have happened if we hadn't come up with such concepts, unknown to the animals, as *refined sugar, beaten egg whites, whipped cream,* and *gelatin.* As the Word speaks a sweet world into being by saying "Let there be!" so all the sweets of our devising come into being by *words.*

Finally, though, there's the creation of mankind in the image of the Spirit — the Mutual Love of the Trinity who in the Beginning broods over the face of the waters, and now shines forth in the warming love that we (again, at our best) confer on our own loves. We show it not only in our "vegetable loves" when we farm, eat, and drink, but also in our love for all other things. It shines out of our delight in beach stones, precious stones, and cathedral stones, and in our inveterate romancing with all the living creatures of the earth. We are the loving priests of creation, ordained to lift everything into the Dancing of the *Creator Spiritus.* Even when our love falls short — even when it fails completely — the Love of the Spirit remains the deepest principle of our lives.

Still, I think there's a further ramification of the image and likeness of God in man. Since the *'adham* in this verse are the crown of everything God makes in this part of *Genesis, the Movie,* it seems to me that the whole created order can be seen as having an equal share in that same priestly gift of God. God's fingerprints are not only on the human race but also on all things — animal, vegetable, and mineral. We see the marks of his hands in the interplay of great and small stones with the mass of the earth. We watch them in the dancing of the plants with soil, air, and sun. We sense them in the choreography of the sometimes harsh ecologies of life and death and good and evil in the animal and human orders, and we feel their power in the frenetic dance of sexuality everywhere.

All of these are nothing less than the participation of the entire universe in the coinherence of the Trinity. Genesis may apply the *imago et similitudo Dei* to us alone, but that's only God's way of inviting us to see his image in every creature over which he gives us dominion. We've been made "higher" to lift up the "lower" ones, not to make wallflowers of them. But more importantly, I think, God has conferred that image and likeness on us just so we'll never make the mistake of calling ourselves nothing but animals. Animals we may be, as this sixth day plainly implies. But *nothing but* remains a false start. When we deny that exalted status to the animals — and then idiotically reduce ourselves to the level to which we've consigned them — we simply deny the image of God in ourselves. In short, we misread the whole world. But, despite our folly, "God's truth abideth still." The rising tide of the divine Coinherence goes right on lifting all the boats of creation. Nothing — not even sticks and stones — is without at least a hint of the image and likeness of God.

But the tide doesn't stop at the creation of man in the *imago Dei.* Verse 27 goes on to say, "So God *creates* man in his *own* image, in the image of God *creates* he him; *male and female creates* he *them.*" (This is KJV, all italics mine, except for *own;* as before, I've put *creates* in the present tense to remind you that this act of creation exists only in the divine Intellect: the rest of my italicizations are intended to underscore the creation of "man" as a male and female "them"). The Hebrew for "create" here is *vayyibhara';* and the word for "in his image" is *b'tsalmô* (this is the same word as before, but as I've said, there's no actual mention of "likeness" here); and the words for "male and female" are *zakhar ûnqebhah.*

One more note. The switch from "him" to "them" as the pronoun for "man" in this verse accentuates the contrast between the "six-day" version of the film in Genesis 1 and the one that will appear in Genesis 2. That second scenario begins with only a male *'adham* and doesn't bring woman into the picture until after the Lord God has planted the Garden of Eden with its two trees, formed all the animals, and given them the names that Adam called them. As a matter of fact, the first time a "they" is heard in the rest of *Genesis, the Movie* is at the end of chapter 2. (If by chance you're keeping tabs on me, the *them* that shows up in Genesis 2:19 refers to the animals — and anyway, as the KJV points out by italicizing it, it's not in the Hebrew.) All in all, then, this joint creation of the *'adham* as male and female bolsters my case (and Augustine's) for taking this first part of the film as creation existing solely in God's Intellect and not in time and space.

Incidentally, I've always found it remarkable that so few people have paid attention to this simultaneous creation of the two sexes in Genesis 1. The making of woman from man's rib is all they remember. But I'm more convinced than ever that taking all six days in Genesis 1 as *within* the One Day of God — and *not* as an act of physical creation — is the right way to go. So just in case I haven't said it clearly enough before now, I want you to consider how many pointless arguments this view can spare you.

If you buy this approach, you'll be liberated from such quibbles as whether the six days were twenty-four-hour periods or whether each lasted for millions or billions of years. Moreover, you'll never again try to prove the Bible true by attempting to square the developmental sequence of the six days with that of science. And, best of all, you won't even attempt to discount evolution by saying it doesn't conform to the timetable of Scripture. With everything in Genesis 1 neatly tucked in God's eternal Mind, you can just sleep through all such fuss and feathers: you'll find no time or space at all in the six days. But if by any chance you're now tempted to reverse field and congratulate me on my liberalism, you can forget that too. I'm still just a conservator, trying to preserve as many endangered truths as I can, whether I find them in the Bible or in science — or even, as you may have noted, in any other reconstructions of creation, factual or fictional.

But on to verse 28 of our script: "And God *blesses* them. . . ." The Hebrew, Greek, and Latin here are *vay'bharêkh 'ôtham Elohim, kai ēulogēsen autous ho theos,* and *benedixitque illis Deus.* The Hebrew word *barakh* means "kneel" or "bless." Applied to God, it means "adore with bended knees"; applied to us, it can mean "bless, salute, or greet" (as in a morning greeting or a farewell), or an expression of gratitude, a congratulation, an act of homage or friendliness. The Greek *eulogein* and the Latin *benedicere* literally mean "to speak well of." But their long-standing use as biblical translations of *barakh* has imported into them all the freight of the Hebrew word. (There is yet another word for *blessed* in the New Testament. In the Greek it's *makarios,* "happy"; and in the Latin it's *beatus,* "blessed" — as in the "Beatitudes" (Matt. 5:1-11): "Blessed are the Meek. . . ." This word is used thirty-eight times in the Septuagint, but never in the book of Genesis. In any case, it too has all the force of *barakh.*)

But the word *barakh* itself is used only three times in the early part of *Genesis, the Movie.* The first occurrence is on the fifth day, in verse 22, when "God *blesses* the great whales and every living creature that moveth, which the waters *bring* forth abundantly, after their kind, and every winged fowl after its kind." The second comes on this sixth day when God *blesses* the *'adham,* male and female. And the third appears on the seventh day (at Gen. 2:3) when God *blesses* the day of his own eternal Rest.

To my mind, therefore, what we have here is an ascending order of blessing. It begins by crowning the animals of sea and air with the blessedness of God himself; it continues by placing the diadem of God's blessedness on man; and it ends with God's coronation (his *congratulation*) of his own blessedness in his endless Sabbath. If this strikes you as an odd way of looking at God's blessings, you're not alone — so I'll try to help you out. People often ask, when confronted with all the biblical passages in which we're told to *bless the Lord,* "How can *we* possibly bless God? Shouldn't we instead ask him to bless us?" But that question is based on a misunderstanding.

In the ancient languages, "to bless" is not an act that *confers* a blessing on something that doesn't yet have it; rather, it's an act that *recognizes* blessedness in something or someone who already has the presence of the Blessed One in itself, himself, or herself. In Luke 1:42, for instance, the pregnant Virgin Mary is greeted by her cousin Elizabeth (carrying the fetus of the future John the Baptist) with the words, "Blessed are you among women, and blessed is the fruit of your womb" — thus making her greeting, in effect, an old woman's recognition of the Blessed One already in the womb of a blessed girl. And when the Palm Sunday crowds shout, "Blessed is he who comes in the Name of the Lord" (Luke 19:38) — or, for that matter, when God appears to Jacob at Peniel and blesses him there (Gen. 32:29-30) — the same thing is true: in both cases, the blessing is pronounced over a person who already enjoys the presence of the blessed God himself.

Therefore the three blessings in the seven days are sacraments of that truth — and it's a truth that Gerard Manley Hopkins beautifully recognized in his poem "God's Grandeur":

> The world is charged with the grandeur of God.
> It will flame out, like shining from shook foil;
> It gathers to a greatness, like the ooze of oil
> Crushed. Why do men then now not reck his rod?
> Generations have trod, have trod, have trod;
> And all is seared with trade; bleared, smeared with toil;
> And wears man's smudge and shares man's smell: the soil
> Is bare now, nor can foot feel, being shod.
>
> And for all this, nature is never spent;
> There lives the dearest freshness deep down things;
> And though the last lights off the black West went
> Oh, morning, at the brown brink eastward, springs —
> Because the Holy Ghost over the bent
> World broods with warm breast and with ah! bright wings.

This "dearest freshness deep down things" is nothing less than the blessing of God spoken to the heart of all creation on the sixth day. Nevertheless, if you take that blessing in conjunction with the image and likeness of God in man (and with Hopkins's poem), I think you'll find that it points straight to a broader view of the Incarnation of the Word of God in our Lord Jesus Christ. Instead of showing it to you as an insertion late in history — or even as an insertion at the beginning of history — it lifts the Incarnation to the status of a Mystery already present not only *from* the foundation of the world but even *before* the foundation of the world. Let me give you some examples of how the New Testament supports this distinction between "from" and "before."

The first is from Matthew 13:35, where Jesus, quoting Psalm 78:2, says, "I will open my mouth in parables; I will speak of things hidden *from the foundation of the world*" (RFC). This clearly refers to the physical creation from its beginning to the present time, as do a number of other such passages (Matthew 25:34, Luke 11:50, and Hebrews 4:3 and 9:26 — just to give you an idea). In all of those, the phrase is *apo katabolēs kosmou* (*apo* being the word for "from"). But elsewhere, the words *pro katabolēs kosmou* appear, *pro* meaning "before." In Ephesians 1:4 we're told that God the Father "has chosen us in him [in Christ] *before* the foundation of the world" (RFC), thus putting the mystery of the Incarnation *prior* to the existence of the physical universe — that is, in the divine Intellect from all eternity, as I've so often insisted. And to corroborate that truth, the same *pro* is used in John 17:24, where Jesus prays that his disciples "may behold my glory that you have given me, for you loved me *before* the foundation of the world." It's also used in 1 Peter 1:20, where, having referred to the precious blood of Christ as of a lamb without spot or blemish, the author then identifies the Christ as the "One who on the one hand was foreknown *before* the foundation of the world but who has now been made manifest in *these last times* for your sakes."

I'll readily admit that Augustine and almost all the fathers and mothers of the church, except possibly the Lady Julian, have not pushed the Incarnation as far back as I would have liked. Most of them tacitly assume that it occurred rather late in time — and that it came into the world as a *remedy,* a medicine for healing the sickness of sin. For that very reason, their views of it to this day have always been open to insertional and transactional interpretations. But even though I have scant company in my preference for seeing the Incarnation as present in the Beginning himself from the start of creation, I do have at least one supporter: John Duns Scotus, the great Franciscan theologian (*circa* 1266-1308). He took the view that the Incarnation of the Father's Word, being the greatest of all works, should not be made contingent on a good of a lower order — namely, the job of dealing with the problem of sin. He therefore held that the Incarnation would have been the Word's chosen relationship with humanity, even if the human race had not sinned.

Scotus thus leaves little theological houseroom for the notion that the

Incarnation was a *temporal insertion* of the Word into human flesh. For him, the Word is just as Incarnate when he creates human nature as its Beginning as he is when he redeems human nature as its End. And in the middle — through the long night of the world's dying — the presence of the Incarnate Word in every human death (*innocent* or *guilty*) is no "afterthought" on God's part. The Word has always willed death to be the engine of our life, even before we sinned. Our sin just gives him a chance to put a new spin on his favorite old top.

Interestingly, Thomas Aquinas was quite aware of the Scotist view of the Incarnation. He brings it up in his *Summa Theologica,* Part III, Question I, Article III, entitled "Whether God would have become Incarnate if man had not sinned" — and he gives it a fair hearing. He first lists five arguments (to me, quite convincing) for saying that the Incarnation would indeed have occurred even without sin. But then, in his response to those arguments, he cites both Scripture and Augustine, and he says they lead him to land on the opposite side.

In other words, he admits that there are differing opinions on the question; but, relying on his conviction that Scripture presents the Incarnation as a *remedial* act of God, he says this: "Therefore, since everywhere in Sacred Scripture the reason for the Incarnation is assigned to the sin of the first man, it's more appropriate to say that the work of Incarnation was ordained by God as a remedy against sin. So much so, that if sin had not existed, there would have been no Incarnation." (As you may have guessed, I think his "*everywhere* in Scripture" is a bit overblown — and I've just given you, a few paragraphs ago, some Bible verses that I think bolster my case.) Thomas does, however, add a significant qualifier at the end of his response: "Although," he says, "the power of God in this matter should not be limited: it is *possible* for God to become Incarnate, even if sin had not existed."

Be that as it may, here ends my effort to convince you that the Incarnation is present not only on the sixth day of creation but even on — *and even before* — day one. If you're kindly disposed to my insistence that the Beginning, namely, the Word by whom all things are made, was already made flesh in the Mind of God at those points, well and good. If not, though, just as well and just as good. We, like both Augustine and Aquinas, were meant to sit at the feet of Scripture, not to dictate to it. To quote E. B. Pusey once again, "Such is the depth of Holy Scripture, that manifold senses may and ought to be extracted from it, and that whatever truth can be obtained from its words does in fact lie concealed in them."

But since I've now been so bold as to pick at least small quarrels with Augustine, Scotus, and even Aquinas — and since I've referred to Augustine only a single time in this chapter so far — I'd like to show you at some length how I think Augustine supports at least a good bit of what I've been saying here. In his *De Genesi ad Litteram*, Book VI, 8, he's dealing with the separate creations of man and woman as they're portrayed in Genesis 2. But even there, he feels constrained to go back to the earlier depiction of their simultaneous creation in Genesis 1. Here's my first citation:

> *Neque enim dicendum est, masculum quidem sexto die factum, feminam vero posterioribus diebus; cum ipso sexto die apertissime dictum sit, Masculum et feminam fecit eos, et benedixit eos, et caetera, quae de ambobus et ad ambos dicuntur. Aliter ergo tunc ambo, et nunc aliter ambo: tunc scilicet potentiam per virtutem Verbum Dei tanquam seminaliter mundo inditam, cum creavit omnia simul, a quibus in die septimo requievit, ex quibus omnia suis temporibus jam per saeculorum ordinem fierent; nunc autem secundum operationem praebendam temporibus, qua usque nunc operatur, et oportebat jam tempore suo fieri Adam de limo terrae, et mulierem ex viri latere.*

For neither is it to be said that the male was made on the sixth day but the female on subsequent days, since on the sixth day itself it is most plainly said, "Male and female he made them, and blessed them, et cetera." And these things are said about both and to both. Therefore, both sexes were involved in one way *then*, and both are involved in another way *now. Then*, of course, they were present as a potentiality put into the world seminally by the power of the Word of God when he created all things at once, from which works he rested on the seventh day, and out of which all things in their own times presently come to be by the order of the ages. But *now* [remember, Augustine is looking at Genesis 2 here], according to the operation furnished to those times, which still operates even now, it was equally fitting that Adam, in his own time, be made from the mud of the earth, and that woman be made from the side of her husband.

There you have a clear view of the contrast between God's creation of "all things at once" *(omnia simul)* and his creation of "all things in their own times" *(omnia suis temporibus)* that I've been insisting on. I think it needs no more comment than I've already worked into my translation, but I just can't resist quoting the paragraph that follows it as well. Not only does it reinforce what Augustine and I have said; the last half of it also contains something that may pass for elliptical humor in an otherwise straight-faced writer. Here it is, from Book VI, 9:

In qua distributione operum Dei, partim ad illos dies invisibiles pertinentium, quibus creavit omnia simul, partim ad istos oppositos, in quibus operatur quotidie quidquid ex illis tanquam involucris primordialibus in tempore evolvitur, si non importune atque absurde Scripturae verba secuti sumus, quae nos ad haec distinguenda duxerant; cavendum est ne propter ipsarum rerum aliquanto difficilem perceptionem, quam tardiores assequi non sufficiunt, putemur aliquid sentire ac dicere, quod scimus nos nec sentire nec dicere. Quanquam enim praecedentibus sermonibus, quantum potuerim, lectorem perstruxerim; plures tamen arbitror caligare in his locis, et putare ita fuisse prius hominem in illo Dei opere quo cuncta simul creata sunt, ut aliquam vitam duceret, ut Dei locutionem ad se directum, cum dixit Deus, "Ecce dedi vobis omne pabulum seminale," discerneret, crederet, intelligeret. Noverit ergo qui hoc putat, non hoc me sensisse, nec dixisse.

In that distribution of the works of God — which pertains partly to those invisible days in which he created all things at once, and partly to those contrasted days in which whatever was primordially wrapped into those things is daily evolved in time (unless we have unfittingly and absurdly followed the words of Scripture which have led us to distinguish these things) — we have to beware lest on account of the sometimes difficult task of comprehension that dull-witted persons are not up to following, we suppose that we may feel and say something which we know we neither feel nor say. For although in my preceding remarks I have, as much as I was able, thoroughly instructed my reader, there are many who cast a dark cloud over these passages.

They believe that man previously came to be in that work of God by which all things were created at once in order that he might lead a life like the one God's speaking pointed out to him when God said, "Behold, I have given you every green herb bearing seed [for food]" — and might discern, and believe, and understand just that. He who thinks this, therefore, will have recognized that I neither thought this nor said it.

This strikes me as a wry if gentle answer to people who try to read vegetarianism into the Bible because only vegetables are mentioned here as food for man (and as a matter of fact, for lions and tigers and bears as well). But there are two problems with grinding that ax on the stone of Scripture. The first is that in the ecology of life and death (which God willed right along with the existence of the creatures of the fifth and sixth days), the animals of sea and air and land obviously eat each other with gusto. So to suggest that the saber-toothed tiger, for instance, was restricted to a diet of hay and hostas puts the poor critter in a theological quandary. He has to wake up every morning (as one wag put it) wondering why God gave him such an inconvenient set of choppers. On the other hand, to imagine that Scripture insists on a vegetarian diet for man is an even bigger stretch, since it runs afoul of God's commandment that his people eat lamb at the Passover — not to mention the fact that he fed them with so many quails that they threw up all over the wilderness. This last, of course, could be (and no doubt has been) construed as God's way of showing his distaste for meat-eating. If you find that approach convincing, you're welcome to it. Just don't try to convert me until you've solved the Paschal lamb problem. I am a devout omnivore, thank you very much.

But Augustine just lets the subject go with as much humor as he can allow himself — which is not a lot. Like almost all of the ancient fathers, he was convinced that *gravitas* was the hallmark of sound theology. In Book XI, 14 of his *Confessions,* he comes as close to a joke as he ever did, but he shies away from it. In that passage he's entertaining a question put by persons "full of their old tricks" (as he characterizes them), who ask, "What was God doing before he made heaven and earth?" But he says he won't answer them as some joker did, "eluding the true force [*violentiam*] of the question, 'He was preparing hell for pryers into mysteries.'" It's one thing, Augustine says, "to answer inquiries, and quite another to make fun of inquirers." He understood the joke, you see; but all he could allow himself was a stern "not funny."

How unlike the Lady Julian he is! She was *merry* in her love of God — utterly serious about her theology, but still able to see the good humor of God in even the least solemn of his designs. At one point in her *Revelations of Divine Love,* as I recall, she even offers a reflection on the anal sphincter — which she marvels at for the way it opens and closes "like a purse."

Augustine, however, goes right back to his theologizing — but with a somewhat lighter touch. If I may give you another example, here's the imaginary conversation he constructs between himself and his rather dense inquirer. It occurs in Book VI, 10, immediately following the preceding quotations. I've abridged it a bit to hold your attention:

Sed rursus, si dixero non ita fuisse hominem in illa prima rerum conditione qua creavit Deus omnia simul, . . . putabit omnino non fuisse. Redeat ergo ad Scripturam; inveniet sexto die hominem factum est ad imaginem Dei, factum est masculum et feminam. Item quaerat quando facta sit femina; inveniet extra illos sex dies; tunc enim facta est, quando Deus e terra finxit adhuc bestias agri et volatilia coeli; non quando volatilia produxerant aquae, et animam vivam, in qua et bestia sunt, produxit terra. Tunc autem factus est homo et masculus et femina: ergo et tunc et postea. Neque enim tunc et non postea; aut vero postea et non tunc; . . . Quaeret ex me quomodo. Respondebo, Postea visibiliter, sicut species humanae constitutionis nota nobis est; non tamen parentibus generantibus, sed ille de limo, illa de costa ejus. Quaeret tunc quomodo. Respondebo, Invisibiliter, potentialiter, causaliter, quomodo fiunt futura non facta.

But again, if I shall say that man did *not* come into being in that first condition of things by which God created all things at once, . . . someone will think man did not come into being at all. Let him go back to Scripture: he will find that on the sixth day [in Genesis 1], man was made in the image of God, and moreover made male and female. But then, should he ask when woman was made, he will find that it occurred outside those six days; for she was then made [in Genesis 2] when God had already made the beasts of the field and the birds of heaven — not when the waters were producing the birds and not when the earth produced the living soul, which includes the beasts. But back then [on the sixth day] man was made both male and female. Therefore, it is a matter of both *then* and *afterwards*. For neither is it a matter of then and not afterwards, nor indeed of afterwards and not then. . . . He will ask me how this can be. I shall respond, "*Afterwards,* it is accomplished visibly, in the same way that the phenomena of human making are known to us; not, however, in terms of the begetting of parents, but rather in terms of man being made from the mud and woman from his rib." He will ask how this happened *then* [on the sixth day]. I shall respond, "Invisibly, potentially, and causally — in the same manner that future things not yet made come into being."

This is one more insistence by Augustine on the two modes of God's creative act — an *intellectual* one in God himself and a *physical* one, outside the six days, in time and space. But it's also a resolution of the often troublesome conflict between chapters 1 and 2 of Genesis. This, of course, has been a long-standing problem. But it's not to be solved by ignoring one or the other of the two accounts — or by reconciling them on the basis of a soft-pedaled approach to chapter 1. Augustine uses both approaches, and as you've seen, he makes his reconciliation by taking the first as an account of the whole of history as it exists in God's Mind, and the second as a depiction of that same history in a temporal and spatial world. His distinctions between *then* and *afterwards,* and between what God makes *visibly* in time and what he makes *invisibly, potentially,* and *causally* in himself, stand as his greatest contribution, I think, to a sensible solution to a problem that has occasioned a good deal of nonsense.

You've been more than patient. Let me give you the wrap-up of his mental dialogue with his opponent, from Book VI, 11:

> *Hic forte non intelligit. Subtrahentur enim ei cuncta quae novit, usque ad ipsam seminum corpulentiam. Neque enim vel tale aliquid homo jam erat cum in prima illa sex dierum conditione factus erat. Datur quidem de seminibus ad hanc rem nonulla similitudo; . . . quid ergo faciam, nisi, quantum possum, salubriter moneam ut Scripturae Dei credat et tunc factum hominem quando Deus, cum factus est dies, fecit coelum et terram, . . . et tunc quando jam non simul, sed suis quaeque temporibus creans, finxit eum de limo terrae, et ex ejus osse mulierem? nam nec isto modo eos illo sexto die factos, nec tamen eos illo sexto die non factos intelligere Scriptura permittit.*

Here, perhaps, he does not understand. All the things he knows have been taken away from him, even what he knows about the bodily nature of seeds. For man was not like that when he was made in that first condition of the six days. Indeed, there is no comparison to seeds in this matter. . . . But still he does not understand. What then shall I do, other than advise him helpfully, as far as I am able, to believe in the God of Scripture and that God *then* made man when God made the [one] day on which he made the heaven and the earth [Gen. 1:1-5] . . . and that he created them *then* even though in creating them *now* in their own times [that is, in Genesis 2], he made man from the mud of the earth and woman from his bone? For Scripture does not permit us to understand either that they were made in this way on that sixth day, or that they were not made in this way on that sixth day.

Once again, Augustine dwells on the *then* and the *now;* but in the end, he returns to his habitually broad view of Scripture. He will not say what Scripture doesn't say. He realizes that the Bible doesn't allow us to resolve our controversies over what it means by claiming either that it supports a physical interpretation of the sixth day or that it repudiates it. As I said, we all sit at Scripture's feet: it's not for us to tell it where to land when it so plainly keeps its travel plans shrouded in Mystery.

*   *   *

On this same sixth day, however, there is a repetition of the divine command that follows God's blessing over the fishes and the birds on the fifth day. At that point God says, "Be fruitful, and multiply, and replenish the earth." But now he says something new, intended for man alone. He adds, ". . . and *subdue it;* and *have dominion* over the fish of the sea, and over the fowl of the air, and over every living thing that moveth upon the earth." Since this is a much-debated passage, let me inset and underline the relevant Hebrew, Greek, and Latin words from verse 28:

> *P'rû ûrbhû ûmil'û 'eth-ha'arets v'khibhshuah, ûrdhû* . . . ("Be fruitful, and multiply, and replenish the earth, and <u>subdue it</u>, and <u>have dominion</u> . . .")
>
> *Auxanesthe kai plērthynesthe tēn gēn kai <u>katakyrieusasthe autēs</u>, kai <u>archete</u> . . . (the same)*
>
> *Crescite et multiplicamini et replete terram et <u>subicite eam</u> et <u>praesit</u>* . . . (the same)

The underlined words that appear here have been a bone of contention in recent times. People may hold "be fruitful and multiply and fill the earth" harmless enough; but "subdue it and have dominion" are seen as an opening for the exploitation of earth's creatures. Well, of course they're an opening: God leaves his human creatures free to do any blessed or damned thing they please.

But, by the same token, he never intended us to take his words as an invitation to beat up on the rest of his works. True enough, man's dominion over the world has been abused to a fare-thee-well: we're coming dangerously close to wrecking the ecology of the earth. But abuses must not be allowed to eclipse legitimate uses. Against all our depredations must be set our successes at lifting creation into ever higher unities. We've lifted the stone of the earth's crust into cathedrals, the wood of its forests into houses and furniture, the eggs of its chickens into *Oeufs à la neige,* the innards of its cattle into *Tripe à la mode de Caen* — and even the tail hairs of its horses and the entrails of its dead cats into violins. You may balk at some of my enthusiasms in that list; but, all in all, I find them warranted. Vegetarians, too, have their *babaghanoosh.*

But since that brings us to verses 29 and 30 — and since Augustine and I have already begged off the hint of vegetarianism in them — I think I have no more to say about it here. Instead, I shall go right to the final words of the script for this sixth day of the world's coronation in the crowning and blessing of man with the image and likeness of God.

LXX Gen. 1:31 καὶ εἶδεν ὁ θεὸς τὰ πάντα ὅσα ἐποίησεν καὶ ἰδοὺ καλὰ λίαν καὶ ἐγένετο ἑσπέρα καὶ ἐγένετο πρωΐ ἡμέρα ἕκτη	וַיַּרְא אֱלֹהִים BHS Gen. 1:31 אֶת־כָּל־אֲשֶׁר עָשָׂה וְהִנֵּה־טוֹב מְאֹד וַיְהִי־עֶרֶב וַיְהִי־בֹקֶר יוֹם הַשִּׁשִּׁי׃	VUL Gen. 1:31 viditque Deus cuncta quae fecit et erant valde bona et factum est vespere et mane dies sextus

KJV Gen. 1:31 And God saw every thing that he had made, and, behold, *it was* very good. And the evening and the morning were the sixth day.

RSV Gen. 1:31 And God saw everything that he had made, and behold, it was very good. And there was evening and there was morning, a sixth day.

NRSV Gen. 1:31 God saw everything that he had made, and indeed, it was very good. And there was evening and there was morning, the sixth day.

You'll be delighted to learn that there are no new words here except for one: the "Very" which this verse adds to the "Good!" that God has so often pronounced over the things he has made on the preceding days. God says, *tôbh m'odh, kala lian, valde bona,* "Very Good!" over *everything* he's made in his divine Mind, from start to finish. From the light on day one (Gen. 1:3), to the fulfillment of all of history in the New Jerusalem which is the Bride of the Lamb (Rev. 21:2), to his "Behold, I make all things new" on the last day (Rev. 21:5), he is utterly delighted with the creation he has beheld from the beginning in his only-begotten Son. And because it all exists in his Word as the Blessed Beginning, this "Very Good" is his ultimate blessing on creation.

A while back, I promised you that I wouldn't annoy you with a running count of God's "Goods!" if you'd keep track of them for yourself. Let's see now if we agree on their numbers. As I recall them, there have been seven, if we reckon them from the Hebrew original and the Latin and English versions; in these, this day has two "Goods," and the third day has two, while the second day has none. But if we count in the Septuagint, there are eight altogether, since that version inserts a "Good" in the second day.

Whatever the tally may be, it seems to me that what we have here is a ringing affirmation of the all-embracing contentment of God with the universe he's thought up in his divine Mind. This final "Very Good" covers not only everything he has *made* but also everything that has *happened* through the whole history of the world. Good or bad, nice or nasty, sinless or sinful — all of it, as he sees it in his only-begotten Son, is Good without let or hindrance. Therefore, I find this unqualified satisfaction of God on the sixth day to be yet another reason for seeing the Incarnation as a fact, in and from the Beginning. If God's Knowledge and Will are as eternal as his being, then everything he knows and wills is present to him before all times and places.

If he can see his creation reconciled in his Incarnate Word even before it exists on its own turf — and even while it is pursuing the unreconciled course of its own history — then everything about that Incarnation fully exists in God's Mind and Purpose from the start. The *Providence* of God cannot be reduced to a mere foreknowing of things and actions that even he must wait to know in fact. To repeat Augustine's great line one more time: *NOTA ERGO*

FECIT, NON FACTA COGNOVIT ("Known things therefore he made, not made things he knew"). If that means anything at all, it means that he sees everything he knows about creation even before he makes it. He sees it as already complete in his own Mind.

But finally, we come to the last line: "And there was evening and there was morning, a sixth day." In Latin, the sixth day is *feria sexta;* and since the sixth day of the week is Friday, these words round out the entire history of the world's salvation. This is the first Friday of the world, and it is Very Good! But it looks forward (as the opening scenes of any great movie do) to another Friday that's even better: to the ultimate Good Friday — the *feria sexta in Parasceve,* the Friday of the Preparation — on which the world will be taken home to the land of the Trinity. It's not just that man is created on the sixth day; it's also that through man, creation is redeemed on the sixth day. So in the drama of the biblical film, the Mystery of the divine Will comes full circle right in the opening scene.

When we first watch the movie, of course, none of that is obvious. But when we review it as it stands complete in our minds, we see that the Director has all along had just that in her Mind. "In my beginning is my end," T. S. Eliot says at the start of *East Coker;* and at the close he says, "In my end is my beginning." So too in the Bible. In this passage, the unbroken circle of Scripture shines before our eyes as one story, glorious from Day One to the Last Day.

Furthermore, Day One is a Sunday, the first day of the week. (Archbishop Ussher, the Primate of Ireland who lived from 1581 to 1656, even went so far as to put God's act of creation on a Sunday morning in 4,004 B.C.) And in the book of Revelation, the Last Day is revealed to John the Divine on the island of Patmos on the *Lord's Day,* which is Sunday. Accordingly, just as there are two Fridays in the film of *Genesis, the Movie* that reveal the redemption of the world, so there are two Sundays that tell the story of the world's creation. On the first Sunday, God makes the heavens and the earth by bringing everything *ex nihilo* — out of the nothing of sheer non-existence. And on the second Sunday (on the first day of the week), he makes everything all over again out of the nothing of the world's death, in the resurrection of our Lord and Savior Jesus Christ. From Friday to Friday, then, and from Sunday to Sunday, the film of the Bible encompasses nothing less than the entire creation that God has had in Mind all along.

At long last, therefore, we're ready for the seventh day — the eternal Sabbath of God.

ELEVEN

The Seventh Day: Genesis 2:1-3

GOD'S ETERNAL REST

My final chapter on the first part of *Genesis, the Movie* will begin with a new twist on an old idea. A good while back, I told you that I thought God's creative act was more like *magic* than manufacturing. Now I want to use the realm of *faerie* as a metaphor for the divine Intellect in which that magic takes place. Webster's Unabridged defines *faerie* as "an imaginary land of enchantment," thus evoking a world that's related to but also different from the physical order. The word comes to us from Middle English, and it conjures up visions of beautiful, ageless creatures whose being is precisely "fairy." In other words, they have an existence that's not, strictly speaking, a matter of time and place.

To my mind, this fits quite well with my insistence throughout this book that the creatures of the six days exist only in the Mind of God and have neither temporal nor spatial qualities of their own. They may indeed be the eternal representations of things here and now, but putting those six days into an *imaginary land of enchantment* (with the Trinity doing the imagining and enchanting) strikes me as a brilliant way of doing them justice.

Enchantment and magic, in fact, lie at the very roots of creation. God is not a general contractor supervising the labors of subordinates, nor is he a lone carpenter shaping the lumber of an "almost-nothing" into a furnished home for his creatures. Rather, he is a *faerie* Magician who brings everything out of nothing by nothing but *words* — by intimately and immediately speaking the names of all things through his eternal Word. A magician's performance is entirely a matter of *incantation*, not hands-on fashioning. The rabbit isn't *made* in the hat; it's *called* out of the nothing within the hat. On day one, for example, the light isn't made out of the darkness; it comes into being

158

when God's Word says, "*Let there be light* [*y'hi 'ôr*]." That command doesn't present us with a manufacturing process; it's simply the *Presto!* of the divine Magician.

The Hebrew mind understood this perfectly. When the Bible wants to refer to a "matter," or a "piece of business," or a "thing done," it uses the word *dabhar* — the ordinary noun for "word." (Look at the KJV translations of Genesis 24:9, or Exodus 18:22, or Deuteronomy 3:26, or 1 Samuel 20:23, 29, or Jeremiah 38:27. All those references are to "a matter" or "matters" — and in the original, every one of them is either the word *dabhar* or its plural, *d'bharim.*) In Hebrew, then, a "word" is an act of power: the mere speaking of it makes things *happen.* And the same thing is true when the Word of God speaks the entire world into existence. Everything comes out of absolutely nothing by the power of the *conversation* between the Persons of the Trinity, not out of any previous stuff that was lying around.

Throughout the six days, therefore, God's intellectual creation comes into being only by *enchantment,* by *incantation,* by *magic.* It is indeed a *faerie* world; and every one of its creatures — and every scrap of their history — is brought forth by the magic of the Word. But if you're tempted to object that this turns history into a fairy tale, don't go there. As I've said several times, history isn't just a list of the things that have happened. That would be mere *chronicle,* and it would give you neither the shape nor the sense of past events. History, by contrast, is made by the words we speak over events to form them into a coherent story. So, in the final analysis, the heart of history is accessible to us only in the world of *faerie. Aesop's Fables* and *Grimm's Fairy Tales* give us a better grasp of human life than all the ledgers of time laid end to end. "The Hare and the Tortoise" doesn't need any proof of its "historicity"; we recognize its truth in the simple act of listening to its *faerie* words.

So too with Scripture, especially in the case of the six days. Our problems with them have come entirely out of our efforts to line them up with some superimposed chronicle of creation. But if we could watch them as the Father and the Son and the Spirit see them in the exchanges of the Trinity — as the Producer, the Star, and the Director of the creation-film view them in their eternal Screening Room — our problems would vanish. Every great movie ever made, even if it's a documentary, is an expedition into the realm of *faerie.* Ken Burns's *The Civil War* is no less a work of imagination than *American Beauty.* And this first and greatest of all movies is no exception: the film of the six days is the truest *faerie* tale ever told.

*   *   *

On now, though, to the seventh day itself. The first thing I want you to note about this day of rest is that, unlike the other days, it contains no mention of either evening or morning. Augustine, true to his habit of careful reading, spends a good deal of time worrying this matter; but I'm not so sure about what he does with it. He observes that it's not until the *end* of day one that Genesis says, "And there was evening and there was morning, one day"; and he also notes that the rest of the days follow the same pattern ("evening . . . morning, a second day"; "evening . . . morning, a third day"; and so on). But for the most part, he decides that the "evening" applies to the day just depicted and the "morning" to the next day. To my mind, however, that gives him more problems than it solves.

First of all, while Augustine might have assigned day one's evening to the *darkness* on the face of the deep and its morning to the creation of the *light*, he might just as easily have given it no morning at all. (As you'll see, that second interpretation will be the one I finally choose.) In addition, even though his shifting of the "mornings" to the next day works fairly well with the second through the fifth days, it's not so clear that it works with the sixth and the seventh. Since he's committed to making the morning mentioned at the end of the sixth day into the morning of the seventh day, he finds himself forced to give the day of rest a morning but no evening — even though neither is actually mentioned in the text. Admittedly, there's a certain theological charm in his insistence that the mornings of day one and the seventh day can be seen as repetitions of the eternal morning of God's all-at-once Today. However, on balance, I don't think that's a completely satisfactory solution.

As you may already suspect, my own preference will be to stick with the Hebrew way of reckoning days. Since the Sabbath runs from sundown to sundown, that is, from its *eve* on Friday to the evening of Saturday, which in turn is the *eve* that begins Sunday, the first day of the week — and since Halloween (All Hallows' *Eve*) is the day whose vespers begin the celebration of All Saints' Day — I shall take all six days as following pretty much that pattern. In general, the "evening" mentioned at the end of each day, besides being the end of that day itself, will also be the *eve* — the beginning, the "first vespers," if you like — of the next day. But since some adjustments are necessary to make that approach work on particular days, let me give you a table that lays out all seven days in sequence and shows you how I treat each of them.

The Seven Days of Genesis 1:1 to 2:3

Day One: Genesis 1:1-5

I take verse 1 of this day ("In the beginning God created the heavens and the earth") as the eternal *eve*, the first proclamation of God's entire creative act as it will be spelled out in the six days that are to follow. With Augustine, I see it as outside all the specific days (as the whole day of Halloween is outside All Saints' Day, perhaps). It exists only in the endless Today of the Trinity, and thus stands "before" all things in the divine Intellect.

But unlike Augustine, I then take verse 2 (the *darkness* on the face of the deep) as the specific *eve* — the "first vespers," if you will — of day one. At that rate, the *light* that was spoken into being, divided from the darkness, and called "day" in verses 3 and 4 becomes the morning, the noon, the afternoon, the late afternoon — and the "sundown" (sans sun) of day one. And that brings us to the "evening" in verse 5, which then becomes the *eve* of

The Second Day: Genesis 1:6-8

Since this day has already begun in the darkness of its "first vespers" on the night of day one, it continues in the same pattern — that is, through its own morning, afternoon, late afternoon, and "sundown" — and itself becomes the *eve* of the third day.

The Third, Fourth, and Fifth Days: Genesis 1:9-23

These follow suit. One after another, they run their courses; and each one, besides having its own "evening," becomes the *eve* of the succeeding day.

The Sixth Day: Genesis 1:24-31

Once again, this day begins with its *eve* in the night of the fifth day. But at its end, there will be no *eve* of the seventh day because God *finished* all his works on the sixth day, and because the seventh day, like the very first verse of day one, stands *outside* God's act of creation. And that brings us at last to

The Seventh Day: Genesis 2:1-3

This final day of God's Rest thus brings us back to the eternity of God in which the whole of this part of *Genesis, the Movie* has been filmed. It has no eve, no morning, and no evening because just as creation began in the eternal Rest of God, so it ends in that same Repose.

I realize that my chart may or may not be as plain as day to you. But I still like it because it has the virtue of bringing the seventh day back to the morningless Today of God with which the movie begins. In short, it makes the whole picture come full circle. The world's consummation in the Sabbath Rest of God becomes its return to the Father who first thought of creating everything through his only-begotten Word, speaking over the brooding of his outbreathed Spirit. And that, I like a lot. Not only does it take creation home to the enchanted Land of the Trinity; it's exactly the kind of thing a Director at the top of her form would do with the film of a *faerie* world — and that, I think, is what the Holy Spirit has already done in *Genesis, the Movie.*

*   *   *

But since the seventh day is the epilogue to the whole of the first part of the movie, I'll go straight to the script and let it speak for itself.

LXX Gen. 2:1 καὶ συνετελέσθησαν ὁ οὐρανὸς καὶ ἡ γῆ καὶ πᾶς ὁ κόσμος αὐτῶν 2 καὶ συνετέλεσεν ὁ θεὸς ἐν τῇ ἡμέρᾳ τῇ ἕκτῃ τὰ ἔργα αὐτοῦ ἃ ἐποίησεν καὶ κατέπαυσεν τῇ ἡμέρᾳ τῇ ἑβδόμῃ ἀπὸ πάντων τῶν ἔργων αὐτοῦ ὧν ἐποίησεν 3 καὶ ηὐλόγησεν ὁ θεὸς τὴν ἡμέραν τὴν ἑβδόμην καὶ ἡγίασεν αὐτήν ὅτι ἐν αὐτῇ κατέπαυσεν ἀπὸ πάντων τῶν ἔργων αὐτοῦ ὧν ἤρξατο ὁ θεὸς ποιῆσαι

BHS Gen. 2:1 וַיְכֻלּוּ הַשָּׁמַיִם וְהָאָרֶץ וְכָל־צְבָאָם: 2 וַיְכַל אֱלֹהִים בַּיּוֹם הַשְּׁבִיעִי מְלַאכְתּוֹ אֲשֶׁר עָשָׂה וַיִּשְׁבֹּת בַּיּוֹם הַשְּׁבִיעִי מִכָּל־מְלַאכְתּוֹ אֲשֶׁר עָשָׂה: 3 וַיְבָרֶךְ אֱלֹהִים אֶת־יוֹם הַשְּׁבִיעִי וַיְקַדֵּשׁ אֹתוֹ כִּי בוֹ שָׁבַת מִכָּל־מְלַאכְתּוֹ אֲשֶׁר־בָּרָא אֱלֹהִים לַעֲשׂוֹת:

VUL Gen. 2:1 igitur perfecti sunt caeli et terra et omnis ornatus eorum 2 conplevitque Deus die septimo opus suum quod fecerat et requievit die septimo ab universo opere quod patrarat 3 et benedixit diei septimo et sanctificavit illum quia in ipso cessaverat ab omni opere suo quod creavit Deus ut faceret

KJV Gen. 2:1 Thus the heavens and the earth were finished, and all the host of them. 2 And on the seventh day God ended his work which he had made; and he rested on the seventh day from all his work which he had made. 3 And God

RSV Gen. 2:1 Thus the heavens and the earth were finished, and all the host of them. 2 And on the seventh day God finished his work which he had done, and he rested on the seventh day from all his work which he had done. 3 So God blessed

NRSV Gen. 2:1 Thus the heavens and the earth were finished, and all their multitude. 2 And on the seventh day God finished the work that he had done, and he rested on the seventh day from all the work that he had done. 3 So God blessed

blessed the seventh day, and sanctified it: because that in it he had rested from all his work which God created and made.	the seventh day and hallowed it, because on it God rested from all his work which he had done in creation.	the seventh day and hallowed it, because on it God rested from all the work that he had done in creation.

Before I turn to my comments on this seventh day, I'd like to mend my fences with Augustine and give you a passage that makes an excellent bridge to what I'll have to say. But first, since the Latin version of Genesis from which he worked was somewhat different from the Vulgate as I've just quoted it (his was a translation based on the Greek of the Septuagint, not on the Hebrew), let me give you that version as it appears in *De Genesi ad Litteram*, Book IV, 1 (noting that, in my translation, I've italicized the words I intend to discuss):

> *Gen 2:1 Et consummata sunt coelum et terra et omnis ornatus eorum. 2 Et consummavit Deus in die sexto opera sua quae fecit; et requievit Deus in die septimo ab omnibus operibus suis quae fecit. 3 Et benedixit Deus diem septimum, et sanctificavit eum; quia in ipso requievit ab omnibus operibus suis quae inchoavit Deus facere.*

Gen. 2:1 And the heaven and the earth were *consummated*, and all the beauty of their adornment. 2 And on the sixth day God *consummated* his works that he made; and God *rested* on the seventh day from all his works that he made. 3 And God blessed the seventh day, and *sanctified* it; because in that same day he *rested* from all his works that God *began* to make.

In the light of that version of the text, I'd like you to pay particular attention to the words *finished (consummata)* and *begun (inchoata)* that occur in the passage I'm about to give you from *De Genesi ad Litteram*, Book VI, 18. Augustine will be at pains to hold that creation is both finished and being begun at the same time — and he'll use the text for the seventh day to support his case. I'll discuss his specific words after you've had a chance to hear him out:

> *Nunc autem quia et consummata quodammodo, et quodammodo inchoata sunt ea ipsa quae consequentibus evolvenda temporibus primitus Deus omnia simul creavit, cum faceret mundum: consummata quidem quia nihil habent illa in naturis propriis, quibus suorum temporum cursus agunt, quod non in istis causaliter factum sit; inchoata vero, quoniam quaedam*

erant quasi semina futurorum, per saeculi tractum ex occulto in manifestum locis congruiis exserenda: ipsius etiam Scripturae verba satis ad hoc admonendum insigniter vigent, si quis in eis evigilet. Nam et consummata ea dicit et inchoata: nisi enim consummata essent, non scriptum esset, "Et consummata sunt coelum et terra, et omnis compositio illorum: et consummavit Deus in sexto die opera sua, quae fecit: et requievit Deus in septimo die ab omnibus operibus suis, quae fecit: et benedixit Deus diem septimum, et sanctificavit eum"; rursusque nisi inchoata essent, non ita sequeretur, quia illa die "requievit ab omnibus operibus suis quae inchoavit Deus facere."

But now, because God created all things at once when he first made the world, those very things which were to evolve in subsequent times are both somehow finished and somehow being begun. On the one hand, they're finished because those things have nothing in their natures that was not causally present in them all along. But on the other hand, they're also in a state of beginning, because certain things were to be sown out in them as "seeds" of future things — things which, by the course of time and in appropriate places, would go from being hidden to being manifest.

And certainly, the words of Scripture itself are sufficiently vigorous to serve as a pointed reminder of this, if one looks at them vigilantly. For it says that things are both *finished* and *beginning*. Because if they were not *finished*, it would not have been written, "And the heaven and the earth were *finished*; and God rested on the seventh day from all his works which he made; and God blessed the seventh day, and sanctified it." But on the other hand, if they were not *beginning*, it would not have followed that on that day "he rested from all his works which God *began* to make."

As you can see, Augustine leans hard here on one side of a textual difficulty. There's no problem with the word *finished* in verses 1 and 2. (*Consummata* and *consummavit* in Augustine's version, *perfecti sunt* and *conplevitque* in the Vulgate, and *synetelesthēsan* and *synetelesen* in the Greek of the Septuagint all mean the same thing.) But the word *begun* in verse 3 is another potful of meaning. The Hebrew words behind *fecit* ("made") here are actually "created [*bara'*] to make [*la'asôth*]." The Vulgate comes the closest to that with *cessaverat ab omni opere suo quod creavit Deus ut faceret:* "He ceased from every work of his which God created that he might make." The Septuagint (which was the basis for Augustine's Latin version) has *katepausen ho theos apo pantōn tōn ergōn autou hōn ērxato ho theos poiēsai:* "He rested from all his works that God *began* to make." (The KJV has "from all his work which

God created and made"; the RSV has "from all his work which he had done in creation"; and the NRSV has "from all the work that he had done in creation.")

Why the Jewish translators of the Septuagint should have rendered the Hebrew *bara'* as the Greek *began (ērxato)* is something of a mystery to me. Perhaps it was because they lived at a time when Hebrew was still a spoken language and they were aware of now-forgotten usages of *bara'* in that sense. Or perhaps they felt that the infinitive *la'asôth* ("to make" or "to do") called for it. After all, the phrase "which God created to make" is awkward — and since creating something clearly causes it to begin, they may have felt that decent Greek style would be better served by "which God *began* to make." Frankly, I just don't know enough to say. But then, the translators of the three English versions seem almost as clueless. One after another, they waffle their way through the text. They remind me of nothing so much as the proverbial difficulty of hunting for a black cat in a coal mine. They make Augustine's *quae inchoavit Deus facere* look as if he saw the beast in broad daylight.

But all that textual nit-picking to one side, the rest of the new words in the script deserve some attention. The first comes at the end of verse 1: "Thus the heavens and the earth were finished, *and all the host of them*" (KJV, RSV; the NRSV has *multitude* for *host*). The Hebrew here is *v'khol-ts'bha'am;* the Septuagint has *kai pas ho kosmos autōn;* and the Vulgate reads *et omnis ornatus eorum. Ts'bha'am* is an augmented form of *tsabha',* the Hebrew word for God's heavenly "hosts" (*tsabha'ôth,* "sabaoth") — the celestial army of God drawn up in full battle array. And because of that notion of *order* and *arrangement,* the Septuagint and the Vulgate felt free to use *kosmos* and *ornatus.* Both of those nouns are from verbs that signify ordering or decoration.

From *kosmos* we get such words as *cosmos,* meaning the ordered universe as opposed to the chaos, and *cosmetics,* meaning facial decorations. And from *ornatus* we have *ornamentation* and *adornment.* The English versions, alas, don't quite catch the charm and breadth in the Hebrew and the earlier versions. *Host* no longer conjures up the splendor of military formations, and *multitude* suggests only quantity, not quality. Still, if I had to choose, I'd go with *host.* The old word, hallowed by use, is at least interesting enough to arouse curiosity; the tiresome clarity of *multitude* simply numbs the mind.

But I cavil. The remaining words I want to flag are less debatable but more important. I think I've done enough with the word *blessed* in the previous chapter, so I'll skip God's blessing of the seventh day and go right to the two phrases I haven't yet covered. They are "he rested" on the seventh day, and "he sanctified it." Let me begin with the latter and work my way back to the first in easy stages.

In the three ancient languages, "he sanctified it" is *vay'qadhêsh 'othô, kai hēgiasen autēn,* and *et sanctificavit illum.* This is the only time the word appears in Genesis, and it's a verb form from the adjective *qadhôsh,* "holy" (as are the Greek *hēgiasen* and the Latin *sanctificavit,* which give us the *Trisagion* in the Greek Liturgy, the *Sanctus* in the Latin Mass, and the "Holy, Holy, Holy" in the English Eucharist). In any case, it's precisely the day of his Rest from all his works that God sanctifies here. But since he has now completed those works and declared them Very Good as he beholds them in himself, this day also becomes his hallowing of the works themselves by giving them a share in his own sanctity. The world is charged not only with the grandeur of God but also with the holiness of God.

But that holiness, as it appears in Scripture, is not a tame or pretty thing. It's nothing like the saccharine halos and Bible-clouds of Victorian stained-glass windows or the tacky "holy cards" handed out by undertakers. Rather, it's something wild and uncontrollable, even dangerous and weird — not a "kindly light" but a million-volt charge of electricity. It doesn't present you with a God who is a pal you can slap on the back; it gives you a God who is Wholly Other than anything you've ever encountered. Your only choices are either to run and hide from him or to stay and tremble. "Tremble, thou earth, at the presence of the Lord, at the presence of the God of Jacob," says Psalm 114:7 (KJV, here and throughout paragraph). And in Exodus 33:18, when Moses asks the LORD to show him his glory, the LORD says,

> I will make all my goodness pass before thee, and I will proclaim the name of the LORD before thee; and will be gracious to whom I will be gracious, and will shew mercy on whom I will shew mercy. And he said, Thou canst not see my face: for there shall no man see me, and live. . . . I will put thee in a clift of the rock, and will cover thee with my hand while I pass by: and I will take away mine hand, and thou shalt see my back parts: but my face shall not be seen. (vv. 18-23)

Even the goodness and the graciousness and the mercy of God are filled with the terror of his holiness.

The world God creates and sanctifies is a place of terrible goodness and terrible holiness. In all its beauty, in all its roughness, in all its lives and deaths, and in all its matter — down to the most minuscule, unpredictable particle of the subatomic realm — it is a place no more tame than God is. All its seas and dry land; all its grasses and plants; all its planets and stars; all its whales, fish, and birds; all its cattle, creeping things, and wild beasts; and all its men and women, even in the thick of their sins — all these are holy and dreadful as well. And so is all the rest of his holy creation. It is made of holy water, holy air, holy earth, holy fire, and even holy smoke. Over every bit of it hovers the benign yet terrifying presence of the Holy Luck by which God draws the whole world into his eternal Rest.

So whether we look at the world as it exists in the seven days of the divine Intellect or as it exists in its own history, the creation that bears his image and likeness is a holy place because it is held in the exchanges of the Holy Father, the Holy Son, and the Holy Spirit. And its ultimate joy is to find that the Holiness of those Three has indwelt it from top to bottom, and world without end.

This brings me at last to my final word: the *requies Dei* that is also *requies nostra* — the Rest of God that is our rest too. In his *De Genesi ad Litteram*, Book IV, 29 and 30, Augustine has some wonderful insights into this grand confluence of holiness and repose, and I shall quote him for you directly. But I must first alert you to two things about my English translation. The first and major one is that it's far less literal than any I've given you so far. This is due not so much to the difficulty of understanding Augustine's Latin (read as Latin, it's not particularly hard to fathom) as it is to the length of his sentences and the way he loads them up with subordinate clauses. My solution to the problem of making readable English out of them involves not only breaking them up into smaller pieces but also relocating some of the pieces and sprinkling in a number of parentheses and dashes. (Augustine loved to dive into a sentence with eleven commas, two colons, and one semicolon, and never let the main verb out of his mouth till he finally broke water at the end. Put a performance like that into word-for-word English, and your readers will drown before they reach the verb.)

The second and minor thing is that every time Augustine uses the word *beatus,* "blessed," I've taken the liberty of translating it as "happy" — partly because that's one of the principal meanings of the word, but mostly because I think "blessed" is now a "churchy" word that conveys more a sense of dull antiquity than of present happiness. In any case, here are Augustine and I going to the mat for you:

29 *Neque enim similitudo pia est, si velimus ita similes esse Deo, ut et nos ab operibus nostris requiescamus in nobis, sicut ipse requievit ab operibus suis. In quodam quippe incommutabili bono requiescere debemus, quod ille nobis est qui nobis fecit. Haec erit igitur summa, minimique superba, et vere pia requies nostra, ut sicut ipse requievit ab omnibus operibus suis, quia non ei opera sua, sed ipse sibi bonum est, quo beatus est: ita et nos ab omnibus operibus, non tantum nostris, verum etiam ipsius, nonnisi in illo requieturos nos esse speremus; idque desideremus post bona opera nostra, quae in nobis agnoscimus illius potius esse quam nostra: ut etiam sic post*

bona opera sua ipse requiescat, cum post bona opera quae ab illo justificati fecerimus, in se nobis requiem praestat. Magnum est enim nobis ab illo exstitisse, sed maius erit in illo requievisse. Sicut ipse non ideo beatus est, quia haec fecit; sed quia etiam factis non egens, in se potius quam in ipsis requievit. Unde non operis, sed quietis diem sanctificavit; quia non haec faciendo, sed eis quae fecit non egendo, se beatum intimavit.

30 Quid ergo tam humile ac facile effatu, et quid tam sublime atque arduun cogitatu, quam Deus requiescens ab omnibus operibus suis quae fecit? Et ubi requiescens nisi in seipso, quia beatus nonnisi seipso? Quando, nisi semper? In diebus autem quibus rerum quae condidit consummatio narratur, et ab eis quietis Dei ordo distinguitur, quando, nisi in septimo die, qui earum sequitur perfectionem? A perfectis enim requiescit, qui nec perfectis eget, quo beatior esse possit.

29 For it isn't just a pious fancy that we should want to be so like God that we should rest in ourselves from our works as he himself rested from his works. For we ought indeed to rest in that unchangeable good which he who made us is for us. Accordingly, this will be our highest and truly pious rest — and by no means a haughty presumption — that just as he rested from all his works (since it is not his works but he himself, for himself, who is the good by which he is happy), so we too shall rest from all [our] works. And not from ours only but also from his — for otherwise we could not hope to be rested in him. But after our good works (which we acknowledge in ourselves to be more his than ours), let us desire this: that just as he could rest after his good works, so, after the good works we will have done as justified by him, he might grant us rest in himself alone. For it is a great thing to have been brought into being by him, but it will be a greater to have rested in him. It's not as if he is happy because he made these things. Rather, it's because he has no need at all of made things that he rested more in himself than in them. So he sanctified the [seventh] day not as a day of works but as a day of quiet, since it was not in his making of these things, but in his not needing the things he made, that he most profoundly intimated his happiness.

30 *What* then is more simple and easy to speak of, and more sublime and difficult to think about, than God resting from all his works that he made? And *where* is he resting, if not in himself, since he is happy only in himself? And *when* is he thus happy if not always? But on the days in which the completion of the things he made is narrated — and by them, the architecture of God's rest is pointed out — *when* did all that take place unless on the seventh day that followed the perfecting of these

things? For he who rests from perfected things is the very one who does not need even perfected things to make him happier than he already is.

In my translation of Augustine's second paragraph, I've italicized the "question" words because I think he realized that saying God doesn't *need* the things he made in order to be happy *(beatus)* might well pose problems for his readers. Yet that's a truism of all sound theology, and it's one of Augustine's most crucial insights. To less subtle minds, making God's act of creation *unnecessary* to his eternal Happiness may seem to make the world a trifle in the sight of God. But instead, it makes it the apple of his eye. It turns it into something he delights in so much that he simply *loves* giving it the time of his eternal Today. ("For it is a great thing to have been brought into being by him, but it will be a greater to have rested in him.") The being of his good creation is a *gift*, not a sop to the divine Ego — and his Rest on the seventh day is his final bestowal of that gift.

In *De Genesi ad Litteram,* Augustine spends quite a bit of time insisting that God's *Requies* on the seventh day should not be taken as mere cessation from labor. First of all, he notes that in chapter 2 of Genesis (which I shall take up next), God is right back in the business of making things. And second, he insists that God will continue to be busy throughout the rest of the Bible with the work of *preserving* and *redeeming* the world he has made. His act of creation is an ongoing work. In Book IV, 21, of *De Genesi ad Litteram,* Augustine wonders whether there isn't a contradiction between God's having rested on the seventh day and his having worked right up to the present day. And he quotes Jesus' words in John 5:17 — "My Father works until now, and I also work" — as the answer to his question. Jesus made this statement, Augustine notes, to those who questioned Jesus' non-observance of the Sabbath rest anciently prescribed on the authority of the God of Scripture. Augustine continues his remarks with this marvelous passage on some concordances to "working" and "resting" that he finds in the New Testament:

Et dici quidem probabiliter potest, observandum sabbatum Judaeis fuisse praeceptum in umbra futuri, quae spiritualem requiem figuraret, quam Deus exemplo hujus quietis suae fidelibus bona opera facientibus arcana significatione pollicebatur. Cujus quietis et ipse Dominus Christus, qui nonnisi quando voluit passus est, etiam sepultura sua mysterium confirmavit. Ipso quippe die sabbati requievit in sepulcro, eumque totum diem habuit sanctae cujusdam vacationis, posteaquam sexto die, id est parasceve, quam dicunt sexta sabbati, consummavit omnia opera sua, cum de illo quae scripta sunt, in ipso crucis patibulo complerentur. Nam et hoc verbo usus est quando ait: "Consummatum est; et inclinao capite tradidit spiritum." Quid ergo mirum si Deum istum diem, quo erat Christus in sepultura quieturus, volens etiam hoc modo praenuntiare, ut ab operibus suis in uno die requievit, deinceps operaturus ordinem saeculorum, ut et illud vere diceretur, "Pater meus usque nunc operatur"?

And indeed it can probably be said that the observance of the Sabbath was commanded for the Jews as a shadow of the future, a figure of the spiritual *rest* that God offered as an example of this quietness of his — that is, as a secret signification of the *rest* laid up for his faithful people when they do good works. And even the Lord Christ himself (who suffered only when he willed to) confirmed the mystery of that *rest* in his burial. Indeed, on that same day of the Sabbath he *rested* in the tomb, and he had that whole day as a kind of holy *vacation*. For after the sixth day, that is, the Friday of the Preparation (which they call the sixth day of the week), he *finished* all his *works* when the things that were written about him were being *fulfilled* on the very gibbet of the cross. For this word *finished* is also used when he said, "It is *finished*, and bowing his head, breathed his last" (John 19:30). What then is there to wonder at here? For if on this day in which Christ was *resting* in the tomb, God wanted to announce beforehand both that Jesus would *rest* from his works on this one day [Holy Saturday] — and that on the succeeding day [the Sunday of the Resurrection] he was still *working* out the order of the ages — that word was also truly being spoken when Jesus said, "My Father is *working* right up to now."

This is another of Augustine's forays through Scripture, and I particularly like the way he equates Christ's "holy vacation" in the tomb with the rest of God on the seventh day of creation. To my mind, this is exactly the kind of thing that preachers and theologians worth their salt should be doing every time they speak or write. Their true calling is to be watchers and reviewers of the greatest movie ever made. Their primary obligation, therefore, is to show us the variations that the Director has played on the themes set forth by the pivotal images of her film. They're not supposed to tell us what its episodes mean — and certainly not to bother us with their notions of what the original scriptwriters could or couldn't have had in mind when they included those episodes.

There can, of course, be room in their spare time for that sort of volunteered information; but when they turn off the bright light of the Director's improvisations on the images, the room becomes a murky place. The best commentary they will ever have on Scripture will always be Scripture itself. So whatever you are — preacher, teacher, or believer — if you take nothing else from this book, I hope it will be a delight in the way Augustine so often manages to make the brilliance of the Holy Spirit's direction shine forth. He may have lived well before the advent of motion pictures, but in my book he rates as one of the best film reviewers of all time.

Still, I think there's one more thing to be said about God's Rest. Just as God's creation of all things in his divine Intellect is accomplished by nothing but the words of his eternal Word spoken in the exchanges of the Trinity, so the ongoing life of that creation, even in his Rest, is utterly dependent on the continuity of the divine Conversation. As I've said, you and I are not here today because we were here yesterday and God hasn't yet foreclosed on our existence. We're here because the Word of God is calling us out of nothing into being at this very moment. Intimately and immediately, he's saying the name of everything he has made; and when he says "Let there be" and "It is so," there ain't no nothin' that can do anything but *be*. In short, we're here not because we have to be but because he wants us to be, here and now. And because the words of his Word are eternal in the Trinity, our being is just as eternal as his speaking.

Were he to stop saying our names, of course, we would be nothing at all. But since he's spoken them once and for all *(simul et sempiterne)* in his endless Today, the non-necessity of our being turns out to be a non-starter. Our poor, contingent existence is backed by the solid gold of God's own Unnecessary Being — in which even a divine Whim is an everlasting Promise. He doesn't have to need us. He doesn't *need* anything. All that's necessary for our being is that somewhere, even in some back alley of his divine Mind, God should just once have liked the sound of our names so much that he mentioned them in the everlasting Sheboygan. Just once. And just anywhere. It makes no difference whether you put it in the six days that are all one day in God, or in the repose of the seventh that has no morning or evening, or in the Word who is the Beginning who always is. Wherever you put that pronouncement of the Great Mentioner, you and I were, and are, and always will be, *there.*

✳   ✳   ✳

We're almost at the end of this first part of my book. For you as the reader and me as the author, there will soon be an intermission in which we'll have a well-deserved rest. But if either of us has understood Augustine, our own work of creation will go on continually, even in rest. I can't guarantee you that, of course, because everything man proposes is subject to God's disposing. All of us live out our lives under the rubric of "if we're spared." Nevertheless, *dum spiro, spero* — "While I draw breath, I have hope." Pray for me.

But I can't move on without a tribute to Augustine. Not as a preacher. Not as a theologian. Not even as one of the most engaging minds I've ever met. Rather, as the new friend I've found him to be. I'm sure he had few doubts, either about his God or about the faith of the church he freely chose to serve. But there are days when I do, and it is on those days that I most cherish his friendship. I sometimes wonder (usually when I'm lying awake in bed at three A.M.) whether the whole business of my belief is just the wish fulfillment of a pleasant dream. Can the consolations of everything I've told you possibly be real? Am I perhaps barking up a tree that isn't there but whose existence I have conjured up out of my need to howl in the lonely night?

It's at those times that Augustine stands closest to me. I'm now going on seventy-eight, one year past his age at his death. I can't say that I've in any way done as much with my time as he did with his. But we do have this much in common: both of us are eminent Victorians in our own day. To be sure, only the "eminent" applies to him; but the "Victorian" goes for each of us — and perhaps for you and the whole modern world as well. He came at the end of a long tradition, and so do I and so do you. The Latin he handled so well had begun its downhill slide into the dark ages, and our English is in the throes of being dumbed down to an equal dimness. He came at a time when the apparently flourishing culture of Rome was in the process of going down the drain — and at a point in history when the barbarians were menacing its gates on all sides. And so have we, with only a few changes of names and places. But in all that, I find myself wonderfully comforted by his unshakable faith. If he could make his decision to trust the revelation of God in Christ in his times — and above all, if he could believe that God was his intimate friend — who am I to do less in my equally waning days?

I know. That's not a good argument if you're trying to convince someone to accept a philosophical system or the structure of a religion. But it's an excellent argument if you're looking for a lover who will help you go on loving. And that's what I've found in Augustine. His love for God is *catching:* his passion warms my too-often cold heart. *"Sero te amavi,"* he told God in his *Confessions:* "Late have I loved you." But then he added the words that strangely take away all my doubts: *pulchritudo tam antiqua et tam nova,* "O Beauty so old and yet so new." He may have been a lover who bordered on the romantic before romanticism, and I may be a romantic after romanticism trying to cross the border back to loving. But it doesn't matter: at my best times his love rubs off on me, and that's enough. So back I go to the work of making something out of my nothing by grace alone, through faith.

But now, while the projectionist changes reels, let's break for refreshments in the lobby.

INTERMISSION

TWELVE

A Conversation with Some History Buffs

"There you are, Robert. Do you have a minute to answer a question for us?"

"Absolutely. Fire away."

"Well, we've been arguing over whether you think the events in the film we just watched are historical or non-historical. Frankly, we find what you've given us so far confusing."

"Well, let me take another crack at it. Your problem, as I see it, is that you're still stuck in the notion that there are two kinds of history: 'real' history and 'made-up' history. You seem to think that the first is an objective fact waiting to be discovered, and that the second is simply a concoction of minds obsessed by myths. Is that a fair summary?"

"Fair enough."

"Good. Because the point I've been trying to make is that even true history has to be made up. History is a story that bare events are incapable of telling. It can be told only by the Mind of God or in our heads; it can't be found by rummaging through what we loosely call the 'facts of history.' So the first thing you have to say is that there's no history until somebody narrates it; and the second thing is that no narrator has to limit himself to literal facts. For his purposes, myths can make the story as well as facts, and the story they tell can be historical — it can give you the real connections between facts — no matter how many imaginary events it may contain."

"But what if it consists entirely of imagined events? That certainly seems to be the case in the first chapter of Genesis, and it will probably be true in the next two chapters as well. Unless, of course, you're a literalist — which you obviously aren't. That pleased some of us who are liberals; but others, who lean harder to the left, suspect you of being a conservative in sheep's clothing. Which is it?"

"Neither. As I said, I'm just a conservator of the historical narrative I've shown you. Even though I didn't interpret any of it literally, my cinematic approach to the Bible enabled me to take every scene, every action, and even every word of the picture as the very thing the Director had in Mind to show me. And it freed me from *all* literalisms, whether from the right or from the left. Conservatives may say that every scrap of the Bible must be taken literally, but liberals do the same thing when they say they can accept only those parts of Scripture that have factual support. The distinction between them turns out to make no difference. The former make the whole Bible literally true, and the latter do the same thing, but only with parts of it. But both are stuck in factuality when they should have been watching an essay on history.

"For example. If you watch a motion picture in a theater or on television, it's not necessary to ask whether the actions of its characters are fictions or facts. Of course they're fictions, because the director made them up to suit his purposes in the film. But, on the other hand, they're also facts, because his movie itself was a historic experience for you as you watched it unfold before your eyes. Indeed, that experience is the *only* history he wants you to watch. As an instance, take the crime series *CSI*. The chief forensic scientist, Gil Grissom (played by William Petersen), gives this bit of advice to a subordinate who's been jumping to conclusions about a murder scene: '*Acquaint yourself* with what you *see*,' he says, 'before you try to *interpret* it.'

"So too with the 'crime scene' of biblical history: Look before you leap. Don't come to any conclusions about what it means until you've watched the Director's entire picture. Only then will you be able to grasp the history she wants to show you."

"Then history is totally made up?"

"Yes and no. Sometimes, when no eye-witness testimony is available, it has to be made out of imaginary events; but at other times, when the events are verifiable, they too can be used to make history. But in both cases, the value of the history produced will lie in the quality of the *mental connections* it makes between the events, not from the qualities of the events themselves. Earlier in this book, I used Ken Burns's *The Civil War* as an example of the aptness of such an approach. The scenes of his motion picture consisted of nothing but still photographs taken during the war. If you will, those photos were precisely the 'events' out of which he made history. But until you absorbed all the 'configurations' he supplied for them, they were opaque to you as history. Only when you listened to his voice-over narration — and to the background music of his solo violin — could you see them as a new *and mov-*

ing picture of history. Only then could you suspend your disbelief and appreciate what he was doing for you."

"We remembered that example. But we still don't see how it solves our problem."

"I know. And it will only get worse when we come to the next part of the movie. In the scenes from chapters 2 and 3 of Genesis, you'll watch history being made out of events that are totally mythic; and you'll be tempted more than ever to try them in the balance of factuality — and find them wanting. I wish you good luck, though: the house lights are already blinking, so perhaps you'd better find your seats."

"Off we go, Robert. But thanks for your time. If you're free after the film, catch up with us, and we'll take you to dinner."

"Fair enough. I always enjoy making history with interesting people."

*   *   *

Back now to you as the reader of this book. To help you appreciate the Director's brilliance in making history of her imagined "evidences," I'm going to enlarge my arsenal of images for the Bible by likening her work to old *radio* dramas. If you remember *The Shadow* or *The Lone Ranger* in the days when radio was more than talk shows, you know that with nothing but the sound track of those programs, you actually made movies of them in your head, becoming both director and cameraman. And if you're too young to have experienced that, you still have something similar available to you when you listen to "talking books" in your car: inevitably, you produce a film from what your hear on tape. But in either case, you've been up to your ears in something very close to the way Scripture has been heard for some three thousand years.

Prior to the invention of printing, few people were able to *read* the Bible. In ancient times, they only listened to it as it was read aloud to the people of Israel — that is, in the "church" of the Old Testament. In Hebrew, that church was called the *qahal,* the "congregation" of Israel. (In the Greek of the Septuagint, *qahal* appeared as *ekklēsia.*) And in the time of the New Testament, the believers in Jesus as Lord and Messiah used the same name for their gatherings: *ekklēsia,* "church." And once again, they mostly *heard* the Scriptures rather than read them. In both of those periods, then — and for all the times since — the people of God have always been listening to the Word of God on the church's radio network.

So let me round out my remarks in this intermission by showing you the difference between the Bible's view of history and the way we too often interpret it. In a nutshell, scriptural history tries to show where the world has always been *going* under God, while our kind of history settles for little more than a description of what the world has been *doing* in and of itself. In our version of history, however, creation has no *destination*. It's little more than a wheel revolving on its axle: if it has any destiny, it's just to keep spinning until it runs out of gas at absolute zero. But in God's version, the wheel of the world's history becomes something very different. While it still revolves on its axle, the axle itself is moving creation *forward* to its ultimate destination — to its final place at the endless Wedding Reception at the Marriage Supper of the Lamb and his Bride (Rev. 21 and 22).

But the history of the world, at least in our hands, does *not* revolve smoothly on the axle of God's intentions for it. Ever since we abandoned God's hands-off management of history at the tree of the knowledge of good and evil, our world has been like a wheel separated from its axle at high speed: it's still spinning, but it's now radically out of control, doing damage to itself and everything in its path. *Unless* it can somehow be put back on the axle, it will eventually come to a crashing halt, even before it enters the final deep-freeze.

But Augustine, and most of the early fathers of the church, held that the "unless" I just gave you has already been taken care of by God himself in the Incarnation of his beloved Son. They held that despite the apparently aimless *circularity* of history as the world sees it, God has always been giving history a *linear* impetus to a destination outside itself. And that destination is none other than the Word of God himself, the Alpha and the Omega of history — the Beginning by whom all things are made, and the Ending in whom all things are restored to their original beauty. And even though our version of history leaves no room for that Mystery of Christ in our minds, our hearts still long for it whether they know it or not. As Augustine said to God in his *Confessions,* "You made us for yourself, and our heart is restless till it rests in you." God's intentions for us, you see, are the driving force of history. The Incarnation of his beloved Son — and, above all, the cross on which he died — are nothing less than the forward-moving axle that brings our revolving history home.

Let me bolster that patristic insistence on the Incarnation as the key to history with some quotations from a more recent writer: T. S. Eliot, in his *Four Quartets.* The first selection is from *Burnt Norton,* the opening poem in that collection:

> At the still point of the turning world. Neither flesh nor fleshless;
> Neither from nor towards; at the still point, there the dance is,
> But neither arrest nor movement. And do not call it fixity,
> Where past and future are gathered.

In the third poem of his *Quartets,* he clearly identifies that still point as the Incarnation of the Word of God. Look at what Eliot says in *The Dry Salvages:*

These are only hints and guesses,
Hints followed by guesses; and the rest
is prayer, observance, discipline, thought and action.
The hint half guessed, the gift half understood, is Incarnation.

But then, summing up the restoration of history's destination in the Incarnation as a present reality, not a future one, he has this to say at the end of the fourth poem, *Little Gidding:*

With the drawing of this Love and the voice of this Calling
We shall not cease from exploration
And the end of all our exploring
Will be to arrive where we started
And know the place for the first time.

It's the cross, you see, that's the still point of the turning world. And in the death of his Incarnate Word, God has driven the axle-tree of the cross back into the hub of history and put it on track to its destination.

In the movie of Genesis so far, I took the view that the Incarnation is not a late-afternoon response to sin on God's part but the truth about his creation from the Beginning. I said clearly that in God's eternal Mind, he doesn't make new "decisions" about his relationship with the world. Everything he does, for us or with us, is decided from all eternity. But in the next part of the film, that eternal, unvarnished making up of the divine Mind will become harder to grasp. You'll be tempted to see his actions toward Adam and Eve (his curses, his expulsion of them from Eden, his placing of the Cherubim and the Flaming Sword at the gate of the Garden) as the *results* of their fall rather than as the *Mystery* of his eternal Good Will toward them.

God never changes his Mind about us as his beloved creatures, and he certainly doesn't wait for us to mend our ways before he accepts us in his beloved Son. In fact, he makes no conditions whatsoever. Everything in the world — even the out-of-control spinning of its sins and disasters — moves into the renewed creation. All the glories of its first state go home in his Incarnate Word, and all the miseries of our history go home as well. We're not saved *from* our sins, we're saved *in* them: "While we were still sinners, Christ died for the ungodly" (Rom. 5:8, RFC); "He made him who knew no sin to become sin for our sakes so that we might become the righteousness of God in him" (2 Cor. 5:21, RFC). Indeed, our sins went into the reconciliation before the foundation of the world: the Christ who takes our history home takes *all* our history home. Even the worst thing we ever did, on a Friday two thousand years ago, ascends to his Father's side in the Glorious Scars of his Sacred Wounds.

Therefore, my view of the Bible as a movie doesn't require you to discard even a scrap of the Bible's history. The Mystery of Christ, by which history moves to its destination, allows you to keep everything — factual or fictional, good, bad, or indifferent — that the Director gives you. Every bit of it is truly your history. And if you stay with the picture to the end, I think you'll find it was a happy history from the beginning.

*   *   *

The house lights are dimming, and the projectionist is ready to roll the film. Time now to watch history being made.

CREATION FLOURISHING ON ITS OWN GROUND

Genesis 2:4-25

THIRTEEN

A View from the Bridge

GENESIS 2:4-6

This part of the movie begins with some footage shot from a car driving across the bridge that leads from the world as it first exists in the Mind of God to the world of time and space. As the camera pans back toward what you're leaving and forward to what you're approaching, you may be tempted to think that the scenery in both places is more myth than history, but I'd like you to avoid that invidious distinction. As I said during our chat in the intermission, myth can give you a better understanding of history than any recitation of facts, however "historical." Because history isn't just about things that happened — it's what we *make of* those events when we think about them. Anyway, since there will obviously be no eyewitnesses to the events and characters of the upcoming part of the film except Adam, Eve, and the snake, everything you'll see will be in the picture strictly because the Director wanted it there. Apparently, she felt she could "make history" even out of old fables — and she chose the ones she did on the basis of their *poetry*, not their "historicity." (*Poiein,* you'll recall, means "to make" in Greek.)

Since verses 4, 5, and 6 of Genesis are the very bridge the Director has provided for her car ride between the two parts of the film, I'm going to show you those verses in two installments: I'll give verse 4 alone here at the beginning of this chapter, and all three verses together at the end. As before, I'll be quoting the biblical passages from the original Hebrew and in five versions. Here's the text of verse 4:

LXX Gen. 2:4 αὕτη ἡ βίβλος γενέσεως οὐρανοῦ καὶ γῆς ὅτε ἐγένετο ἡ ἡμέρᾳ ἐποίησεν ὁ θεὸς τὸν οὐρανὸν καὶ τὴν γῆν

אֵלֶּה תוֹלְדוֹת BHS Gen. 2:4
הַשָּׁמַיִם וְהָאָרֶץ בְּהִבָּרְאָם בְּיוֹם
עֲשׂוֹת יְהוָה אֱלֹהִים אֶרֶץ
וְשָׁמָיִם׃

VUL Gen. 2:4 istae generationes caeli et terrae quando creatae sunt in die quo fecit Dominus Deus caelum et terram

KJV Gen. 2:4 These *are* the generations of the heavens and of the earth when they were created, in the day that the LORD God made the earth and the heavens . . .

RSV Gen. 2:4 These are the generations of the heavens and the earth when they were created. In the day that the LORD God made the earth and the heavens . . .

NRSV Gen. 2:4 These are the generations of the heavens and the earth when they were created. In the day that the LORD God made the earth and the heavens . . .

Rather than give you a lengthy dose of word study with my comments bunched together at the end, let me take up the significant words in the order in which they occur and make my remarks as I go along.

The first word is *generations,* which is the translation given in all three English versions. In the Hebrew, the word is *tôl'dôth,* a feminine plural noun from the verb *yaladh,* meaning "to bear, to bring forth, to beget, to give birth." Its prime significance here, of course, is that it introduces a world whose successive generations provide it with the makings of a *history.* But since my remarks in the intermission have already given you my view of the grand sweep of history, I'll confine myself here to just one of the mechanisms that enable us to create it — namely, the fact that our generations perpetuate themselves over time by sexual reproduction. Sex may be the main reason for our birth, and being born may be the ultimate cause of our death. But in the meanwhile, every living thing survives only by the death of other living things.

Accordingly, this marvelous reciprocity of sex and death turns both of them into the engine of life itself. Some modern writers have even gone so far as to describe sex as the gene pool's strategy for ensuring its own immortality. That's fair enough, but only as long as you don't trap yourself into saying that sex is "nothing but" a genetic insurance policy. That would be reductionism of the worst sort; and it's always a no-no, especially in this context. Sex and death are a complex mystery to be explored, not a simple puzzle to be solved. Reduce either one of them to a mere anything, and you'll promptly lose your grip on both. I've already spent a good deal of time calling this mystery "the ecology of life and death." Here, I'll be returning to it again and again.

But back to the passage at hand. If we look at the Greek of the Septuagint, we find a quite different reading, probably because the Hebrew text the translators used wasn't the same as the one that eventually came to be the standard. Their translation reads, *haute hē biblos geneseōs:* "this is the book of the 'origin, source, birth, race, or descent.'" Clearly, these meanings of the word *geneseōs* are still close to the notion of "generations"; but the preceding word, *biblos* (a feminine noun meaning "book" and originally denoting the inner bark of the papyrus), appears in none of the other versions. The Vulgate, of course, working from a later Hebrew text, has the word as *generationes:* "generations" pure and simple.

Please remember that in this second account of creation there will be very little about the other creatures that the first account displayed as existing in the divine Intellect. There won't be a word here about the earth *without form and void,* nor any mention of the darkness *on the face of the deep,* nor any reference to the Spirit of God *brooding upon the face of the waters.* (Indeed, this creation story begins with a totally *dry* earth, with no explanation of how God made it.) And you won't find any of the other wonders you saw in the first part of the movie: not the *light* created on day one; not the creatures of the second through the sixth days: no *firmament,* no *seas,* no *dry land,* no *sun, moon,* or *stars,* no *fish, birds,* or *land animals* (till later on in chapter 2); and not even any *human beings* as yet (no male and female *'adham,* as God made them on the sixth day). All in all, it's as different from the first half of the film as anything you could imagine.

The next words in order are "the heavens and the earth," whose generations are being introduced. Once again, the Vulgate and all three English versions translate the Hebrew *hashshamayim,* "the heavens," as the plural it always is. But back in the first creation story, the Septuagint, the Vulgate, the KJV, and the RSV — following not only the older versions but also the tradition of the fathers of the church — rendered it in the singular, "the heaven." I have two reasons for preferring the plural translation throughout. For one thing, it's faithful to the Hebrew; and for the other, it applies nicely here because it's obviously the *physical* universe that's being referred to. While *hashshamayim* can indeed mean either the "heaven" of God himself or of the angelic orders, it can also mean simply the "skies" — which we quite easily speak of as the "heavens." But in this bridge text, the Septuagint alone renders the word in the singular: "the *heaven* and the earth."

Translating it here as "the heavens," though, also helps you see more clearly the territories at either end of the bridge. First of all, it harks back to the creation of everything in the Mind of God the Father as he holds it in his "heaven of heavens" and to the making of everything by the Father's only-begotten Word, who is none other than his eternal *Beginning* (see John 8:25). And second, it also allows you to see the physical heavens of our earth as the "skies, the "deep space" into which we peer on every clear night. And it does the same thing for your perception of "the earth." This blue planet of ours is not the only thing you can include under the image of *terra firma:* all other spheres of existence, wherever they might be in the universe — and all the home bases of other creatures (mineral, vegetable, or animal) that may exist — can fairly be called their "earth."

As a matter of fact, Augustine said that compared to the heaven of God himself, even the "heaven" of the angels (whom he named God's *supercelestial folk*) could be called earth. More than that, insofar as those angels intervene in the world of time and space, they become actors in the drama of the temporal world. Indeed, when we come to the serpent who appears in chapter 3 of Genesis, he will qualify as just such an angelic impersonator. While that particular fancy may not please biblical critics who find it unhebraic, it hasn't kept most of us from seeing him as a fallen angel — as the Prince of Darkness out on the town, playing hob with the splendid innocence of Adam and Eve in their first state.

Moving along, though, the next words we need to look at are "when they were created." That's the translation given in the three English versions; but in the Hebrew, they're a single word, *b'hibbaram* — a participle with a pronominal suffix that can be translated literally as "in the creating of them." Here again, the Septuagint clouds things a bit. Having said "This is the book of the beginning [*geneseōs*] of the heaven and the earth," it then goes on to say "when it came into being [*egeneto,* "it happened, it came to pass"]." In short, the Septuagint quite plainly makes "beginning" the subject of the verb "happened." The Vulgate goes along with the "when" (*quando*), but it makes the "heavens and the earth" the subject of the verb "*they* were created" (*creatae sunt*).

But the most important thing to note is that the Hebrew (and all the versions except the Septuagint) clearly return to the word *create,* which has already been used six times so far in Genesis — and they stay away from the word *made* (*epoiēsen* in the Greek). This is partly due to the fact that while Greek uses the verb *poieō* for many purposes ("make, do, create") — and while it does have a verb, *ktizō,* that means simply "create" — the translators of the Septuagint didn't choose to employ *ektisen* ("he created") here. In any event, since the Hebrew word *bara* ("create") is such a "Sunday punch" word in Genesis, its use here ties both parts of the movie together; therefore, of all the words in this verse, it's one of the two main piers on which the bridge between them rests.

This brings us to the other pier, the word *day.* Augustine was fond of seeing all six days of the first account as one day, and he even went so far as to suggest that they were all repetitions of the "day one" in which God's act of creation began. In the Bible, the phrase "the day" doesn't denote just a twenty-four-hour period, let alone something that will happen a week from some Tuesday. In its deepest meaning, it has nothing to do with clocks or calendars, or with any other devices we use to tell time as mere *chronos* ("clock time"). Rather, it points us to the "high time," the *kairos,* the "due season" of God himself — and to the high times of our own lives: our births, our deaths, and everything else that happens to us within those two brackets.

Interestingly, when we begin a faerie tale of deep significance, we commonly use the phrase "Once upon a time," thus locating it not at some point in calendar or clock time but putting it in time as *kairos.* But the tale can also start with a simple "One day," or if it happens to be in German, with *"Eines Tages,"* which reads literally as "Of a day," meaning "There was once a day. . . ." This is yet another device that the Director, following the Hebrew, has used to underscore her notion that "day one" (or the "one day") is *outside* the days of the physical world.

Do you see the fabulous links that she can forge with this word *day?* Watch. She has God create our world on a Day One, without which it would never have existed at all; and she has him bring us to a happy ending on a Last Day, without which we would cease to exist forever. And in the meanwhile, she will be able to portray every one of our days as holy to the Lord: "*This* is the day that the Lord has made; we will rejoice and be glad in it" (Ps. 118:24, RFC). Or, as she managed to get John Donne to say (picking up on Ps. 95:7), "To day, if you will heare his voice, to day he will heare you." And thus the words "in the day" as they appear in this text comprise all our days and all our times, high and low. They are all the day of the *parousia,* the real presence, of the Father's Word himself. (To be sure, *parousia* may be translated as the "second coming" of Christ, but its literal meaning is simply the "presence" of the Incarnate Word at every point in time. You can make his coming at the Last Day as real an event as you like, but its deepest reality will always be the "arrival" of Someone who never left.) Therefore, every one of our days, despite our "estrangèd faces," is both the hopeful beginning and the triumphant ending of our due season in the endless Today of God.

"Estrangèd faces," by the way, is from Francis Thompson's "The Kingdom of God." Let me quote the last three verses of the poem for you:

> The angels keep their ancient places; —
> Turn but a stone, and start a wing!
> 'Tis ye, 'tis your estrangèd faces,
> That miss the many-splendoured thing.
>
> But (when so sad thou canst not sadder)
> Cry; — and upon thy so sore loss

Shall shine the traffic of Jacob's ladder
Pitched betwixt Heaven and Charing Cross.

Yea, in the night, my Soul, my daughter,
Cry, — clinging Heaven by the hems;
And lo, Christ walking on the water,
Not of Gennesareth, but Thames!

I just couldn't resist giving you that: it's been haunting my mind for some fifty years. Back to our text.

The Hebrew for "in the day" is *b'yôm.* While the preposition *b'* can mean either "in" or "on," it seems to me that its sense here is best expressed in English by "in." Because when we say "on the day" (as in "I'll meet you on next Wednesday"), we simply locate that day at a narrow point in time; but when we say "in the day" (as in "What shall we do in the day of our victory?"), we turn that day into a mansion for a many-splendored party. But the most wonderful thing about the phrase "in the day" here is that it uses the same word for both God's original party and our current one. This "day," then, faces in two directions: back to God's first celebration of creation in his own Mind, and forward to whatever celebrations we ourselves will be able to manage. Not a bad day's work for a three-letter word.

But I think the biggest surprise in the text we have in hand lies in the words immediately after "in the day" — namely, "when the LORD God made the earth and the heavens." Let me touch briefly on the word *made* before I come to the larger point I want to make. In the Hebrew, it's *'asôth,* which is an infinitive of the verb *'asah,* "to make" — and which Genesis uses more often than *bara',* "create" (nine times as opposed to six so far in these opening chapters). In the Septuagint, as I've said, it's translated by that word of all work, *epoiēsen;* but in the Vulgate it's *fecit,* "he made," to distinguish it from *creatae sunt,* a passive form meaning "they were created."

It's the words "LORD God," however, that deserve the most attention. This is the first appearance of the personal name of God in the Bible, so I should remind you of some peculiarities in its presentation. Whenever the word *LORD* is printed in English versions with large and small capitals, you should realize that it's meant to alert you to the fact that it's a circumlocution for God's proper name, *YHWH,* as it appears in the Hebrew text. But among Jewish believers (and even in Christian usage), that name is considered too sacred to pronounce out loud. Instead, it's spoken (or printed out) as *adhonai,* an ordinary word for "Lord." That's the reason for "LORD" in all three English versions, as well as for *Dominus* in the Vulgate. (Oddly, though, the Septuagint doesn't have the word Lord — *kyrios* — anywhere in these bridge verses: instead of "Lord God," it reads simply "God," *ho theos*. In fact, in my copy of the Septuagint, *kyrios ho theos* doesn't show up until verse 8 — and even at that, it's still omitted in some places where the Hebrew has it. Go figure.) In any event, biblical scholars have been bold enough to sound out YHWH as *Yahweh,* or if they're German scholars, as *Jahveh.* So, at the risk of enlarging on something I said previously, let me give you a little background on the consequences of all that.

As a result of the German spelling of *Jahveh* (and of the prominence of Germans in biblical criticism), this second story of creation in Genesis has come to be known as the "J" account, to distinguish it from the first story, which is called the "E" account. "J" is considered to be a ninth-century B.C.E. "document," while "E" (for *Elohim,* "God") is assumed to be an eighth-century source which used only that word when referring to God. "E," however, was updated after the Babylonian captivity in the fifth century by a group called "P" (for "priestly" editors) and is therefore now referred to as the "E/P" account. (The "J" document, as you can see, seems also to have been updated, since the form in which we now have it commonly uses both words when speaking of God, just as it does here: *Yahweh Elohim,* "Lord God.")

But far more important than any of that scholarly slicing and dicing is the bare fact that *Yahweh,* as a proper name, tells you *who* God is, whereas *Elohim* tells you only *what* he is — it gives you his *identity,* if you will, rather than his *occupation.* Accordingly, let me make a slightly impudent suggestion about what's going on here. It's almost as if, having seen just plain *God* in action all through the first part of the movie, we've suddenly been surprised to learn that he's actually *Irving.* Alternatively, I could put it in terms of the film's first viewers and make it no surprise at all: since the Jews had been worshipping *Irving* for centuries before "E" wrote him up as *God,* they might simply have said, "Oh, we already knew who you were talking about. We were just too polite to mention it."

Now, however, I'm going to take an even bolder leap and join the writers of the New Testament and the fathers of the church in identifying the *Irving* of the Hebrew Scriptures with the holy and undivided Trinity: the Father, the Son, and the Holy Spirit. The Gospel according to John, for example, begins its first chapter's takeoff on Genesis by saying, "In the beginning was the Word, and the Word was with God, and the Word was God" (KJV). But then, after a brief interlude that ties its narrative to Jesus' precursor, John the Baptist, it heads straight for the Christ himself and says, "And the Word became flesh and dwelt among us." What is that, if not the same recognition of a *who* formerly hidden under a bushel of *whats?* "Aha!" John says in effect. "I know who that *Beginning* in Genesis really is — and I'm not too polite to mention that his name is Jesus."

While I'm on the subject of John's Gospel, I'd like to insert a few parenthetical paragraphs touting my cinematic approach to Scripture. A great deal of breath and ink has been wasted on the so-called problems of the Fourth Gospel. People have wondered who John really was (the son of Zebedee? the Beloved Disciple? a second-century Platonist?) — and even if his book was written by any John at all. Those who put the date of its authorship around A.D. 110 (as even I do) have complained that it came too late to be of any historical value whatsoever (which I wouldn't think of doing). But if you watch this Gospel as the Holy Spirit did when she first inspired John to write it, you're mercifully delivered from such trivia.

Look at her direction of him this way. She'd already decided to put all (and perhaps somewhat more than all) she had of Paul into her picture; and she'd made the same decision about Matthew, Mark, and Luke. But after those last three, she wished she could find something, by someone who really understood Paul, to bring her accounts of the Good News back to his insights into the Person of Christ. She seems to have felt that none of her first-century scriptwriters had fully grasped what Paul was getting at; and when she found John at the beginning of the second century, her wish was granted. "My, my," she said. "Here at last is somebody who actually 'got' Paul. It took a while, but he was worth the wait."

Do you see my point? The critics' difficulties with the Fourth Gospel pale into insignificance when you see it from the Director's point of view. Gone are all the quibbles over date, style, and authorship. Gone too is all the nonsense about the relevance or irrelevance of its "hellenisms." All you have left is the elation of the Director when she saw the most obvious thing about it: it's practically the best piece of script-writing in the whole biblical movie. And as generations of film-watchers have discovered to their own delight, it was a box-office hit from the moment it was produced. Do I need to tell you that this Director-oriented approach works wonders with the rest of the biblical movie as well? I think not. I'll only remind you of what I said in the intermission: *acquaint* yourself with the film of Scripture before you try to interpret it. Write your review of the Bible only after you've watched the whole picture — and even then, be open to rewriting it after further viewings.

But that takes me back to the God of the Hebrew Bible as "Irving," and to the church's identification of "Irving" with the Trinity. To begin with, one of the clearest things about the movie of Scripture is that the God of the Old Testament loves the sound of his own name. Just to keep my references to the name "Irving" consistent with the custom of not pronouncing it, I'll suggest that its Hebrew form might be *'RVNG;* and for the next paragraph, I'll follow the practice of using a circumlocution of my own devising every time the tetragrammaton *YHWH* appears in the quotations I'm about to give you. Since LORD is a four-letter word, I'll use *BOSS* as a substitute for it.

Here then are some "evidences" for the BOSS's preoccupation with his own name, all taken from the Ten Commandments (found in Exodus 20). In the first commandment, we find "I am the BOSS your God, who brought you out of the land of Egypt." In the second, there is "You shall not make for yourself any graven image . . . for I the BOSS your God am a jealous God." In the third, there's "You shall not take the name of the BOSS your God in vain." In the fourth, we have "Remember the Sabbath day, to keep it holy. . . . But the seventh day is the Sabbath of the BOSS your God . . . for in six days the BOSS made heaven and earth, and all that is in them; and rested the seventh day: therefore the Boss blessed the Sabbath day and hallowed it." And for the fifth commandment's concluding reference to the BOSS's name, we read "Honor your father and your mother, that your days may be long upon the land that the BOSS your God gives you."

It's that last appearance of God's sacred Name that I want to take special notice of here. My father's name was Fred, and my mother's, Maybelle. But like almost all children now in their seventies, I always used titles like "father" and "mother" or "mommy" and "daddy" for them and never their first names — even when I spoke of them to other people. Therefore it strikes me that the fifth commandment may have been given to me as a kind of training program for my observance of the third. No doubt this traditional carefulness about the identity of a child's significant others has long since been put in mothballs. But I'm not sorry that my parents drummed it into me — to the point of requiring me to call their friends and drinking companions "Uncle" and "Aunt." As a result, I think, I was kept light years away from the regrettable familiarity of treating God as my cosmic Pal. My sense of the holiness of my Most Significant Other is all the greater for having never had parents who I thought were my buddies. With a little circumlocution, the longest way 'round can sometimes be the shortest way home.

Incidentally, while we're on the subject of the Ten Commandments, it occurs to me that our usual division of them into four about duty to God and six about duty to neighbor might be improved by splitting them up five and five. For one thing, "LORD" (for God's sacred Name) appears only in the first five and not in the rest. Which leads me to two new images for the Commandments. It lets me take numbers one through five as the part of Israel's "Constitution" that sets forth the Presidency of the LORD — as a charter defining the uniqueness of the Hebrew community and the sovereignty of the

LORD its God over all the competing gods that surrounded it. And in turn, that image leads to my revised view of commandments six through ten. They become the earliest amendments to Israel's Constitution, designed to prohibit the community from copying the offensive social behavior of the peoples who worshipped those gods. In short, it lets me see those "duty to neighbor" laws as analogous to the American Bill of Rights — that is, as Israel's first Bill of Wrongs to be avoided at all costs.

That was just a bit of biblical throwaway for you to take or leave as you like. Either way, on with the rest of this chapter.

*　　　*　　　*

Let me return to the image of the bridge between the two creation stories and now give you all three verses of its text, and then a glimpse of how Augustine, despite the inadequacies of his Latin version, managed not only to see it as a bridge but also to see all six days of the first account as a single day in God. First, then, the full text:

LXX Gen. 2:4 αὕτη ἡ βίβλος γενέσεως οὐρανοῦ καὶ γῆς ὅτε ἐγένετο ἡ ἡμέρα ἐποίησεν ὁ θεὸς τὸν οὐρανὸν καὶ τὴν γῆν 5 καὶ πᾶν χλωρὸν ἀγροῦ πρὸ τοῦ γενέσθαι ἐπὶ τῆς γῆς καὶ πάντα χόρτον ἀγροῦ πρὸ τοῦ ἀνατεῖλαι οὐ γὰρ ἔβρεξεν ὁ θεὸς ἐπὶ τὴν γῆν καὶ ἄνθρωπος οὐκ ἦν ἐργάζεσθαι τὴν γῆν 6 πηγὴ δὲ ἀνέβαινεν ἐκ τῆς γῆς καὶ ἐπότιζεν πᾶν τὸ πρόσωπον τῆς γῆς	BHS Gen. 2:4 אֵלֶּה תוֹלְדוֹת הַשָּׁמַיִם וְהָאָרֶץ בְּהִבָּרְאָם בְּיוֹם עֲשׂוֹת יְהוָה אֱלֹהִים אֶרֶץ וְשָׁמָיִם: 5 וְכֹל שִׂיחַ הַשָּׂדֶה טֶרֶם יִהְיֶה בָאָרֶץ וְכָל־עֵשֶׂב הַשָּׂדֶה טֶרֶם יִצְמָח כִּי לֹא הִמְטִיר יְהוָה אֱלֹהִים עַל־הָאָרֶץ וְאָדָם אַיִן לַעֲבֹד אֶת־הָאֲדָמָה: 6 וְאֵד יַעֲלֶה מִן־הָאָרֶץ וְהִשְׁקָה אֶת־כָּל־פְּנֵי־הָאֲדָמָה:	VUL Gen. 2:4 istae generationes caeli et terrae quando creatae sunt in die quo fecit Dominus Deus caelum et terram 5 et omne virgultum agri antequam oreretur in terra omnemque herbam regionis priusquam germinaret non enim pluerat Dominus Deus super terram et homo non erat qui operaretur terram 6 sed fons ascendebat e terra inrigans universam superficiem terrae
KJV Gen. 2:4 These *are* the generations of the heavens and of the earth when they were created, in the day that the LORD God made the earth and the heavens, 5 And every plant of the	RSV Gen. 2:4 These are the generations of the heavens and the earth when they were created. In the day that the LORD God made the earth and the heavens, 5 when no plant of the field	NRSV Gen. 2:4 These are the generations of the heavens and the earth when they were created. In the day that the LORD God made the earth and the heavens, 5 when no plant of the field

field before it was in the earth, and every herb of the field before it grew: for the LORD God had not caused it to rain upon the earth, and *there was* not a man to till the ground. 6 But there went up a mist from the earth, and watered the whole face of the ground.

was yet in the earth and no herb of the field had yet sprung up — for the LORD God had not caused it to rain upon the earth, and there was no man to till the ground; 6 but a mist went up from the earth and watered the whole face of the ground —

was yet in the earth and no herb of the field had yet sprung up — for the LORD God had not caused it to rain upon the earth, and there was no one to till the ground; 6 but a stream would rise from the earth, and water the whole face of the ground —

As a bridge of my own to Augustine, though, I'm going to get to him in four steps. First, I'll give you this text in the old Latin version (called the *Itala*, a late-second-century rendering of the Septuagint) from which he was working, then a rather literal translation of it, then some difficulties in the various translations of the Hebrew you've seen so far, and finally a passage from Augustine himself that I particularly want you to see. For openers, then, here's the biblical text as he quotes it in his *De Genesi ad Litteram,* Book V, chapter 1:

> *4 Hic est liber creaturae coeli et terrae, cum factus est dies, fecit Deus coelum et terram, 5 et omne viride agri, antequam esset super terram, et omne foenum agri, antequam exortum est. Non enim pluerat super terram Deus: at homo non erat qui operatur terram. 6 Fons autem ascendebat de terra, et irrigabat omnem faciem terrae.*

> 4 This is the book of the creature of heaven and earth, when the day was made when God made the heaven and the earth, 5 and every green plant of the field before it was upon the earth, and every herb of the field before it arose; for it had not yet rained upon the earth, and there was no man who might work the earth. 6 But a fountain was coming up from the earth, and it watered the whole face of the ground.

The upshot of having to deal with this text is that Augustine found it necessary to spend a lot of time fiddling with the first account of creation and worrying the question of whether the *vegetation* on the third day or the *sun* on the fourth day (which makes plant life possible) is being alluded to here — or even whether those days were to be taken as physical or spiritual periods of "time." Finally, though, he decides that we're being admonished by Scripture to "investigate the word *day* with our intellect even though we know nothing about whether it was a corporeal day in I know not what light, or whether it was a spiritual day in the fellowship of angelic unity" (*De Genesi ad Litteram*, V, 4). As you can see, even Augustine could be uncertain of what his version meant.

But now for the difficulties in our English versions. Look at the texts I just gave you, and you'll see them. Augustine is not the only one at a loss over what to do with these verses. The first thing you need to remember is that the Hebrew, at least in its earliest, strictly consonantal form, had almost no punctuation. (When I translated Augustine, I ignored many of his merely grammatical periods, commas, colons, and semicolons.) The other thing, as I've said, is that his Latin version was translated not from the Hebrew but from the Greek of the Septuagint. Hence the "This is the book" (*Hic est liber*) in his *Itala* version and the rest of the peculiarities it inherited from the Greek text — especially its reading of *tol'dôth*, "generations," as *geneseōs* ("origin, source, birth, race, or descent") and the *Itala's* translation of *geneseōs* as "of the creature" *(creaturae)* — not to mention the general confusion in both versions over which words should be considered the antecedent of the word *day*. It wasn't until Jerome produced the Vulgate that Latin readers saw anything based on the Hebrew; and if you compare Augustine's Latin text with Jerome's, you'll realize what a superb and even "modern" translation his Vulgate really is.

Indeed, of all the translations, I find it the most straightforward and faithful to the original — and the Septuagint the least so. But parts of the English versions strike me as likewise deficient. The KJV has the fewest defects: it puts periods at the end of verses 5 and 6, thus avoiding the inconvenient run-on sentence in the RSV and the NRSV, and letting each verse stand as a complete thought. My only objection to the KJV is its failure to put a full stop at the end of verse 4 as well. Needless to say, I also dislike the dashes in the other two (printed by my *Bible Works* Scripture program as " — "). As you already know, I'm addicted to dashes in my own writing; but in translations of Scripture, I find them a bit too trendy. Call me old-fashioned, if you like; but I have the same objection to the NRSV's rendering of the KJV's "not a man" and the RSV's "no man" as "no one." It did that, of course, in the interest of gender neutrality. Nevertheless, I still wish it hadn't because it obscures the recurrences of the word *man* (*'adham*) in the Hebrew. If there's anything I'm more enthusiastic about than periods, it's the preservation of the "concordances" in the original text. Fudge those "Director's flags" out of the text (as political correctness so often does), and you lose the threads of imagery with which she weaves the Bible's narratives into a moving picture.

One final drawback in all three English versions. By failing to put a period at the end of verse 4, they pretty much close out the possibility of seeing it as a bridge connecting two territories: the realm of God's *intellectual* act of creation in chapter 1 and the realm of God's *physical* act of creation in chapter 2. Not only does that remove the connection between them; it also (to my ear at least) misrepresents the Hebrew. I think the right way to hear it would be to imagine the Director writing out "stage directions" for her Narrator in this part of the film. Let me try to spell them out for you.

"*Director to Narrator:* Here are my suggestions as to how you should prepare yourself for what you'll be reading (I've put the text in italics and underscored the key words): *These will be the <u>generations</u>* [pause here as if you were gesturing to your right to alert the viewer to the forthcoming physical order] *of the heavens and the earth <u>when they were created</u>* [pause again as if gesturing to your left to indicate the previous act of creation in God's Mind] *<u>in the day</u> in which the* LORD *God made the heavens and the earth* [hear yourself as reminding the viewer not only of day one but of all six days of God's first creation as repetitions of that day], *<u>and</u>* [change of tone here: you're now returning us to your opening subject of physical *<u>generations</u>*] *every plant of the field before it was in the earth, and every herb of the field before it grew* [and so on to the end of verse 6 — or even verse 7]. I realize this won't be easy, but I trust your talent. Good luck!"

Needless to say, my excursion into the Director's mind does little more than reproduce what Jerome did with that passage in the Vulgate. But with that off my chest (and with a promise to name the actor who'll play the Narrator in the next chapter), let me deliver the final item I invoiced to you eight paragraphs ago: Augustine's remarkable excursus on verses 5 and 6, where he not only makes them the bridge from the first account to the second but also ties them to God's simultaneous creation of all things *(omnia simul)* in day one. True to his wide-ranging form, he leaves all his interpretive options open (as our English versions do not). He had a roomy mind. In any case, the passage appears in his *De Genesi ad Litteram*, Book V, 6; and it's a perfect example of both the complexity and the warmth of his thinking. In my translation, I'll not only sit loose to his punctuation and word order; I'll also break his single paragraph into two for the sake of clarity:

> *Porro autem superior narratio factum diem primitus indicat, eumque unum diem deputat; post quem secundum annumerat, quo factum est firmamentum; et tertium, quo species terrae marisque digestae sunt, et lignum atque herbam terra produxit. An forte hoc illud est, quod in libro superiore simul moliebamur ostendere, simul Deum fecisse omnia, quandoquidem narrationis illa contextio cum sex dierum ordine creata cuncta et consummata memorasset, nunc ad unum diem omnia rediguntur nomine coeli et terrae, adjuncto etiam fruticum genere? Nimirum, propter*

quod supra dixi, ut si fortassis ex hac nostra consuetudine intelligeretur dies, corrigeretur lector, cum recoleret viride agri ante istum solarem diem Deum dixisse ut terra produceret. Ita jam non ex alio Scripturae sanctae libro profertur testimonium quod omnia simul Deus creaverit; sed vicina testificatio paginae consequentis ex hac re admonet, dicens, "Cum factus est dies, fecit Deus coelum et terram, et omne viride agri"; ut istum diem et septies intelligas repetitum, ut fierent septem dies; et cum audis tunc facta omnia simul, cum factus est dies, illam senariam vel septenariam repetitionem sine intervallis morarum spatiorumque temporalium factam, si possis apprehendas; si nondum possis, haec relinquas conspicienda valentibus: tu autem cum Scriptura non deserente infirmitatem tuam, et materno incessu tecum tardius ambulante proficias; quae sic loquitur, ut altitudine superbos irrideat, profunditate attentos terreat, veritate magnos pascat, affabilitate parvulos nutriat.

But furthermore, the preceding narration first indicates that a day was made and then singles it out as "one day," after which it enumerates a "second day" in which the firmament was made, and then a "third" in which the beauties of land and sea were separated from each other, and the earth brought forth tree and herb. But by any chance is this what we were struggling to show in the preceding book, namely, that *God made all things at once?* Indeed it is; because that same form of narrative (which related both the creation and the consummation of all things by a succession of six days) is now re-introduced to bring all things back to the one day by including those things under the name of "the heaven and the earth," and by adding in vegetable creatures for good measure. Undoubtedly, as I said above, it does this for a good reason. For if our usual way of speaking should by chance lead someone to understand "day" as merely a single circuit of the sun, such a reader would be corrected when he recalls that God said the earth should bring forth the green herb of the field *before* there was any sun to define a day.

So now it is not from some other book of holy Scripture that testimony is offered for God's creation of all things at once [Augustine has in mind Ecclesiasticus 18:1, which reads, "He who lives forever created all things at once"]; rather, the neighboring testimony of the very next page reminds us of this when it says, "when the day was made when God made the heaven and the earth, and every green herb of the field." And it does this not only that you might understand that this day was repeated seven times so there would be seven days, but also that when you hear that *then* all things were made at once when that day was made, you might, if you're able, take that sixfold or sevenfold repetition as having been made without any intervals of temporal times or spaces. If you're not yet able to do that, you'd best leave these matters to more robust minds; but since Scripture does not desert your weakness, you will also, by her motherly dogging of your footsteps, eventually become proficient in walking. For as she thus holds your hand, she speaks in high things that she might mock the proud, in deep things that she might terrify the nitpickers, in truth that she might feed the mature, and in pleasantness that she might nourish the young.

This is Augustine at his complex finest. He plays with many possible interpretations of this text of Scripture, but he finally leaves you free to choose between them, if you're able to — though if you're not, he still gives you encouragement. Admittedly, he can pick professorial nits with the best of them — so much so that he can keep you knee-deep in nit-droppings for pages on end. But then he can turn on a dime (hence my paragraph break) and speak words more comforting than any you ever expected. Moreover, he can execute this leap from abstract analysis to personal concern almost without notice — except that the element of surprise exists only in our minds, not his. Having read him for years now (and much more diligently of late), I've often had the feeling that no matter how heavily the black and white of his prose may plod along, he always has a purple passage lurking in the back of his mind. (Look at the last three lines of his Latin: their color is only deepened by their terseness.) So, for all the coolness of his intellect, he's never far from either his warmth as a friend or his ardor as a lover of God. As I said earlier, he was a romantic before the invention of romanticism — and he's not ashamed to let it show. If I can turn you on to him — even a little — I'll be a happy man.

*   *   *

But we've reached the end of the bridge, and it's time to let the Director take us out of the car and focus her camera on the soil of the physical world.

FOURTEEN

The Making of the 'adham *in Time and Space*

GENESIS 2:7

Only one thing has actually happened since the Director landed us on this side of the bridge. For most of the ride across, she's had us either looking back at "day one" in the first part of her film or listening to a Narrator who, by reading verses 4 and 5 of Genesis, has told us all the things that *haven't* happened yet: he mentions the plants before they were in the earth, the herbs before they grew, the rain that hadn't fallen, and the man who wasn't there to till the ground. But when he reaches verse 6, we finally hear about the first event in this part of the movie: the "fountain" or "spring" or "mist" or "stream" that "comes up from the earth to water the whole face of the ground." (None of our versions seems to know quite what to do with the Hebrew word *'edh.*)

But who is it that the Director casts as the Narrator? If I may make a suggestion, I think she might well choose Anthony Hopkins. For one thing, Hopkins did play C. S. Lewis in *Shadowlands,* and Lewis had no qualms about telling people what God was up to. True enough, you might object that Hopkins's role as Hannibal Lecter in *The Silence of the Lambs* makes him a poor choice for a reader of Scripture. But even at that, I have to disagree. Not only is the divine Director about to show us God planting a tree of the knowledge of "good *and* evil" in his garden east of Eden; she's eventually going to bring on the serpent who tempts Adam and Eve to violate that ecology of opposites and to decide (as God does not) to choose *between* good and evil rather than (as God does) *let both be.* So what better voice and accent for such a reptilian character than the man who came to dine *on,* instead of *with,* his friends?

Now, however, I need to give you the verse that will be the *locus classicus,* the prime text for this chapter, Genesis 2:7. It brings up both the hero and the

villain of this part of the movie: the "man," the *'adham,* who in both his innocence and his guilt is none other than we ourselves.

LXX Gen. 2:7 καὶ ἔπλασεν ὁ
θεὸς τὸν ἄνθρωπον χοῦν
ἀπὸ τῆς γῆς καὶ ἐνεφύσησεν
εἰς τὸ πρόσωπον αὐτοῦ
πνοὴν ζωῆς καὶ ἐγένετο ὁ
ἄνθρωπος εἰς ψυχὴν ζῶσαν

וַיִּיצֶר יְהוָה BHS Gen. 2:7
אֱלֹהִים אֶת־הָאָדָם עָפָר
מִן־הָאֲדָמָה וַיִּפַּח בְּאַפָּיו נִשְׁמַת
חַיִּים וַיְהִי הָאָדָם לְנֶפֶשׁ חַיָּה:

VUL Gen. 2:7 formavit
igitur Dominus Deus
hominem de limo terrae et
inspiravit in faciem eius
spiraculum vitae et factus
est homo in animam
viventem

KJV Gen. 2:7 And the LORD
God formed man *of* the
dust of the ground, and
breathed into his nostrils
the breath of life; and man
became a living soul.

RSV Gen. 2:7 then the LORD
God formed man of dust
from the ground, and
breathed into his nostrils the
breath of life; and man became a living being.

NRSV Gen. 2:7 then the
LORD God formed man
from the dust of the
ground, and breathed into
his nostrils the breath of
life; and the man became a
living being.

What the Director shows us here is the LORD God getting out of the car
to dabble in the mud made by the fountain that watered the face of the dusty
earth. All the English versions (following the Hebrew) say that God made
man of the *dust* from the ground. But that dust is now mud, and Augustine
(like Jerome) is inordinately fond of saying that God made man *de limo
terrae,* from the "slime" or "clay" of the earth. In effect, then, the Director
gives us God's act of creation here as play rather than work. She films him
more as a kid making mud pies than as a laborer sweating over a project. In
fact, what she most wants us to see is that the human race will be the crowning expression of the divine Fun of the Trinity. I know. I've mentioned that at
great length earlier in this book. But in a world seriously short of fun, it's just
more fun to keep repeating it.

But before turning in earnest to Genesis 2:7, with its formation of the
man from the clay of the ground, I want to give you a little rundown on the
'adham who is made at this point. So far, the movie of Genesis has designated
this *'adham* in two ways. On the sixth day, in Genesis 1:26-27, we first heard
the Narrator speak *generically* about God making the human race as kings
and queens of creation. In verse 26, he reads us God's words: "Let us make
man in our image, after our likeness: and let them have dominion over the
fish of the sea, and over the fowl of the air, and over the cattle, and over all the
earth, and over every creeping thing that creepeth upon the earth." But then,
in verse 27, God seems to shift from the generic to the specific: "So God cre-

ated man in his *own* image; in the image of God created he him, male and female created he them" (both quotations, KJV).

The Hebrew of Genesis 1:26 has *'adham* without the definite article;
verse 27 has it with the article, as *ha'adham* (which is by far the more common form in Genesis). The Septuagint translates it as *ton anthrōpon*, the Vulgate as *hominem*, the RSV (like the KJV) has "man," and the NRSV renders it
as "humankind" — thus underscoring the fact that the word is being used as
a reference to humanity as a whole, not as a specific allusion to an individual
human male. However, had I been involved in producing the NRSV, I might
have argued that when *ha'adham* reappears in Genesis 1:27, it should be translated literally as "the man" rather than the redundant "humankind," since the
verse will end up including both sexes anyway. (In my own writing, I've used
"the *'adham*" instead of "humankind" for the same reason.) But I would also
have insisted that the NRSV's fudging of the Hebrew's "in the image of God
created he *him*" by changing "him" to "them" subjugates accurate translation
to the interests of gender neutrality and political correctness. (The Hebrew of
Genesis 1:27 literally reads, "And God created the *'adham* in his image
[*b'tsalmô*], in a likeness [*b'tselem*] he created *him* [*bara' 'ôthô*], male and female created he *them* [*bara' 'ôtham*].")

The Hebrew words for maleness and femaleness in that verse are *zakhar
ûnqebhah*, "male and female"; the Septuagint reads them as *arsen kai thēly*,
ditto, the Vulgate as *masculum et feminam*, ditto, and the English versions all
agree on "male and female." The specific Hebrew words for "a man" and "a
woman" (that is, a male person or husband, as contrasted with a female person or wife) won't appear until Genesis 2:23, when Adam says of the woman
God has made from his rib, "This *is* now bone of my bones, and flesh of my
flesh: she shall be called Woman [*'ishshah*] because she was taken out of Man
[*'ish*]" (KJV). I'll have more to say on this when we reach that text.

Getting back to the *'adham* in chapter 2, however, there remain two
more problems with the word. The first is that the Hebrew of chapter 2 stead-
fastly uses the masculine singular pronouns *he* or *him* when referring to the
'adham. You're probably going to see this as contradicting what I said above
about *'adham* being a generic noun for *humanity*, and thus including woman.
But I think you shouldn't give in to that temptation. Even this second account, with its production of woman from man's rib, portrays woman as
equally human with man. As I see it, the only reason for the "he's" and "him's"
in both the original and the translations is an economy of convenience: this
part of the movie will arrive at the two sexes by a leisurely process in which
God will first offer *'adham* the animals to be his helpers. Only later, when this
gambit fails, will he get around to making woman. On the other hand, in the

first part of the movie (the creation of the 'adham in the Mind of God rather than in time and space), God creates both sexes *simultaneously.* Nevertheless, there's still no male chauvinism here in Genesis 1:27, only a cinematic style suited to a world of sequentially developing events.

The second problem, though, is a bit different. While the Hebrew uses *ha'adham* ("*the* 'adham," with the definite article) almost everywhere in chapter 2, the word as it appears in the various translations eventually shifts from being a designation for generic humanity to being a proper noun — that is, to being the name of the first man: "Adam." The Septuagint makes this transition to Adam in verse 16 and continues that practice for almost all the rest of the chapter. (Before that, it consistently used *anthrōpos* for *ha'adham*.) The Vulgate uses *Adam* from verse 19 on (having used *homo* and *hominem* prior to that). The KJV likewise begins to use "Adam" in verse 19 ("and brought them unto Adam . . ."); the RSV doesn't introduce it until Genesis 3:17, where the word appears as *l"adham;* "*to* 'adham" ("And to Adam he said . . ."); and the NRSV doesn't use "Adam" anywhere in chapters 2 or 3, bringing in the name only when it reaches Genesis 4:25 ("And Adam knew his wife again . . ."). The "man" in 2:24, by the way, is *'ish,* not 'adham.

I give you all this because I think the use of "Adam" as a proper noun comes to us mostly out of ancient tradition, not out of any necessary connection with the Hebrew text. Still, I have a kind word to say for it. Even though it's plainly a man's name, the KJV's use of it from verse 19 on strikes me as less chauvinistic than the other English versions' gender-specific persistence in using "man" beyond that point. As I said, it's quite close to what I've tried to do with "the 'adham": it makes our first father — not to mention our first mother, who was made of Adam's rib and declared "one flesh" with him at the end of chapter 2 — a *sacramental person* rather than just a guy who preceded us. But that's far too fast a shuffle, so let me develop this point more gradually for you.

When the 'adham were made on the sixth day of the movie, God said, "Let *us* make man in *our* image, after *our* likeness." Many biblical critics now balk at seeing those first-person plurals as references to the Trinity, but I think that's only because they're reading Scripture as a book rather than watching it as a movie. Of course it's true that the original authors of the Hebrew text never thought of such a "Christian" identification. But that doesn't bother the Director of *Genesis, the Movie.* Even though her scriptwriters were working in ignorance of her intentions for the rest of the film, she nevertheless holds the entire picture, start to finish, in her own Mind. So even though they violated their strict monotheism and put (or more likely, *left*) that strange "Let *us* make" in their text, she lets it stand in her picture as a way of tipping her hand to what she'll be doing when she gets around to revealing the Trinity in the New Testament portion of the film.

But since you might be almost as perturbed as the critics to hear me speak of the Father, the Son, and the Holy Spirit this early in the film, I'm going to cushion the shock a bit by referring to the Three-in-One cinematically rather than theologically. As I've done extensively in this book, I'll call them the Producer, the Star, and the Director of the movie, and I'll insist that they're so at one with each other that they constitute a single, undivided Production Company. Accordingly, what we have here in the making of the *'adham* from the dust of the ground is the first physical manifestation of the movie's Star — or, if you'll allow me one large slip into theology for a moment, the first appearance of the second Person of the Production Company, the first "advent," if you will, of the Word of God Incarnate — in the world of time and space.

No doubt my discovery of the Incarnation in the second chapter of the Bible may be just as irksome to you as my unearthing of the Trinity in the first. But that's because you underestimate the talents of the Director. Later in the film, she'll have Paul refer to this very verse in 1 Corinthians 15:45 (RFC): "Thus it is also written, 'The first man Adam became a living soul; the last Adam, a life-giving spirit.'" In other words, she gets Paul to *identify* Christ, the Incarnate Word, with Adam. Accordingly, I feel quite free to reverse Paul's formulation and ask this question: "If Christ can be the last Adam, why can't Adam be the first sacramental appearance (the first *real presence*) of Christ in the movie?"

That's what my fast shuffle was all about. If you think that's tampering with history, I need to remind you that the so-called historical Jesus is not the movie's first manifestation of the Star. The story that the Director makes of the events in her film is the only history she wants us to watch; and in making that history, she can bring the Star into the picture anywhere she wants him to show up — before, during, or after her definitive presentation of Jesus of Nazareth as the Incarnate Word of God. So, to demonstrate her fondness for presenting the Star in various guises throughout the movie, here are just some of the places at which she has him appear.

We've already noted his presence on-screen as the *'adham* in Genesis 2:7. But the Star also appears as *Isaac* when God commands Abraham to sacrifice his son in chapter 22 of Genesis, and as *Joseph* in chapters 37 to 48, where Jacob's eleventh son, despite his brothers' nastiness to him, becomes their savior. In Exodus 12, the Star turns up dressed as the *Passover lamb* (who of course is Christ himself, as Paul says in 1 Corinthians 5:7: "Christ, our Passover, is sacrificed for us"). In Exodus 16, he reappears as the *manna*, the bread from heaven — which Jesus, in John 6, identifies with himself three times. In verse 35, he says, "I am the Bread of life"; in verse 48, he repeats, "I am that Bread of life"; and in verse 51, he caps it all off with "I am the living Bread that came down from heaven" (RFC).

But there's more. Every time we hear the prophets speak about the *Word* of the LORD, we recognize that the Star is being shown as one with the Producer. And in Psalm 33:6, we even hear him made one with the entire Production Company: "By the *Word* of the LORD were the heavens made; and all the host of them by the *Breath* of his mouth" (KJV, italics mine; the fathers easily took this verse as an early revelation of the Three-in-One). And finally, *after* Jesus' thirty-three years among us, the Director has the Star continue to appear in the movie: first as the risen and ascended Lord to Paul on the road to Damascus, then as the glorified Christ to John the Divine on Patmos, and finally as the Bridegroom who takes the new heavens and the new earth as his bride at the Marriage Supper of the Lamb.

Now that's a history worth writing home about. In fact, it's the only history that gives us a home worth hoping for.

*   *   *

But back to the text at hand. In the Hebrew, we read, "And the LORD God formed [*vayyitsar*] the man [*ha'adham*] dust [*'aphar*] from the ground [*min-ha'adhamah*]*." Note that this last word is not *'arets*, "earth," but *'adhamah*, the feminine of *'adham*. It gives us a picture of the ground as the wife of man, as the soil upon which he procreates living things as a husband does in making love to his marriage partner. (While this may sound odd, it isn't: even in English, we refer to a farmer as a "*husband*man.") In the Septuagint, the words are *eplasen ho theos ton anthrōpon choun apo tēs gēs* — literally, "God made man dust from the earth." *Eplasen* is from *plassein*, "to form, mold, shape, fashion," and *choun* is a "bank, mound, heap of dirt" from the earth. (It's in the New Testament that *chous* is translated as "dust" — see Mark 6:11 and Revelation 18:19, where the Vulgate translates it as *pulvis*, the ordinary word for "dust.") In the Vulgate, however, the word is rendered as *limus*. The full phrase is *formavit igitur Dominus Deus hominem de limo terrae:* "God formed man from the 'slime, mud, mire, clay, dirt' of the earth." (The three English versions have only minor differences between them; examine them if you like.)

When Augustine comes to *de limo terrae* in this text, he takes *limus* as "clay" — thus opening up the possibility of seeing God as the divine Potter, putting life into the clay figure of a man. He actually makes this identification in his *Enarratio*, his long sermon on Psalm 94. When he takes up the words "he who formed the eye, shall he not see?" he fastens on the word *finxit,* "formed," and his mind jumps to *figulus,* "Potter": he asks, "Is not God a Potter when he makes fragile, weak, and earthly creatures?" And then, after recalling Paul's reference to God as a Potter in Romans 9:20-21, he makes a grand leap to Jesus' making of clay to restore the sight of the blind man in John 9. "Look at the Lord Christ himself," he says, "because he shows himself as a Potter. For just as he had made man from clay [*de limo*], so also from clay he supplied an anointing for the one whose eyes he had made less than adequately in the womb."

That's typical of Augustine's clever handling of the concordances of Scripture. But now I want to show you how he plays with the verses of Genesis we've been watching so far — and how he'll eventually do even more remarkable things with the clay in the phrase *de limo terrae.* First, though, to introduce you to the way he's been handling our film so far, I'll give you a short passage from Book II, 4 of his *De Genesi contra Manichaeos,* "On Genesis against the Manichaeans." Here he's considering the words of Genesis 2:5, where no rain had as yet fallen on the earth:

> "*Nondum enim pluerat Deus super terram, nec erat homo qui operetur in ea.*" *Laborantium enim homini in terra imber de nubibus est necessarius, de quibus nubibus jam dictum est. Post peccatum autem homo laborare coepit in terra, et necessarias habere illas nubes. Ante peccatum vero, cum viride agri et pabulum fecisset Deus, quo nomine invisibilem creaturam significari discimus. Irrigabat eam fonte interiore loquens in intellectum ejus: ut non extrinsecus verba exciperet, tanquam ex supradictis nubibus pluviam; sed fonte suo, hoc est de intimis suis manente veritate, satiaretur.*

"For God had not yet made it rain in the earth, nor was there a man to work it." Rain from the clouds is a necessity if man is to work the earth, and it's about those clouds that the text has now spoken. But it was *after sin* that man actually began to work the earth and to have need of those clouds. *Before sin,* though — when God made the "green herb of the field [*before* it was in the earth] and the edible plants [*before* they grew]," it's by those words that we learn that an *invisible* creation is being signified — God watered [the earth] by a Fountain internal to himself, speaking to his own Intellect. And he did this so that the words might not be taken extrinsically, as rain from the above-mentioned clouds, but as an outpouring by his own Fountain, that is, by the Truth that abides in his innermost being.

Just one word about the internal Fountain that Augustine ascribes to God in that last sentence: he's actually referring to the Spirit of Truth —

God's Holy Spirit. In the classic hymn *Veni Creator Spiritus* ("Come, Holy Ghost, Our Souls Inspire"), the Spirit is given, among other titles, the names *Fons Vivus, Ingis, Caritas,/et Spiritalis Unctio:* "Living Fountain" (that is, Fountain of *flowing* Water), "Fire," "Love,"/and "Spiritual Anointing." This hymn postdates Augustine by some four hundred years; but his writings might well have been in the mind of its author (Hrabanus Maurus?). More importantly, though, in John 7:38, where Jesus says, "He who believes in me, as the Scripture said, 'Rivers of *living water* will flow out of his belly'" (RFC), that Living Water has been taken by the church as the Holy Spirit, whom Jesus promises to send, and who, in the words of the Nicene Creed, "proceeds from the Father and the Son." As a matter of fact, that verse is one of the bases for the Western doctrine of the "double procession," the "joint outbreathing" of the Spirit, by the first two Persons of the Trinity. All in all, then, the church that cherished Augustine has always heard the words *Fons Vivus* in the hymn *Veni Creator Spiritus* as an attribution of the title "Living Fountain" to the Holy Spirit.

In *De Genesi contra Manichaeos*, Book II, 8, however, Augustine turns to the "mystery" of the *limus*, the clay from which God actually formed man, and he addresses the Manichees themselves. Among their many mistaken notions was the idea that the Old Testament could have only a physical interpretation. And since they themselves were convinced that human nature was a strictly spiritual phenomenon, they despised the "clay" in this verse and said it had no relevance whatsoever. Augustine, of course, spotted the obvious setup in that approach: he felt it was dirty pool to say the Bible is unspiritual when it's your own insistence on physical meanings that's precluded spiritual interpretations. So in the passage I'm about to give you, Augustine goes after these Bible sharks with gusto. He reminds them that he sees the entire first account of creation (Gen. 1:1–2:3) as a world existing in the divine Intellect alone; and that now, in this second account (Gen. 2–3), he sees a world existing on its own turf. But he insists that in this text, even the "clay" leaves room for both the physical and the spiritual meanings. Here's the passage:

> *Nunc videamus post universae creaturae insinuationem tam visibilis quam invisibilis, et universale beneficium divini fontis erga invisibilem creaturam, quid de homine specialiter intimetur, quod ad nos maxime pertinet. Primo enim quod de limo terrae Deus hominem finxit, solet habere questionem qualis ille limo fuerit, vel quae materia nomine limi significata sit. Illi autem inimici veterum librorum, omnia carnaliter intuentes, et propterea semper errantes, etiam hoc reprehendere mordaciter solent, quod de limo Deus hominem finxit. Dicunt enim; "Quare de limo fecit Deus hominem? an*

defuerat ei melior et coelestis materia, unde hominem faceret, ut de labe
terrena tam fragilem mortalemque formaret?" Non intelligentes primo
quam multis significationibus vel terra vel aqua in Scripturis ponatur: limus
enim aquae et terrae commixtio est. Dicimus enim tabidum, et fragile, et
morti destinatum corpus humanum post peccatum esse coepisse. Non enim
in nostro corpore isti exhorrescunt nisi mortalitatem, quam damnatione
meruimus. Quid autem mirum, aut difficile Deo, etiamsi de limo istius
terrae hominem fecit, tale tamen corpus ejus efficere, quod corruptione non
subjaceret, si homo praeceptum Dei custodiens peccare noluisset? Si enim
coeli ipsius de nihilo, vel de informi materia dicimus factam, quia
omnipotentem artificem credimus: quid mirum si corpus quod de limo
qualicumque factum est, potuit ab omnipotente artifice tale fieri, ut nulla
molestia, nulla indigentia cruciaret hominem ante peccatum, et nulla
corruptione tabesceret?

Now then — after the introduction of the universal creation, both visible
and invisible, and the universal beneficence of the divine Fountain [God
himself] toward the invisible creation — let's see what might be specifically intimated here about man, and what pertains particularly to us. Because first of all, the fact that God formed man from the clay of the earth
raises the question of what sort of thing that clay might be, or what material might be signified by the name of "clay." But those enemies of the old
Books [the Manichees, who rejected the Old Testament], taking everything carnally and thus always being in error [about those Books], also
have the nasty habit of seizing on this one, where God formed man from
clay, and biting the heart out of it. For they say, "Why did God make man
from clay? Was it perhaps because he lacked a better and heavenly matter
from which he might make man that he used a disgusting thing of the
earth to form such a fragile and mortal creature?" To begin with, they
don't understand the many senses of *earth* and *water* that are set forth in
Scripture, for clay is a commixture of water and earth. For we [who be-
lieve] say that it was only *after sin* that the human body began to be a
wasted and fragile thing, and to be destined for death. So these people are
horrified at nothing in our body except the mortality that we deserved by
damnation. But how is it astonishing or difficult for God, even though he
made man from the clay of this earth, nonetheless to make man's body
such that it would not be subject to decay if he were to avoid sin by keeping the commandment of God? For if we say that the beauty of heaven itself was made from nothing or from unformed matter (Gen. 1:2) because
we believe in an omnipotent maker, why is it astonishing if a body that

was made from clay of whatever sort was able, thanks to the omnipotent maker, to become such that *before sin* man should be tormented by no shame, no want, and should waste away by no process of decay?

This raises the thorny problem of the *sinlessness* and *deathlessness* that Augustine (and most of the fathers) ascribed to the *'adham* before the Fall. I'll be dealing with it again and again as I go along in this book, so be patient if I don't go into detail about it here. All I'll say now is that Augustine is only partly responsible for the more far-fetched solutions that have sometimes been given to the problem. True enough, later Augustinians often turned the *prelapsarian* Adam into a stainless-steel specimen who lived in a Teflon paradise. And, equally true, many anti-Augustinians have gleefully jumped on such excesses as proof of Augustine's folly. But blaming an author for what his readers do with his writings is an unfair game: Augustine was so good at making distinctions that he actually closed many of the doors his posterity thought he opened.

In this instance, he came at the question from two different directions. On the one hand, he held that man, like the rest of the animals, was mortal (though sinless) even *before* the Fall; but on the other hand, he saw nothing remarkable in maintaining that the human race's mortality was *forestalled* at that point by a special gift from God — sacramentalized by the Tree of Life. In other words, he felt that if God wanted to do such a thing, who's to say him nay? So he had no difficulty with the idea that death as we now experience it is an *infralapsarian* condition — a *consequence* of sin rather than the primordial will of God. And while I find that unobjectionable (it seems to me quite true that, had we not messed up God's ecology of life and death, our death would have been a mystery to be embraced rather than a conundrum to be solved), I do think Augustine deserves a bit of reworking by sympathetic minds if we're to commend him to our contemporaries. Indeed, that's one way of describing what I'm up to in this book.

I do realize, however, that I've just given you two more problems. The first stems from the Latinisms I just threw at you: *prelapsarian* and *infralapsarian*. *Pre-* means "before," *infra-* (below) means "after," and *lapsus* is "fall." Problem solved. Why then did I give it to you in the first place? To tell the truth, I did it because I have an incurable addiction to Latin theology. If that bothers you even more, it only goes to show that some problems can't be solved by honest answers.

But the second problem is too important to deal with on short notice. It reared its head (as you may recall) in the parenthesis near the end of the paragraph just before the preceding one. I made a terse reference there to our fiddling with the ecology of life and death, and to my notion that death as we now know it is a consequence of sin only because our sin was precisely an attempt to convert the mystery of death into a riddle we could solve by control. But even that summary is too fast, so take it only as a teaser to whet your appetite for my eventual reformulation of Augustine's position. Still, since everything we've seen so far is *prelapsarian* (and will continue to be until the beginning of Genesis 3), Adam at this juncture is both sinless and deathless. Don't worry, though — death as a result of sin is sure to come. Like the spinach soup at the Waldorf, you'll get it one way or another.

Back to Augustine on the creation of the human body. In *De Genesi contra Manichaeos*, Book II, 9, he picks up from where he left off in the previous passage. He uses his ability to find spiritual interpretations in physical events (to "make history" of them), and he comes up with this wonderful linkage between creation in the Mind of God and creation in its own right:

> *Itaque superflue quaeritur unde hominis corpus Deus fecerit; si tamen nunc de corporis formatione dicitur. Sic enim nonnullos nostros intelligere accepi, qui dicunt, posteaquam dictum est, "Finxit Deus hominem de limo terrae"; propterea non additum, "Ad imaginem et similitudinem suam," quoniam nunc de corporis formatione dicitur. Tunc autem homo interior significabatur, quando dictum est: "Fecit Deus hominem ad imaginem et similitudinem Dei." Sed etiamsi nunc quoque hominem ex corpore et anima factum intelligamus, ut non alicujus novi operis inchoatio, sed superius breviter insinuati diligentior retractatio isto sermone explicetur; si ergo, ut dixi, hoc loco ex corpore et anima factum intelligamus, non absurde ipsa commixtione limi nomen accepit. Sicut enim aqua terram colligit, et conglutinat, et continet quando ejus commixtione limus ejus efficitur; sic anima corporis materiam vivificando in unitatem concordem conformat, et non permittit labi et resolvi.*

And so it's superfluous to ask what God made the body of man from if now it's only the formation of the body that's being discussed. For so even some of our own [he has Tertullian and Hilary in mind] are taken to understand that fact: they say that after it was said, "God formed man from the clay of the earth," the reason why "in his image and likeness" was not added here was because this discourse is *now* about the formation of the body. But back *then* [on the sixth day, Gen. 1:26], when it was said, "God made man in his image and likeness," the *interior* man [the soul] was being signified. But even if we might now also understand man as made of body and soul, what is being explicated in this discourse is not the beginning of some new work, but a more meticulous re-envisioning of what was briefly insinuated earlier [that is, on the sixth day]. If, therefore, as I said, we may understand man in this context as being made of body and soul, it's not absurd that this same commixture should itself be given the name of clay. For just as water assembles earth, and glues it together, and keeps it together when its clay is made by its commixture [with earth], so the soul, by vivifying the matter of the body, forms it into a concordant unity and does not allow it to be blemished and dissolved [just as clay, once solidified by fire, is unchanging and indissoluble].

This is Augustine's bow to the Director, who can take pairings of different images and use them to illuminate and reinforce one another. Just as she can make an ecology of apparent opposites (light and darkness, life and death, good and evil), so Augustine can make matching unities of such disparate things as earth and water, body and soul — even to the point of calling soul and body the "clay" from which the *'adham* was made. It's all a matter of seeing his underlying trick of *hendiadys,* of being able to say one thing by means of two. Lesser minds always think they have to decide between opposites. But Augustine's mind, formed by Scripture, was free to join God in rejoicing over the harmony, the *unitatem concordem,* the agreeable unity of their commixture. He was able to see them all in the light of the *Coincidentia Oppositorum* himself — of the undivided One who goes all the opposites one better by being Three at once.

*   *   *

But having arrived, courtesy of Augustine, at the *soul* that the LORD God breathes into the body of the *'adham* in the final part of verse 7, we can now set aside his identification of water with soul and look at the words we haven't yet dealt with. I'll take the Hebrew and all the versions in one fell swoop. They read as follows: "*And he breathed* [in the Hebrew, it's *vayyipach;* in the Septuagint, they're *kai enephysen;* in the Vulgate, they're *et inspiravit;* and in all three English versions, they're "and he breathed"] *into his nostrils* [*b"aphav,* "into his nose, nostrils, face"; *eis to prosōpon autou,* "into his face"; *in faciem eius,* "into his face"; and in the English versions, "into his nostrils"] *the breath of life* [*nishmath chayyim,* "the breath of lives"; *pnoēn zōēs,* "the breath of life"; *spiraculum vitae,* "the breath of life"; and in the English versions, "the breath of life"]."

But then comes the most problematical part of the verse: "and man became a _____ _____." I'll underline the various words that fill those blanks as I proceed. In the Hebrew, they're *vay'hi ha'adham l'nephesh chayyah*, literally, "and behold [or, and so] the man a soul of life, a living soul, an ensouled being"; in the Septuagint, they're *kai egeneto ho anthrōpos eis psychēn zōsan*, "and the man became a living soul"; in the Vulgate, they're *et factus est homo in animam viventem*, "and man [Latin has no definite article, so you have to guess at the "the"] was made a living soul." In the KJV, they're "and man became a living soul"; in the RSV, the same; and in the NRSV, "and the man became a living being."

This is where some inattentive people think the brouhaha over the soul's immortality or mortality got its start in the Bible. It's worth noting, though, that *nephesh chayyah* ("living soul") has already appeared in the movie of creation on the fifth and six days of Genesis 1. At 1:21, it was applied to the swarming "ensouled creatures" of the sea; and at 1:24, it was spoken over the land animals. (In the Septuagint and the Vulgate, in fact, it's given the same translations it gets here: *psychēn zōsan* and *animam viventem*.) So on the face of the Scriptures, there's nothing here about the "immortality" of the soul. In this film, it's simply the "informing principle" of the body: it's what makes animals *animate* rather than *inanimate* beings. Indeed, Thomas Aquinas, following Aristotle, called the soul (the *anima*) the *motor corporis*, the "mover" of the body — and he held that all vegetable and animal souls (except man's) perished with the deaths of the bodies they inhabited.

True enough, the notion of the deathlessness of man's soul has now been around so long that most Christians think it's a biblically revealed truth. But it's not. The Old Testament knows nothing of it; and the Good News of the New Testament can be proclaimed better without it than with it: it just waters down the resurrection of the dead and makes Jesus a Santa Claus helper rather than the Incarnate Lord by whom all things are made. Jesus is the Word of God, for crying out loud. He makes all things out of nothing in their beginning; and as the Resurrection and the Life, he raises all the dead from the nothing of their death. Nothing is his favorite material. So if you've been deluding yourself with the notion that after your death you'll only be half-dead (that is, dead in body but not in soul) — or if you're afraid that if your soul dies, God won't be able to help you — just stop all that anti-Gospel nonsense. We believe that Jesus is God Almighty in Person. We most emphatically do not believe that he is some quasi-spiritual mechanic who will, a week from some Tuesday, bolt your immortal soul back onto a resuscitated corpse. Jesus himself is your resurrection and your life *right now*. He's got better tricks up his sleeve than reassembling your parts.

Still, I have little hope of convincing the general public of that. I once saw a Christmas episode of *Ally McBeal* on television. It was about a minister who "lost his faith" when his wife was shot by a mugger. He felt he couldn't preach about Christmas because he missed his wife so much that he no longer believed in the immortality of the soul that God promised in the birth of Jesus. All the "comfort" he'd ever given to bereaved parishioners ("The soul of your loved one still lives on") had turned to ashes in his mouth. His crisis of faith, though, was resolved when all the cast members assured him they still thought the immortality of the soul was the true meaning of the Nativity, so he should just bite the bullet and celebrate Christmas for Christmas's sake.

I muttered my way through the whole show. To me, it was just one more tacky proof that the church has allowed the immortality of the soul to pull the teeth out of the Gospel's mouth. It confirmed my abiding suspicion that as a priest, I could sooner propose getting rid of Baptism, the Bible, the Creeds, the Eucharist, and even the church itself than breathe a word suggesting that maybe the soul dies with the body. The troops have become so enamored of its deathlessness that they'd only conclude (as the minister's official board did) that I should look for another line of work. But for my money, if that's the church's idea of the consolation of the Gospel — well, by George, the quicker it turns to ashes the better. It's theological *schlock*, not Christian faith. If you don't like hearing that, I'm sorry. But as I've said many times from the pulpit, I wasn't ordained to make you happy.

These last three paragraphs of ranting, however, threaten to take me into another subject, if not a whole 'nother book. Back to the more fruitful aspects of the soul.

$$* \qquad * \qquad *$$

The Director of *Genesis, the Movie* presents the breathing of a soul into the *'adham* in this verse in a way that disappoints many mere readers of her script. Such people like to ask irrelevant questions about extraneous subjects instead of watching her fascinating picture of a clay figure that suddenly becomes a living creature. For one thing, they ask how this depiction can be squared with an evolutionary view of human nature. For another, they'd like to know when this inbreathing of a soul took place. And for a third, they're dying to tell me that, since I've already said that *nephesh chayyim* has been applied to mere animals, I should admit that man has no particular excellence or dignity at all. Let me dispose of these questions as briefly as I can — in reverse order.

As to the final one, the Director has already filmed the pre-eminence of the *'adham* in her portrayal of the sixth day. She has God say, "Let us make man in our image, after our likeness: and let them have *dominion* over the fish of the sea, and over the fowl of the air, and over the cattle, and over all the earth, and over every creeping thing that creepeth on the earth" (KJV). 'Nuff said, because I've already said that.

But now for the second and first questions (which involve just one matter). *When* the "ensouling" of the *'adham* took place and *how* it might fit into an evolutionary schedule deserve only one simple response: *It hardly matters.* The emergence of man in time and space, no matter what timetable you put it on, is a rather recent piece of business. If you follow Archbishop Ussher's biblical chronology, you put man's first appearance at 4,004 B.C. If you follow evolution, you put it somewhere around 25,000 to 50,000 B.C. But if you look at any of those dates in the light of the scientific estimates of the age of the universe, the differences between them practically disappear. In the first part of the movie, I gave a graphic illustration of their negligibility in the form of a timetable comprising the billions of years from the beginning of the physical universe to the present day. Here it is again, now boiled down to a single line:

_____ !

The line represents billions of years, and the exclamation point at the end represents the last relatively few years — 52,002, 27,002, or 6,006 years, just as you choose. Do you see? The point of the diagram is that no matter which number you pick, the "!" at the end will always be so narrow a window in time that *it hardly matters* in the grand sweep of the universe's existence. Which is exactly what I just said, so QED — and here endeth my response to the nitpickers.

The Director, however, cares about no such matters. Her cinematic approach to the emergence of man gets closer to "making history" than all the evolutionary accounts laid end to end. Not that I'm against evolution. I object only to certain evolutionists who think they're making history when all they're doing is rattling off sequences of events. As I've said, events are not history: history is what we make when we weave events into a story that gives them some *traction* — something that will give them a grip on the ground of history. That's what the great evolutionist Teilhard de Chardin did in *The Divine Milieu*, where he made Christ the Omega Point, the End who through the whole time of creation has been drawing (at*tracting*, from *tractare*, "to lead, haul, or pull") all things to himself. I'm sure the Director found him much to her liking, because in her film she chose an "evolutionary" format even for creation in the divine Mind — a format that comes remarkably close to evolution's sequences, even though it doesn't quite win the rewarding cigar.

Therefore, let me try to flesh out her approach to this second part of her movie for you with a little script-writing of my own. She assumes that you've already watched her film of the "intellectual" creation, and that you realize she's presented you with a complete history of the universe. Not, of course, history as we gradually make it up in time and space, but nonetheless that very same history we sneak up on as it's been held simultaneously in the eternal conversation between the Producer, the Star, and the Director. There isn't a scrap of our being, however momentary or transitory, or a word of our history — short or long, important or unimportant, accidental or deliberate, good or bad — that hasn't been contemplated forever by those Three.

But now, as she comes to the filming of the beginning of human history in this verse, I think she might come up with a "shooting script" that looks something like this:

SCENARIO FOR END OF CREATION OF ADAM

(Background MUSIC: Vivaldi's FOUR SEASONS, SPRING)

As the NARRATOR begins to read the words about the MIST from the earth at the beginning of verse 6, WE CONTINUE in the ANIMATED-DRAWING format we've been using since the beginning of verse 4. The NARRATOR is silent; the MUSIC continues.

WE WATCH as a FOUNTAIN turns the dusty ground into MUD. Then WE SEE the LORD GOD appear as a bright, roughly triangular WHITE CLOUD. In its UPPER CORNER, WE SEE two GOLDEN EYES; in its CENTER, a pair of GOLDEN LIPS; and in the LOWER LEFT and RIGHT CORNERS, WE SEE two GOLDEN HANDS (a RIGHT and a LEFT HAND, respectively). The MUSIC continues; the NARRATOR is silent.

WE SEE the hands reach out of the cloud and begin to form something from the MUD. The MUSIC is softer. The NARRATOR reads, "And the LORD God formed man from the dust of the earth." The NARRATOR goes silent again; the MUSIC comes up.

WE WATCH as a CLAYMATION figure of the thing being formed appears. (The rest of the screen is still in straight ANIMATION format.) And WE SEE the figure

---

> take on human form. The MUSIC continues; the NARRA-
> TOR is still silent.
>
> WE WATCH as the HANDS lift the MOTIONLESS FIGURE to
> the EYES of the CLOUD and then LOWER IT so that its
> NOSE is directly below the LIPS in the center of the
> CLOUD, and the NARRATOR begins the words "And he
> breathed in his nostrils . . . and man became a liv-
> ing soul." The FIGURE begins to MOVE, the LIPS
> SMILE, and the MUSIC makes a crescendo to the end of
> the scene.

These HANDS, by the way, are straight out of Irenaeus (second century), who called the Son and the Holy Spirit the two hands of the Father. The rest is just the amateurish imagining of my fevered brain, but perhaps it's enough to give you an idea of what I have in mind for the Director. The *'adham* is now a living being; and though he may be mortal by nature, the LORD God not only sees him as the crown of creation but also — as God said of all things at the end of the sixth day — finds him "Very Good." The Director has given us a history after our own hearts.

What now stands before our eyes is not a creature who came up from the slime or down from the trees but our very own great great great great grandfather without a single bad habit. However much our estrangèd faces may look down on the innocence of our beginning — and however we might be tempted to write it off as wishful longing for a lost golden age — it still stands as the history that we, but for our sins, would most like to have written. No one in his right mind wants to hear that things were never better than they are now. Because only someone out of his mind could hope for a bright future on the basis of a perpetually dim past. Either there was once a real possibility that the human condition might have a glorious denouement, or there was never any hope for a future at all. You can't make a silk purse out of a sow's ear, and you can't make a happy history out of two hundred generations of rotten ancestors.

On to the next chapter then, and to a world of really serious — and delightful — innocence.

FIFTEEN

The Garden, the Tree of Life, and the City

GENESIS 2:8-9

Let's begin this chapter by going directly to the script that the Director has handed the Narrator at this point — and to the pregnant images she sets before us:

LXX Gen. 2:8 καὶ ἐφύτευσεν κύριος ὁ θεὸς παράδεισον ἐν Εδεμ κατὰ ἀνατολὰς καὶ ἔθετο ἐκεῖ τὸν ἄνθρωπον ὃν ἔπλασεν 9 καὶ ἐξανέτειλεν ὁ θεὸς ἔτι ἐκ τῆς γῆς πᾶν ξύλον ὡραῖον εἰς ὅρασιν καὶ καλὸν εἰς βρῶσιν καὶ τὸ ξύλον τῆς ζωῆς ἐν μέσῳ τῷ παραδείσῳ καὶ τὸ ξύλον τοῦ εἰδέναι γνωστὸν καλοῦ καὶ πονηροῦ

וַיִּטַּע יְהוָה BHS Gen. 2:8
אֱלֹהִים גַּן־בְּעֵדֶן מִקֶּדֶם
וַיָּשֶׂם שָׁם אֶת־הָאָדָם אֲשֶׁר
יָצָר: 9 וַיַּצְמַח יְהוָה אֱלֹהִים
מִן־הָאֲדָמָה כָּל־עֵץ נֶחְמָד
לְמַרְאֶה וְטוֹב לְמַאֲכָל וְעֵץ
הַחַיִּים בְּתוֹךְ הַגָּן וְעֵץ
הַדַּעַת טוֹב וָרָע:

VUL Gen. 2:8 plantaverat autem Dominus Deus paradisum voluptatis a principio in quo posuit hominem quem formaverat 9 produxitque Dominus Deus de humo omne lignum pulchrum visu et ad vescendum suave lignum etiam vitae in medio paradisi lignumque scientiae boni et mali

KJV Gen. 2:8 And the LORD God planted a garden eastward in Eden; and there he put the man whom he had formed. 9 And out of the ground made the LORD God to grow every tree that is pleasant to the sight, and

RSV Gen. 2:8 And the LORD God planted a garden in Eden, in the east; and there he put the man whom he had formed. 9 And out of the ground the LORD God made to grow every tree that is pleasant to the sight and

NRSV Gen. 2:8 And the LORD God planted a garden in Eden, in the east; and there he put the man whom he had formed. 9 Out of the ground the LORD God made to grow every tree that is pleasant to the sight and

good for food; the tree of life also in the midst of the garden, and the tree of knowledge of good and evil.	good for food, the tree of life also in the midst of the garden, and the tree of the knowledge of good and evil.	good for food, the tree of life also in the midst of the garden, and the tree of the knowledge of good and evil.

The Hebrew reads, "And the Lord God planted [*vayyita'*] a garden [*gan*, a "fertile enclosure"] in the east [*miqqedhem*, literally, "from the before, or on the before side"] in Eden [*b'êdhen*, "in a place of delight"], and he put there [*vayyasem sham*] the man [*ha'adham*] whom he formed [*'asher yatsar*]." As you'll see, the versions differ considerably in their translations of these words.

The Septuagint does have "planted [*ephyteusen*] a garden," but then it renders *gan*, "garden," as *paradeison*, "a paradise, a park." Furthermore, it takes the word *'êdhen* in *b'êdhen* as the proper name of a place and simply transliterates it as *en Edem*, "in Eden." But when the Septuagint comes to the word *miqqedhem*, it translates that as *kata anatolas*, "on the east." (*Anatolē* is from the verb *anatellein*, "to rise up" — and since it's also used for the sun's rising, it becomes the ordinary Greek word for "east.") The remainder of the verse stays close to the Hebrew: "and he put there [*kai etheto ekei*] the man whom he made [*ton anthrōpon hon eplasen*]."

It's the Vulgate, however, that contains the most interesting translations. It reads, "But the Lord God planted a paradise [*paradisum*] of pleasure [*voluptatis*] from the beginning [*a principio*], in which he put [*in quo posuit*] the man whom he had formed [*hominem quem formaverat*]." Jerome agrees with the Greek text on "paradise" as a translation for *gan*, but he decides not to take Eden as a place name; instead, he takes *'êdhen* in its root sense as "a place of delight" — hence *paradisum voluptatis*. But when he comes to the Hebrew *miqqedhem*, "from the before," he doesn't use the Latin word for "from the east" (*ab oriente*, from the "sunrise," or "the east" — which would have echoed the Greek); rather, he chooses a variation on its root meaning and comes up with the translation *a principio*, "from the beginning."

Initially, I found this merely puzzling; but on second thought it began to look more like a Mystery inserted at the Director's prodding. Since Jerome had already used *In principio* to translate the very first word of Genesis 1:1, *B'reshith*, "In the beginning," I saw his *a principio* here in Genesis 2:8 as a harking back to the six-day account in the first chapter of Genesis, where the entire creation exists solely in the Mind of God. So, expecting that old Latin version of Genesis 2:8 (the *Itala*, which Augustine used) would also have *a principio*, I looked up his reference to it in *De Genesi ad Litteram*, Book VIII, 1. But to my surprise, the *Itala* at this point began with *Et plantavit Deus paradisum in Eden ad orientem*, "And God planted a paradise in Eden to the east" (thus following the Septuagint, from which it was translated). However, when Augustine commented previously on the words *in principio* in Genesis 1:1 (in *De Genesi ad Literam,* Book I, 3), he capitalized *Principio* to indicate that he took it as a reference to the Incarnate Word — to the eternal Son, the divine Wisdom, the second Person of the Trinity — by whom and in whom all things are made.

That was what led me to see Jerome's use of *a principio* in connection with the Garden as a hint that the Garden itself — and, in particular, the Incarnation of the Word — had been in the Mind of the Trinity from the start. And that in turn led me to see that all the events in the second and third chapters of Genesis (which appear *sequentially* in times and places) were present *simultaneously* and *eternally* in the first chapter's account of the world in the divine Intellect. For when God makes all things *simul et sempiterne,* "at once and forever," in his only-begotten Beginning, he sees not only the *existence* of the beings he creates but *every smitch of their history* — even before those beings have had a chance to make it on their own.

The Three-in-One do not have to wait for things to exist in order to know them; they simply know everything that will ever be known as it's held *in the Beloved* from all eternity. And that includes not only the free choices of his creatures but even the "accidents" of their whims. In this book I've frequently quoted (in capital letters) Augustine's concise summary of that Mystery of the divine Knowledge — *NOTA ERGO FECIT, NON FACTA COGNOVIT:* "God made things he already knew; he didn't need them to be facts in order to know them."

I realize that such a hundred-proof distillation of God's Knowing may taste like a stiff shot of predestination to you, but it isn't. God doesn't *fore*-know our history; he just sits in his eternity watching us make it. Our problem with it lies in our habit of poking in words like *pre-* and *fore-* and *before* when we talk about God. So, for a cure, let me lend you my old mantra on the subject: "God knows what I *did tomorrow* in the same way he knows what I did yesterday." Do you see? God knows all things and all events *eternally,* not *temporally.* His Knowledge of time and space is independent of time and space. But if that's still too strong a drink to swallow neat, let me add a splash of branch water to it. If it wasn't Jerome who went back to the bar of Genesis 1 for another glass of the old divine Knowledge, then it was the Director herself, who throughout her movie has a fondness for "the Beginning" as one of her favorite toasts to the Incarnate Word. Throughout her film, she raises her glass and says, "Here's to the Beginning, who holds all of history in his eternal Now. Cheers!"

*　　　*　　　*

But since all the English versions agree nicely with the Hebrew — and since the Director has already given us at least three images to watch closely — let's take a break from the script at this point and concentrate on what I consider her principal image so far: the *Garden* as a sacrament of the *City*.

God puts the *'adham* in a "garden," a *paradeison*, a *paradisum*, a "paradise" that he planted. And I think he puts the *'adham* there in order to show us our role as human beings in the *shaping* of the world that he makes. Accordingly, the placing of the human race in an earthly paradise marks the beginning of our history-making career. But note well that God doesn't put us into a jungle, or a desert, or any other "wild" place. Instead, he puts us into a place that he's already begun to shape, to "civilize" by making a garden of it. Perhaps he did this by arranging three flowering shrubs in a neat triangle, or by setting three perfectly round pools of water in a straight line. But by whatever devices God "citified" the Garden, he put us there because he wants us to take that hint of *civilization* (from the Latin *civis*, "city") and run with it.

In short, he wants us to become the *builders* of the City he has in Mind for the world. The Garden, however, is only the first of many sacraments of the City that the Director will give us in her film of the Bible. Indeed, if you look at the others she has up her sleeve, you can review her entire movie just by keeping your eye on the bouncing ball of the City as it appears in the rest of her film. Watch, and I'll insert my own review of the whole film to show you how it's done:

> The City to be built by human hands first dawns in Eden, and its light breaks on the *innocence* of the *'adham*, on our blameless humanity, which thus becomes the first sacrament of the Word Incarnate in our flesh. And that splendid sinlessness prevails all through chapter 2 of Genesis, even at the end, where the man and his wife are "one flesh" and are "naked and not ashamed." They're celebrating the world's first and only unqualifiedly happy marriage, and that *Marriage* thus becomes another sacrament of the City: one that will find its fulfillment at the Marriage Supper of the Lamb in the book of Revelation. Next, though, we watch the start of the City's downfall at the tree of the knowledge of good and evil, where Adam and his wife (the name "Eve" doesn't appear till Genesis 3:20) *reject* God's hands-off management of good and evil, thus losing the true Key to the City. Instead, they choose a hands-on key of their own devising and steal the peace of God's ecology of good and evil, turning it into a perpetual state of war between the two.
>
> After that, our failure to build the City leads us straight downhill. In Genesis 4, we see Cain murder his brother Abel in an argument over reli-

218

gion; and in chapters 6 through 8, we watch as God drowns the fallen City in the flood. But then we see his Covenant of the Rainbow, in which he changes his Mind and swears never to do anything like that again. At the end of this sequence, however — in Genesis 11 — we witness the last gasp of humanity's perverse effort to build the City at the Tower of Babel.

But now the history of the City that God will eventually build by our hands begins to appear as the mystery it really is. In chapters 12 through 22 of Genesis, God makes a Covenant with Abraham (the Covenant of Circumcision), in which he promises him that in his seed (that is, in his son Isaac and in Isaac's descendants) "all the nations of the earth shall be blessed." In other words, despite our failures to perfect the City, God still intends us to be its builders. Now, though, in the midst of our relentless tracking of mud over the carpet of God's world, it will be built *under the carpet* of our fallen history. And it will rise up in glory by the Mystery of God's indwelling of our humanity. The promised "Seed of Abraham" will turn out to be none other than Jesus the Christ, who is the ultimate manifestation of the Word of God present in our flesh.

But in the meanwhile, the Director's history of the City moves slowly but inexorably to its triumphant end. Israel, the sacramental community of the City, goes down to slavery in Egypt; it is liberated at the Passover and wanders forty years in the wilderness; it receives the Law on Mount Sinai; it conquers the Promised Land and eventually occupies Jerusalem — which then becomes the name of the City itself all the way to the end of the film. But its troubles are not yet over. The City next falls into captivity in Babylon, and after forty years, the exiles once more return to Jerusalem. And when God finally reveals the Mystery of his Presence in Jesus, he weeps over the City that rejects him, he is crucified outside the City, he rises from the dead and ascends to his Father's right hand, and the Mystery of his death and resurrection is proclaimed to the whole world "beginning at *Jerusalem.*"

But it's only at the end of the biblical film that the City finally appears in triumph as the New Jerusalem, the Bride at the Marriage Supper of the Lamb. The old sacraments of City and Marriage now come together in a new and open reality that fulfills them both. After all is said and done, the City is indeed built by human hands (by the hands of the Carpenter of Nazareth, who made all things to begin with); and the happy Marriage between God and creation finally reappears in an endless consummation (with the world in the arms of the God who became man for our sakes). And as the Bridegroom himself passes us the eschatological Champagne at the eternal Party, we see the eternal *cost* of the divine-human Builder's

219

labors. The final evidences of the City's triumph and the Marriage's success are the nail prints, the Sacred Wounds, in the hands that serve us history done to a turn at the everlasting Wedding Reception.

Please note carefully, though, what those endless festivities are *not*. They don't occur in some airy-fairy, eschatological "otherwhere" in which we become totally spiritual beings, nor do they take place in a boring "heaven" where bed-sheeted saints sit on clouds. They're the celebration at which we ourselves are restored to our full humanity in the resurrection of our bodies. They're celebrated in the New Jerusalem itself, with all its transfigured but still earthy splendor: twelve foundations of precious stones, gates of pearl, streets of gold, and the wood of life growing on both sides of the river of life.

I can't resist a joke here. A dying man is visited by an angel who tells him he can take to heaven any treasure he likes. The man says he wants to take three bars of gold bullion: one for the Father, one for the Son, and one for the Holy Spirit. The angel says "Done!" And then the man dies. On arriving at the pearly gates, he meets St. Peter and shows him his gifts. Peter looks at them in disbelief and says, "You brought *pavement?*"

Despite the skepticism of the keeper of the keys, the man's gift was entirely appropriate: his gold Belgian blocks could only make the City grander. The "heaven" of Scripture is chock-full of the stuff of this world. Our final destiny is not an escape from history, let alone from our failure to build the City; it's the recapitulation and renewal of all our history — good, bad, or indifferent — by the Incarnate Builder himself. Nothing gets lost on the way to our final destination, even if we insist on going home the hard way. Our redemption is a case of *per aspera ad astra:* "through hardship to the stars." The City is civilized by the very incivility with which we defaced it: it is built by lifting the passion of the world into the Passion of the Word — and Jesus takes that Passion to the Father's right hand. Our sins, our failures to build the City, go home in the body of our Lord — but they go as Glorious Scars, not as marks of disgrace.

In our final state, then, we will be risen human beings, not angels. And, like Christ, we will take our humanity home "with flesh, bones, and all things appertaining to the perfection of human nature" (as it says in the "Articles of Religion" in the Book of Common Prayer). We will have risen hands, risen feet, risen eyes, risen brains — and even risen hearts, lungs, livers, and kidneys. I'll gladly admit that I haven't a clue about how any of those components might actually show up in the eschatological City. But I do believe that without them I will have no City that fulfills what God promised me in Eden.

I believe in the resurrection of this earthy body I've lived in all my life.

Either everything about me goes home, or nothing much about me makes the trip. The City was always mine to build. But if I have to walk the streets of the New Jerusalem in something other than my body, I'll have a hard time feeling it's my City. If the Incarnate Word who made me in his image can tread those pavements on risen feet, "Why then, oh why can't I?"

Still, it's not just human beings who are made in the image of the City-building Word. Our *civilizing* proclivities are shared in no small way by our brothers and sisters in the animal orders. The anthill, the beehive, the birds' nest, the lodge under the beaver dam, and yes, even the courteous exchanges of the wolf pack — all are evidences of a craving for community. Furthermore, the schooling of bluefish, the upstream struggles of salmon to spawn, and the parental ministrations of whales and porpoises are sacraments of that same Mystery. And so too are the cities of life out of death that are built by the vegetable orders. Seeds, in cooperation with their fellow citizens of sun, earth, air, and water, make parks and palaces for the enjoyment of the whole creation. All of these activities — high or low, great or small, animal or vegetable — are nothing less than civic triumphs over the loneliness of individual existence.

But there's more to be said about them than that. The Greek word for city is *polis* — from which we get "politics," "policy," and "polity." And our lesser but equally political companions in the City are almost as addicted to those pursuits as we are. We're not the only alpha males or females in the world. The lion vies with other males for political supremacy over his pride of wives; and the lioness rules her cubs with a paw of iron, but she has a policy of sheathing her claws to spare them harm. Even vegetation has its policies: pinecones wait for forest fires to release their seeds; lentils left in a pyramid for thousands of years are simply biding their time until water gives them a political break.

Above and beyond them all, however, there lies the promise of the Peaceable Kingdom — of the City as the Word restores the world to itself, the eschatological Community where the political cunning of every one of God's creatures will be transfigured, not abolished. In Isaiah we read, "The wolf also shall dwell with the lamb, and the leopard shall lie down with the kid; and the calf and the young lion and the fatling together; and a little child shall lead them. And the cow and the bear shall feed; their young ones shall lie down together: and the lion shall eat straw like the ox. And the sucking child shall play on the hole of the asp, and the weaned child shall put his hand on the cockatrice' den. They shall not hurt nor destroy in all my holy mountain: for the earth shall be full of the knowledge of the LORD, as the waters cover the sea" (11:6-9, KJV).

That may sound like an *abolition* of nature, but in fact it's nothing less than the *triumph* of nature through the courtesies of the City: it comes about by the political wisdom of creatures who respect God's paradoxical ecology of opposites. The lion doesn't have to replace his fangs with horse dentures in order to eat straw like the ox; he has only to make a policy decision, for the good of the City, not to use them unwisely in the eschaton. The sucking child will be safe — not because the asp has lost its bite, but because the asp has decided, in the renewed politics of the reconciliation, that the child is as much her family as her own asplets.

But the lion still has lion's teeth, and the asp still has its poison: God's ecology of good and evil, of life and death, arrives at its destination *intact*, not abolished. The earth will be filled with the knowledge of the Lord — with the political know-how by which the Wisdom of God reaches from one end of creation to the other and *fortiter suaviterque*, "mightily and sweetly," orders all things (Wisd. of Sol. 8:1). To repeat myself, the Word of God does *not* take good and evil or life and death as problems to be solved; he takes them as Mysteries to be embraced. And in his human arms, the City — which we have so long tried to build by warfare between those opposites — finally comes back to the peace of the *coincidentia oppositorum* in which the mystery of their ecology was first held.

*　　*　　*

With that, however, we've reached the next verse in the narration of our text. The Hebrew of Genesis 2:9, taken more or less literally, reads as follows: "And the Lord God made to grow [*vayyatsmach*] from the ground [*min-ha'adhamah*] every tree [*kol-'ets*] pleasing to the sight [*nechmad l'mar'eh*] and good to eat [*v'tôb l'ma'akhol*], and the tree of life in the midst of the garden [*v"êts hachayyim b'thok haggan*], and the tree of the knowledge of good and evil [*v'yets hadda'ath tôbh vara'*]."

The Septuagint translates this as "*kai exaneteilen ho theos eti ek tēs gēs* [and God, moreover, raised up out of the earth] *pan xylon hōraion eis horasin kai kalon eis brōsin* [every tree beautiful to the sight and good for food], *kai to xylon tēs zōēs en mesōi tōi paradeisōi* [and the tree of life in mid-paradise] *kai to xylon tou eidenai kalou kai ponērou* [and the tree by which to know good and evil]."

The Vulgate has "*produxitque Dominus Deus de humo* [and the Lord God produced from the soil] *omne lignum pulchrum visu et ad vescendum suave* [every tree beautiful to the sight and sweet for eating] *lignum etiam vitae in medio paradisi* [and also the tree of life in the midst of the paradise] *lignumque scientiae boni et mali* [and the tree of the knowledge of good and evil]." Once again, the English versions have no significant differences for us to consider.

I'm tempted to write a scenario for the filming of all that, but having already given you one at the end of the previous chapter, I won't try your patience with another. I'll only suggest that in her treatment of both this verse and the preceding one, the Director might well have switched from her animated-drawing format to a live actor for the *'adham*, and to onsite photography for the Garden itself. But whatever she's done, it will probably be wise for us to linger a bit here on the production of the trees — and on what must have been the *'adham's* astonishment at the sight of them, his delight in the sweetness of their fruits. Right in the middle of verse 9, we need to give ourselves time to appreciate the *'adham's* liking for the "ordinary" trees of the Garden before we watch him size up the two trees that will be the Director's major plot device all the way to the end of chapter 3, not to mention the rest of her movie of Scripture. So take a pause here, to let the felicity of her filming sink in. . . .

But now, after that moment of silence, it's time to look at the Tree of Life. It will reappear later on at the two defining points of the film: at the death of Jesus, where it will become the Tree of the Cross, and at the consummation, where it will become the Wood, the Arboretum of Life, whose leaves are for the healing of the nations. But here the Director must hope that we'll see some visual connection between it and those two others. I wouldn't expect her to make the connection too obvious, of course: maybe just a preponderance of the color red in the fruits of the Tree of Life to suggest the crucifixion; or maybe twelve different kinds of fruit on the largest tree in the Garden to serve as an anticipation of the end of the movie. But however she might have done it, this Tree, in all its upper-case glory, must spring forth in the very center of the Garden.

This matter of the *size* of the Tree of Life seems crucial to me: it just has to be huge. In the fevered imaginations of many Christians, the tree of the knowledge of good and evil looms so large that it overshadows everything else. Its fascinating, forbidden fruit convinces them that sin was practically inevitable from the start — so much so that they hardly notice two far more important matters. First, only the fruit of the tree of the knowledge of good and evil was forbidden; and second, the *'adham* could "freely eat of all the other trees," including the Tree of Life. In my estimation, then, the tree of the knowledge of good and evil has to appear in as "lower-case" a way as possible: as smaller than the rest of the trees, perhaps, and bearing no fruit that wasn't already on the other trees.

In any case, the point that needs to be made is that our sin of messing up God's ecology of good and evil was *not* the easiest thing in the world to bring off. In fact, in the midst of all the goodness of the Garden, we (in the persons of Adam and Eve) had to take a million-mile mind trip to commit such a sin. After all, when everything around us was just dandy, why would we have bollixed it up by doing something with a single, forbidden tree that we were already allowed to do with any other tree we liked? The sane answer, of course, is that we wouldn't have; but since we long ago lost our right minds, the only adequate answer is that God let us do it for his own mysterious purposes. That's why I opted for a large, gorgeous Tree of Life, and for a tree of the knowledge of good and evil that's nothing more than a bush overshadowed by it. I wanted to make the "temptation" look as untempting as possible; otherwise, we'd turn God's honoring of our freedom into a nasty setup — which, in fact, is exactly what we've done.

In addition, though, we need to imagine the Tree of Life as *including* life and death from the start, since death has already been portrayed as the engine of life in the first part of the movie (on the third, fifth, and sixth days). It must be seen as a sacrament of that same ecology of opposites. I do realize that this wasn't Augustine's view. While he held that man was indeed mortal in his first state, he insisted that the natural mortality of the *'adham* was forestalled by a *donum superadditum*, a gift over and above nature, given to man by his lawful partaking of the Tree of Life. Provided only that we stayed clear of the tree of the knowledge of good and evil, Augustine thought, we would never have experienced death.

Needless to say, very few modern Bible scholars are able to accept that view. Even I shall have to revise it a bit when I come to the other references to the tree of the knowledge of good and evil later in this book. But I think I owe you at least a word here about my eventual revision. The main text in question appears at Genesis 3:1-5. In that passage, the serpent (the father of lies in slinky drag) begins his testing of the woman by asking, "Did God say, 'You shall not eat of any tree of the garden'?" To which Eve replies, "We may eat of the fruit of the trees of the garden; but God said, 'You shall not eat of the fruit of the tree which is in the midst of the garden, neither shall you touch it, lest you die.'" But the serpent says to her, "You will not die. For God knows that when you eat of it your eyes will be opened, and *you will be like God, knowing good and evil*" (RSV). I put those last words in italics because they were the beginning of the lie. They were a nasty hook concealed in a clever half-truth — but I think that the scholars' worrying of the text hid both the hook and the other half of the truth from them. So if I may, I'm going to reformulate the serpent's dialogue with Eve to make clear what I think they've missed. Here goes:

The snake's first question to Eve ("Did God say . . . ?"), is just a rhetorical come-on to lead her astray. He already knows what God said about freely eating of all the trees of the garden. What he's really interested in is seeing if he can get Eve to make a mistake when she repeats what God said. And she does. She takes God's words in Genesis 2:17 ("but of the fruit of the tree of the knowledge of good and evil you shall not eat, for in the day that you eat of it you shall surely die," RFC), and she interprets them as a threat of literal death, right on the spot of the transgression.

But she fails to notice something far more important. The *knowledge* the tree represents is not meant to be a recognition that good is pleasing to God while evil is not, or that God wants never the twain to meet. Rather, it's a knowledge of how to *manage both good and evil at the same time* as God manages them in his ecology of opposites — that is, by *letting each of them be itself.* For when all is said and done, that's in fact the way God runs the world. Despite all the assurances of unscriptural piety, he doesn't manage creation by abolishing evil and allowing only the good to flourish. To be sure, he loves goodness with all his heart, and he reserves his right to bring off the odd intervention here or there to show his championship of it. But he exercises that right only on rare occasions. If you honestly compare the total number of times he puts a goodness-protecting finger into the pie of history with all the times he doesn't (Jesus, for example, may heal a handful of the sick, but he leaves the great majority of the world's afflicted unhelped), you get a proportion that's something like one ameliorated evil in a billion billion billion instances of no *present* amelioration at all.

Now, though, having gotten Eve to misread God as a controller, the snake has her where he wants her. She says, "If I touch the tree, I'll die"; and he, knowing that God never meant anything as un-mysterious as that, quite correctly replies, "You will not die" — which of course she does not. Then, however, he unleashes the Big Lie. If I may paraphrase him for you, he says, "For God knows that when you decide to choose *between* good and evil, your eyes will be opened, and you will be like God, *controlling* good and evil."

That was the Great Prevarication, because choosing only good and putting the arm on every instance of evil is precisely what God does not do. In Jesus on the Tree of the Cross, we see the ultimate revelation of the modus operandi that God first revealed at the tree of the knowledge of good and evil: he takes the evil of the world into himself, restores its ecology with the good, and then takes the whole shooting match home to his Father.

In the Director's overall view of her film, of course, the serpent knows all that. So if I may give him, like members of Congress, the privilege of revising and extending his remarks, he goes on to say, *sotto voce,* "Actually, my dear girl, what will happen is that you, who were made in the image of God, will end up re-creating God in your own image — after which, you'll have to invent the strictures of religion to deal with the ungodly monster you've made. And that, honey, is what I had in mind all along. On my test, therefore, you get an 'A'; on God's, unfortunately, you get an 'F.' So three cheers for me: I've gotten you addicted to something God never wanted you to touch at all."

But enough of the old deceiver. There was no religion in Eden to begin with; and at the end, there will be no religion in the New Jerusalem. But in the meanwhile, religion has been our cup of poisoned tea. Our first, dead-earnest taste of it came as soon as Adam and Eve left the Garden — the quarrel between Cain and Abel was over whose religion the God they'd manufactured liked best. And the same hassle has been our meat and drink ever since. It's given us all the religious wars of history (dare I say *all* wars, period?); and it's been the story of every argument over who's right and who's wrong in every corner of creation: in every marriage, in every friendship, in every business, and in every vendetta. It certainly hasn't been a pretty story; but it's been *our history,* and but for the grace of the true God, we've been stuck in it.

"But for the grace of God": religion may have been deadly for us from the moment we invented it, but the Incarnation that brought us "grace upon grace" (John 1:16) has always been the death of religion. Although we've spent two thousand years insisting that Jesus is the founder of a new religion called Christianity, and that the Gospels are religious documents, none of that was ever true. Religion is bad news, not Good News. It enslaves us to the impossible notion that there's something we must do in order to find favor with God. But Paul, in Romans 5:8, put that to rest once and for all: "While we were *still sinners,* Christ died for us." God never sat up in heaven waiting for us to straighten up our act; he was always Incarnate in the world, restoring us to the religionless innocence of Eden in which the *'adham* was made the first sacrament of Christ. Everything that religion ever tried (and failed) to do has been perpetually done in the Person of the Incarnate Word — of the Alpha and Omega who is the Beginning and the Ending of our history. The world was always all right in him, even when it was all wrong in our hands. It was sweet before, during, and after every one of our efforts to turn it sour.

The Word who becomes flesh and dwells among us is the uncreated Light who said "Let there be light" in Genesis 1:3. In John 1:9 that same Word is the true Light who, at his coming into the world from the beginning, lightens every man. That light shines backward over every scrap of our dismal history. And it shines forward to the reconciliation of history: in Revelation 21:23, in the New Jerusalem, he reveals himself one last time as the Light of the renewed world: "And the City has no need of the sun or of the moon to shine on it, for the glory of God lights it up and its Lamp is the Lamb" (RFC). The Light of the Word, in short, was never not here.

Every now and then I come across people who ask whether there might not be (or once have been) other Incarnations than the one finally revealed in Jesus of Nazareth. They seem to think that an Incarnation of the Word next year in a man from Scranton, or three centuries ago in a woman from Beijing, or yesterday in a child from Mozambique would better serve the interests of divine Inclusiveness. But I always tell them that if only they could see the Incarnation as something true of the whole world from the Beginning — and not as an insertion of the Word at a specific time and place — their thirst for inclusivity would be completely quenched. The Person who meets us in Jesus is already the Person by whom all things are made and held in being. There's no need of multiple lamps or candles to lighten the world's darkness; the one Light who is the Word can enlighten everyone to whom he's already intimately and immediately present. In one shot, he does the job better than all the birthday candles the world could ever light.

To sum it up, the trouble with plural incarnations is that they turn God's relationship with the world into a game of tag. When I played tag as a boy in Queens, my friends and I had a quasi-religious maneuver we called "electricity" to help our playmates. One of us would put a hand on the "home base" phone pole and stretch out his other hand. The next one would hold that hand, and the rest would do likewise, making a long chain of players that would shorten the distance that the one being chased had to run. Then we would all shout, "'Lectricity!" — and if the last player being pursued by the one who was "it" touched the chain soon enough, he'd be saved from the fate of being the next "it."

That, it seems to me, is exactly how God does *not* deal with the world in the Incarnation — even though, alas, it's very much the way we've preached it for far too long. We've acted as if people had to make some connection of their own with Jesus before they could have the benefit of his salvation, and we've made the church into the "'lectricity" chain that hooks them up to him. But the Good News of the Gospel is that no such religious shenanigans are necessary. God has already (and from the Beginning) brought everyone "home" in his Word: he's taken away the sins of the *world*, not just the sins of the cooperative, or the repentant, or even the faithful. We're saved by grace, not works. True enough, Ephesians 2:8 says, "You are saved by grace through faith"; but it adds, "and this is not of your doing; it's the gift of God" (RFC). Your act of believing is in no way the cause of the grace that saves you; it simply enables your enjoyment of the safety you already have in the grace of the Incarnate Word.

Indeed, you could spend your whole life grunting and groaning your faith in God's promise of grace; but if he hadn't delivered on that promise in the first place, your faith wouldn't do a thing for you. Faith is not a gadget for saving yourself; it's just *trust* in the Incarnate Word himself. If you have it, you're safe. If you lose it, you're safe. And if you never had it at all, you're still safe. The Word is not a phone pole you need to touch; he's the root and ground of your being — and no matter what you do, you can never lose him.

*   *   *

Let me go back to my notes and finish this chapter with a couple of items I haven't yet given enough breathing room.

The Tree of Life and the tree of the knowledge of good and evil are best seen as another instance of hendiadys — of saying one thing by means of two. The "one thing" is that both of them are about the ecology of good and evil. Admittedly, that ecology isn't mentioned in connection with the Tree of Life; but since the Director has already showed us death as the engine of life in chapter 1 of Genesis, I felt free to imagine some blood-red fruits on that Tree to remind you that it stands for the ecology of life and death. The tree of the knowledge of good and evil, however, clearly stands for the coinciding of those opposites in the Mind of God. Taking the two trees together, then, I think it's fair to say that they represent not only a single planting by God but even, perhaps, a single tree with a double meaning.

And *there's* the hendiadys: one thing (the ecology of opposites) presented by means of two different possibilities for managing that ecology (by God's hands-off management of good and evil, and by our own hands-on efforts to control them). But they're still one planting; and when the Director finally brings both of them to fulfillment, she'll do so by making them into a single tree: first, into the Tree of the Cross, on which the mistake at the tree of the knowledge of good and evil is undone; and second, into the Wood of Life in the midst of the City, where the Tree of Life returns as the centerpiece of the New Jerusalem. (If you already understood all that, I apologize for the repetition; if you didn't, I hope you now have at least an inkling.)

The other item addresses the question of whether all this "tree business" that the Director puts so prominently into her movie is historical or non-historical. The usual modern answer is to say that it's not history but myth; but that won't work because history is something we make — and myth can be just as good a tool for the job as "historically" verifiable events. A moving picture like the Bible can propel its story line by fictions as well as by facts; all you need to remember is that either way, the Director will be able to illuminate our own history by the history of her characters. And that's what she does here in Genesis. Not only does she set before us the unhappy crisis-management that's given us what we brazenly call the "real world"; she also gives us a glimpse of the divine Management by which reality is actually run. In short, she shows us both sides of our history — its successes and its failures — as they are.

However, since the failures are yet to come in her movie, let me say a kind word about the evolution of species as one of the successes of God's hands-off management. I have no doubt that the war between science and religion, or between theology and evolution, is still going strong. But it was always a stupid war, based on the empirically false assumption that God acts in a direct, hands-on way when he creates. But he doesn't. He doesn't *make* the species evolve; he *lets them* evolve. Luther said that redemption is God's *opus alienum,* his "strange work," the work of God's "left hand." But his act of creation is a left-handed piece of business as well. It bursts forth as a rhapsody of divine Permission in which everything is free (within the limits of its nature) to do anything it has the luck to get a chance at. And the most wonderful thing about evolution is that it shows there's no ecology-destroying conflict between chance and design. As I've said before, chance *is* the design: under God's management by the luck of the draw, all luck is holy. And that truth is precisely what evolution gives us: the mystery by which a world that has the bad luck to be running downhill to absolute zero can also have the good luck to run uphill at the same time.

And that Mystery applies to us individually as well. Even in our sins — even in the thick of our mismanagement of good and evil — we've been able to achieve a considerable degree of civilization. Not enough, of course, to turn the world into the City of God by our own efforts; but enough to convince ourselves of two things. One, that for as long as we can remember, we haven't gotten there yet; and two, that it remains the only place worth going. But if we take seriously my favorite evolutionist, Teilhard de Chardin, we're still being inexorably drawn there. The Word Incarnate, who is the Omega Point of our history, has always been drawing all things to himself (John 12:32). He will never *force* us to get to that Point; but, by the same token, neither will he ever stop *attracting* us to it.

*   *   *

Meanwhile, though, the City still leads us on. In the words of Peter Abelard's hymn to the heavenly Jerusalem, *O quanta qualia,*

Nostrum est interim mentem erigere,
et totis patriam votis appetere,
et ad Jerusalem a Babylonia
post longa regredi tandem exsilia.

Here's a fairly literal, line-by-line translation of that — without Abelard's rhyme scheme, but with a stab at his original meter:

Our task in the meanwhile is to lift up our mind,
and to long for that country in all of our prayers,
and then to Jerusalem from Babylonia
after long exile at last to return.

Or, if you'd like to see what a real poet did with it, here's John Mason Neale's translation:

Now in the meanwhile with hearts raised on high,
we for that country must yearn and must sigh,
seeking Jerusalem, dear native land,
through our long exile on Babylon's strand.

But, as Monty Python used to say, now for something completely different.

SIXTEEN

Detour

For one short chapter, I'm going to interrupt my progress to answer a question you may have about my method. While I've obviously been trying to proceed in a straight line through the verses of Genesis 2, you've no doubt noticed that my comments on them have been less than linear. This was especially clear in the preceding chapter when I was dealing with the Tree of Life. In the midst of my comments, I fell back to the ecology of life and death as it appeared on the third, fifth, and sixth days of Genesis 1 — and then I immediately sprang ahead to the Tree of the Cross in the Gospels and the Wood of Life in the book of Revelation. Moreover, when I commented on the tree of the knowledge of good and evil, I plunged at some length into the serpent's dialogue with Eve, which won't occur until Genesis 3. You may have felt, therefore, that I was cheating on my principle that the Director's movie of creation should be re-viewed only after we've seen the whole picture. Instead of having me as a silent partner in the theater of your mind, you found yourself sitting next to a pest who insisted on reminding you of scenes you remembered perfectly well, or on spoiling future ones by giving them away too soon.

You have a point. But rather than argue it, let me drop my image of the Bible as a film for this chapter and give you two completely different ones: the waxing of a car; and the harpsichord I've been building, on and (mostly) off, for the past sixteen years.

*   *   *

When you polish your car, you don't first wax the whole vehicle front to back and then make a second trip to buff it up. You wax and buff one section at a time, and you're free to deal with those sections in any order that strikes your fancy. Most people start with the engine hood because it's easier; but if you want to begin at the rear end of the car and work your way to the front, who's to stop you? The car's original finish (pun intended) is already under your hands no matter where you begin; and the beginning of the manufacturer's creation of it is just as present to you as the end. Therefore, a *linear* approach to the job on your part is fundamentally irrelevant. And so it is with the Bible: the order (or disorder) of your polishing makes no difference because, wherever you wax, you're highlighting something that's already there.

But there's more to the image than that. The experts who wrote the instructions on the can of polish all agree that while you're progressing, you shouldn't use *longitudinal* strokes of the waxing pad. Instead, they tell you to use a *circular* motion: round and round and round, carefully repeating yourself till you've covered the whole section. And they make that suggestion because going in circles is more likely to prevent "holidays" in your application of the wax. So too with the car of Scripture: its finish is best enhanced by preachers who apply the carnauba of their comments on it by making them over and over, not by taking a single pass and letting it go at that.

In any case, what I've been doing in this book is very much the same thing. I've been trying to restore the original shine of the Bible, taking care that no spot fails to get a generous coat of its concordances with other spots. So I'll admit that I've dealt with some parts of the biblical car out of sequence. Earlier, I polished the hood over its engine (creation in the Mind of God, Genesis 1). But when I reached the roof over its passenger compartment in Genesis 2 (where the *'adham* sits for his trip into the City of the Garden), I couldn't resist taking you back for a look at the work I'd done on the engine hood. Likewise, in the midst of polishing the roof, I took you forward for a glimpse of the shine I want to put on the trunk lid (the book of Revelation) under which the City will ultimately be stowed.

I suppose I got this habit of leaping around in Scripture from Augustine: he was never afraid to buff up a passage he'd previously polished while he was working on a later one, and he was equally fearless about shining a future passage in the midst of a present one. But I think the main reason his mind flitted about so easily was his inveterate love of teaching. A good teacher is always convinced that his students will get more out of hearing him say something again and again than they would out of trying to follow the logic of a linear argument. Augustine doesn't give us the beginning of the story only at the beginning and the end only at the end; he continually gives us both everywhere.

I agree with his approach entirely. So as you watch me polish the biblical car, be patient with my repetitious circling. I've been doing it that way for ages, and I don't intend to stop now. In the fifty-three years I've been preaching, I've kept harping on the Good News that Jesus takes away the sins of the whole world — and that the "whole world" includes absolutely everybody. Some people wince when I hammer that home with a list of folks they'd just as soon not look at forever (Osama Bin Laden, Adolf Hitler, Vlad the Impaler, and their brother-in-law); but at least I've faithfully applied the Gospel wax. Sooner or later, they may even help me buff it up.

But since I'm a teacher at heart — and since the Bible's teaching is far less plausible than many of my students think it is — I have no more fear of reiterating its mysteries than Augustine did. Now, though, let me give you my other illustration, which will become an image for the finish the Holy Spirit applied to the Bible. As promised, it will be based on the two-manual harpsichord that sits in my basement, four-fifths completed. The history of my relationship with it bears repeating.

*   *   *

True to form for an amateur enthusiast, I began work on it in 1986 and went at it hammer and plane, chisel and sandpaper, brush and paint for two years. But then (man proposes, God disposes), a series of intrusions hampered my progress. In 1988, my landlord on Shelter Island wanted his house back, so my wife Valerie and I had to move everything — dolls, dishes, four floors' worth of furniture that my mother had since 1923, and the harpsichord — to East Hampton, where I was working as an assistant priest. By 1990, the work of painting the instrument was done, and I was ready to get back to the "musical" part of the project. But in that year I had a major retinal detachment in my left eye. It derailed me for months; and since I already had a profusion of "floaters" in the same eye, having to do one-eyed stringing and voicing turned out to be more than I could handle.

At the end of 1993, through a combination of smoke, mirrors, and financial fudging, we managed to finagle a mortgage on a house of our own on Shelter Island — necessitating a move back in the nasty winter of '94 and a fair amount of home carpentry on my part. But, to add insult to injury, from 1990 to the present I've also had to put the vintage Studebaker of my body in the shop for a series of repairs: emergency surgery on a strangulated colon, a less-than-satisfactory cataract operation on the already bad eye, and the mending of two hernias. All in all, between the time I've spent on the hospital lift, and the time I've spent writing, lecturing, and putting in three half-days a week as supply priest at a small parish, I haven't been able to do any more work on the harpsichord. Everyone who sees it admires its gorgeous, hand-rubbed finish, but not a note can be played on it.

I apologize for boring you with medical and occupational excuses, but at least they've brought me to the nub of my second illustration: the paint job that Valerie and I did on the instrument so long ago. We began our work with two coats of filler, sanded them down, and then applied three coats of Chinese Red enamel, each carefully rubbed flat. Then came the task of applying about eleven coats of varnish that had been tinted with Alizarin Crimson and lots of dark wood stain to produce the look of a black cherry lacquer box. (Valerie made all the color decisions: in addition to my other infirmities, I'm slightly color-blind when it comes to red and green.) We rubbed the earlier coats of varnish down to the Chinese Red in varying degrees and at random places, and then continued the process until we'd produced a richly colored and subtly patterned surface. The final touch consisted of three coats of un-tinted clear varnish, each rubbed to a high polish with pumice and rottenstone. At several points since then, we were about to wax our pride and joy; but the changes and chances of this mortal life kept interfering with our plans. As you can see, though, we do know something about what goes into the production of a fine finish.

I can't now recall the order in which we tackled our painting, sanding, and rubbing, but I do remember two things: from one coat to the next, we seldom tackled the work in the same linear order; and we spent a lot of time going in circles over the surfaces of the harpsichord. And there is the analogy I'm after: my harpsichord as an image of the Spirit's creation of the "factory finish" of the Bible. If it wasn't necessary for her first "Valeries" (the actual writers of Scripture) to understand the mysteries of her circling hand, neither do you or I need to fathom them. All we have to do is follow her methods. The goal of our polishing must always be to bring out the strange and fascinating colors of her work, not to obscure them with an overlay we find easier to look at. Scripture has a communicable beauty; we should try our best to catch its glorious contagion.

*   *   *

Thank you for following me through this detour of circular images. Now, though, it's time to get back to my main one: the movie of God's original Garden Party.

SEVENTEEN

The River, the Watering of the World, and the Tree of the Knowledge of Good and Evil

GENESIS 2:10-17

Let's begin by going straight to the text — Genesis 2:10-14, on the River that flowed out of the Garden — for the first part of this chapter. First, then, the full text:

LXX Gen. 2:10 ποταμὸς δὲ ἐκπορεύεται ἐξ Εδεμ ποτίζειν τὸν παράδεισον ἐκεῖθεν ἀφορίζεται εἰς τέσσαρας ἀρχάς 11 ὄνομα τῷ ἑνὶ Φισων οὗτος ὁ κυκλῶν πᾶσαν τὴν γῆν Ευιλατ ἐκεῖ οὗ ἐστιν τὸ χρυσίον 12 τὸ δὲ χρυσίον τῆς γῆς ἐκείνης καλόν καὶ ἐκεῖ ἐστιν ὁ ἄνθραξ καὶ ὁ λίθος ὁ πράσινος 13 καὶ ὄνομα τῷ ποταμῷ τῷ δευτέρῳ Γηων οὗτος ὁ κυκλῶν πᾶσαν τὴν γῆν Αἰθιοπίας 14 καὶ ὁ ποταμὸς ὁ τρίτος Τίγρις οὗτος ὁ πορευόμενος κατέναντι Ἀσσυρίων ὁ δὲ ποταμὸς ὁ τέταρτος οὗτος Εὐφράτης

וְנָהָר יֹצֵא מֵעֵדֶן BHS Gen. 2:10 לְהַשְׁקוֹת אֶת־הַגָּן וּמִשָּׁם יִפָּרֵד וְהָיָה לְאַרְבָּעָה רָאשִׁים: 11 שֵׁם הָאֶחָד פִּישׁוֹן הוּא הַסֹּבֵב אֵת כָּל־אֶרֶץ הַחֲוִילָה אֲשֶׁר־שָׁם הַזָּהָב: 12 וּזֲהַב הָאָרֶץ הַהִוא טוֹב שָׁם הַבְּדֹלַח וְאֶבֶן הַשֹּׁהַם: 13 וְשֵׁם־הַנָּהָר הַשֵּׁנִי גִּיחוֹן הוּא הַסּוֹבֵב אֵת כָּל־אֶרֶץ כּוּשׁ: 14 וְשֵׁם הַנָּהָר הַשְּׁלִישִׁי חִדֶּקֶל הוּא הַהֹלֵךְ קִדְמַת אַשּׁוּר וְהַנָּהָר הָרְבִיעִי הוּא פְרָת:

VUL Gen. 2:10 et fluvius egrediebatur de loco volup-tatis ad irrigandum para-disum qui inde dividitur in quattuor capita 11 nomen uni Phison ipse est qui cir-cuit omnem terram Evilat ubi nascitur aurum 12 et aurum terrae illius opti-mum est ibique invenitur bdellium et lapis onychinus 13 et nomen fluvio secundo Geon ipse est qui circuit omnem terram Aethiopiae 14 nomen vero fluminis tertii Tigris ipse vadit con-tra Assyrios fluvius autem quartus ipse est Eufrates

KJV Gen. 2:10 And a river went out of Eden to water the garden; and from thence it was parted, and became into four heads. 11 The name of the first is Pison: that is it which compasseth the whole land of Havilah, where there is gold; 12 And the gold of that land is good: there is bdellium and the onyx stone. 13 And the name of the second river is Gihon: the same is it that compasseth the whole land of Ethiopia. 14 And the name of the third river is Hiddekel: that is it which goeth toward the east of Assyria. And the fourth river is Euphrates.

RSV Gen. 2:10 A river flowed out of Eden to water the garden, and there it divided and became four rivers. 11 The name of the first is Pishon; it is the one which flows around the whole land of Havilah, where there is gold; 12 and the gold of that land is good; bdellium and onyx stone are there. 13 The name of the second river is Gihon; it is the one which flows around the whole land of Cush. 14 And the name of the third river is Tigris, which flows east of Assyria. And the fourth river is the Euphrates.

NRSV Gen. 2:10 A river flows out of Eden to water the garden, and from there it divides and becomes four branches. 11 The name of the first is Pishon; it is the one that flows around the whole land of Havilah, where there is gold; 12 and the gold of that land is good; bdellium and onyx stone are there. 13 The name of the second river is Gihon; it is the one that flows around the whole land of Cush. 14 The name of the third river is Tigris, which flows east of Assyria. And the fourth river is the Euphrates.

Since I plan to deal with the Director's image of the River at some length, I'm going to leave its four branches till later and limit myself to verse 10 for now. The Hebrew reads, "And a river [v'nahar] went out [yôtse'] from Eden [me'edhen] to water the garden [l'hashqôth 'eth-haggan], and from there [ûmishsham] it was divided [yippârêdh] and became four headwaters [v'hayah l'arba'ah ro'shim]" — the last two words are literally "into four heads." The Septuagint has much the same thing: "A river [potamos] went out [ekporeuetai] of Eden [ex Edem] to water [potizein] the garden [ton paradeison]; from there [ekeithen] it was divided [aphorizetai] into four heads [eis tessaras archas]" — the last word is literally "beginnings." In the Vulgate, however, Jerome follows his previous renderings of salient words: "And a river [fluvius] went out [egrediebatur] of the place of pleasure [de loco voluptatis] to water [ad irrigandum] the paradise [paradisum] which from there [qui inde] was divided [dividitur] into four heads [in quattuor capita]." The English versions all follow the Hebrew quite closely, with only minor differences: in verse 10, the KJV has "four heads," the RSV, "four rivers," and the NRSV, "four branches."

In the spirit of Augustine, my opening comments on this verse will be about the Director's image of the River, and the assorted water-balloons she

236

juggles along with it, as they bounce their way through her entire movie. To alert you to them, I'll capitalize the Rivers and italicize the balloons.

Looking backward over what we've seen so far, we notice that *water* has already been the Director's major image in part one of her film. On day one, darkness is on the face of the *deep,* and the Spirit of God broods on the face of the *waters.* On the second day, God makes a firmament in the midst of the *waters* and divides the *waters* under the firmament from the *waters* above it, and he calls the firmament heavens. On the third day, the *waters* under the heavens are gathered together into one place, and the dry land appears, and God calls the dry land Earth, and the gathering together of the *waters* he calls *Seas.* On the fourth day, no *waters* are mentioned, but the sun, moon, and stars are *in* the firmament of the heavens — thus putting them in the remarkable position of being *under the waters* above the firmament. (Indeed, Augustine was bold enough to read those *"waters above"* as the angelic orders of creation who exist in God's own heaven of heavens beyond all times, places, and things.) On the fifth day, the denizens of the *deep* and the birds who *swim* in the air are created. And finally, on the sixth day, while no *water* is specifically mentioned, the animals that are made and the human beings who are created, male and female, are far and away mostly *water.* As you can see, the Director's first account of creation in the Mind of God richly deserves the title of the "wet version."

By contrast, if we look straight ahead at her second version that's now on our screen, we'll find it doesn't deserve to be called, as it sometimes is, the "dry account." To be sure, her film of this sequence does begin with a dusty, unwatered earth; but things don't stay that way for long. First, she brings up a *mist,* or *stream,* or *fountain* to *water* the whole face of the ground; second, she has God form the 'adham from the resultant *mud;* third, she promptly puts the man into a Garden that will need *watering;* and finally, as if that weren't enough *wetness* for one short scene, she sends the whole subject upstairs and introduces a River that will *water* the entire earth.

But if we now look forward to the rest of her movie, we'll find that it wasn't enough for her. She'll give us *waters* upon *waters* in all their guises. In the Joseph stories (Gen. 37–50), she'll take the Jews to Egypt because the Nile has kept it fertile in the midst of a worldwide drought; and when things go badly for them there, she'll put the baby Moses in a basket and set him adrift in the same *river* so he can live and become the savior of his people. (Pharaoh's daughter names him "Moses" because she "drew him out of the *water*"; Exod. 2:1-10.)

And on and on she goes. She has the *rivers* of Egypt turn to *blood* during the plagues (Exod. 7:19-25); she makes the *blood* of the Paschal Lamb a sacrament of life out of death for the people of Israel (Exod. 12); after the Passover, she makes the parting of the *waters* of the Red Sea into an image of the same redemption (Exod. 14–15); she shows us *streams* flowing in the desert when Moses strikes the rock in the wilderness (Exod. 17); she has Joshua lead the people across the River Jordan on dry ground (Josh. 3); she has Elijah cross the Jordan by smiting its *waters* with his cloak, and she makes Elisha recross it by the same device after he's become Elijah's successor (2 Kings 2). And as a bridge to her New Testament scenes yet to come, she inspires the Psalmist to include in Psalm 46:4, "There is a River whose *streams* make glad the city of God" (RSV, italics mine) — thus foreshadowing the Pentecostal gift of the Holy Spirit.

But even before she gets that far, she begins her climactic rhapsody on the *waters* as sacraments of Christ. She shows us Jesus being *baptized* in the Jordan (Mark 1); she films the dialogue between Jesus and the Samaritan woman at the *well*, where he says, "Whoever drinks of the *water* that I will give him will not thirst forever" (John 4:14, RFC, here and throughout paragraph); and in John 7:38, she has him say (of the Spirit whom the believers in him are about to receive), "The one who believes in me, as the Scripture says [Prov. 18:4; Isa. 58:11], '*rivers* of living *water* will flow out of his belly.'" Then she returns to the images of *blood* and *water* in the piercing of Christ's side at the crucifixion (John 19:34). And at the end, she makes John the Divine give him a voice like the voice of many *waters* (Rev. 1:15), she has the glorified Jesus promise that he will freely give to the thirsty from the *spring* of the *water* of life (Rev. 21:6), and she wraps it all up by bringing back both the River and the Tree of Life. In the midst of the plaza of the City and on either side of the River of the *water* of Life, there is now the Wood of Life: the Tree has been *watered* into a great Forest, the Garden has returned as the ultimate Park, and the River has become the emblem of eternal Life for the world (Rev. 22:2).

It may have taken me five paragraphs to splash all those fluids around, but they're still only a sprinkling of what the Director has given us. Be that as it may, I'm now ready to give you my own thoughts about the River presently before us.

*   *   *

The rivers of the earth empty into the sea, and the sea is the source of all life. Living creatures first appear in the waters of the deep, and when our precursors emerge onto dry land, those waters provide them with lifelong nourishment. Evaporation and condensation send their roots rain, the rain runs back into the rivers, the rivers overflow their banks, their flood plains and deltas become fertile fields, and when we appear, we live off the fat of those lands, chin-deep in water from start to finish. We spend nine months in the womb surrounded by amniotic fluid; the breaking of that water signals our debut in the world; our life in faith begins in the waters of Baptism (some churches even keep holy water near the front door so the faithful can remind themselves of that Mystery); and at the end of our days we go to our rest — if you'll allow me an extravagance — under a heavier rain of earth and stones, to await our ultimate watering by the River of Life in the New Jerusalem.

But the world's rivers also have another function: they're the *arteries* of creation's economic life. We've floated our goods and services down them for as long as we've been human — and it's our riding of their floods that brings me to my principal comment on the River that went out of Eden: it has both a *centrifugal* and a *centripetal* force. In its centrifugal motion, it flows away from the Garden to water the earth, becoming the main artery of the world's economy; and in its centripetal motion, it carries all the freight of our economic occupations back to that same Garden in the New Jerusalem. The River of Eden, if you will, is the Director's way of imaging for us the deepest truth of our being: as Augustine put it in his prayer to God, "You made us for yourself, and our hearts are restless till they rest in you." In *returning* and *rest* we shall be saved: economics is the paradigm of our journey back to God.

The word *economy* is from the Greek *oikonomia*. Literally, it means the "law" *(nomos)* of creation's "housekeeping" (*oikos* is "house"); but, by extension, it refers to all the legitimate ways the world *plays house*. Please don't overlook that word *legitimate*. We must never forget that in chapter 2 of Genesis — in the un-fallen condition of our first parents — everything that happens is lawful and right. Nothing has as yet gone wrong; "economics" still has a good name. However rudimentary the commercial activities of the first human beings may have been (a little hunting here, a bit of gardening there), they were all about "dressing and keeping" the Garden of the world.

Still more importantly, the New Testament applies the word *oikonomia* to the house-keeping, the "economies" of the three Persons of the Trinity in their own commercial relationships with the world. This is not as clear as it might be in our English versions, having been obscured by varying (and unfortunate) translations. In the Pauline letters, for example, the *oikonomia* of God is sometimes tied more closely to Paul than to God. In Ephesians 3:2, for instance, the KJV translates *oikonomia* as "the *dispensation* of the grace of God which is given me" — implying that it's more about Paul's business activities than God's. The RSV does better in Ephesians 3:9, where it renders the word as "the *plan* of the mystery hidden for ages in God who created all things."

Accordingly, if I were translating Paul's letters, I would use the word *economy* every time *oikonomia* appears. In Colossians 1:24-26, for instance, I'd keep all my theological options open and read it as ". . . of the church, of which I became a servant according to *the economy* of God given to me for you, to fulfill the Word of God — that is, the *mystery* hidden from the ages and the generations but now made manifest to his saints." In other words, I'd try to tie the River on which the world's economy rides as closely as possible to the mysterious Current flowing from and to God himself.

Hence the twofold significance that the Director has given the River. Its centrifugal, *outbound* flow is the Current of the Holy Spirit who first brooded over the face of the waters, and its centripetal, *return* flow is the Current by which the Incarnate Word of God draws the world back to the right hand of the Father. In formal theology these are referred to as the divine *Economies* of the Persons of the Trinity. The Economy of the Father as the Fountain of Divinity is to *think up* the whole of creation in his eternal Mind (Gen. 1:1). The Economy of the Son as the Father's Word by whom all things are made (John 1:3) is to *make creation exist* in its own right and to *draw it back* to the Father (John 12:32). And the Economy of the Spirit as the Breath proceeding from the Father and the Son is to *inbreathe* creation with life (Gen. 1:2) and to *take* what belongs to the Son and *proclaim* it to the world (John 16:14).

In addition to this world-oriented, "economic" view of the Trinity, however, theologians also speak of an "essential" view that looks only at the relationships between the three Persons themselves in what are called the "processions" of the Trinity. In that light, the role of the Father is to be the unbegotten Source of Deity who "generates" the Son by an eternal "begetting." The role of the Son is to "be begotten" of the Father: it's his "filiation," his status as the only-begotten Son of the Father before all worlds. And the role of the Spirit, the *amor mutuus,* the "mutual love" of the three Persons, is precisely to be "breathed forth" — or, as theologians put it, to be "spirated" by the Father and the Son. (I could apologize for all the theological jargon, but I won't: I just love it.)

To sum it up, then, creation lives by an invisible stream of Knowledge and Love that runs between and from and to the Three-in-One. We've been bobbing along in the River of their economies from all eternity, and at no moment of our history will we ever escape it. No one can swim against the current of the divine Mississippi. We have no choice about being carried into the divine Ocean. Willy-nilly, we'll all reach it; the most we can do is complain forever about the unavoidable trip home. And just in case you were itching for me to say there is a hell after all, there you have my vision of it: a perpetual, upstream struggle against the Love that will not let us go.

Meanwhile, though, the River flowing out of Eden bears along all the economies of the world itself. Commerce, manufacture, the stock market are buoyed up by it — as is even the airline industry so recently in the doldrums. The air of the skies has its currents as well, and if we ever achieve economically feasible space travel, we'll still be going with a flow of our goods and services. Economics may have come by its reputation as the "dismal science" because economists seldom agree on much. But if we see that science under the image of the River, we won't find it dismal at all: rather than being a study of how to make a buck off each other, it will become a sacrament of the divine Current that takes the world home.

Our inveterate love of doing business, therefore, has its roots in the River of Eden — but not in any literalistic sense that would require me to "verify" the historical existence of that River. The history that the Bible gives us is no mere recitation of verifiable past events; rather, the Bible "makes history" for us by impregnating even unverifiable events with sacramental significance. I no more want to make Genesis 2 into a literal account of the first businessman on earth than I want to turn Genesis 3 into a simple depiction of a crime once committed by the first couple. Both accounts are far too deeply historical for that. The Man, the Garden, the Two Trees, the River, the Animals, the Woman, and the Marriage in chapter 2 are all images of the housekeeping successes of our race — just as the Serpent, the Disobedience, the Curses, and the Expulsion from the Garden are images of our failures. And both those successes and those failures are *simultaneously* present in every moment of our history.

At its deepest, then, nothing here is merely sequential. The Director is not telling us that we were once good, then later turned bad — and now, if we're lucky, might work our own way back to goodness again. She's telling us that we've always been all three at once. And in the fourth chapter of Genesis, God affirms his mysterious tolerance of that strange triplicity. The first thing he does after he evicts Adam and Eve from the Garden is to station the Cherubim and a Flaming Sword between them and the Garden to guard the way of the Tree of Life. That is indeed a warning that we can never go back to innocence by our own devices — and that we can only go forward into the mess we've made. But on the basis of the rest of the Bible, it's also a promise that he will follow us into the mess. Its messiness won't matter to his ecology of good and evil because he himself, in his Incarnate Word, will always be making all things right, even in the midst of our making them wrong: "While we were still sinners, Christ died for us." For him to do anything less — for him to wait until we'd straightened up our own history before reconciling us to himself — would be to renege on his Rainbow promise to Noah. It would make him a literalist stuck in his own simplicities rather than the Master of mysterious images he always is.

Now, though, at the end of verse 10, we come to the four rivers into which the River of Eden was divided. But instead of doing a line-by-line study of the words in verses 11-14, I'll just go directly to what I think the Director has in mind when she includes geographical specifics about the rivers she mentions in her film. Her main purpose, of course, is to extend her imagery of the Garden to cover the whole earth. In a sense, she's had only marginal success in achieving that objective. Too many viewers of her film have either exhausted themselves with efforts to puzzle out which actual rivers of the earth she had in mind, or else they've given up and ignored her imagery completely.

The first river, the Pishon, gets the most exposure. It flows around the whole land of Havilah, a district referred to elsewhere in the Bible as in the vicinity of Arabia. Here, however, the "whole land" seems to indicate an even larger region (possibly including India), in which case, the Director's scriptwriters may have assumed she was thinking about the Ganges or the Indus. But whatever they thought, it seems to me more likely that she's definitely trying to accentuate the *economic* implications of its wide-ranging flow. Her mention of *gold* clearly suggests *commerce*, bringing up the subjects of money and trade; and her references to *bdellium* (a gum resin used in the making of incense and perfumes, and as a topical medicine) and to the *onyx stone* (used in the manufacture of cameos — a luxury if ever there was one) just as plainly signify the same thing.

The Gihon, which flows around the "whole land of Cush" (Ethiopia?) has sometimes been identified as the Nile. But since the least unlikely "location" for the Garden of Eden seems to be somewhere north of Palestine, the fact that the Nile rises in Africa would seem to rule it out as an identification for the Gihon. The Tigris and the Euphrates, however, are hardly problems at all. Both rise in what is now the vicinity of Armenia, and both flow southeast, coming as close to each other as thirty-five miles near the present city of Baghdad before going their separate ways toward the Persian Gulf.

However inconclusive the geography of the four rivers may seem to us, the Director is unfazed by it. What she wants us to see in her movie is as plain as day to anyone but a diehard literalist — namely, that the River flows out of Eden to water every part of the world. She's not as interested in the physical details of its four branches as she is in the cinematic continuity that the image of its waters will provide for her film. And when she reaches its ending in the New Jerusalem, she will have rolled everything I've mentioned in this chapter — all the waters, all the lives they support, all the freight they carry, all the economies of the world they make possible, and even the three divine Economies that make its economics possible in the first place — into the River of Life itself. As in every great film, we'll see that she's had all of those images in mind, even before her opening credits began to roll.

* * *

However, having given us that quick trip around the world of getting and gaining that's so very much with us, the Director now seems eager to get back to the Garden and the *'adham* she put in it. First, then, the remainder of her shooting script for this chapter:

LXX Gen. 2:15 καὶ ἔλαβεν κύριος ὁ θεὸς τὸν ἄνθρωπον ὃν ἔπλασεν καὶ ἔθετο αὐτὸν ἐν τῷ παραδείσῳ ἐργάζεσθαι αὐτὸν καὶ φυλάσσειν 16 καὶ ἐνετείλατο κύριος ὁ θεὸς τῷ Αδαμ λέγων ἀπὸ παντὸς ξύλου τοῦ ἐν τῷ παραδείσῳ βρώσει φάγῃ 17 ἀπὸ δὲ τοῦ ξύλου τοῦ γινώσκειν καλὸν καὶ πονηρόν οὐ φάγεσθε ἀπ' αὐτοῦ ᾗ δ' ἂν ἡμέρᾳ φάγητε ἀπ' αὐτοῦ θανάτῳ ἀποθανεῖσθε

BHS Gen. 2:15 וַיִּקַּח יְהוָה אֱלֹהִים אֶת־הָאָדָם וַיַּנִּחֵהוּ בְגַן־עֵדֶן לְעָבְדָהּ וּלְשָׁמְרָהּ׃ 16 וַיְצַו יְהוָה אֱלֹהִים עַל־הָאָדָם לֵאמֹר מִכֹּל עֵץ־הַגָּן אָכֹל תֹּאכֵל׃ 17 וּמֵעֵץ הַדַּעַת טוֹב וָרָע לֹא תֹאכַל מִמֶּנּוּ כִּי בְּיוֹם אֲכָלְךָ מִמֶּנּוּ מוֹת תָּמוּת׃

VUL Gen. 2:15 tulit ergo Dominus Deus hominem et posuit eum in paradiso voluptatis ut operaretur et custodiret illum 16 prae-cepitque ei dicens ex omni ligno paradisi comede 17 de ligno autem scientiae boni et mali ne comedas in quo-cumque enim die comederis ex eo morte morieris

KJV Gen. 2:15 And the LORD God took the man, and put him into the garden of Eden to dress it and to keep it. 16 And the LORD God commanded the man, say-ing, Of every tree of the garden thou mayest freely eat: 17 But of the tree of the knowledge of good and evil, thou shalt not eat of it: for in the day that thou eatest thereof thou shalt surely die.

RSV Gen. 2:15 The LORD God took the man and put him in the garden of Eden to till it and keep it. 16 And the LORD God commanded the man, saying, "You may freely eat of every tree of the gar-den; 17 but of the tree of the knowledge of good and evil you shall not eat, for in the day that you eat of it you shall die."

NRSV Gen. 2:15 The LORD God took the man and put him in the garden of Eden to till it and keep it. 16 And the LORD God commanded the man, "You may freely eat of every tree of the gar-den; 17 but of the tree of the knowledge of good and evil you shall not eat, for in the day that you eat of it you shall die."

As you can see, she begins here with a recapitulation of verse 7, so I won't repeat my comments on anything she's already shown us; but she does add several new elements. The first two come at the end of verse 15, where she introduces the reason why the *'adham* was put in the Garden to begin with:

"And the LORD God took the man and he put him in the garden to till it [*l"abh'dhah*, "to work it"] and to keep it [*ûlsham'rah*, "to keep it safe, guard, protect it"]." The Septuagint has "to work it and to guard it" (*ergazesthai auton kai phylassein)*; the Vulgate has much the same thing (*ut operaretur et custodiret illum)*; the KJV has "dress it and keep it"; and the RSV and NRSV both update "dress" to "till." In any case, it seems to me that the Director has made the economics, the housekeeping of the *'adham,* abundantly clear.

The most important new element, however, is God's commandment about the tree of the knowledge of good and evil. Back in verse 9, the Director simply showed us the LORD God making all kinds of trees, both pleasant to look at and good for food, and she then had him add the two trees that would be central to her film. But at that point she didn't give him a word to say about what the *'adham* was to do, or not do, about them. The question therefore arises: Why did she interrupt herself with the apparent distractions of the River in Eden and the four rivers that water the earth?

Notice, if you will, the way I've put that question. Many people have spotted this interruption, but they've tried to solve their difficulties with it the wrong way around. They've asked, "Why did the *writers* of the original account poke in this digression?" And having put it in those terms, they wandered off into speculations on the mind-set (or mindlessness) of the author(s) of the "J" account. But on the basis of my cinematic approach to Scripture, that's a false start. What you actually see in a finished film has nothing to do with the original scriptwriters' motives for using the words they did, and it has everything to do with the Director's intentions for her picture. Fussing about what they might have meant only distracts you from what she was thinking of. That's why I addressed my question to the Director's motives, and here's my answer to it.

Her "interruption" wasn't an interruption at all. Right after verse 9, she wanted to stress something central to the *mise-en-scène* she'd just given us. Having set her stage with the two trees, she felt the need of *rivers* to stress the worldwide implications, the *cosmic* significance, of the ecology of life and death and good and evil that the rivers represent *before* she introduced the image of a "forbidden" tree. Her reason? Well, I think it was to ensure that the tree of the knowledge of good and evil, which might prove fatal for the human species, could be seen as *not fatal at all* in God's original intention. That tree was as much a part of the ecology of good and evil as the Tree of Life was. As I've said many times, if the Tree of Life was a sacrament of our life, it had to include the mystery of death, because in the world the Director has been showing us, death has always been the engine of life.

Indeed, I would maintain that the Director's excursion down the rivers which water the whole earth indicates that despite the roughness and may-hem of God's ecology of life and death, the Garden and its two trees represent a totally *innocent* world. There may have been hurt and harm in it back then; but there was no malice as we know it — any more than there is malice now in the natural order, save for our obnoxious influence. Therefore, her cine-matic tour of that non-noxious world in Genesis 2:8-14 simply had to be filmed before she could give us her portrayal of the damage that might be done by our misperceptions of the tree of the knowledge of good and evil. Ac-cordingly, her River sequence stands as a bridge between the outflowing inno-cence of the Garden and the possibility (but not yet the actuality) of our fall from that innocence (a disaster that will materialize only after we've reached chapter 3). In the meanwhile, here's a sneak (if cryptic) preview of the ending of chapter 2 — which will be as much a success story as its beginning.

When we watch the creation of the animals in verses 18-20, we'll see the *priesthood* of the human race. The *'adham* have already been made in the *im-age and likeness* of God on the sixth day in chapter 1; and the specific Person of the Trinity in whose image they were then created is the great High Priest himself, the Word of God who speaks all things into being as their Beginning and who restores all things in his Incarnation as their Ending. When we watch the making of woman from man's rib in verses 21-22, we'll see the al-ready pervasive *sexuality* of the world (on the third, fifth, and sixth days) ele-vated into a sacrament of the mutual attractions of the Three-in-One. And when we hear the Director introduce the man and his wife as *one flesh* in the opening of her movie, we'll be prepared for her use of that *marriage* when she finally closes it. At the end, she'll show us the Marriage of the Lamb and the New Jerusalem — the eternal Wedding Reception at which the Incarnate Bridegroom celebrates his Union with the City that has become his Bride.

But back to verses 16 and 17. The Narrator of the film now gives us God's warning about the possible but by no means necessary consequences of our mismanagement of the tree of the knowledge of good and evil: "And the LORD God commanded [*vay'tsav*] the man, saying, 'Of every tree of the gar-den you may freely eat [*mikkol 'ets-haggan 'akhol to'khêl*].' " The last two words are "eating you may eat" — the duplication being a common Hebrew idiom that intensifies any verb it embraces. "But of the tree of the knowledge of good and evil you shall not eat [*lo' to'khal*] because in the day you eat of it [*kî b'yôm 'akholkha mimmennû*] you shall surely die [*môth tamûth*, same id-iom again: "dying you will die"]." The Septuagint reads the first occurrence of the idiom as *brōsei phagēi*, "for food you may eat [it]," and the second as *thanatōi apothaneisthe*, "in a death you will die." The Vulgate fudges the id-iom in the first instance (it has only *comede*, "eat," in the imperative); but in the second instance it does have *morte morieris,* "in [or by] a death you will die." The English versions all reproduce the idiom as "freely eat" in verse 16. But only the KJV has "thou shalt surely die" in verse 17; the RSV and the NRSV ignore it there, having a bare "you shall die."

By the way. Please note that the tree of the knowledge of good and evil should never be called simply "the tree of knowledge." That careless habit introduces a gross misunderstanding. The knowledge represented by the tree of the knowledge of good and evil isn't just an awareness that good is to be chosen and evil avoided; rather, it stands for a mysterious knowing of good and evil as inseparable elements in the ecology of the world God has made. It's the knowledge (despite many commentators to the contrary) that God does *not* have to abolish evil in order to make the good flourish.

As I've noted, God only *seems* to take that vengeful tack at the beginning of the Flood story (Gen. 6–9). At the end of it, he sets up the Rainbow as a sign to the world that he'll never do anything like that again. And in the final representation of that first proclamation of the Gospel — in the ultimate renewal of the Covenant of Mercy with Noah — God's Word Incarnate takes all the evils of history down into his death on the cross; and in his resurrection he rises with the marks of a perpetual presence of evil in his glorified hands, feet, and side. He remembers evil forever, you see; but he holds it in its restored relationship with his own goodness.

The Hebrew verb "to know" signifies not just information stored in memory but an intimate relationship of the knower with the thing known. In Genesis 4:1, for example, we read, "Adam *knew* his wife; and she conceived, and bore Cain." (*Knew* is the ordinary biblical way of referring to sexual intercourse.) Consequently, in that larger sense of "knowledge" (and in particular when it's used in connection with the tree of the knowledge of good and evil), I think we should read it not as an awareness that we must choose *between* good and evil but as the knowledge of how to cope with *both at once.*

Moreover, when the Director presents the "testing" of the human race in the persons of Adam and Eve in chapter 3, she doesn't portray it as their choice of some evil particle of creation. There wasn't a single evil *thing* for Eve to choose: *everything* in the film so far (including, presumably, the tree of the knowledge of good and evil) was pronounced "Very Good" by God at the end of the sixth day. Indeed, Thomas Aquinas said that that there is no material wrongness, no *ontological* evil anywhere in the world; there is only the immaterial *possibility* of evil in the decisions of human will. And that possibility can become an actuality only if we make it so by choosing to *perceive* the good in an evil way. Aquinas defined the will as an infallible appetite for the good: it simply can't choose evil *as such.* In other words, we can never do evil until we can dress it up as a good in our minds. Evil, he said, can be chosen only *ad instar boni,* only under the guise of good. It has to hide before it can go public.

I have no idea what you think of Aquinas's philosophical analysis, but I find it utterly true to life. I never choose to lie unless I can convince myself that my untruth is somehow better than the truth. And to carry Aquinas's insight all the way to 9/11, Al Qaeda could never have assassinated three thousand people with hijacked planes until it convinced itself that the good of Islam required such a monstrous act. None of this, of course, diminishes the devastating consequences that murders or lies can bring into the world: real beings suffer real agonies because of them. But the taproot of their horror lies in a fundamentally unreal perversion of a genuine good.

Nevertheless, the God of the Bible goes right on preserving his original ecology of real goods and unavoidable evils, even while we're turning them into implacable enemies. In spite of all our wars in the name of good, it's a simple fact of history that evil has never actually been eliminated from the material world. And the reason why it can't be is made quite clear in Scripture: the father of lies tempts Eve with a *spiritual* choice: "If you eat [a material act], you will be as gods [an immaterial benefit that was unavailable to her in God's physical world]." As a matter of fact, the only real consequence of the human race's efforts to be like God, knowing good and evil, has not been to make us in the likeness of God; it's been to make God in the image of ourselves. We've turned the God of Scripture, who lets both good and evil be, into a celestial cop on the beat, constantly on the lookout for evildoers to put in the infernal slammer. In short, we've invented the God of *religion* in the worst sense of the word. That hasn't hurt God himself, of course: he had nothing to do with religion in Eden, and he'll have no room for it in the New Jerusalem. But sure as the hell it brought in its tow, we've been stuck in religion's fire and brimstone ever since.

At this point, though, I feel some revisions and extensions of my comments about the tree of the knowledge of good and evil coming on. In Chapter Fifteen of this book I said that Eve, in her dialogue with the serpent, misquoted God's commandment about not eating the fruit of that tree. Her words (as recorded in Genesis 3:2-3) were, "We may eat of the fruit of the trees of the Garden; but of the fruit of the tree which is in the midst of the Garden, God has said, 'You shall not eat of it, neither shall you touch it, lest you die.'" There are two things that I think are right about that reply. One is the implication that the Tree of Life was included among the *permitted* trees, and thus was eaten of by Adam and Eve for as long as they were in the Garden. The other is the more debatable notion that they would not have died as long as they could continue to eat of it. I'll have more to say about this second point shortly; but before that, I want to note *four* things that I find suspicious in Eve's answer to the serpent.

One small non-footnote here. You've probably noticed that I've now dropped my possibly annoying repetitions of "the *'adham*" and begun to use the names Adam and Eve. That's because I was waiting until at least one of the Bible versions we're using made the shift from *'adham* to Adam. That moment has now come. The Septuagint switches to Adam in verse 16; good-bye and good riddance to "the *'adham*."

Back to my four suspicions. First, when Eve refers to the forbidden tree as the one in the midst of the Garden, she's saying more than the Director's cut of the movie does. Not that she could have looked up Genesis 2:9 in her Bible, but the fact of the film is that only the Tree of Life has been explicitly put in the center of things so far. As you'll recall, when I was dealing with this matter two chapters ago, I was even tempted to put the tree of the knowledge of good and evil on the outskirts of the Garden to show its *non-centrality* in God's original arrangements for Adam; but I settled for putting it next to the Tree of Life and making it just a bush overshadowed by it. Still, I wasn't trying to be a literalist; I was only having fun with the fascinating peculiarities of her film.

Second, when Eve quotes God in her answer to the snake, she puts in something that hasn't been heard on the sound track of the movie. She adds an eisegesis of her own to God's command not to eat of the tree of the knowledge of good and evil: "neither shall you touch it." Third, throughout her entire answer, she's telling the serpent about things she simply wasn't around to witness. In verse 17 of chapter 2, where the LORD God commands Adam not to eat of the tree of the knowledge of good and evil, Eve was just a rib in her husband's side. Accordingly (thinking as a movie director would), I would have to assume that Eve acquired her misinformation about not touching it from her husband — possibly in one of their after-supper talks. To be sure, the Director of the biblical movie doesn't burden herself with any such scene; but if you want to indulge in the fussiness of imagining it, I think you have two alternatives. You can blame the "no touching" command on Adam, thus making him responsible for misquoting God; or you can chalk it up to Eve, making her guilty of misquoting her husband. In either case, though, somebody committed the crime of eisegesis. Maybe biblical criticism was the first sin after all.

Frivolity aside, however, the fourth suspicious matter is the most important one. When Eve concludes her answer to the serpent by incorrectly quoting the LORD God ("lest you die" instead of "you shall surely die"), she goes straight to a misreading that for ages has made all sorts of theological mischief. She seems to think that God has threatened them with an instantaneous zap of death at the moment of their disobedience. But as the serpent said to her (the old deceiver can even tell the truth when it serves his purposes), "*lo' môth t'muthûn*," meaning "You shall not surely die," or better, "You shall not actually die in that death" (with the unexpressed kicker, "You will suffer a fate worse than literal death: the death of God's ecology at your hands, which is just fine by me").

I admit I've just imported my theological conclusions into the serpent's mind, but the events of Genesis 3 do support the facts behind my theology: the serpent certainly knows that Eve thinks she and Adam will die on the spot of their eating — and he just as certainly knows they won't. So as I see his words, "You shall not surely die" show his suspicion that God had something more profound in Mind than mere physical death. I realize that this may strike you as something of a stretch — that you may think it makes the devil the first theologian in the Bible. But that's not all bad: maybe his reply to Eve might have enlightened other theologians, if only they hadn't been so preoccupied with the liar that they missed the truth that passed his lips. (I know: snakes don't have lips. But neither do they make speeches. I thought we were above literalism here.)

Speaking of those other theologians, it pains me to say that Augustine was one of them — and so were a great many commentators who followed him. They've all assumed something quite like what Eve thought — namely, that the Tree of Life was originally meant to forestall the natural mortality of the human race, and that the reason we now die was its removal from our reach at the end of Genesis 3. I, of course, have been taking that Tree as something different: as a sacrament of the ecology of life and death — of the "togetherness" of the good of life and the evil of death, even "in the time of man's innocency" in the Garden. Thus, in my thinking, the Tree of Life becomes a sign of both life and death for us: like all the other living things in the primeval Garden, we would have experienced death even there. But our deaths in that situation would have been triumphs of the ecology rather than contradictions of it. They would have been freely offered *gifts* that we gave to other creatures within the ecology and not *robberies* perpetrated against us on its premises.

The distinction between *offering* and *robbery* is crucial to what I'm getting at — and it's not as far-fetched as it first seems. Even in our fallen state, we can see many deaths as affirmations of life rather than outrages against it. Martyrs give their lives as witnesses to the truth. Firefighters offer up their lives to save others. Even some suicides among the terminally ill remove themselves from life as a relief for their long-suffering families. And Jesus is the Captain of all gift givers. He died voluntarily that the world might live, and he praised such deaths as the highest offering: "Greater love has no one than this, that he lay down his life for his friends" (John 15:13, RFC). Even among our lesser brothers and sisters in the animal and vegetable orders, their deaths are a service to others. The chicken dies to feed the fox; the squirrel is run over to feed the crow; the crow dies to feed the maggots; and everything on earth dies to feed the worms and the bacteria.

So even in a fallen world, death is never unqualified robbery. How nice it would have been if our estrangement from the ecology of life and death had not made us so afraid of dying. But it did — and that, I think, leads us to the right way of looking at our mistake at the tree of the knowledge of good and evil. The death we died there is a death in fear; and the worst thing about it is that unlike death itself, which happens only once to each of us, the dread of it haunts us every minute of our time here. "*In the day* that you eat of it, you shall surely die." That *day* is every day of our lives.

But God has reconciled all our days, good and bad, in the Sabbath Rest of his endless Today. He may begin that reconciliation with a stern warning: "Today, if you will hear his voice, harden not your hearts as in the provocation, as in the day of testing in the wilderness" (Psalm 95:7-8, RFC, as quoted in Hebrews 3:7-11). In the Psalm, that "today" refers to Israel's time in the Sinai desert. But I think that Hebrews allows us to apply it backwards and forwards to every day mentioned in Scripture. Back to the day at the tree of the knowledge of good and evil, and all the way forward to the day of the cross in which our "F" on the test was given a vindicating "A+" by Jesus. Back to day one of the Beginning of the world, and forward to the last day of its Ending. And finally, back to the seventh day — to the eternal Today of God, in which the Father, the Son, and the Holy Spirit invite the whole world into their everlasting Rest.

True enough, in Psalm 95 God goes on to say, "I swore in my wrath, 'They shall not enter into my rest.'" But those words are yet another Hebrew idiom: it reads, "*if* they shall enter into my rest" (with a silent "I'll be a monkey's Uncle" appended at the end in God's Mind). However, since that once-unavailable rest is now extended to the entire world in Jesus, the "if" has been removed, and the certainty of our Sabbath Rest in God is now ours in his beloved Son. (The whole of chapters 3 and 4 of Hebrews is worthy of the closest study you can give it; it may be the best exegetical sermon you'll ever hear.)

*   *   *

Admittedly, this has been a weighty chapter. You deserve a change of pace; so turn the page, and see what I have in store for you.

EIGHTEEN

Scenario for a Short Subject

"ROBERT AND THE DAY VISITORS"

PRODUCER'S NOTE: Whenever a CHARACTER is quoting something in LATIN (ITALIAN pronunciation, please), the ENGLISH will appear on the SCREEN in a SUBTITLE, noted in this script by [ENG. SUB.: ". . ."]. Likewise, whenever the quote is in ENGLISH, the LATIN will appear as an *italicized* SUBTITLE, noted by [LAT. SUB.: ". . ."].

> SCENE: A HOUSE on Shelter Island
> INTERIOR: A small, book-cluttered STUDY

(As the LIGHT comes up on the SCREEN, WE SEE the AUTHOR working at his computer with the door closed. REVERSE on the CLOSED DOOR. Unnoticed by the AUTHOR, two VISITORS materialize in the room without opening the DOOR. One is a young, handsome person in a sky-blue Armani SUIT; the other is a fiftyish fat man wearing a black ROBE. The SUIT speaks first.)

SUIT: Ahem! We beg your pardon, Robert . . .

ROBERT: (REVERSE on the AUTHOR, suddenly SWIVELING AROUND in his chair) I'm sorry. I didn't hear you come in.

SUIT: People seldom do. But no matter. We're from

the City, and we bring you greetings from Augustine.

ROBERT: Wow, is that ever a coincidence! I was just about to begin a chapter on him.

ROBE: We know. Unfortunately, Augie is reading Hebrew with Jerry right now, so he sent us instead.

ROBERT: You're on a nickname basis with those guys?

SUIT: Of course, my dear. But while we have all the time in the world, you don't. Why don't you simply ask us who we are?

ROBERT: Who are you?

ROBE: My name is Thomas . . .

SUIT: . . . and mine is Gabriel . . .

THOMAS: . . . and you may ask us any questions you like about Augustine. Especially me. I'm not the anti-Augustinian some people have made me out to be.

ROBERT: I never thought you were. That's one of the points I've been trying to make in this book.

GABRIEL: We know that too, Robert. We've been fond of you for ages — and we've been on tippy toes watching you write this book.

ROBERT: I thought only my wife was doing that.

THOMAS: We've been watching Valerie as well. You're lucky to live with such a good editor.

ROBERT: I certainly am. But what a terrible host I am. Let me move some of these papers off the couch so you can sit down. Please. Would you

like some coffee? A glass of wine? (THEY
SIT.)

GABRIEL: Thank you, no. But enough of this badinage.
We've noticed that you have some problems
with Augustine's teachings about the tree of
the knowledge of good and evil. Why don't
you go straight to those? Is that all right
with you, Tom?

THOMAS: Perfectly fine. Proceed, Robert.

ROBERT: Very well. My first problem with him is
scriptural. In effect, he turns the tree of
the *knowledge* of good *and* evil into a tree
of *choosing* good *or* evil. For example, in
his *De Genesi ad Litteram, VIII, 12* [ENG.
SUB.: "On Genesis to the Letter"], he introduces his comments on the tree by using a
name that has a word Genesis doesn't use.
"It follows," he says, "that we should look
at the tree of the knowledge of how to *distinguish between* good and evil." [LAT. SUB.:
*Sequitur ut videamus de ligno scientiae
dignoscendi bonum et malum.*] I think Augustine is being led astray here by the old
Latin translation he had in hand. When Jerome
translated these words from an apparently
better Hebrew text, he stuck close to the
letter and rendered them simply as "the tree
of the knowledge of good and evil" [LAT.
SUB.: *lignum scientiae boni et mali*]. Therefore, it's Augustine's *dignoscendi* [ENG.
SUB.: "of how to distinguish between"] that
bothers me.

THOMAS: Ah, yes. It certainly does seems to go
against your notion of the "ecology" of good
and evil — as does much of what the rest of
the fathers said, I might add.

ROBERT: True. But dare I ask if anything I've said
about that ecology in this book has made you

wish you'd had such a concept around when you were writing?

THOMAS: You may. But as a writer yourself, you must know that one writes only out of one's past, and only in and for one's own time. A dead writer survives only in the minds of his successors. It's up to the living to say what he might or might not have done had he had the benefit of subsequent thinking. So let me answer you by saying that in my present state I find what you're trying to do quite interesting.

ROBERT: That sounds suspiciously like the Chinese curse "May you live in interesting times."

THOMAS: No offense. Some of my best friends in the City are Chinese. Please go on.

ROBERT: Thank you. Augustine then goes on about his tree of the knowledge of how to distinguish between good and evil. He says that it's not to be doubted that it was a real tree, but why it got this name needs looking into. And he begins his inquiry with an intellectual toss-up: "But having thought about it over and over, it's not possible for me to say to what extent those words support the opinion that the tree was not harmful as food; but then, neither did he who had made all things very good (Gen. 1:31) put anything of evil in paradise." [LAT. SUB.: *Mihi autem etiam atque etiam consideranti dici non potest quantum placeat illa sententia, non fuisse illam arborem cibo noxiam; neque enim qui fecerat omnia bona valde, in paradiso instituerat aliquid mali.*] But then he comes to this unqualified conclusion: "Rather, the evil for the man was the transgression of the commandment." [LAT. SUB.: *sed malum fuisse homini transgressionem praecepti.*]

GABRIEL: Let me congratulate you on your talent for translating and interpreting at the same time. But frankly, I don't see how you can have a difficulty with Augustine on that.

ROBERT: I'm just about to get to it. But rather than call it a difficulty, I'd prefer to say that Augustine creates a problem for me by missing a major theological opportunity. First, the problem. Augustine says, "But it was fitting that a man placed under the Lord God should receive a prohibition from somewhere, so that his very *obedience* might be the virtue by which his Lord accounts him as deserving. . . ." [LAT. SUB.: *Opportebat autem ut homo sub Domino Deo positus alicunde prohiberetur, ut ei promerendi Dominum suum virtus esset ipsa obedientia. . . .*]

    The problem, as I see it, arises when we combine this passage with the first one I cited from Augustine, where he makes the tree a sign that man was to choose between good and evil — to do only good and to have nothing whatsoever to do with evil. Here, though, he pretty much reduces that choice to a decision to obey or not obey a divine Command. Accordingly, it seems to me that he makes it a tree of *obedience* rather than a tree of *knowledge.*

THOMAS: Well! As you know, I agreed with his formulation. In Question XCVII, Article I of my *Summa Theologica*, entitled *Utrum Homo in Statu Innocentiae esset Immortalis* [ENG. SUB.: "Whether Man might be Immortal in the State of Innocence"], I first posited, as usual, a number of arguments for a *negative* answer. The fourth one was this: *Immortalitas promittitur homini in praemium, secundum illud Apoc. 21, "Mors ultra non erit,"* sed homo non fuit conditus in statu praemii, sed ut praemium mereretur [ENG. SUB.: "Immortality is promised to man as a *reward*, accord-

255

ing to that saying in Revelation 21, 'Death shall be no more,' but man was not made in a state of reward, but that he might *merit* a reward."]

Having read deeply in the fathers, I found them almost unanimous on this subject. They agree that a reward for meritorious obedience was the very thing the tree represented. Had it been used in obedience to God's command, it would have led man to immortality, even though he was made mortal by nature. I just never saw that as a problem. But I can see how your metaphor of an ecology might lead you to think otherwise.

ROBERT: I appreciate your fairness. Ever since my seminary days, I've been an enthusiastic Thomist. All I'm doing here is what you said a while back — suggesting possible reworkings of Thomism in the light of subsequent developments. But since I, like Luther, am an heir not only of the Catholic tradition but also of the Reformed one, a flag goes up in my mind whenever anyone brings up the subject of human merit. To be sure, there's some truth in that notion, but it's been used far too often to put the *sole merit of Christ* in the shade. I always watch it like a hawk.

THOMAS: I understand perfectly. Martin and I have had more conversations than you may think. The City is nothing if not a place of reconciliation.

ROBERT: If only the church on earth could take that hint! But since we interrupted Augustine in mid-paragraph, let me get back to where we left off and indicate the opportunity I think he missed. He continues, "I can say most truly that [obedience] is the sole virtue for every rational creature acting under *the power of God*, and the first and greatest vice of the prideful swelling that leads man

256

to ruin is his desire to use *his own power* —
and the name of that vice is *disobedience."*
[LAT. SUB.: *quam [obedientiam] possum*
verissime dicere solam esse virtutem omni
creaturae rationali agenti sub Dei potestate
primumque esse maximum vitium tumoris ad
ruinam sua potestate velle uti, cujus vitii
nomen est inobedientia.]

Those words about *power* are a missed opportunity because I think they show that Augustine comes very close to the bull's-eye of
the ecology of good and evil, but still
fails to win the rewarding cigar. Even though
he begins by making the tree of the knowledge of good and evil a test of *obedience,*
at the end he does suggest that the main
question on the test was *"Whose power,* God's
or man's, will the human race use to manage
good and evil?"

Had he made more of that insight, he
might have seen that the great divide is not
between good and evil as such but between
two diametrically opposed ways of *dealing*
with good and evil.

The God of Scripture handles good and evil
(barring the odd miraculous intervention here
or there) by *letting both be* — by *not* poking
his divine Finger into the pie of creation.
We, on the other hand, try to handle them by
control — by manhandling the good into what
we think are "improvements" of it, and by
trying to elbow evil out of the picture entirely. Our power is plausible and right-
handed. God's power is mysterious and left-
handed. His work is an *opus alienum,* a
"strange work" that leaves creation free to
do anything it likes. Ours is just the same
old business as usual by which we've been
turning the world into a war zone ever since
Eve.

THOMAS: Hmmm. That certainly is innovative. But then,
           I too was something of an innovator in my

own day, so I applaud your efforts to raise the level of theological discourse with new insights. I know how hard it is to go against received opinion. When I introduced Aristotle into Western theology, many old-line Platonists (who took their cues from Augustine) seemed to think I'd betrayed him. But I didn't think I had. In the final analysis, I believed that God's relationship with good and evil is more a mystery than a plausibility. And even when that mystery is finally revealed in his Son on the cross, it remains fundamentally unintelligible. We must always be suspicious of theologians who take the mystery only as a problem to be solved by the human mind. Looking back from here, I suppose I might have taken that advice more seriously myself.

ROBERT: But as I recall, you did. I read somewhere that at the end of your life you said you had seen things that made everything you wrote seem like ashes (or words to that effect). That strikes me as a quite sufficient grasp of the mystery.

GABRIEL: May I break in? Now that you've brought up the subject of mystery, let me put in a word or two as an Archangel. We immaterial beings are even more baffled by the cross than you bodily creatures are. There's a seventeenth-century Palm Sunday hymn that sums us up nicely:

> Ride on! ride on in majesty!
> The angel armies of the sky
> Look down with sad and wond'ring eyes
> To see the approaching sacrifice.

That word *wondering* gets us exactly right. We just haven't a clue about mystery. As a matter of fact, in 1 Corinthians 1:17, Paul himself pointed this out. He said that Christ didn't send him to run around doing things, not even baptisms. Rather, he sent him to proclaim the Good News, "not in the wisdom of reasonable discourse — not in the wisdom of a logical 'word,' lest the cross of Christ be emptied of its power." And if you think that such wisdom is less opaque to us than to you, you're mistaken. We may have, as Thomas said, *infused knowledge* of the things that our angelic minds know; but knowledge of God's *mysteries* is simply beyond us.

But the clearest indication of our invincible ignorance of mystery comes in Ephesians 3:8-11. It says that Paul was given grace "to proclaim to the Gentiles the Good News of the untraceable footprints of the richness of the Christ, and to enlighten all people about the *economy*" — I liked your word, Robert — "of the *mystery* hidden from the world in the God who made all things, and now" — here comes the nub of it — "to make known *through the church*, for the benefit of the *principalities and powers* in the *heavenly places*, the fantastically varied wisdom of God."

In effect, those words "through the church" effectively mean that we disembodied spirits have no talent for mystery. It's only you down-to-earth creatures who have enough whimsy to love *secrets*. All we have is the high-flown knowledge that God gives us. What he keeps to himself, we can't grasp at all. We just wait for you to let us in on what he's whispered in your ears. We can only wish, as 1 Peter 1:12 says, that we could "stoop down low enough to look into" the things he's told you.

ROBERT: I like that a lot, Gabriel. And it gives me an idea. In a way, your angelic minds are like the "computer intelligence" we so often overestimate. We've played too long with the notion that we'll someday succeed in making

computers that will be the equal of human
intelligence. But I don't think that day will
ever come. Until we can make a computer capable of totally unpredictable whimsy, it
will remain only an electronic imitation of a
very bright angel. It will never be earthy
enough to have a sense of humor.

In fact, it won't be able even to *begin* a
joke. By what software could you program a
computer to come up with an opening line
like, "Two nuns went into a cocktail lounge,
and the first one says to the bar-
tender. . . ." Or with something like this:

> A corpulent maiden named Kroll
> Had a notion exceedingly droll;
> At a masquerade ball,
> Dressed in nothing at all,
> She backed in as a Parker House roll.

You can program a machine to play chess,
but that's because chess isn't funny. It's
about *prudence,* about making merely congru-
ent, rational moves. Humor is the sudden perception of incongruity. It's about the *impu-
dence* of making irrational moves — and you'd
have a hard time writing a program for that.

But even if you succeeded, you'd never
trust a computer that could say, on its own
whim, "To hell with it all!" You could lose
all your information, not to mention your
shirt and your freedom. And why? Because your
entire effort would be to program all the
foolish moves out of your electrical mini-
world, which is precisely what Adam and Eve
thought they were being told to do at the
tree — and what God emphatically does *not*
do. To be sure, Adam and Eve sinned. But in
Greek, "to sin" is *hamartanein:* "to miss the
mark, to miss the point." *That's* what people
who don't get jokes do. And it's exactly
what our first parents did at the tree. They
refused to see the whimsy of God's ecology

and chose instead to put good and evil at war with each other.

But as Paul says in 1 Corinthians 1, God's program for history is a foolishness and a weakness that allows evil free rein — "for the foolishness of God is wiser than men, and the weakness of God is stronger than men" [v. 25, RFC]. He hasn't provided the universe with a Doomsday Machine that will automatically erase everything bad. And therefore the real problem with anything that can say "To hell with it all" is that it's *not funny*. It misses the point of the divine Joke — the tall tale of how God can put up with evil forever, yet still have the last laugh.

THOMAS: I must say, Robert, you *are* fun! I know I've been called the Angelic Doctor. But if I may, like you, revise and extend my remarks, I think I have something funny of my own to add. In the light of your film metaphor and my knowledge of old Peter Sellers movies, I'd be tempted to say that the angels are the "straight men" of creation, playing Commissioner Dreyfus to God's Inspector Clouseau.

GABRIEL: You never cease to surprise me, Thomas. You should have told Robert the other "pastime" Augie and Jerry enjoy in the eternal Present. After they read Hebrew, they think up new jokes to tell the angels, just for the fun of seeing us not laugh.

ROBERT: How comforting. We'll never have to stop acting like kids, even in the eschaton. We can go right on finding each other impossible *and* delightful.

THOMAS: Still, I want to say a kind word for the angelic intellect. Angels may not have a sense of humor, but they can still recognize behavior that indicates its absence. They have an intense dislike of cruelty and torture. Even Lucifer, as I now see him, may not have had a mean streak. The so-called torments of the damned may not have been invented by him at all, and perhaps not even by God. It just might be that they were thought up by the inmates of hell for use on other inmates — and that they're tolerated by God (as Origen held) while he waits for the occupants of the city of despair to wake up and see the real City all around them. So while Gabriel understands straight faces quite well, he just doesn't get the joke God played on the father of lies in the Garden. Lucifer has to live forever in the company of humorless in-grates.

ROBERT: By the way, when I read the Office today, the Gospel reading was John 5:1-18, the story of Jesus and the sick man at the Pool of Bethzatha. As always in the Fourth Gospel, Jesus is not without a sense of humor. He asks the man, "Do you want to become well?" And instead of giving him a simple "Yes," the man goes into a rigamarole, telling him all the troubles he's had getting into the Pool. Jesus ignores this completely. He just says, "Get up, take up your cot, and walk!" (*In Jesus,* you see, the man is already well — just as Lazarus was already risen before Jesus called him out of the tomb.)

   And even when the bystanders tell the man he shouldn't be traveling around with his cot on the Sabbath, he still doesn't see the fun Jesus is having with him (and them). With a straight face, he puts the blame for breaking the Sabbath on the person who healed him. So Jesus — who had immediately made himself scarce after healing the man — finds him and says, "Look, you're well; don't sin anymore." In the Greek, that's *mēketi hamartane:* "Stop with this missing of the point, lest some-thing worse happen to you." But the man goes

262

right on. He runs back to the bystanders
and snitches that it was *Jesus* who made him
well, thus getting our Lord himself in Dutch.

One more point. Fascinatingly, every time
Jesus does a "sign" in John's Gospel, somebody *believes* in him — except here. This man
is stuck in his humorless whining. Which is
what I've described in this book as the essence of hell, the totally unfunny missing of
the point of the nose on our risen faces.
The nose, in fact, is one of God's best
jokes. It's an incongruous appendage that defines our appearance better than almost anything else. Think of what a *risen* nose could
do for you.

GABRIEL: Not having a body to call my own, I have to
take that on faith. But I must say, you're
delightful, Robert. Still, Thomas and I must
soon be about other business, so if you have
further questions, now is your last chance to
get them in. [He runs his FOREFINGER across
his THROAT.)

ROBERT: I must say, for someone who has no proper
hands you express yourself forcefully with
the apparent ones sticking out of your Armani
jacket. But in deference to your time con-
straints — or should I say "eternity con-
straints"? — let me limit myself to just one
item. It concerns Thomas's Article IV of the
same Question we've been discussing. He enti-
tles it, "Whether Man in the State of Innocence obtained Immortality by the Tree of
Life" [LAT. SUB.: *Utrum Homo in Statu
Innocentiae per Lignum Vitae Immortalitatem
consecutus fuisset*]. Is that all right with
you, Thomas?

THOMAS: Indeed it is. Proceed.

ROBERT: As usual, you begin in the negative, with
three reasons why the Tree could *not* have

been the cause of immortality. I find them
all fascinating examples of your ability to
slice and dice even the most intractable in-
gredients in the recipe of Scripture.

Your first reason is philosophical. You
note that an effect cannot exceed its cause.
But since the Tree of Life was perishable
(for otherwise it could not have been taken
in as nourishment) — and since food is converted into the substance of the thing it
nourishes — therefore the Tree of Life could
not have conferred imperishability or immortality.

Your second reason is taken from nature.
You say that the *effects* caused by the powers of plants and other natural things are
themselves natural. Therefore, if the Tree of
Life were to be the cause of immortality,
that immortality itself would have to have
been natural to man — which in fact it is
not.

But your third reason is the most interesting of all. You say that this whole business of a Tree that can confer immortality
seems to hark back to those old fables in
which the gods, who ate of a certain special
food, were made immortal by it. And you
rather gleefully dismiss that notion with
just three words, *quod irridebat Philosophus*
[ENG. SUB.: "which Aristotle *made fun of*"].

THOMAS: I hope you'll make it clear that in those
negative reasons, I was simply setting up a
distinction that I would use when I came to
affirm the Tree as the cause of immortality
for man.

ROBERT: Of course. Right after that, you do indeed
turn the corner and argue in the affirmative.
First, you bolster your case with Genesis
3:22: ". . . lest he put forth his hand, and
take also of the Tree of Life, and eat, and
live forever." But then you add something

264

from Augustine (in question 19 of his "Questions of the Old and New Testament"): "The
tasting of the Tree of Life inhibited the
perishing of the body. In short, even after
sin, man would have been able to remain in-
dissoluble, if only he'd been permitted to
eat of the Tree of Life." [LAT. SUB.: *Gustus
arboris vitae corruptionem corporis
inhibebat, denique et post peccatum potuit
insolubilis manere, si permissum esset illi
edere de arbore vitae.*]

THOMAS: That's a fair enough summary. I can hardly
wait for your comments on the body of my Article.

ROBERT: I know it will take up precious time, but I
can't resist quoting some more of your Latin.
You now begin your argument itself: *Respondeo
dicendum, quod lignum vitae quodammodo
immortalitatem causabat, non autem
simpliciter.* [ENG. SUB.: "I respond by saying
that the Tree of Life did in some way cause
immortality, but not simply."] And you go on:
*Ad cujus evidentiam considerandum est, quod
duo remedia ad conservationem vitae habebat
homo in primo statu, contra duos defectus.*
[ENG. SUB.: "As to the evidence for that, it
should be considered that man in his first
state had two remedies for the conservation
of life, directed against two defects."]
    I love the orderliness of your mind,
Thomas, and I suppose I always will. Valerie,
in one of her kinder remarks about my own
love of order, once said, "We certainly lead
an ordered life!" Being unable to resist a
straight line when I hear one, I said, "Yes,
you give the orders and I'm in for life."
Nothing snide intended, but I feel the same
way about you.

THOMAS: I take that as a compliment. Still, I must
also congratulate Valerie on her patience in

living with *you*. Humor can be wonderful and wearing at the same time. Do go on.

ROBERT: You spell out the first defect as the depletion of the body's moisture by the action of the natural heat that is the soul's means of animating the body. This, you say, was remedied for man by his eating of the other trees of the Garden, just as it is for us even now by the foods we take in. But for the second defect, you bring in Aristotle and argue from his premises. Let me paraphrase your subtle — if not cagey — analysis of him.

First, you quote him: "That which is produced from something outside itself is joined to it." But then you refer to the "moisture" that the activating power of man's specific nature threatened. And you go on to give an illustration. You say that just as water joined to wine is at first converted into the taste of wine, so also, to the degree that more or less is added, it diminishes the strength of the wine — until at last the wine becomes watery. Thus we see, you say, that in the beginning, the activating power of human nature is strong enough to turn food not only into something that can restore what was depleted but also into a cause of further growth. After the Fall, though, even the food that enabled those processes isn't up to the task of causing growth — it's limited only to the restoration of what was depleted, and in the end not even to that. In the state of old age, it can restore neither the conditions that follow man's depletion nor the dissolution of the body that finally ensues.

THOMAS: That is a paraphrase indeed! But at least it puts what I said into idiomatic English. Continue. And don't rush yourself on our account.

ROBERT: Thank you. You then get to the real thrust of your argument. You say that it was against *this* defect that man was helped by the Tree of Life. For it had the strength to fortify the power of human nature against the debility that was caused by the introduction of something foreign to it (to man as God created him). And you support that by quoting from the fourteenth part of Augustine's "On the City of God": "Food was present to man that he might not hunger, drink that he might not thirst — and the Tree of Life that old age might not dissolve him." And you add that in his "Questions of the Old and New Testament," Augustine says that the Tree of Life, *in a medicinal way,* prevented the perishing of men.

Nevertheless, you go back to your *non simpliciter* and say that the Tree did not cause immortality in any simple sense. For the soul's natural power to conserve the body was not caused by the Tree of Life, nor was the Tree, as such, able to give the body a disposition toward immortality that might never be dissolved. Which is clear, you say, from the fact that the power of any kind of body is finite, and therefore the power of the Tree of Life could not extend to giving a body the power of lasting for an *infinite* time, but only of lasting for a *determinate* time. For it's clear that to the extent that a power is greater, it imprints a more durable effect. Therefore, although the power of the Tree of Life was finite, once eaten of, it preserved man from perishing for a determinate time — at the end of which, either man would have been carried over into a spiritual life, or he would have needed to eat of the Tree of Life again.

THOMAS: Bravo! Why don't you take a rest and let me give my concluding paragraph myself?

ROBERT: I'd be delighted. But only if you'll guarantee me one last chance to compliment both of
you after you've finished.

THOMAS: Agreed — *in quantum possum*. Here, then, is
how I took care of all three objections to
the Tree of Life as a source of immortality.
I said I'd answered all of them at once in
the body of the Article you just rendered so
nicely: *Et per hoc patet responsio AD
OBJECTA. Nam primae rationes concludunt, quod
non causabat incorruptibilitatem simpliciter.
Aliae vero concludunt, quod causabat
incorruptibilitatem, impediendo corruptionem,
secundum modum praedictum (in corp. art.)*
[ENG. SUB.: "And by this, the response TO
THE OBJECTIONS is obvious. Because the *first*
reasons lead only to the conclusion that the
Tree didn't cause imperishability *in a simple
sense*, and the *others* conclude that it did
cause imperishability by *impeding perishability* — and both of those I worked into
the body of the Article."] *There*, I argued
that the Tree caused imperishability precisely by impeding perishability.

(As the NEXT WORDS are spoken, GABRIEL and THOMAS
begin to FADE from the SCREEN, leaving only ROBERT
in the room at the end.)

ROBERT: Now it's my turn to say "Bravo!" You're
right, Gabriel. Thomas never ceases to amaze.
And you yourself have been a joy to meet.
You have an angelic spontaneity I never sus-
pected. And you, Thomas? You are my hero of
careful discourse. If I had an eighth of
your way with words, I'd be . . .
    Aw, shucks . . .

FADE TO BLACK

NINETEEN

The Animals, the Priesthood of Adam, and the Man and His Wife as One Flesh

GENESIS 2:18-25

I hope that was as much a breather for you as it was for me: I feel both exhilarated and chastened by such exalted company. Still, we must get back to our own business, so let me go straight to the overarching subject of this chapter: the *Priesthood* of Adam and Eve — and priesthood itself as the hallmark of God's whole creation.

As I see it, priestliness in its widest sense is the offering up of separated, individual things into a dance that makes them one — the exaltation of mere units into unity. It has its root, of course, in the divine Three-in-One. The Son, who offers all things to the Father on the Altar of the Spirit, was from the beginning a Priest forever after the order of Melchizedek (Gen. 14:17-20, as quoted in Ps. 110:4 and Heb. 5:6, 6:10, and 7:17). The Word doesn't *become* a Great High Priest in Jesus; he simply *reveals* that he's been one all along. Indeed, as I've tried to say many times, the Word doesn't even *become* Incarnate in Jesus. He's *always* been Incarnate in the world he made: he just took his time to disclose that fact. And his earliest shots at both those disclosures come right at the beginning of Genesis. The first is the creation of male and female, humanity as a priestly race on the sixth day; and the second is the bringing of the animals to the priestly Adam to receive their names.

But it's not just human beings who are made in the image of his Priesthood. *All things* are engaged in a priestly Dance of mutual offering. Let me spell out more fully how the Director has already shown us this dance in her film. In the beginning, she brings on God himself as the Lord of the Dance, the Originator of the ballet of creation. But then, in ascending order, she introduces the *dancers:* the *Nothing,* the *Darkness,* the *Light,* the *Firmament,* the *Seas* and *Dry Land,* the *Plants* and *Herbs,* the *Fishes* and *Birds,* the *Animals* of the *Earth,* and Adam, by whom and in whom the whole priestly *corps de ballet* will find its priesthood fulfilled. Finally, she brings back the divine *Maître de Ballet* for an eternal curtain call on the Seventh Day. In the endless Sabbath of the Trinity, creation itself rests in its own priestly goodness.

In this part of the movie, however, the Director films the world's priestliness with a different cast, and in another order. She still begins with the LORD God; but she introduces him here as the second Person of the Trinity — as the priestly Word responsible for all the ballet's priests, the divine Stage Manager without whom the dry-as-dust dance would never have made it out of New Haven. And she arranges for this Manager to show us an even clearer succession of priesthoods. He wets down the dust to make the clay from which Adam will be formed. But when Adam has finally been made, the Manager promptly sends the budding priest into a Garden to study pastoral theology. He then plants attractive and tasty trees to please all creatures; he sets up a priestly Eucharist in which those trees will transubstantiate carbon dioxide into oxygen; he causes the Tree of Life to rise up from the stage of the Garden as a sacrament of the right use of all priesthoods — of the *White Mass* in which everything will be offered up into ever higher unities; and he sets up the tree of the knowledge of good and evil as a warning against the *black mass* — against the perversion of man's priesthood that will bring the world only to war.

The Stage Manager goes further still. He makes the River and its tributaries carry the priestly results of man's labors across the whole earth; he reiterates the warning against the black mass; and he makes every beast of the field and every bird of the air, all of whom have their own share in the priesthood of Adam. Next, he sends in the animals so Adam can claim his priesthood by naming them. But then, since Adam is still looking for proper company in his priesthood, the Word puts him to sleep, makes a woman from one of his ribs, and brings her to him. And Adam says, in a triumph of priestly naming, "This is now bone of my bone and flesh of my flesh, and she shall be called Woman, because she was taken out of Man." And finally the Manager has both of them pirouette across the stage, stark naked and gloriously unashamed. The priesthood of Adam and Eve, at the end of their *grand jeté,* now stands revealed in the *one flesh* of the man and his wife.

*   *   *

Now, though, a look at the first part of the script on which this chapter's scenes of that priesthood's success will be based:

LXX Gen. 2:18 καὶ εἶπεν κύριος ὁ θεός οὐ καλὸν εἶναι τὸν ἄνθρωπον μόνον ποιήσωμεν αὐτῷ βοηθὸν κατ' αὐτόν 19 καὶ ἔπλασεν ὁ θεὸς ἔτι ἐκ τῆς γῆς πάντα τὰ θηρία τοῦ ἀγροῦ καὶ πάντα τὰ πετεινὰ τοῦ οὐρανοῦ καὶ ἤγαγεν αὐτὰ πρὸς τὸν Αδαμ ἰδεῖν τί καλέσει αὐτά καὶ πᾶν ὃ ἐὰν ἐκάλεσεν αὐτὸ Αδαμ ψυχὴν ζῶσαν τοῦτο ὄνομα αὐτοῦ 20 καὶ ἐκάλεσεν Αδαμ ὀνόματα πᾶσιν τοῖς κτήνεσιν καὶ πᾶσι τοῖς πετεινοῖς τοῦ οὐρανοῦ καὶ πᾶσι τοῖς θηρίοις τοῦ ἀγροῦ τῷ δὲ Αδαμ οὐχ εὑρέθη βοηθὸς ὅμοιος αὐτῷ

BHS Gen. 2:18 וַיֹּאמֶר יְהוָה אֱלֹהִים לֹא־טוֹב הֱיוֹת הָאָדָם לְבַדּוֹ אֶעֱשֶׂה־לּוֹ עֵזֶר כְּנֶגְדּוֹ: 19 וַיִּצֶר יְהוָה אֱלֹהִים מִן־הָאֲדָמָה כָּל־חַיַּת הַשָּׂדֶה וְאֵת כָּל־עוֹף הַשָּׁמַיִם וַיָּבֵא אֶל־הָאָדָם לִרְאוֹת מַה־יִּקְרָא־לוֹ וְכֹל אֲשֶׁר יִקְרָא־לוֹ הָאָדָם נֶפֶשׁ חַיָּה הוּא שְׁמוֹ: 20 וַיִּקְרָא הָאָדָם שֵׁמוֹת לְכָל־הַבְּהֵמָה וּלְעוֹף הַשָּׁמַיִם וּלְכֹל חַיַּת הַשָּׂדֶה וּלְאָדָם לֹא־מָצָא עֵזֶר כְּנֶגְדּוֹ:

VUL Gen. 2:18 dixit quoque Dominus Deus non est bonum esse hominem solum faciamus ei adiutorium similem sui 19 formatis igitur Dominus Deus de humo cunctis animantibus terrae et universis volatilibus caeli adduxit ea ad Adam ut videret quid vocaret ea omne enim quod vocavit Adam animae viventis ipsum est nomen eius 20 appellavitque Adam nominibus suis cuncta animantia et universa volatilia caeli et omnes bestias terrae Adam vero non inveniebatur adiutor similis eius

KJV Gen. 2:18 And the LORD God said, *It is* not good that the man should be alone; I will make him an help meet for him. 19 And out of the ground the LORD God formed every beast of the field, and every fowl of the air; and brought *them* unto Adam to see what he would call them: and whatsoever Adam called every living creature, that *was* the name thereof. 20 And Adam gave names to all cattle, and to the fowl of the air, and to every beast of the field; but for Adam there was not found an help meet for him.

RSV Gen. 2:18 Then the Lord God said, "It is not good that the man should be alone; I will make him a helper fit for him." 19 So out of the ground the Lord God formed every beast of the field and every bird of the air, and brought them to the man to see what he would call them; and whatever the man called every living creature, that was its name. 20 The man gave names to all cattle, and to the birds of the air, and to every beast of the field; but for the man there was not found a helper fit for him.

NRSV Gen. 2:18 Then the LORD God said, "It is not good that the man should be alone; I will make him a helper as his partner." 19 So out of the ground the LORD God formed every animal of the field and every bird of the air, and brought them to the man to see what he would call them; and whatever the man called every living creature, that was its name. 20 The man gave names to all cattle, and to the birds of the air, and to every animal of the field; but for the man there was not found a helper as his partner.

Let's look only at the new words in the ancient languages. (The English versions pretty much speak for themselves.) I'll do the old texts verse by verse, quoting only the RSV as a guide to what I'm talking about. In verse 18, the Hebrew for "a helper" is *'ezer k'neghdô*, literally, "a helper as over against him"; the Septuagint has *boēthon kat' auton*, "a help in accordance with himself"; and the Vulgate has *adiutorium similem sui*, "a help like himself." In verse 19, when the LORD God brings all the animals and birds to Adam to see what he will call them, the Hebrew word for the "name" Adam gives them is *sh'mô*, "its name"; in the Septuagint, it's *onoma autou*, "its name"; and in the Vulgate, it's *nomen eius*, "its name." And in verse 20, while the Hebrew of "a helper fit for him" is *'ezer k'neghdô* as before, the Septuagint has *boēthos homoios autōi*, "a helper like him," and the Vulgate has *adiutor similis eius*, "a helper like him."

Obviously, it's Adam's act of *naming* that most interests me, because it's the clearest manifestation of the priesthood by which the human race lifts all things into unity. And that priesthood, as I've said, is the sign that we've been made not only in the general image of God but in the specific image of the Word of God, the second Person of the Trinity. It's precisely our priestly elevation of things and persons by the names we give them that enables us to lift them into the City of God. Our "dominion" over the world isn't a license to *obliterate* other creatures by force; it's an invitation to *offer them up* in love by the priestly power of our words — by our eucharistic bestowal of new names on things that, but for us, would never have heard them.

Some thirty years ago, when I wrote *Hunting the Divine Fox: An Introduction to the Language of Theology*, I included a bit of whimsy about the first caveman's experience with naming. That book, incidentally — along with two others, *An Offering of Uncles: The Priesthood of Adam and the Shape of the World*, and *The Third Peacock: The Problem of God and Evil* — has been republished most recently in a single volume entitled *The Romance of the Word: One Man's Love Affair with Theology* (Eerdmans, 1995). If you can find it (try Amazon.com), I think you'll like all three of them. In any case, here's my illustration from *Hunting the Divine Fox:*

> Housebuilding was impossible until someone, somewhere, spoke a word. The human race was provided with no instinctual architectural faculties. The bees built hives, the birds made nests, and the beavers worked like beavers, practicing housebuilding and stream control at the same time. But no one built *houses* until the day when one fellow who had sense enough to come in out of the rain sat down on a fallen tree he had dragged into his cave.

And it was so damp and dark and unpleasant that he got to thinking how wonderful it would be if he could arrange things so that he never saw the inside of a cave again. And as he thought, his eye fell on the tree on which he was sitting, and all of a sudden, an internal word sprang up noiselessly in his mind. He wasn't thinking the word *tree,* and he wasn't thinking the word *seat.* He was thinking a word he had never thought before. So he opened his mouth to hear what it was and, lo and behold, out came the word *lumber.*

It was such an odd word that he just sat there for a while. And all of a sudden, it happened again. Two new internal words in one day! Wait till his wife got home! But he couldn't wait, so he opened his mouth again, and this time, out came *house.*

Well, he was so enthused that he picked up a phone and dialed a friend.

"Irving?"

"Speaking."

"Irving, have I got news for you! You and I are going to make a bundle. You know that *ax* of yours? And all those *trees* you've got in that *yard* I thought up for you last week? You're going to split them up, and we're going to sell them for *lumber.*"

"For *what?*"

"No, Irving. Not for *what.* For *lumber.*"

"What good is *lumber?* Who'd buy it? Nobody even knows what it is."

"Irving, Irving. Think big. When there's no market, you create one. We're going to sell the lumber to people who want *houses.*"

"What's *houses?*"

"It's the plural of *house,* Irving. I just thought up both words this afternoon."

"What have you been smoking over there?"

"Nothing. I've just been thinking."

"That's even worse. Every time you think, I end up working."

"Believe me, Irving, this time you'll thank me. I've even got the name of our business picked out. In honor of your place, we'll call it The Lumber Yard. So hang up now and start chopping. I'm going to think up *writing* so I can letter the sign."

Needless to say, that dialogue with Irving was only a baby step into the priesthood of Adam and Eve, but all the giant steps of our human priesthood are implicit in it. Think once again of the first violin: it became feasible only after the human race had spent innumerable Saturday afternoons thinking about the insides of trees, the entrails of cats, and the hairs in horses' tails. Or consider the first really decent stone building: it wasn't possible until we thought of the *blocks* into which stone could be cut and the *saws* we would use to do the job. And all the other priestly firsts we've achieved by naming follow the same pattern. They run from the double-hung window, whose every component we've given a name of its own (*mullion, meeting rail, water table, sill*), to the house itself with its *studs, shoes,* and *plates,* its *joists, rafters,* and *ridge poles,* to the renaming of common salt as *sodium chloride,* and to all the other new names that have made the city of the sciences possible. And these new, priestly names elucidate the entire universe, from the farthest star down to the very bottom on which the physical order sits (quarks, antimatter, indeterminacy, entropy). Even though the objective existence of such concepts may be problematical, they enable us to lift up the physical exchanges of objective reality.

And this we do — provided, of course, that we say a White Mass over those exchanges rather than a black one. The second chapter of Genesis doesn't present us with a *once-upon-a-time* priesthood of the human race that's since become inoperative; it proclaims that even now, after the countless black masses we've said over the world, we can still act as the priests of creation. Its picture of a sinless earth is not meant to leave us with only nostalgia for what can no longer be. Rather, chapter 2's picture has to be taken in tandem not only with chapter 3's warning that our failed priesthood can never take us back to Eden, but also with the rest of Scripture's assurance that our priesthood has already been restored in the Great High Priest himself. Even in the midst of everything we may have lost, all is not lost.

But while it cannot be said too often that the animals are priests every bit as much as you and I, that statement does need a little qualification. When your cat presents you with a dead mouse, she no doubt has an inkling of sorts about the priestly offering she's made by giving you the victim of her sacrifice; but for all that, her mind doesn't seem to have a concept of *priesthood* with which to understand her ritual, any more than she has a concept of *starvation* with which to interpret her experience of an empty stomach. And the reason for that limitation is her lack of *words,* and in particular, of abstract *nouns. Noun* comes from the Latin *nomen,* "name." But as far as we know, the animals don't give names to anything — in all likelihood not even to themselves, and certainly not to other creatures, to the best of our knowledge.

As cat fanciers, you and your pet Felicity may bristle at that. Don't. For your comfort, I have almost unlimited sympathy with feline mysticism. At the height of my children's catmania, we had twenty-one of them in the rectory, a few actually having their *accouchements* in a closet on the premises. And I've always been fond of T. S. Eliot's *The Old Possum's Book of Practical Cats* (from which the musical was adapted). In his poem "On the Naming of Cats," he first gives instances of names that are plain, fancy, and just plain peculiar. But then he says this:

> But above and beyond there's still one name left over,
>   And that is the name that you never will guess;
> The name that no human research can discover —
>   But THE CAT HIMSELF KNOWS, and will never confess.

But despite Eliot's exploration of the feline mind (and the family planning of my children's cats), I still don't think cats rise to the level of tossing around abstract nouns.

In this, I stand foursquare with Thomas Aquinas. Consider. To the animals, he assigned a *sensitive* intellect: one that knew things by seeing the *sensible species,* the "sense images" of them in their minds. To human beings, he assigned a *rational* intellect that could grasp things by words, by nouns, by names *abstracted* from the perceptions of their senses. For the angels (who had no bodies and therefore no senses to abstract from), he developed the notion of *rational species,* of "immaterial images" *infused* directly into their minds by God. And in the case of God himself, he held that God's knowledge of all things was *immediate* — without any intervening help from anything.

Perhaps borrowing from Augustine, Thomas said that the divine Mind's knowledge, while totally immaterial, is the *intimate cause* of all material being. God only has to *know* your cat, and presto, *there she is!* In other words (if I may repeat myself), the Father just thinks up Felicity, the Word just mentions the name "Felicity" in the heavenly Sheboygan, the Spirit sighs in admiration over the creature whose name the Word has spoken — and there is a real Felicity at your feet, with a really dead mouse. And if I may once again quote my favorite words from Augustine: *NOTA ERGO FECIT, NON FACTA COGNVOVIT:* "God made things that *already existed* in his Mind; he didn't have to wait for them to be facts for him to know them."

But enough of this theological epistemology; back to the priesthood of the animals beyond the bees, birds, and beavers I've already given you. I once watched a pack of wild African dogs on a television nature program. They pursued their prey as a single hunter, yet I'm sure they never had a coach who lectured them on the abstract subject of *teamwork.* Likewise, in my watching of the deer that overrun Shelter Island, I've seen an experienced doe put herself in front of her fawn to protect it from an approaching car; but I hardly think she did it on the basis of a concept like *traffic.* All such behavior of animals in the wild, therefore, is priestly without a shred of knowledge about *priesthood.*

It's when we make *pets* of animals, however, that we lift them into something quite like our own priesthood. We lift them to the level of *persons* who can join us in our offerings of the world. Old "Tom" (the black-and-tan mongrel who was another of our household's pets) certainly knew his proper name; and he also knew, far better than I, all the shortcuts that could take him from the outer marches of my morning run back to the rectory. In those halcyon days before leash laws, I'd just say, "Tom, go home," and off he would go. As fast as I might run, I never beat him back once. In his doggy, non-conceptual way — with no *map* in his mind and no *directions* to confuse him — he was always there first, waiting to give me a welcoming bark when I returned to *his* porch.

In fact, it's those dreadful leash laws that bring me back to Adam's naming of the animals — and to our own priestly relationships with them. In its deepest sense, the "dominion" over them that we were given on the sixth day was to be precisely *sacerdotal.* Far from issuing man a license to lord it over them by craft and force, God was inviting us to be their protectors and nurturers — to lift them up rather than to keep them down.

There's an old saying that every time you put a leash on a dog, the dog has a leash on you. Your attempts to manage other creatures by control and constraint always backfire — for the simple reason that they're violations of the priesthood that alone can make you a free agent of the Coinherence. And that violation extends to all your activities, from the leashing of your dogs (cats, at least, have the sense not to put up with such nonsense) to the forgiveness of your brother's sins. One of the rules of priestliness is that you must be willing to lay down your life for your friends. A true priest must be willing to be a dead priest: if you can't manage to be dead to your brother's lies about you, you'll never be able to hold your brother as a "keeper." Even the Great High Priest himself, whom death cannot hold, dies as dead as a doornail for your sake. And when he rises, he still carries his death with him, held forever in his Sacred Wounds. Unless you emulate his Priesthood by dropping dead for at least one creature's sake, you'll lose the only grip you have on everything else.

*   *   *

Even at the end of all Adam's priestly naming, however, there is still "no helper fit for him." Though he is surrounded by "animals with friendly faces," no creature is as yet really like him — just as he himself, though made in the image of God, is not really the same as the God who reigns in the priestly

Coinherence of the Father, the Son, and the Holy Spirit. Nevertheless, God keeps on trying. He comes up with the brilliant idea of making a helper who will be *different* from Adam and yet made in the *same image* as Adam. The LORD God causes a "deep sleep" to fall upon the man. (The Hebrew calls it a *tardemah*, a "heavy sleep"; the Septuagint translates it as *ekstasin*, a "trance"; and the Vulgate renders it as *soporem*, a "deep sleep.") Since that brings us nicely to the rest of the scenes in this chapter, here's the script for them:

LXX Gen. 2:21 καὶ ἐπέβαλεν ὁ θεὸς ἔκστασιν ἐπὶ τὸν Αδαμ καὶ ὕπνωσεν καὶ ἔλαβεν μίαν τῶν πλευρῶν αὐτοῦ καὶ ἀνεπλήρωσεν σάρκα ἀντ' αὐτῆς 22 καὶ ᾠκοδόμησεν κύριος ὁ θεὸς τὴν πλευράν ἣν ἔλαβεν ἀπὸ τοῦ Αδαμ εἰς γυναῖκα καὶ ἤγαγεν αὐτὴν πρὸς τὸν Αδαμ 23 καὶ εἶπεν Αδαμ τοῦτο νῦν ὀστοῦν ἐκ τῶν ὀστέων μου καὶ σὰρξ ἐκ τῆς σαρκός μου αὕτη κληθήσεται γυνή ὅτι ἐκ τοῦ ἀνδρὸς αὐτῆς ἐλήμφθη αὕτη 24 ἕνεκεν τούτου καταλείψει ἄνθρωπος τὸν πατέρα αὐτοῦ καὶ τὴν μητέρα αὐτοῦ καὶ προσκολληθήσεται πρὸς τὴν γυναῖκα αὐτοῦ καὶ ἔσονται οἱ δύο εἰς σάρκα μίαν 25 καὶ ἦσαν οἱ δύο γυμνοί ὅ τε Αδαμ καὶ ἡ γυνὴ αὐτοῦ καὶ οὐκ ᾐσχύνοντο

BHS Gen. 2:21 וַיַּפֵּל יְהוָה אֱלֹהִים תַּרְדֵּמָה עַל־הָאָדָם וַיִּישָׁן וַיִּקַּח אַחַת מִצַּלְעֹתָיו וַיִּסְגֹּר בָּשָׂר תַּחְתֶּנָּה: 22 וַיִּבֶן יְהוָה אֱלֹהִים אֶת־הַצֵּלָע אֲשֶׁר־לָקַח מִן־הָאָדָם לְאִשָּׁה וַיְבִאֶהָ אֶל־הָאָדָם: 23 וַיֹּאמֶר הָאָדָם זֹאת הַפַּעַם עֶצֶם מֵעֲצָמַי וּבָשָׂר מִבְּשָׂרִי לְזֹאת יִקָּרֵא אִשָּׁה כִּי מֵאִישׁ לֻקֳחָה־זֹּאת: 24 עַל־כֵּן יַעֲזָב־אִישׁ אֶת־אָבִיו וְאֶת־אִמּוֹ וְדָבַק בְּאִשְׁתּוֹ וְהָיוּ לְבָשָׂר אֶחָד: 25 וַיִּהְיוּ שְׁנֵיהֶם עֲרוּמִּים הָאָדָם וְאִשְׁתּוֹ וְלֹא יִתְבֹּשָׁשׁוּ:

VUL Gen. 2:21 inmisit ergo Dominus Deus soporem in Adam cumque obdormisset tulit unam de costis eius et replevit carnem pro ea 22 et aedificavit Dominus Deus costam quam tulerat de Adam in mulierem et adduxit eam ad Adam 23 dixitque Adam hoc nunc os ex ossibus meis et caro de carne mea haec vocabitur virago quoniam de viro sumpta est 24 quam ob rem relinquet homo patrem suum et matrem et adherebit uxori suae et erunt duo in carne una 25 erant autem uterque nudi Adam scilicet et uxor eius et non erubescebant

KJV Gen. 2:21 And the LORD God caused a deep sleep to fall upon Adam, and he slept: and he took one of his ribs, and closed up the flesh instead thereof; 22 And the rib, which the

RSV Gen. 2:21 So the LORD God caused a deep sleep to fall upon the man, and while he slept took one of his ribs and closed up its place with flesh; 22 and the rib which the LORD God had taken

NRSV Gen. 2:21 So the LORD God caused a deep sleep to fall upon the man, and he slept; then he took one of his ribs and closed up its place with flesh. 22 And the rib that the

LORD God had taken from man, made he a woman, and brought her unto the man. 23 And Adam said, This *is* now bone of my bones, and flesh of my flesh: she shall be called Woman, because she was taken out of Man. 24 Therefore shall a man leave his father and his mother, and shall cleave unto his wife: and they shall be one flesh. 25 And they were both naked, the man and his wife, and were not ashamed.

from the man he made into a woman and brought her to the man. 23 Then the man said, "This at last is bone of my bones and flesh of my flesh; she shall be called Woman, because she was taken out of Man." 24 Therefore a man leaves his father and his mother and cleaves to his wife, and they become one flesh. 25 And the man and his wife were both naked, and were not ashamed.

LORD God had taken from the man he made into a woman and brought her to the man. 23 Then the man said, "This at last is bone of my bones and flesh of my flesh; this one shall be called Woman, for out of Man this one was taken." 24 Therefore a man leaves his father and his mother and clings to his wife, and they become one flesh. 25 And the man and his wife were both naked, and were not ashamed.

This, of course, brings up the subject of sex. But while I work up the nerve to tackle our sovereign source of mirth and misery, let me warm to the task with some off-the-wall comments on the "sex-change operation" the LORD God performed in the Garden of Eden.

To begin with, verse 21 gives us the biblical movie's first instance of anesthesia. Without drugs or gasses — indeed, with nothing more than a kind of divine Hypnosis — the LORD puts Adam into an *ekstasin,* a "standing outside himself." And the surgical procedure that ensues has all the hallmarks of futuristic medicine. A single rib is painlessly removed, tissue is implanted in its place, the "incision" leaves no mark, and the patient spends not a minute in the recovery room. The scene is straight out of *Star Trek,* where the in-house physician of the *Starship Enterprise* punches almost instantaneous healing into her patient with a gadget that looks, for all the galaxy, like a cell phone.

And there's more of the same. In verse 22, the Director shows us the divine Physician taking the rib to his laboratory for the Bible's first successful *cloning.* I know. The analogy is shaky. Barring further developments in that controversial science, the genetic material in a man's rib would yield only a male clone. Maybe the entire process is impossible. But then again, maybe the LORD was, as he so easily can be, ahead of our time. In any case, it happens right before our eyes in the movie, giving it quite enough historicity for all but the most foolish film-watchers. The words the Director uses to describe the divine Geneticist's labors in this experiment are "and he built": in the three ancient languages they are *vayyibhen, kai ōikodomēsen,* and *et aedificavit.* (The English versions dilute the earthy Hebraism to a mild "he made.") But then comes the successful — and gorgeous — result of the experiment. What is constructed from "the rib" *(hatstsela', tēn pleuran, costam)* turns out to be precisely a "woman" *('ishshah, gynaika, mulierem).*

Notice, if you will, how my lark through genetics has nailed the irrelevancy of interpretations that find a derogation of the "weaker sex" in this passage. There's nothing of the sort, because however God may have circumvented the rules of DNA, he obviously succeeded in producing a woman who has the *same nature* as the man. Moreover, inspired by his replication of that *unitary* aspect of his Being, God also makes her attractively — even wildly — *different* from the man, thus making mankind's "two for the price of one" an echo of his own better deal: Threeness at the divine Bargain of Oneness. But just before the Director's transition to verse 23, she hands her assistant a stage direction: "God now takes the woman 'and brings her' [*vay'bhi'eha, kai ēgagen autēn, et adduxit eam*] to the man."

In verse 23 itself, though, I find something that argues for God's increasing confidence in the priesthood of Adam. There's no divine "Let's see what the man will call her" here (as there was with the animals); instead, the camera holds on the man and his woman, and Adam simply blurts out his recognition of her (his *re-knowing* of her, his *naming* of her) in vividly specific terms. And Adam says, "This is at last bone of my bone [*zoth happa'am 'etsem me'atsmai, touto nyn ostoun ek tōn osteōn mou, hoc nunc os ex ossibus meis*], and flesh of my flesh [*ûbhasar mibb'sari, sarx ek tēs sarkos mou, caro de carne mea*]" — thus recognizing her as the very spit and image of his own priesthood.

Next, though, comes a bit of pedantry on Adam's part. His seminary training rears its ugly head, and he shows off his knowledge of etymology with a didactic aside to his non-existent class: "To this feminine creature will be given the name of Woman, because she was taken out of Man [*l'zo'th yiqqare' 'ishshah kî meîsh luqachah zo'th, hautē klēthēsetal gynē hoti ek tou andros elēmphthē hautē, haec vocabitur virago quoniam de viro sumpta est*]." Notice that all the versions, except the Greek, manage to reproduce the pun on *'ishshah/'îsh* in the original Hebrew: with <u>*virago/vir*</u> in the Latin, and Wo<u>man</u>/<u>Man</u> in the English.

Jerome, I think, was making a bit of a reach for the play on words when he tried to save it with the overly specific *virago* (a "man-like woman," a "female warrior," a "heroine") instead of the more general *mulier* for the woman. To him, I suppose, it may have sounded like a compliment; but at least some of its meanings have opened the door to less-than-kind male jokes. The English translators were luckier with "Woman/Man." The Hebrew wordplay was already built into their native language; had they been Germans, they would have been stuck with Luther's *Männin/Manne* — which is more awkward, and even less complimentary, than *virago/vir*.

Have I told you that the Hebrew text is *not* a version? I have? Well, I shall just tell you again. The word *version* comes from the Latin *vertere*, "to turn around"; and in its root sense it always means a translation — a *turning* of the original language of a document into another tongue. *Ergo,* we've been working throughout this book with one *original* (in Hebrew) and five *versions* in other languages.

In any case, Professor Adam is unable to shut himself up. He next delivers himself of a short disquisition on moral theology — the unlikelihood of which the Director gladly overlooks because it introduces the image of *Marriage*. In verse 24, she has Adam say, "Therefore a man leaves his father and mother [a flagrant anachronism, since Adam had neither] and cleaves to his wife, and they become *one flesh*." The Hebrew for this is *'al-ken ya'azabh-'ish'eth-'abhiv v"eth 'immō v'dhabhaq b"ishtō v'hayû l'bhasar 'echad;* the Greek is *heneken toutou kataleipsei anthropos ton patera autou kai tēn mētera kai proskollēthēsetai pros tēn gynaika autou kai esontai hoi dyo eis sarka mian;* and the Latin is *quam ob rem relinquet homo patrem suum et matrem et adherebit uxori suae et erunt duo in carne una.*

The Director, in short (in fact, at some length), now fetches the image of Adam as male and female from the sixth day and plants it here as an image of humanity in the likeness of the *Trinity.* As I've already intimated, the marriage that makes the two one flesh becomes a sacrament of the Coinherence by which the Three are one God. So I take back my slur about the academic tone of Adam's moral-theology lecture. Here, he's doing *dogmatic* theology at warp speed — which is the very thing I've been trying to do, perhaps less speedily (and less charmingly), in this chapter. The marriage of the man and his wife now stands as a sacrament of the Word by whom all things are made and returned to the Father. And so do all our marriages, whether of convenience or inconvenience — and whether they're sanctioned by state, or church, or personal choice.

Every one of the sacraments is a real presence of something that's already present *outside* itself. In the Eucharist, Jesus does not show up in a room from which he was previously absent. In Baptism, the candidate does not receive a Jesus he or she didn't have before. In Confession, the priest does not add a thing except assurance of the forgiveness that Jesus already gave, once and for all, to the whole world. And every one of our joinings — in business or pleasure, in love or friendship, in wisdom or folly, in marriage or divorce (no marriage ever really gets out of our system) — is a *communion* by which the Love who holds us reiterates his long-standing policy of never letting us go. They are not to be justified by the human affection they may or may not achieve. Their ultimate justification lies in Love himself. The only thing we can do is rest, or grow restless, in his arms.

In verse 25, however, the Director wraps up her scenes of the Garden so far by showing us the sheer success of God's experiment with sexuality. She has her Narrator read (over the strains of *Alle Menschen werden Brüder* from Beethoven's Ninth Symphony) these words: "And they were both naked, the man and his wife, and they were not ashamed" (*vayih'yû sh'nêhem 'arûmmîm ha'adham v'aiishtô v'lo' yithboshashû; kai ēsan hoi dyo gymnoi ho te Adam kai hē gynaika autou kai ouk ēschynonto; erant autem uterque nudi Adam scilicet et uxor eius et non erubescebant*).

I'm aware that I promised to deal with both the mirth and the misery of sex after my warm-up to it. But on second thought, the warmth of that scene has changed my mind. If I get to the other edge of the two-edged sword of sexuality at all, it will be later in this book — where Adam will come up with his excuse for hiding in the bushes after he's made sex a problem it never was. The LORD God, out for an evening stroll in his Garden, says, "Adam, where are you?" And Adam says, "I heard your voice in the Garden, and I was afraid because I was *naked*." And the LORD says, "Who gave you that egregious piece of non-information? Have you eaten of the fruit of the tree of which I commanded you not to eat? In case you hadn't noticed, I rather liked your nakedness." Until we reach that point, therefore, *tacet* the darker side of sexuality.

I think I remember once reading, in the reductionist ramblings of an otherwise fine scientist, that "the purpose of sexuality was to insure [*sic*] the immortality of the gene pool." Alas, that actuarial solecism makes a glorious activity duller than a death benefit, and the gene pool as dry as a desert. The impetuousness of sex was not ordained by an actuary. It was instituted by the *impetus Fluminis*, by the rush of the River that makes glad the City of God — by the impetus of God's own *Amor Mutuus*, his Mutual Love, his Holy Spirit, who proceeds from the Father and the Son. Nor was the gene pool dug out by day laborers. Sex was the cavity excavated by the Word to become the Municipal Swimming Pool of the City of God — the *Water Park* in which every creature with soul enough could splash its way to freedom.

Therefore, what I shall give you here will be neither a statistical analysis of the odds on insuring ourselves against inactivity between the sheets nor a lecture on the political benefits that might come from our sexual congresses. Rather, it will be my personal tribute to sex — my very own (if I may be so bold) *orgasm recital*.

It opens with a *Toccata* on the theme *Komm Süsser Tod*, "Come, Sweet Death." Our orgasms are not only the beginning of life; they are also the grand sacrament of the end of life, of the *letting go* and the *letting be* that carry us out of our own control into the uncontrollable and uncontrolling joy of God. They're not a ride we take with our wits about us; they're a ride that *takes us,* as Auden said, beyond all liking and happening. They're the *Wave* of the Spirit herself — of the *Breaker* that slowly gathers beneath us until it crests and sends us speeding out of our minds toward the beach of delicious exhaustion.

Next comes the *fugue* — on the theme of our inveterate *running* after orgasms. None of them are fully controllable, and some are beyond all control. Augustine, of course, could see this fact only as evidence that our fall robbed us of rational control over our lives. That was understandable, I suppose. His times, and the history of his own days, left him with no other conclusion. But the influence of his bad days was as much the bane of posterity as his better days were a blessing. The governing power of reason is vastly overrated. It may be able to build houses and form societies, to make omelets and negotiate treaties; but ever since Eden, it's been unable to produce a life worth living, and in all the millennia of our history, it has never brought peace to our world. Our fleeting orgasms are a constant witness to the truth that life with its changes and chances — and liberty with its unpredictability, and the pursuit of happiness with its risk that we will never catch up — are always waiting for us just beyond the reach of reason, and quite outside the scope of our good intentions. We don't run the race of sex; the race runs us. It was a sport meant for racers willing to chance it, not for grim competitors who want to win medals.

Full organ now: this is "the time of man's innocency." The man and his wife, naked and not ashamed, are one with all the living things of earth — with the *plants* because, like Adam and Eve, they too reproduce in a dance of sex and death; and with the *animals* because, just as the Man and his Woman frolicked among the trees like squirrels in springtime, they too flit through the bushes playing hard to get. *Nothing is wrong here.* And in the glorious End, when we shall rise in the fullness of our restored sexuality, we shall have it all back.

But in the meanwhile . . .

THE CORRUPTION OF GOD'S ECOLOGY OF GOOD AND EVIL

Genesis 3:1-24

TWENTY

The Beginning of the Misery

GENESIS 3:1-7

Let me begin as far as possible from the subject of misery. I was born in Queens, with the sounds of New York Jewish humor ringing in my ears. Practically from birth, I was an assimilated Gentile: the Borscht Belt was the girdle of my mind. And, predictably, the comedians I was most drawn to when I grew up were Shelly Berman, Jackie Mason, and Alan King. They may have had Anglicized names, but I had a Yiddish heart. The first girl I fell in love with in grade school was a perfect Ruth, with lovely breasts and dark hair: she lived down the block from P.S. 89 in an *apartment* — which, to my twelve-year-old Episcopalian mind, was the quintessence of Jewishness.

But even before then, I made afternoon friends with Ralphie Goldenkopf and Jackie Resnick. Ralphie's father was only a rumor to me, but his mother was the original cookie pusher. I can still taste her *Hamantaschen.* On the other hand, Jackie's father was a real presence in his family. They lived over his paint store under the Roosevelt Avenue El — and he knew from paint. He would have loved the finish on my harpsichord, but I can hear him saying, "So, Bobby, how come you still haven't finished the job?"

I lost track of those early loves when I went to Stuyvesant High School in Manhattan. Another Alan, cut from the same cloth, became my best friend. He too lived in Queens, and after school we used to go to the abandoned Holmes's Airport and declaim poetry at each other in the high wind. And then came my competitors for highest grade average at Stuyvesant. In our junior and senior years, the five of us vied with each other to see who would come first in the second decimal place of the 98th percentile. There was J. Arthur Greenwood the mathematician, Alan Turner (*né* Dreher) the English specialist, and (New York being New York) a Lutheran named Robert Schrage and a Roman Catholic named William Shanahan — all of them so bright you could read by their light.

Every one of us of was infected with Jewish humor. Jokes were the staples of our lunch hours. Let me give you a sampler:

> A man goes into a Lower East Side delicatessen. He looks at his soup and says, "Waiter, what's this fly doing in my soup?" The waiter says, "The backstroke."

> Same man, same restaurant, same question. The waiter says, "There wasn't room in the potato salad."

> Four men go into a delicatessen. The first says, "I'll have a glass tea," and the second and third say, "I also will have a glass tea." But the fourth says, "Bring me a glass tea; but in a clean glass." The waiter ambles off and eventually comes back with four glasses on a tray. He says, "Who ordered in a clean glass?"

Or, for the pick of the literature — and as a bridge to the misery that dawned on us in the Garden of Eden — try this one.

> A man comes up to a rabbi as he's walking home after Friday-night services. He says, "Rabbi, tell me. Why does a rabbi always answer a question with a question?" The rabbi strokes his beard and says, "Why shouldn't a rabbi always answer a question with a question?"

In the scenes you're about to watch, God is exactly like that rabbi. When Adam hides in the bushes after he's eaten the fruit of the tree, the response of the divine Nudge — in the best tradition of the Catskills — is all questions:

> The LORD calls to Adam and says, "Adam, where are you?" And Adam says, "I heard your voice in the Garden, and I was afraid because I was naked." And God says, "Who told you you were naked?"

This is a God who knows from timing. His "Who told you you were naked?" is history's first one-liner: *six words* and Adam is the butt of a Jewish joke. God does bring up the subject of sin, and he does mention sexuality — but just barely. So the one thing I'm *not* about to do here is encourage the notion that the sin of Adam and Eve was a sexual trespass. Sex will indeed go down the tubes in this story, but in the same way as all other human activities:

not by a deliberate choice of evil over good, but by a mindless missing of God's point in holding good and evil as an ecology. Instead of letting both be, as God does, our first parents will propel us into a perpetual war between white hats and black hats — a war that can finally be un-declared only by God himself on the cross. Nevertheless, at this point in the Director's film, the war hasn't even started. There is only innocency in the midst of fun.

So the first thing I want to note about the sequence that's coming up is that the Director leaves no break whatsoever between it and the innocency of Adam and Eve. (As you may have noticed, the ancient languages are not fond of breaks, either: the Hebrew has only minimal punctuation, and the Septuagint and the Vulgate dispense with it entirely.) Be that as it may, when the serpent comes on-screen, Adam and Eve are still naked and unashamed. Their innocency is not simply an absence of criminality; it's the positive presence of their pleasure in their own skins. In fact, the snake slithers up to Eve while she's taking a voluptuous breather from the *naked dance* of their nuptials.

For that's precisely what marriage itself was meant to be: a *romp* through life with no clothes, material or mental, to hide our nakedness. (This is not to disparage the fashion industry. As you'll see later on, God's sense of humor joins hands with his fashion sense. Even in his annoyance with Adam and Eve, he won't allow them to walk out of Eden in tacky aprons.) At this point, however, they haven't a stitch to cover themselves. "Which things," as Paul said, "are an allegory" (Gal. 4:24). Everything about us is "naked and opened" to anyone "with whom we have to do" (Heb. 4:13). Our marriages, willy-nilly, are sacraments of what all human relationships are: our others know us better than we know ourselves. Our foibles don't fool them. They recognize our follies the minute we commit them; even our lies are bare-necked, scarf-less transparencies to them. We may run, but we can't hide.

Now, however, as the Stage Manager prepares to send the serpent "oozing charm from every pore" and "oiling his way across the floor" of Eden, there's nothing here to hide. Everything is just peachy. There are no rules against any *real* thing Adam and Eve might want to do. There is only God's warning that they should not do something *unreal* with the tree of the knowledge of good and evil.

At this point, though, I have two suggestions for the Director. Back at Genesis 2:17-18, she could have reintroduced the triangular, golden Cloud of the Trinity and shown the two divine Hands putting up a NO TRESPASSING sign on the forbidden tree. And now, at the beginning of chapter 3, I think she should hire *Alan King* as the voice of the serpent. The snake is a rabbi too, and Alan has not only the beardy tone but also the rabbinical speech patterns to go with the part.

But otherwise, Adam and Eve haven't yet had a problem in the world. Like the plants of the dry land and the beasts of the field, they've had the sense to stay clear of nonsense. And that *original innocence* of theirs is crucial to our understanding of what's about to happen. *For if we were never as good as God said we were in the beginning, he would never have gotten as upset with us as he did.*

*   *   *

That, however, gets us ahead of the film. Here at last is the script for this chapter:

LXX Gen. 3:1 ὁ δὲ ὄφις ἦν φρονιμώτατος πάντων τῶν θηρίων τῶν ἐπὶ τῆς γῆς ὧν ἐποίησεν κύριος ὁ θεός καὶ εἶπεν ὁ ὄφις τῇ γυναικί τί ὅτι εἶπεν ὁ θεὸς οὐ μὴ φάγητε ἀπὸ παντὸς ξύλου τοῦ ἐν τῷ παραδείσῳ 2 καὶ εἶπεν ἡ γυνὴ τῷ ὄφει ἀπὸ καρποῦ ξύλου τοῦ παραδείσου φαγόμεθα 3 ἀπὸ δὲ καρποῦ τοῦ ξύλου ὅ ἐστιν ἐν μέσῳ τοῦ παραδείσου εἶπεν ὁ θεὸς οὐ φάγεσθε ἀπ' αὐτοῦ οὐδὲ μὴ ἄψησθε αὐτοῦ ἵνα μὴ ἀποθάνητε 4 καὶ εἶπεν ὁ ὄφις τῇ γυναικί οὐ θανάτῳ ἀποθανεῖσθε 5 ᾔδει γὰρ ὁ θεὸς ὅτι ἐν ᾗ ἂν ἡμέρᾳ φάγητε ἀπ' αὐτοῦ διανοιχθήσονται ὑμῶν οἱ ὀφθαλμοί καὶ ἔσεσθε ὡς θεοὶ γινώσκοντες καλὸν καὶ πονηρόν 6 καὶ εἶδεν ἡ γυνὴ ὅτι καλὸν τὸ ξύλον εἰς βρῶσιν καὶ ὅτι ἀρεστὸν τοῖς ὀφθαλμοῖς ἰδεῖν καὶ ὡραῖόν ἐστιν τοῦ κατανοῆσαι καὶ λαβοῦσα τοῦ καρποῦ αὐτοῦ

BHS Gen. 3:1 וְהַנָּחָשׁ הָיָה עָרוּם מִכֹּל חַיַּת הַשָּׂדֶה אֲשֶׁר עָשָׂה יְהוָה אֱלֹהִים וַיֹּאמֶר אֶל־הָאִשָּׁה אַף כִּי־אָמַר אֱלֹהִים לֹא תֹאכְלוּ מִכֹּל עֵץ הַגָּן: 2 וַתֹּאמֶר הָאִשָּׁה אֶל־הַנָּחָשׁ מִפְּרִי עֵץ־הַגָּן נֹאכֵל: 3 וּמִפְּרִי הָעֵץ אֲשֶׁר בְּתוֹךְ־הַגָּן אָמַר אֱלֹהִים לֹא תֹאכְלוּ מִמֶּנּוּ וְלֹא תִגְּעוּ בּוֹ פֶּן־תְּמֻתוּן: 4 וַיֹּאמֶר הַנָּחָשׁ אֶל־הָאִשָּׁה לֹא־מוֹת תְּמֻתוּן: 5 כִּי יֹדֵעַ אֱלֹהִים כִּי בְּיוֹם אֲכָלְכֶם מִמֶּנּוּ וְנִפְקְחוּ עֵינֵיכֶם וִהְיִיתֶם כֵּאלֹהִים יֹדְעֵי טוֹב וָרָע: 6 וַתֵּרֶא הָאִשָּׁה כִּי טוֹב הָעֵץ לְמַאֲכָל וְכִי תַאֲוָה־הוּא לָעֵינַיִם וְנֶחְמָד הָעֵץ לְהַשְׂכִּיל וַתִּקַּח מִפִּרְיוֹ וַתֹּאכַל וַתִּתֵּן גַּם־לְאִישָׁהּ עִמָּהּ וַיֹּאכַל: 7 וַתִּפָּקַחְנָה עֵינֵי שְׁנֵיהֶם וַיֵּדְעוּ כִּי עֵירֻמִּם הֵם וַיִּתְפְּרוּ עֲלֵה תְאֵנָה וַיַּעֲשׂוּ לָהֶם חֲגֹרֹת:

VUL Gen. 3:1 sed et serpens erat callidior cunctis animantibus terrae quae fecerat Dominus Deus qui dixit ad mulierem cur praecepit vobis Deus ut non comederetis de omni ligno paradisi 2 cui respondit mulier de fructu lignorum quae sunt in paradiso 3 de fructu vero ligni quod est in medio paradisi praecepit nobis Deus ne comederemus et ne tangeremus illud ne forte moriamur 4 dixit autem serpens ad mulierem nequaquam morte moriemini 5 scit enim Deus quod in quocumque die comederitis ex eo aperientur oculi vestri et eritis sicut dii scientes bonum et malum 6 vidit igitur mulier quod bonum esset lignum ad vescendum et pulchrum oculis aspectuque delectabile et tulit de fructu illius et comedit deditque viro suo qui comedit 7 et aperti sunt

ἔφαγεν καὶ ἔδωκεν καὶ τῷ
ἀνδρὶ αὐτῆς μετ᾽ αὐτῆς καὶ
ἔφαγον 7 καὶ διηνοίχθησαν
οἱ ὀφθαλμοὶ τῶν δύο καὶ
ἔγνωσαν ὅτι γυμνοὶ ἦσαν
καὶ ἔρραψαν φύλλα συκῆς
καὶ ἐποίησαν ἑαυτοῖς
περιζώματα

oculi amborum cumque
cognovissent esse se nudos
consuerunt folia ficus et
fecerunt sibi perizomata

KJV Gen. 3:1 Now the serpent was more subtil than any beast of the field which the LORD God had made. And he said unto the woman, Yea, hath God said, Ye shall not eat of every tree of the garden? 2 And the woman said unto the serpent, We may eat of the fruit of the trees of the garden: 3 But of the fruit of the tree which *is* in the midst of the garden, God hath said, Ye shall not eat of it, neither shall ye touch it, lest ye die. 4 And the serpent said unto the woman, Ye shall not surely die: 5 For God doth know that in the day ye eat thereof, then your eyes shall be opened, and ye shall be as gods, knowing good and evil.
6 And when the woman saw that the tree *was* good for food, and that it *was* pleasant to the eyes, and a tree to be desired to make *one* wise, she took of the fruit thereof, and did eat, and gave also unto her husband with her; and he did eat. 7 And the eyes of them both were

RSV Gen. 3:1 Now the serpent was more subtle than any other wild creature that the LORD God had made. He said to the woman, "Did God say, 'You shall not eat of any tree of the garden'?"
2 And the woman said to the serpent, "We may eat of the fruit of the trees of the garden; 3 but God said, 'You shall not eat of the fruit of the tree which is in the midst of the garden, neither shall you touch it, lest you die.'" 4 But the serpent said to the woman, "You will not die. 5 For God knows that when you eat of it your eyes will be opened, and you will be like God, knowing good and evil." 6 So when the woman saw that the tree was good for food, and that it was a delight to the eyes, and that the tree was to be desired to make one wise, she took of its fruit and ate; and she also gave some to her husband, and he ate.
7 Then the eyes of both were opened, and they knew that they were naked; and they sewed fig leaves

NRSV Gen. 3:1 Now the serpent was more crafty than any other wild animal that the LORD God had made. He said to the woman, "Did God say, 'You shall not eat from any tree in the garden'?" 2 The woman said to the serpent, "We may eat of the fruit of the trees in the garden; 3 but God said, 'You shall not eat of the fruit of the tree that is in the middle of the garden, nor shall you touch it, or you shall die.'" 4 But the serpent said to the woman, "You will not die; 5 for God knows that when you eat of it your eyes will be opened, and you will be like God, knowing good and evil." 6 So when the woman saw that the tree was good for food, and that it was a delight to the eyes, and that the tree was to be desired to make one wise, she took of its fruit and ate; and she also gave some to her husband, who was with her, and he ate. 7 Then the eyes of both were opened, and they knew that they were naked; and they sewed opened, and they knew that they *were* naked; and they sewed fig leaves together, and made themselves aprons.

together and made themselves aprons.

fig leaves together and made loincloths for themselves.

What I need to dispose of first in this scenario are questions you may have about this character who confronts Eve. You want to ask, "Who exactly is this *nachash,* this *ophis,* this *serpens?* Is he only a snake who talks like Alan King, or is he the devil in disguise, the father of lies out on the prowl? Or is he just an old myth, not made for modern minds?" Frankly, I don't much care one way or the other. As your movie reviewer, I'm content simply to watch him and listen to what he says. So I can answer you with an "all of the above," or a "both," or a "neither" — as long as I remember that what I think doesn't amount to a hill of beans compared to what I see and hear. Whoever he may be, it's the rabbinically devious thrust of his questions that fascinates me.

As you've heard, the Director tells us he is "'more subtle" than any other beast of the field. That's how the KJV and the RSV describe him; and the NRSV has "crafty." The Hebrew has *v'hannachash hayah 'arûm mikkol chayyath hassadheh;* the Septuagint renders this as *ho de ophis ēn phroni-mōtatos pantōn tōn thēriōn epi tēs gēs;* and the Vulgate has *sed et serpens erat callidior cunctis animantibus terrae.* '*Arûm* means "shrewd"; *phronimōtatos* means "the most sensible, thoughtful, or worldly-wise"; and *callidior* means "the more clever, skillful, sly, or cunning." All three words leave room for the serpent to tell the *truth* when it suits his purposes.

In any case, his first question to the woman in verse 1 is a set-up, a rhetorical sucker-pitch that he knows is way off the plate. "Has God said," he asks in Alan King's voice, "'You shall not eat of any tree of the Garden'?" She almost doesn't swing at it; but then, missing the point of his shrewdness, she can't resist a half-swing that strikes her out. Her best response, of course, would have been to just say "No" and stare the pitcher down. But instead she tries to correct him — always a bad tactic when you're dealing with a star closer. She says, "Goodness gracious! That's not true at all! We may certainly eat of the fruit of the trees of the Garden; but of the fruit of the tree that is in the midst of the Garden, God has said, 'You shall not eat of it, neither shall you touch it, lest you die.'" By my count, that's fifty-two words too many when you're up against a rabbi who can pitch.

But since I've already reviewed this scene back in Chapter Seventeen (not to mention the scenes in verses 2 through 5), let me add only one thing about this sequence so far. The serpent is testing the woman to see if she'll fall for his hidden agenda. He's trying to trick her into turning the Garden into the *control room* of creation — and the tree of the knowledge of good and evil into a stuck throttle that will choke the world with gas. We preachers love to go on about the *vastness* of Adam's and Eve's sin. But their sin, in itself, wasn't vast at all. Compared to the reality of their surroundings, it was tiny: a triviality, a minuscule act, a belch in the history of the universe. To mix metaphors completely, they created a little closet in their heads where they could keep control over what God refuses to touch.

God (as I've said to the point of wearing you down) holds good and evil as an ecology. And that ecology goes right on being the way the real world works, no matter what we do. The man and the woman can *think* they're controlling things — just as we've *thought* we could control them ever since. But outside the closet of our minds, the only thing our vaunted control can do is go against the grain of reality. But the *results* of our contrariness are truly vast. Adam's and Eve's sin was a small thing, but it was enough to undo God's whole harmony — as we're now learning to our sorrow. We are quite able — and dangerously willing — to assassinate life on earth in the name of the "higher" goods we've concocted in our minds. The nuclear winter that our missile defenses are designed to prevent may just as easily come because of them. With nothing but mental power at our disposal, our self-deception can overpower the world.

Let me move on, then, to verses 6 and 7, where the seeds of our misery begin to sprout. The woman now sees three things about the tree in her mind's eye, but only two of them are true. She sees that "the tree is good for food" (*tôbh ha'ets l'ma'akhol; kalon to xylon eis brōsin; bonum esset lignum ad vescendum*), and "a delight to the eyes" (*ta'avah la'ênayîm; areston tois ophthalmois; pulchrum oculis*). But when she comes to her third mental eye-balling of the tree, she produces a wild falsehood. The Bible (RSV) says she saw that "the tree was to be desired to make one wise." The Hebrew has just that: *nechmadh ha'ets l'haskîl,* "the tree was to be coveted to make wise." The Septuagint has something close: *hōraion estin tou katanoēsai,* "it is beautiful to the understanding." And the Vulgate, a bit oddly, has *aspectuque delectabile,* "and delectable in being seen."

This at last is the trick of perception that brought the gorgeousness of God's creation down like a house of cards. Admittedly, Eve got a 66.6 on the serpent's test. But while it may have been a barely passing grade, it was not enough to keep old 666 himself from demoting her to a lower grade in his school for scandal. And it was certainly not enough for God to have much hope of promoting her on the spot. The unfixable fix was in, and the rest is history — our sorry school record in the Kindergarten of the world. In jumping to her final conclusion, our first mother didn't leap out of a basement window; she plunged from the pinnacle of creation in a fall that still hasn't hit bottom — and she took her husband down with her. That all her children are now in danger of ending up in hell is too obvious to mention. But it's important to note that God has put his own Wisdom in our flesh — and but for our refusal to trust his Word's word that we're already in heaven, we need never go to hell. "If I go down to hell, thou art there also." In Jesus, the whole world is home free, whether it likes its surroundings or not. What a shame to argue with such a gallant promise.

But now comes the proof of our insistence on arguing with it anyway. In verse 7, the damage done in the human mind spills over into the real world. In the KJV it reads, "And the eyes of them both were *opened,* and they *knew* that they were *naked;* and they sewed *fig leaves* together, and made themselves *aprons*" (italics mine). The words I've italicized appear in the Hebrew as *tippaqachnah, yedh'û, 'erumîm, 'alêh t'aienah,* and *chaghoroth;* in the Septuagint as *diēnoichthēsan, egnōsan, gymnoi, phylla sykēs,* and *perizōmata;* and in the Vulgate as *aperti sunt, cognovissent, nudos, folia ficus,* and *perizomata.* But since the tree was precisely about the *knowledge* of good and evil, let's begin with Adam's and Eve's stunningly stupid discovery of the *nakedness* they suddenly thought they knew for the first time.

It's all baloney. From the moment they were made, they'd never been anything *but* naked. Adam's vision of Eve as "bone of my bones and flesh of my flesh" was not a glimpse through a nightgown or a bathrobe. The naked man simply recognized, in the naked woman, the same being as himself — with some delightful if puzzling differences. And the naked Eve (assuming she looked at herself first) must have seen the naked Adam, if not with fear and trembling, then at least with admiration for God's sense of humor. As I've said, the knowledge of their nakedness could not possibly have been news — unless it was a dangerously perverse knowledge of something that *wasn't there.* And that's exactly what it was: the gratuitous manufacture of a shame, of a guilt they'd never known before. The sin in the Fall, therefore, was internal, not external. It sprang not from the *fruit* of the tree but from the *eating* of the fruit — from the *digesting* of a lie about reality. And from there on, it was only a matter of time until it spilled over into the as yet innocent world.

Hebrew is not a language of abstractions. It's a tissue of concrete nouns, verbs, and adjectives that can deal with high subjects in an earthy way *(reigning you will reign, dying you will die).* And even though *eating you will eat* does not appear in the text, its meaning is plain: "You will metabolize this lie until it becomes the truth of your miserable lives." It would be hilarious if it weren't so sad. The sin of Adam and Eve in the Garden was a bad joke on the human intellect — a silly extravagance, a pointless peripatation around the simple truth of their being. And it took them clean (or murkily) out of their minds. They didn't learn anything here. They focused on the unlearnable, and they paid the price. They became fools — and they took us into their folly with them.

That leaves only the fig leaves with which they covered their privy parts — their *pudenda* (to use the shame-filled Latinism). *That* was what the "aprons" were all about, you know. They weren't gowns to flatter their figures, or headdresses to glorify their faces, or shoes to save their feet. They were itchy little chastity belts to protect their newfound — and useless — embarrassment. Enter here, then, the *guilt* for which the Bible is unjustly famous — unjustly, because the God of Holy Scripture is embarrassed by nothing. He can see a man pissing against a wall and declare him a soldier fit to do battle. And he can see King David leering from his rooftop at the nude Bathsheba, and then (after a few "Ahems" over the contract David put out on her husband Uriah) make her David's wife, the mother of Solomon — the spoiled little bastard whom the Director makes the wisest king in the history of Israel.

But above all, in the Incarnation of God's Word in Jesus, God makes shamelessness his supreme virtue. Our Lord hangs out with prostitutes and crooked tax collectors, he welcomes sinners and eats with them, he breaks the Holy Sabbath — and, to cap the climax, he takes an endlessly sinning world into his sinless self on the cross and drops all its guilt into the eternal Forgettery of his dead human mind. As a matter of fact, guilt barely makes it into the Bible. "Jewish guilt" is over-rated: most likely it was invented by Jewish mothers-in-law (of both sexes) who thought they could keep their families in line by shaming them. And "Christian guilt" is a total non-starter. Peter, Paul, the Apostles, the Apostolic Succession, the squabbling Church Militant — and everybody else, all the way down to you and me — are all guilty as hell. *But it doesn't matter to Jesus.* "God made him who knew no sin *become sin for us,* that we might become the righteousness of God in him" (2 Cor. 5:21, RFC). Guilt is *gone.* "Sin is behovely, and all shall be well, and all shall be well, and all manner of thing shall be well." At least the Lady Julian got it right.

*   *   *

Do you at last see the *Mystery* of God's ecology in all this? Everything that Adam and Eve had in the Garden of the world has changed, and yet nothing real has happened. The germ of misery has been injected into the veins of the human mind; but as yet, no one has even sneezed. The serpent was right: they did not die. But he also lied, because the seeds of a world living in fear of death have now been planted. This is what Hannah Arendt called "the banality of evil," the *triteness* of how little it takes to make a whole world go wrong. T. S. Eliot has some lines in "The Hollow Men" that sum it up nicely enough:

> This is the way the world ends
> This is the way the world ends
> This is the way the world ends
> Not with a bang but a whimper.

The Incarnate Word, though, sums it up better when he dies on the cross. He says, *Tetelestai:* "It is finished — it is done to perfection." Yet nothing on earth gets any better as a result of his death: misery is still our lot here and now. We believe, of course, that in his resurrection everything is made new. But even when he rises, the misery goes on: *nothing changes here.* The warriors keep on warring, the dying still end up dead — and the world he has already translated into heaven continues to go to hell in a handbasket. In his mysterious love of goodness — and in his even more mysterious tolerance of evil — he still lets both be, because in him their harmony is already restored.

But even the world itself can remind us of the ecology we've wrecked. No matter how hard we try, we cannot do away with earth's faithfulness to the harmonies of God that we've violated. As Francis Thompson said in "The Hound of Heaven,"

> I tempted all His servitors, but to find
> My own betrayal in their constancy,
> In faith to Him their fickleness to me,
>   Their traitorous trueness, and their loyal deceit.

For all our efforts to make things happen to our liking, the things themselves have stayed with the One beyond all liking and happening. We may sink everything we were meant to lift up, but we can never drown out creation's passion for the Incarnate Word, who draws it to himself. Look at this splendid poem by James Stephens:

What Thomas an Buile Said in a Pub

> I saw God. Do you doubt it?
>   Do you dare to doubt it?
> I saw the Almighty Man. His hand
> Was resting on a mountain, and
> He looked upon the World and all about it:

I saw him plainer than you see me now,
   You mustn't doubt it.

He was not satisfied;
   His look was all dissatisfied.
His beard swung on a wind far out of sight
Behind the world's curve, and there was light
Most fearful from His forehead, and He sighed,
"That star went always wrong, and from the start
   I was dissatisfied."

He lifted up His hand —
   I say He heaved a dreadful hand
Over the spinning earth. Then I said, "Stay,
You must not strike it, God; I'm in the way;
And I will never move from where I stand."
He said, "Dear child, I feared that you were dead,"
   And stayed his hand.

The "I" in that poem is not just Thomas an Buile, who is plainly drunk. He's also the Word of God whose cross stands in the way of our destruction — and who, before his passion, prayed to his Father at the end of his Supper Discourse in the seventeenth chapter of the Gospel according to Saint John. That passage has been called The Great High Priestly Prayer of Jesus. But let me rinse the solemnity of that name out of my mouth with some wine of humor.

It's taken me fifty-three years to recuperate completely from the hangover of higher criticism I suffered in seminary. But now I have; so good-bye and good riddance to all the times I've coughed out the words "The Fourth Gospel" in order to please the Doctors. Lord knows, I should have gotten an obedience prize from them for not ascribing it to the Beloved Disciple. I even went so far as to revise the old Sunday school rhyme to remind myself to drink their cheap whiskey. I changed it from "Matthew, Mark, Luke, and John,/Hold my horse till I get on" to "Matthew, Mark, Luke, and Fourth,/Speak not that name from South to North."

But with the phlegm of such fussiness at last out of my throat — and "with me haart no longer in it," as Thomas the Irishman might say — I can finally see what Luther had in mind when he gave the Supper Discourse the beery name *Tischrede*. It was precisely "table talk," tipsy but serious chitchat before a short and nasty death. It was *gallows humor* (dare I say Gallo's humor?). Jesus was being funny and funereal, wry yet real at the same time; but he got in everything on his agenda with well-chosen, winey words. The Temperance Union and the League of Anti-alcohol Clinicians to the contrary notwithstanding, Jesus was in his cups — even, quite properly, drunk as a Lord. *In vino veritas.*

For there was indeed wine at that table — and Jesus was no mean winebibber. If you listen closely to what he says in front of his friends, you'll hear the unmistakable rhythms of inebriation (which St. Ignatius of Loyola picked up in his *Anima Christi:* "Soul of Christ, sanctify me. . . . Blood of Christ, *inebriate* me"). Jesus never married; but if he had, I'm sure his wife would have told him not to drink so much. She'd say it was the drink talking when he said, over and over, *Amēn, Amēn, legō hymin:* "Verily, Verily, I say to you." But she wouldn't see that, in his relentless circling over the same subjects, she was hearing the Truth himself, full of a stronger Spirit than wine, discoursing on everything under the sun. On *love,* on the *world,* on his *glory,* on *eternal life,* and on the *oneness* of everyone in the Unity he has with his Father. Socrates kept talking after the hemlock went down. Jesus goes on and on after he's drunk the wine that is the blood of the New Covenant in his death.

Strangely, John spends five chapters on this dinner conversation without saying a word about Jesus' institution of the Lord's Supper. But even more strangely, at the end of chapter 14 John puts in something that all the other Gospel writers seem to have missed. After only two chapters of table talk, John records that Jesus does something odd. Abruptly signaling the waiter for the check, Jesus takes everybody out of the Upper Room for an outdoor stroll. *Egeiresthe, agōmen enteuthen,* John has him say: "Up you go — let's get out of here."

But Jesus never stops talking. Do you know what I think that means? It means he was so enchanted by wine and words that he just had to begin his walk to the cross. His Great High Priestly Prayer in chapter 17, therefore, was an ambulatory prayer — a walking conversation with his Father that was itself a parable of his obedience. I commend that notion to you because it makes perfect sense of the beginning of the chapter that immediately follows the Supper Discourse. John 18:1 reads, "And having said these things, Jesus went out with his disciples across the Kidron valley where there was a garden, which he and his disciples entered" (RFC). Having spoken to his Father, he realizes that the season of evening strolls is over, and it's time to head for the garden of his betrayal.

It's possible, of course, that the words at the end of chapter 14 should have been blue-penciled from the start — that John too was in his cups that night. But I don't think so. His memory strikes me as better than anybody's, and he certainly has no qualms about insisting on what he saw and heard.

(See John 21:24: "This is the disciple who's bearing witness about these things and who wrote these things, and we know that his witness is true," RFC). More likely, they were all drunk *except* for John, who seems to have had his wits about him the whole night — and to have been anything but hung over the next day. (Peter might get a little credit for following Jesus to the house of the high priest, but he left after his third denial of Jesus and went out to weep tears of drunken desperation.) But the rest of them? "They all forsook him and fled" — like bleary-eyed fraidycats whose three years of listening to Jesus went whistling down the wind of their run for cover.

*   *   *

I know. My ruminations on John's Gospel may themselves have struck you as unsober, if not as an affront to your piety. But I've given them to you as an object lesson in seeing the Bible as a movie to be *taken in* rather than a book to be *deciphered*. They show you the liberation from literalism you might find if you can stop asking questions of the biblical text and just watch it. But now, perhaps, a darker question occurs to you. You wonder whether any of this (from John or Genesis or me) can be true at all. The only honest answer I can give you is that I think the question is irrelevant.

Truths are like puppies. There's no point in arguing over whose truth is the best, any more than there is in quarreling about whose puppy is the cuddliest. Truths or puppies, we care about them because we find them *delightful,* not because we understand them. They appeal more to our sense of humor than to our sense of importance. So if there's even a grain of *veritas* in that vinous comparison, the most any of us can say is, "I like my truth-doggy better than yours." Anything more pretentious, and we forget that we can keep truth only as a *pet.* It's fun to have around, even if it wets our floors and chews up our slippers; but we really know very little about the beast. Only God knows the truth, the whole truth, and nothing but the truth. We just pat its head, pull its tail, and hope for the best. Only the Father, who holds Truth Itself in his beloved Son, actually *owns* It.

Before we end this chapter, I have two surprises for you. Earlier in this book, I suggested that the Director might use *four voices* for the lines spoken by God on the six days of creation. I said she might cast an alto voice for the Spirit; two voices, soprano and tenor, for the Son (to capture his femininity as the divine Wisdom and his masculinity as the divine Word); a bass voice to represent the *gravitas* of the Father Almighty; and *all four voices in unison* for lines redolent of the Trinity. I can now make that more specific. In the *first* chapter of Genesis, the bass voice of God should have a timbre of Authority, a tone that suggests the divine Omni-Competence — the Self-Assurance of a Deity who can bring everything out of nothing as easily as saying "*THIS* IS CNN." *James Earl Jones* is the man for the job.

But in the second and third chapters, I think the Director should switch to a voice more suited to the Central Park West character who appears here as the LORD God. This LORD is a God who dabbles in mud, who fails before he succeeds at making a helper fit for Adam, and who has a short but funny divine Fuse. And who better for the voice of this NUDGE God than *Billy Crystal*, the God of the Academy Awards. Not only would his diffident, whining masculinity be comic relief from the sonorities of Mr. Jones; it would also send a subtle signal that we are now in the presence of a Creator who understands stand-up. Bear that in mind, if you will, as we proceed into the rest of Genesis 3 — and please do remember my entire cast of off-screen actors: Liv Ullmann as the Director, Anthony Hopkins as the Narrator, Alan King as the Snake, and Messrs. Jones and Crystal as the Two-Sided Three-in-One.

On we go, then — into the tragicomic consequences of our Fall.

TWENTY-ONE

The Passing of the Buck
and the Beginning of God's Curses

GENESIS 3:8-15

Since I've already touched on this scene at some length, I'll try not to repeat myself. But in the light of my recent showbiz imagery, I'd like to give you a whimsical update of the Director's movie so far, plus some "coming attractions" of the scene we're about to watch.

As I now see God's work in Genesis 1, he finished his first creative engagement at the heavenly Concord with a James Earl Jones wrap-up: in his best CNN voice, he pronounced everything "VERY GOOD!" In Genesis 2, however, the LORD God booked himself into the earthly Grossinger's (as Billy Crystal) and did a comedy act whose ending is equally happy: the man and his wife are "NAKED AND NOT ASHAMED." But then, at the beginning of Genesis 3 (still at Grossinger's), he sent in the serpent (Alan King) to do a warm-up routine before his best act of all: his send-up of the tragedy of the Fall, beginning with the zinger, "WHO TOLD YOU YOU WERE NAKED?"

Now the LORD God will really strut his stuff. He'll take a late-afternoon stroll in the Garden — puffing on creation's first Havana cigar and watching his favorite spaniel scamper ahead of him. He's looking, of course, for the unhappy couple, but in his rabbinical Omniscience, he already knows everything about their nonsense: they've *eaten* of the tree of the knowledge of good and evil, and they're *hiding* in the woods out of *fear*.

We need to ask, "Fear of what?" Of the LORD whom Adam was never terrified at before? No. Of the serpent that Eve spoke with so fearlessly? No again. The fear-mongering villain of this tragicomic shtick will turn out to be an abstraction they concoct out of thin air in their heads. In short, they'll invent *RELIGION*. They'll become their own godawful parents and give themselves the willies with all the rules and laws they've made up for themselves. *That's* what made them think they could no longer stand before God in their nakedness. And that's what now makes them *ashamed*.

I know. I've milked the Solomon County imagery almost to the point of exhausting your patience; so let's CUT to the Garden as the Narrator begins to read from the script:

LXX Gen. 3:8 καὶ ἤκουσαν τὴν φωνὴν κυρίου τοῦ θεοῦ περιπατοῦντος ἐν τῷ παραδείσῳ τὸ δειλινόν καὶ ἐκρύβησαν ὅ τε Αδαμ καὶ ἡ γυνὴ αὐτοῦ ἀπὸ προσώπου κυρίου τοῦ θεοῦ ἐν μέσῳ τοῦ ξύλου τοῦ παραδείσου 9 καὶ ἐκάλεσεν κύριος ὁ θεὸς τὸν Αδαμ καὶ εἶπεν αὐτῷ Αδαμ ποῦ εἶ 10 καὶ εἶπεν αὐτῷ τὴν φωνήν σου ἤκουσα περιπατοῦντος ἐν τῷ παραδείσῳ καὶ ἐφοβήθην ὅτι γυμνός εἰμι καὶ ἐκρύβην 11 καὶ εἶπεν αὐτῷ τίς ἀνήγγειλέν σοι ὅτι γυμνὸς εἶ μὴ ἀπὸ τοῦ ξύλου οὗ ἐνετειλάμην σοι τούτου μόνου μὴ φαγεῖν ἀπ' αὐτοῦ ἔφαγες 12 καὶ εἶπεν ὁ Αδαμ ἡ γυνή ἣν ἔδωκας μετ' ἐμοῦ αὕτη μοι ἔδωκεν ἀπὸ τοῦ ξύλου καὶ ἔφαγον 13 καὶ εἶπεν κύριος ὁ θεὸς τῇ γυναικί τί τοῦτο ἐποίησας καὶ εἶπεν ἡ γυνή ὁ ὄφις ἠπάτησέν με καὶ ἔφαγον

BHS Gen. 3:8 וַיִּשְׁמְע֞וּ אֶת־ק֨וֹל יְהוָ֧ה אֱלֹהִ֛ים מִתְהַלֵּ֥ךְ בַּגָּ֖ן לְר֣וּחַ הַיּ֑וֹם וַיִּתְחַבֵּ֨א הָֽאָדָ֜ם וְאִשְׁתּ֗וֹ מִפְּנֵי֙ יְהוָ֣ה אֱלֹהִ֔ים בְּת֖וֹךְ עֵ֥ץ הַגָּֽן: 9 וַיִּקְרָ֛א יְהוָ֥ה אֱלֹהִ֖ים אֶל־הָֽאָדָ֑ם וַיֹּ֥אמֶר ל֖וֹ אַיֶּֽכָּה: 10 וַיֹּ֕אמֶר אֶת־קֹלְךָ֥ שָׁמַ֖עְתִּי בַּגָּ֑ן וָאִירָ֛א כִּֽי־עֵירֹ֥ם אָנֹ֖כִי וָאֵחָבֵֽא: 11 וַיֹּ֕אמֶר מִ֚י הִגִּ֣יד לְךָ֔ כִּ֥י עֵירֹ֖ם אָ֑תָּה הֲמִן־הָעֵ֗ץ אֲשֶׁ֧ר צִוִּיתִ֛יךָ לְבִלְתִּ֥י אֲכָל־מִמֶּ֖נּוּ אָכָֽלְתָּ: 12 וַיֹּ֖אמֶר הָֽאָדָ֑ם הָֽאִשָּׁה֙ אֲשֶׁ֣ר נָתַ֣תָּה עִמָּדִ֔י הִ֛וא נָֽתְנָה־לִּ֥י מִן־הָעֵ֖ץ וָאֹכֵֽל: 13 וַיֹּ֨אמֶר יְהוָ֧ה אֱלֹהִ֛ים לָאִשָּׁ֖ה מַה־זֹּ֣את עָשִׂ֑ית וַתֹּ֙אמֶר֙ הָֽאִשָּׁ֔ה הַנָּחָ֥שׁ הִשִּׁיאַ֖נִי וָאֹכֵֽל:

VUL Gen. 3:8 et cum audissent vocem Domini Dei deambulantis in paradiso ad auram post meridiem abscondit se Adam et uxor eius a facie Domini Dei in medio ligni paradisi 9 vocavitque Dominus Deus Adam et dixit ei ubi es 10 qui ait vocem tuam audivi in paradiso et timui eo quod nudus essem et abscondi me 11 cui dixit quis enim indicavit tibi quod nudus esses nisi quod ex ligno de quo tibi praeceperam ne comederes comedisti 12 dixitque Adam mulier quam dedisti sociam mihi dedit mihi de ligno et comedi 13 et dixit Dominus Deus ad mulierem quare hoc fecisti quae respondit serpens decepit me et comedi

KJV Gen. 3:8 And they heard the voice of the LORD God walking in the garden in the cool of the day: and Adam and his wife hid

RSV Gen. 3:8 And they heard the sound of the LORD God walking in the garden in the cool of the day, and the man and his wife hid themselves

NRSV Gen. 3:8 They heard the sound of the LORD God walking in the garden at the time of the evening breeze, and the man and his wife themselves from the presence of the LORD God amongst the trees of the garden. 9 And the LORD God called unto Adam, and said unto him, Where *art* thou? 10 And he said, I heard thy voice in the garden, and I was afraid, because I *was* naked; and I hid myself. 11 And he said, Who told thee that thou *wast* naked? Hast thou eaten of the tree, whereof I commanded thee that thou shouldest not eat? 12 And the man said, The woman whom thou gavest *to be* with me, she gave me of the tree, and I did eat. 13 And the LORD God said unto the woman, What *is* this *that* thou hast done? And the woman said, The serpent beguiled me, and I did eat.

from the presence of the LORD God among the trees of the garden. 9 But the LORD God called to the man, and said to him, "Where are you?" 10 And he said, "I heard the sound of thee in the garden, and I was afraid, because I was naked; and I hid myself." 11 He said, "Who told you that you were naked? Have you eaten of the tree of which I commanded you not to eat?" 12 The man said, "The woman whom thou gavest to be with me, she gave me fruit of the tree, and I ate." 13 Then the LORD God said to the woman, "What is this that you have done?" The woman said, "The serpent beguiled me, and I ate."

hid themselves from the presence of the LORD God among the trees of the garden. 9 But the LORD God called to the man, and said to him, "Where are you?" 10 He said, "I heard the sound of you in the garden, and I was afraid, because I was naked; and I hid myself." 11 He said, "Who told you that you were naked? Have you eaten from the tree of which I commanded you not to eat?" 12 The man said, "The woman whom you gave to be with me, she gave me fruit from the tree, and I ate." 13 Then the LORD God said to the woman, "What is this that you have done?" The woman said, "The serpent tricked me, and I ate."

Note first that Adam and Eve's fear has nothing to do with God and everything to do with themselves. They're cringing at a god they made up in their own minds; and they now compound their panic by inventing a world that will need an endless string of lies to keep it going.

Their new "un-creation" begins quietly enough. In verse 8, Adam and Eve hear God's Voice as he's *walking* in the Garden: "walking" is *mithhalekh, peripatountos,* and *deambulantis* — all of which mean "walking around." In fact, it was from the Greek *peripatountos* that I got the six-bit word *peripatation* with which I described this walk "in the cool of the day" (*l'rûach hayyôm,* "at the wind, the breath of the day"; *to deilinon,* "at evening"; *ad auram post meridiem,* "at the late-afternoon breeze"). And Adam and his wife *hid* themselves (*vayyithchabbê; ekrybēsan; abscondit se*) from *the face* (*mipp'nê; apo prosōpou; a facie*) of the LORD God in the midst of the wood of the Garden. But before I move on to the tissue of lies they weave, let me give you a few unkind paragraphs about the English versions of this passage.

All of them (even the KJV) avoid the vivid imagery of the Hebrew phrase "from *the face of* the LORD God" and substitute *from the presence of* for it. Why? Well, I think the reason is that their compilers had a less-than-perfect understanding of what translations of Scripture ought to be. *Translate* is from the Latin *transfero, transferre, transtuli, translatus* — "to carry over, to *bring over.*" But what is it that good translators are supposed to *bring over* into a second language? Is it just the *meaning* of the original? I think not. Meaning is the province of expositors, scholars, and preachers. But it can be the province of translators only if they can explain what a word means without sacrificing its status as an *image* in the whole of Scripture. If their explanations obscure its "concordances" with the rest of the film, they're not only out of their province, they're in Outer Mongolia. The *face of the* LORD *God* is simply too big an image to lose.

Our translations, regrettably, have too often lost the images of Scripture in a fog of interpretation. Generally speaking, the KJV is the least guilty of this loss, the RSV is more so, and the NRSV is as guilty as hell of this crime against faithful translation. Paul's brilliant use of the concordances of the word *seed* in Galatians 3:15-16 is a case in point. He knew that the "seed" (meaning the "descendants" that Abraham was promised in Genesis 12:7) was *singular* in the Hebrew (*l'zar"akha,* "to your *seed*") — and he also knew that in the Septuagint (which was what he quoted from for the benefit of his Greek-speaking readers), it appeared in the singular as "to your *seed* [*tōi spermati sou*] will I give this land." Paul observes that God did not say "to seeds" *(tois spermasin),* as if he were talking about many descendants, but to your "seed," as if he had only *one* such person in mind.

Do you see what I'm getting at? Had Paul been an over-explanatory Englishman — and thus tempted to use the RSV's "descendants" (or, worse yet, the NRSV's vague "offspring") — his entire argument would have gone up in smoke. He could never have gotten himself to the double meaning of that single seed. He would never have realized that while its primary referent in Genesis is Isaac (Abraham's promised heir, his link to the history of Israel), its ultimate referent in the complete film of Scripture is the *Mashiach,* the Messiah of the Chosen People — the *Christos,* the Word of God Incarnate in the Lord Jesus.

But enough of translations that betray images by interpretation. In Genesis 3:9, we hear the nudging, singsong voice of Billy Crystal as he gives God's almost Yiddish reaction to the lies he knows are waiting to be told. The LORD God *calls* to Adam. "AA-DAM! *AA*-DAM? ADAM *SCHMADAM,* where *ARE* you?" This is God as the divine Rabbi who knows all the answers but prefers to confront cluelessness with questions. (One small but interesting note here, suggested by the "quotes" I put around Billy Crystal's lines. No doubt you've read the KJV often enough; but have you realized that it never uses quotation marks? Instead, it simply capitalizes the first word of its quotations. This is not important to you? Not even *interesting?* What happened to your curiosity?)

On to verses 10 and 11. Adam says (KJV), "I *heard* thy voice in the Garden, and I was *afraid,* because I was *naked;* and I *hid* myself" (italics mine). That's nine words in the Hebrew, fifteen in the Greek, and fourteen in the Latin. But in that short space, Adam manages to include one obvious truth, two silly reactions, and one totally useless program of action. The *truth* is his "I heard" (*sham'atî, ēkousa,* and *audivi*). The *reactions* are "I was afraid" (*'îra', ephobēthēn,* and *timui),* and "because I was naked" *(kî-'êrom, hoti gymnos eimi,* and *eo quod nudus essem).* And the *useless program* is "I hid" (*'echabhe', ekrybēn,* and *abscondi me).* And why does he hand the LORD God such a grab bag of excuses? Because his mind is focused only on his idiotic efforts to do something — anything — that would undo what was undoable to begin with. Because one lie is never enough to support a world that doesn't exist, and which he never once thought of before.

Back in Genesis 2, Adam had heard the LORD God's warning about the tree of the knowledge of good and evil without batting an eye. He wasn't afraid at the beginning of that chapter; and all through it, he was as pleased with his nakedness as God was. But here, he announces his discovery of this non-news as if it were hot off the presses. The real news, however, lies precisely in his *shame* at something that was never shameful — and in his *fear* of something that never needed to exist. Adam's dread of God isn't the holy fear that's the beginning of Wisdom. It's the beginning of our unholy fear, of our self-induced trembling, at the face of a Friend who will never forsake us. As the old hymn has it, "His wrath is ever slow to rise, and ready to abate."

God is indeed easily provoked; but his beatific Peevishness is only his Mercy as it's seen by people who insist on burying themselves in a grave inside their own heads — by the incorrigibly stupid, who richly deserve God's "Oh, damn!" but whom he will never consign to damnation unless they insist on it. His Mercy draws *all* to himself. The only place we can go to hell from is the heaven of his Grace; and the only thing we can do wrong with that "happy issue out of all our afflictions" is to object forever, for whatever dumb reasons, to its hilarious graciousness. But nothing — not death, not life, not angels, not principalities, not things present, not things to come, not powers, not height, not depth, not any other created thing — can separate us from the Love of God in Christ Jesus our Lord (Rom. 8:38-39, RFC).

Thus our terror at the curses of God and our fear of hell come only and entirely out of the lies we tell ourselves — out of the dread-filled *religions* we've saddled ourselves with — not out of anything remotely resembling the final Will of God for us. It comes from the self-invented laws of retribution with which we've bound not only mankind but also (sadly) the God whose anger leads him only to the Passion of his love. But "the Word of God is not bound" (2 Tim. 2:9) — except by his inexorable Mercy. On the cross, he submits himself to death so that in our own deaths he might set us free. At the heart of the Mystery of Christ, therefore, is the truth that he never *seriously* meant a single one of his damning words. And our failure to take *that* seriously stems from all the solemn pieties that have made us miss the point of Grace.

Nevertheless, we are free. Nevertheless, there is *no law* that can stand before Grace. As Paul said in Romans 4:14-16, "For if we can be heirs only by the law, faith is emptied of its meaning, and the promise [to Abraham] is nullified; for the law produces wrath, but where there is no law, there is no transgression. For this reason, everything depends on faith, in order that it all might go home by Grace, so that the promise to every seed of Abraham might be made firm . . ." (RFC).

Back to Adam's and Eve's missing of that point. I've already given you my thoughts about God's "Who told you you were naked?" so let's move on to Adam's reply in verse 12. He now finds the inevitable rhyme for shame — and out of his mouth comes *blame.* The rule of the fallen world is, "When you can't think of a defense, pin your crime on someone else." And Adam does just that. He says, "The woman [*ha'ishshah, hē gynē, mulier*] that you gave to be with me [*'asher nathattah 'immadhî, hēn edokas met' emou, quam dedesti sociam mihi*], SHE gave me [*HÎ' nathnah-lî, HAUTĒ moi edoken, dedit mihi*] of the tree, and I ate [*min-ha'ets va'okhel, apo tou xylou kai ephagon, de ligno et comedi*]."

That capitalized SHE is not just the first instance of bad manners in the Bible (only an oaf uses the third person to talk about someone in the room); it's the birth of male chauvinism. To be sure, Adam used the word before, back in Genesis 2:23. But there, he was admiring his wife, not criticizing her. He said (more to himself than to God), "*THIS* [*zo'th* is a feminine demonstrative pronoun] is now bone of my bone and flesh of my flesh: *SHE* shall be called Woman, because SHE was taken out of Man."

In this verse, though, it's pure derogation — hardly more than a snide "this little woman." He hasn't given her the name Eve yet; but even if he had, it would have made no difference in his tone. Like a nasty husband giving his wife a dig in front of company, he tells God, "That's a woman for you. She read the map wrong. She couldn't find her way out of a wet paper bag." The failed history of the human race begins with a man who uses sexist humor to evade responsibility.

But he doesn't stop at that. Eve is not just "the woman" to Adam now; he tells the LORD that she's the woman "*YOU* gave me." Once the blame game has started, you see, it will stoop to anything to avoid a time out — even if it might give us a respite from battling God's offensive line-up. On and on we've gone, complaining but never letting up. "Why does God allow terrorists to fly planes into buildings?" "What sort of God would let my innocent baby die of leukemia?" "If God is just, why do the wicked prosper?" "Why did he give me a wife who can't tell north from south?" We will take even God himself down with us, if that will assuage our indignation at a deity we ourselves invented.

And from there it's only a short step to our fixation on the evils of other people — to the paranoid style not only of American politics but of every place and nation. We all do it. You and I, with our stigmatization of former friends as "rotten apples"; and those more highly placed than we, with their lumping of North Korea, Iran, and Iraq into an "axis of evil" that may cost us the friendship of wiser, less bellicose nations. We will put others to tests we ourselves cannot pass, just to avoid the self-examination we most fear. And we won't even notice we're doing it, because our wars between good and evil (which have never solved anything) demand the extermination of evil — even if it means the death of everything good. Still, "The war made me do it" is no better an excuse than "The dog ate my homework." As long as we persist in self-justification, just that long do we keep ourselves from seeing ourselves as others see us, God included.

Now, though, in verse 13, the divine Rabbi turns his questioning to the woman. "What's this that you've done?" he asks *(mah-zoth 'asîth, ti touto epoiēsas, quare hoc fecisti)*. And she answers, "The serpent [*hannachash, ho ophis, serpens*] deceived me [*hishshî'anî, ēpatēsen me, decepit me*], and I ate [*va'o'khel, kai ephagon, et comedi*]." This is the second passing of the counterfeit buck of blame — and it's fake for two reasons. First, the snake only *half-deceived* her. Back in Genesis 3:5, when he said, "You will be like God, knowing good and evil," he was speaking to someone who had *already* been made in the image and likeness of God — which made only his use of the future tense ("you *will be*") a lie. And second, God *allowed* the bogus bill to be passed because he'd made Eve free to violate even his no-fault ecology of good and evil. Either way, though, her blaming was irrelevant — and God shows his impatience with her by turning his attention to the serpent.

Here are the opening lines of the LORD God's curses on the folly of everyone in the Garden. (I'll leave the rest of them for the next chapter.)

LXX Gen. 3:14 καὶ εἶπεν κύριος ὁ θεὸς τῷ ὄφει ὅτι ἐποίησας τοῦτο ἐπικατάρατος σὺ ἀπὸ πάντων τῶν κτηνῶν καὶ ἀπὸ πάντων τῶν θηρίων τῆς γῆς ἐπὶ τῷ στήθει σου καὶ τῇ κοιλίᾳ πορεύσῃ καὶ γῆν φάγῃ πάσας τὰς ἡμέρας τῆς ζωῆς σου 15 καὶ ἔχθραν θήσω ἀνὰ μέσον σου καὶ ἀνὰ μέσον τῆς γυναικὸς καὶ ἀνὰ μέσον τοῦ σπέρματός σου καὶ ἀνὰ μέσον τοῦ σπέρματος αὐτῆς αὐτός σου τηρήσει κεφαλήν καὶ σὺ τηρήσεις αὐτοῦ πτέρναν

BHS Gen. 3:14 וַיֹּאמֶר יְהֹוָה אֱלֹהִים אֶל־הַנָּחָשׁ כִּי עָשִׂיתָ זֹּאת אָרוּר אַתָּה מִכָּל־הַבְּהֵמָה וּמִכֹּל חַיַּת הַשָּׂדֶה עַל־גְּחֹנְךָ תֵלֵךְ וְעָפָר תֹּאכַל כָּל־יְמֵי חַיֶּיךָ: 15 וְאֵיבָה אָשִׁית בֵּינְךָ וּבֵין הָאִשָּׁה וּבֵין זַרְעֲךָ וּבֵין זַרְעָהּ הוּא יְשׁוּפְךָ רֹאשׁ וְאַתָּה תְּשׁוּפֶנּוּ עָקֵב:

VUL Gen. 3:14 et ait Dominus Deus ad serpentem quia fecisti hoc maledictus es inter omnia animantia et bestias terrae super pectus tuum gradieris et terram comedes cunctis diebus vitae tuae 15 inimicitias ponam inter te et mulierem et semen tuum et semen illius ipsa conteret caput tuum et tu insidiaberis calcaneo eius

KJV Gen. 3:14 And the LORD God said unto the serpent, Because thou hast done this, thou *art* cursed above all cattle, and above every beast of the field; upon thy belly shalt thou go, and dust shalt thou eat all the days of thy life: 15 And I will put enmity between thee and the woman, and between thy seed and her seed; it shall bruise thy head, and thou shalt bruise his heel.

RSV Gen. 3:14 The LORD God said to the serpent, "Because you have done this, cursed are you above all cattle, and above all wild animals; upon your belly you shall go, and dust you shall eat all the days of your life. 15 I will put enmity between you and the woman, and between your seed and her seed; he shall bruise your head, and you shall bruise his heel."

NRSV Gen. 3:14 The LORD God said to the serpent, "Because you have done this, cursed are you among all animals and among all wild creatures; upon your belly you shall go, and dust you shall eat all the days of your life. 15 I will put enmity between you and the woman, and between your offspring and hers; he will strike your head, and you will strike his heel."

In these two verses, the LORD God momentarily loses interest in the woman and turns his attention to the snake — whom he recognizes as having a rabbinic mind much like his own. Have you noticed that the serpent doesn't say a word or ask a question about God's curse on him? Do you realize that Alan King is now temporarily out of work? I have, and it leads me to suggest that we underestimate the devil's role in the movie of the Bible. Satan may well be the "adversary" of God, but he's an adversary whose advances God *welcomes*.

In the book of Job, the devil is right up there in God's eternal Boardroom, questioning the policies of the divine CEO. Alan King returns as the voice of Satan, and James Earl Jones is back as the voice of God. Let me give you the script as the Narrator begins it:

> KJV: Job 1:6 Now there was a day when the sons of God came to present themselves before the LORD, and Satan came also among them. 7 And the LORD said unto Satan, Whence comest thou? Then Satan answered the LORD, and said, From going to and fro in the earth, and from walking up and down in it. 8 And the LORD said unto Satan, Hast thou considered my servant Job, that *there is* none like him in the earth, a perfect and an upright man, one that feareth God, and escheweth evil? 9 Then Satan answered the LORD, and said, Doth Job fear God for nought? 10 Hast not thou made an hedge about him, and about his house, and about all that he hath on every side? thou hast blessed the work of his hands, and his substance is increased in the land. 11 But put forth thine hand now, and touch all that he hath, and he will curse thee to thy face. 12 And the LORD said unto Satan, Behold, all that he hath *is* in thy power; only upon himself put not forth thine hand. So Satan went forth from the presence of the LORD.

Plainly, this is not God arguing with someone alien to himself. It's an inseparable pair of Rabbis in the divine Mind going at each other with pointed questions. Two posers are from Rabbi God, and two from Rabbi Satan — and the dark side wins the game, at least for openers. With only slightly qualified divine Permission, Satan goes out and, during a party in the house of Job's sons and daughters, plays havoc with everything Job has. Job's oxen and asses are stolen by the Sabeans. They kill all his servants except the poor wretch who reports the disaster, and the "fire of *God*" (note how the text supports my contention that Satan and God are two in One) falls from heaven and burns up all his sheep and shepherds. Next, the Chaldeans steal his camels and kill the camel-keepers. And finally, a great wind from the desert collapses the house on Job's children and kills them all.

Job shaves his head, falls down upon the ground, and *worships*. And he says, "Naked came I out of my mother's womb, and naked shall I return thither: the LORD gave, and the LORD hath taken away; blessed be the name of the LORD." In all this, the Bible says, "Job sinned not, nor charged God foolishly."

But in chapter 2 of Job, Rabbi Satan comes back for another visit to the heavenly council-chamber:

> KJV: Job 2:1 Again there was a day when the sons of God came to present themselves before the LORD, and Satan came also among them to present himself before the LORD. 2 And the LORD said unto Satan, From whence

comest thou? And Satan answered the LORD, and said, From going to and fro in the earth, and from walking up and down in it. 3 And the LORD said unto Satan, Hast thou considered my servant Job, that *there is* none like him in the earth, a perfect and an upright man, one that feareth God, and escheweth evil? and still he holdeth fast his integrity, although thou movedst me against him, to destroy him without cause. 4 And Satan answered the LORD, and said, Skin for skin, yea, all that a man hath will he give for his life. 5 But put forth thine hand now, and touch his bone and his flesh, and he will curse thee to thy face. 6 And the LORD said unto Satan, Behold, he *is* in thine hand; but save his life. 7 So went Satan forth from the presence of the LORD, and smote Job with sore boils from the sole of his foot unto his crown. 8 And he took him a potsherd to scrape himself withal; and he sat down among the ashes.

God's two internal Rabbis are still bickering endlessly, but this time only Rabbi God tries to stick to his guns. His first query is just a repeat of the set-up question he asked the first time around. But when he comes to his second, he can't resist a bit of divine Bragging. "So what do you think of my servant Job *now?*" But Rabbi Satan has him where he wants him. "Hurt Job himself," he answers, "and he will curse you to your face." And Rabbi God gives in: he lets his opposite number go out and give Job the world's worst case of boils. But then, enter Job's wife (who is something less than the soul of sympathy, yet still a bit of a rabbi herself). She says to Job, "So? You're still going to play Mr. Longsuffering? Curse God and die." But he says to her (male chauvinism by now having become a fixture of human behavior), "Just like a woman! What's with you? We can receive good from the hand of God, and not evil?" And "in all this did not Job sin with his lips."

Nevertheless, Job now launches into thirty-five chapters of invective against God's two-facedness. It's a rant that will end only when the LORD himself appears to Job in the whirlwind. It reminds me of nothing so much as the old story about the prizefighter who staggers to his corner after a particularly punishing round:

> Handler: "Don't worry, Champ; he never laid a glove on you."
> Fighter: "Keep an eye on the Referee then, 'cause somebody in there's beatin' the hell out of me."

Ex ore infantium et lactantium perfecisti laudem (Ps. 8:2). Out of the mouth of the tongue-tied and the sucker-punched, thou hast perfected praise — for thy Conspiracy in the wounding of the world.

Fascinatingly, when God finally does speak from the whirlwind, he adds nothing to what Job's miserable comforters have been saying all along. The real point of the book of Job is that his comforters are just pious snobs in love with their theology, while Job is the only one who's actually in love with God. The book of Job is the story of a lovers' quarrel. Job's tirades are part and parcel of his infatuation with God, and they stop the minute he lays eyes on his Beloved: "I have heard you by the hearing of the ear; but now my eye sees you. Therefore I abhor myself, and repent in dust and ashes. I love you, and I'm sorry." And *nevertheless,* Job gets everything back — double.

I think *nevertheless* is almost the most important word in the Bible. And its most significant appearance is in 2 Kings 23:26 — where it shows up as *'akh* in the Hebrew, as *plēn* in the Septuagint, as *verumtamen* in the Vulgate, and as "Notwithstanding," "Still," and "Still" in the three English versions.

As clever writers do, the author of that verse has been setting up this "Grand Adversative," this All-Confounding "Nevertheless," from the beginning of 1 Samuel. But now he comes out with his final BUT to religion's false expectation that we will receive only good, and not evil, from the hand of God. For one hundred chapters of the books of Kings, he's been like a shareholder whose opening remarks to the annual meeting give the CEO nothing but *hope.* "Mr. Chairman," he begins, "I cannot tell you how much I admire your integrity and the boldness with which you maintain it. You are fair to a fault, and I would be the last to suggest that any corrupt design could find room in your thinking. Not only have you served us well in your management of our successes and by the unfailing wisdom with which you have managed our . . ." But enough. No matter how many praises you may hear him sing, you've known all along that the adversarial shoe was just waiting to drop.

So too with our author here. After all those chapters in which he laid the blame for Judah's woes on bad kings — after his relentlessly religious theory of history in which God would one day send a good King to make the sun shine on his people — God actually sends them Josiah, a King after his own heart. Josiah finds the long-neglected Law in the House of the LORD. He reads it, *and he actually keeps it.* He abolishes the worship of idols; he tears down the high places that Solomon had built for the abominable human sacrifices of the heathen; and he keeps such a Passover as had never been held before in Israel or Judah. "And like unto him was there no king before him, that turned to the LORD with all his heart, and with all his soul, and with all his might, according to all the law of Moses; neither after him arose there any like him" (2 Kings 23:25, KJV).

But then, in verses 26-27, God himself drops the other shoe with a clap of thunder. "*Notwithstanding* the LORD turned not from the fierceness of his great wrath. . . . And the LORD said, I will remove Judah also out of my sight, as I have removed Israel, and will cast off this city Jerusalem which I have chosen, and the house of which I said, My name shall be there." Josiah is slain by the Egyptians at Megiddo in 609 B.C.; and in 597, Jerusalem is sacked, and the Jews are led away captive to Babylon (Iraq!).

With one grand adversative, the life's work of the author of the books of Kings becomes just so much scrap paper in the trash can of *realpolitik*. The God of good reneges on his promises, and the God of evil licks his chops in satisfaction. And yet they are not two Gods but One. The God who holds good and evil as an ecology not only tolerates the evil — he takes full responsibility for it. Indeed, I'm even tempted to say that, for all biblical and practical purposes, Satan is the alter Ego of the great I AM.

No doubt that *really* bothers you. I've tried to soften it a bit by calling it God's "tolerance" of evil. But what's the point of that? For the Almighty to allow evil can mean only one of two things. Either he's not Almighty and *can't* stop it, or he is, and he *permits* it. Only the second represents the Bible's view, and it alone squares with common sense. If you see an eighteen-month-old toddling toward the edge of a cliff — and if you have the power to stop her but don't use it — *you* are the agent of her death.

*   *   *

But to convince you that the same is true of God throughout Scripture, I need to take you on an even longer detour than the one I've just made through the book of Job. I want to give you two more "testings" of God by God, two more debates between God and his equally significant Other, whose very existence he carries in his own Being. One will be the testing of the Incarnate Word in Matthew 4, after Jesus has fasted forty days in the wilderness; and the other will be the story of the Flood in chapters 6–9 of Genesis.

I'm aware that this may be a stretch for you. Like most people, you've probably watched the first of those scenes as the testing of God by someone other than God, and the second as the story of an angry God who at the end promises, inexplicably, never to destroy the world again. Your viewing habits are such that it will take a lot of looking before you can even consider another way of watching either of them. But be patient with me. With luck, this exercise may limber up your mind's eye.

First, then, the testing of Jesus by the devil. What takes place in the desert is not a contest between a good Jesus and a bad Satan. The Director may accept Matthew's version of the scene for its cinematic possibilities, but I think she knows better. That dialogue is actually a conversation of Jesus with Jesus — a debate between his left brain and his right brain.

Notice first what precedes it. It comes right after his baptism, where the Spirit hovered over him like a dove, and a Voice from heaven said, "This is my Son, the Beloved, in whom I am well pleased." Plainly, he now knows he has a spectacular career ahead of him; but logically, he needs some quiet time to consider what it will involve. So off he goes to fast and pray his way through the conflicts of his calling. Will he be, as some of the Scriptures suggest, a man-on-horseback Messiah, punching out the enemies of the Lord and making Israel the top dog of the world? Or did that most recent Voice, even though it spoke only of love, have something darker in his mind? In either case, those questions finally dramatize themselves in Jesus' mind at the end of his fast. He thinks through his options, checks them all against the Scriptures, and has a showdown — *with himself.*

But notice too that Jesus' "temptations," as we misleadingly call them, are not temptations to *sin.* Every choice he presents himself with is a possible good. A little bread after forty days of no food is not a crime. A death-defying leap from a tall building could be the very thing the troops need to strengthen their faith in God's power. And some effective measures to stop the ravages of politics-as-usual might be just what the doctor ordered. The *test,* therefore, is not to do wrong things; it is to do right things for the wrong reason — to do good by the methods of the Prince of this world rather than to follow the paradoxical methods of the King of the universe.

It's worth noting that the scene of this test is presented unevenly in the Gospels. Matthew and Luke give it a full, dramatic treatment; Mark devotes only a passing, two-verse reference to it; and John doesn't mention it at all. Furthermore, for all its prominence as the opening gun of Jesus' responses to his calling, none of the Gospel-writers record that Jesus ever mentioned it again. Why? Well, I think there are a couple of reasons. One is pure speculation on my part: since none of the disciples were present with Jesus in the wilderness, they could have learned about the testing only from Jesus himself. And as far as I'm concerned, there's only one place where that could have happened: during the forty days between his resurrection and his ascension, when he opened the disciples' minds to understand all the things that were written about him in the law of Moses, and in the prophets and the Psalms, *concerning himself* (Luke 24:44-45).

A second reason might well be that the Gospel-writers knew they were dealing with the same test every time they recorded people's objections to Jesus' predictions of his death. When Peter rebukes him for saying he will be a Messiah who will die, Jesus snaps back at him with a withering "Get thee behind me, Satan" (Matt. 16:23, and parallels). And when the Jews at Capernaum (who thought he'd make a dandy king) are perplexed by Jesus' weird allusions to his death, he just perplexes them further: "*Unless* you eat my flesh and drink my blood, you have no life in you" (John 6, verse 53 and passim). In both cases, however, the showdown over his career choices has occurred first and foremost in the mind of Jesus himself.

So try looking at the testing in the desert in that light. Jesus saw the role of a conquering Messiah as a tempting proposition. He could do a lot of good as a wonder-worker, if he put his mind to it. Not only could he make himself a stone sandwich any time he felt like it; he could also solve the world's hunger problem. He could abandon his dark, dense parables and give people visible signs of the anti-evil God they were desperately looking for. He could jump off the top of the temple and let them watch the angels catch him six inches from the sidewalk. "But then," he thinks. Always the "but then." What would he have to do to apply that right-handed power to an incorrigibly left-handed world — to all the kingdoms committed to the use of force? His Father, no doubt, was committed to letting their goods and evils co-exist. But then, wasn't he also *against* evil? Wasn't Lucifer right? Didn't the world that the Messiah would preside over respect only control?

Thus Jesus begins his imaginary conversation with the devil as Matthew records it. Alan King, of course, is the voice of the devil in Jesus' head, and he begins his first two tests with "If you're the Son of God." But then he backs up the suggestions he makes for Jesus' career moves with *messianic* passages of Scripture that promise divine Help and Protection to the LORD's Anointed. To both of those tests, Jesus responds with nothing but *commandment* passages that promise only the presence of the hands-off God. But when Alan comes to his third test, he drops the "if."

"Look," he says to Jesus. "I know who you are, and you know who I am. We're both *you*. So why don't we skip all this waltzing around and talk about the world everybody else lives in? Sure, you like solitude; but why should you be *lonely?* It's all so simple: with your power and my brains, we could turn this dump back into Eden in a month. A little responsible arm-twisting here and there, some attention-getting death penalties for people who deserve them, and lots of life sentences without parole for all the bleeding hearts who have no stomach for sensible solutions — why, we'd have a world that even your Father could be proud of. Just fall down and worship me, and you'll have all the right people on your side." But Jesus nixes that one too, and Alan's voice departs from his mind.

But only for a while. As I've said, that test will be repeated every time anyone objects to Jesus' being the Jesus he'll finally decide to be — to the Jesus who will heal a handful of sick people, cast out a few demons, and raise three corpses — but (and *nevertheless,* and *notwithstanding,* and *still,* and *still,* and *still*) *who will let the rest of the world continue in unrelieved misery.* The Mystery of the cross will be his only answer to the problem of evil to which Alan thought only control could be the solution.

As I promised, my final stop on this trip around the barn in which God stores his ecology of good and evil will be the story of Noah and the Flood in Genesis 6–9. It's the clincher of my case — so much so, that I think the Director should use only one voice (that of James Earl Jones) to speak for both sides of the divine Mind. There's no Lord/serpent contest here, no God/Satan fencing match, no Jesus/devil testing of wills. There's just the one God going off in two directions. And those directions are presented in stark contrast: two and five-sixths chapters on the angry God who can flush the human race down the drain without flinching, and one and one-sixth chapters on his exact opposite, the God who swears he'll never do anything like that again. Here's the point in the story at which he abruptly shifts into reverse:

> KJV: Gen. 8:20 And Noah builded an altar unto the Lord; and took of every clean beast, and of every clean fowl, and offered burnt offerings on the altar. 21 And the Lord smelled a sweet savour; and the Lord said in his heart, I will not again curse the ground any more for man's sake; for the imagination of man's heart *is* evil from his youth; neither will I again smite any more every thing living, as I have done. 22 While the earth remaineth, seedtime and harvest, and cold and heat, and summer and winter, and day and night shall not cease.

This test, you see, is entirely within God himself; and he passes the examination not on the basis of fancy theological distinctions but by his sense of smell. He gets one whiff of burnt fat, and his heart melts. The Lord *repents* himself of the evil that he thought to do, and he does it not. In the Hebrew, the verb "to repent" is *nacham.* It's used some forty times in the Bible, and in the vast majority of instances, it's applied not to God's people but to God himself. But however frequently theologians may have had problems with this God they treated as a manic-depressive — and however often they suggested drugs to palliate his symptoms — the God of Scripture seems never to have taken their prescriptions to the pharmacy.

For two good reasons. One, *he's* not maladjusted; the world is. And two, even the psychiatric fraternity has graduated from the term "manic-depression" to "*bipolar* disorder." And *there,* I think, is the word we've been looking for. "Bipolar" may be the very ticket we need to get us out of the mental-health clinic in which we've kept God waiting while the doctors tried to find a cure for his two minds about good and evil. (By the way, I have no *theological* use for the "disorder" part of that diagnosis. God's manic ordering of the universe may be too much for us to handle, but it's hardly the work of a clinically depressed Mind. A *bipolar* Mind, however, fills the bill nicely.)

Because if we don't fault a magnet for having a north and a south pole, we certainly don't have to fault God for having a good one and an evil one. A magnet without poles wouldn't be a *magnet;* and a God without a polarity of good and evil wouldn't be the *one* God who's got the whole world in his left and right hands — almost gleefully. Almost *reveling* in his bipolarity, in fact. "I form the light, and create darkness," the LORD says in Isaiah 45:7: "I make peace, and create evil: I the LORD do all these *things*" (KJV). And — best and worst yet — when he comes across evils he didn't make, he lets *them* be as well. The God of Scripture is no smug moralist trying to save the world by dispensing free advice and dire consequences. He's the Bipolar God of the Rainbow who can love his job and hate it at the same time.

The end of the Noah story makes that perfectly clear. After the LORD has set up his perennial sign of Mercy, Noah — his "safe bet" for a new beginning of the human race — scratches himself from the running. He plants a vineyard and gets drunk, and his son Ham tries to get his jollies by watching his father's erection during a hung-over nap. His two other sons — Shem, the forefather of the Semites, and Japheth, the ancestor of their friends — do slightly better. They're prudish enough to back into his bedroom with a blanket to "cover their father's nakedness." But when you think about it, that's a less-than-encouraging start on a new creation.

It doesn't discourage the LORD, though — any more than the fiasco at the Tower of Babel does. Yes, I know. The reductionists say that Genesis 11 is nothing but the Bible's way of explaining earth's diversity of languages. Sure, that's part of it. But it's not the main part. Its true *biblical* thrust lies in the fact that it comes *after* the Rainbow Covenant in Genesis 9, and just *before* the Covenant with Abram/Abraham, the Covenant of Circumcision in Genesis 12–22 — the Covenant of the *Promise* to God's Chosen People. It says that the LORD *knows* he won't manhandle the world into a better place by rearranging the furniture *on top of the carpet of creation.* Instead, he'll let the world go on keeping its own, messy house and go down *under the carpet of history.* He'll save the world by the absurdity of doing *nothing much.*

He'll promise an heir to a 75-year-old man with a barren wife. He'll send him out mapless to wander around the Middle East. He'll watch him lie his way out of trouble. He'll make him wait twenty-four years for the Promise to be fulfilled. But when Abraham finally has his son Isaac to laugh with, God will tell him to kill him as a sacrifice. And all that, just to set up the *Mystery of faith* — just to give Paul a shot at God's attractive and repulsive Polarities. Just to hear him ring the changes, in Romans, on Faith versus Knowledge, on Good News versus Bad News, on Grace versus Law, and in 1 Corinthians, on the Foolishness of God that's Wiser than men and the Weakness of God that's Stronger than men. As I said, God *revels* in his Bipolarity. North or south, plus or minus, right or left, clockwise or counter-clockwise — he's never happier than when he's going in two directions at once.

*   *   *

No, I haven't forgotten the script I introduced so many pages ago. And no, I won't apologize for the detours I just took you through. But yes, back we go to verses 14 and 15.

These are the beginning of God's ambivalent curses — of the steel-centered marshmallows of his Mercy. But rather than make you thumb back to the script, let me re-quote it for you from the KJV:

> 14 And the LORD God said unto the serpent, Because thou hast done this, thou *art* cursed above all cattle, and above every beast of the field; upon thy belly shalt thou go, and dust shalt thou eat all the days of thy life:
> 15 And I will put enmity between thee and the woman, and between thy seed and her seed; it shall bruise thy head, and thou shalt bruise his heel.

That's all of God's curse as far as the snake is concerned. But rather than waste your time with reductionist dismissals ("The story is nothing but a myth") or literalistic quibbles ("Did the serpent really walk on his hind feet before this?"), I want you to note just two things about this passage. One is that it makes for wonderful cinema. If my bipolar take on the film is any-where near the truth, the LORD God is cursing his alter Ego here. And what a conversation it is! On and on he'll roll, entranced by the sound of his own voice. This is only the beginning of the rhetoric with which he'll warm to his self-criticism by damning everything in sight. Even God knows that when you can't or won't fix something, a few well-chosen cusswords can do wonders for your disposition.

But the other thing to note is that neither the snake, nor Eve (who'll be-come his next target), nor Adam (who'll get his fullest attention) has a word to say in reply. It's almost as if God cares only for his own concerns. "Rats!" he says. "I know I made them capable of this nonsense, but my hopes for them are still intact. If they weren't, I would have dematerialized the lot of them

315

back at the beginning of this chapter. But I didn't, so I'll just read them the riot act. I'll let them know that life itself will be quite enough punishment for their foolishness — and for Mine, if I'm going to be honest. They may cheat their Father God, but they can't fool Mother Nature. If snakes can't see how much fun I have watching the patterns they make in the sand, then let them see what women will make of them after this. Let little boys stamp on them, and let them bite their heels. Serves them all right."

Nevertheless, this has been a long chapter. Rather than drag you through another wordfest on the Hebrew and five versions, I think I'll call it a day. You think I shouldn't end so abruptly?

Too bad. I just did. I feel the need for an Augustinian fix.

TWENTY-TWO

On the Other Hand

In this chapter I'll be looking at Augustine's take on the scenes I've just covered in Genesis 3:1-15 — with two purposes in mind. On the one hand, I'll show you how he actually supports my newish — if not Jewish — watching of them. On the other hand, I may have a few bones to pick with him on his approach to the testing of Adam and Eve, and to the curses God put on all concerned. In any case, at the beginning of Book XI, 1 of Augustine's *De Genesi ad Litteram*, he quotes the entire third chapter of Genesis from the old Latin version, the *Itala*. (There are twelve books altogether in his *On Genesis to the Letter*, but Book XI is the last one in which he addresses the text as such; Book XII deals with more general considerations.)

Having set out his text in section 1, he next offers a short preface on the necessity of looking at Scripture in the right way. Here is section 2, in both Augustine's Latin and my translation:

> *2. Antequam hujus propositae Scripturae textum ex ordine pertractemus, admonendum arbitror, quod jam me et alibi in hoc opere memini praelocutum, illud a nobis esse flagitandum ut ad proprietatem litterae defendatur quod gestum narrat ipse qui scripsit. Si autem in verbis Dei, vel cujusquam personae in officium propheticum assumptae, dicitur aliquid quod ad litteram nisi absurde possit intelligi, procul dubio figurate dictum ob aliquam significationem accipi debet; dictum tamen esse dubitare fas non est: hoc enim a fide narratoris, et pollicitatione expositoris exigitur.*

Before we deal with the text of this proposed Scripture, I think I should tell you what I now remember having said elsewhere in this work; that is, my earnest plea that what a writer narrates as a *thing done* should be defended by staying as close as possible to the letter of his words. But if something is said that can be understood only *absurdly* according to the letter (whether it's in the words of God, or of some person he's taken to himself in a prophetic capacity), there's no doubt that it ought to be taken *figuratively,* as signifying something else. Nevertheless, the fact of its having been said is not to be doubted, because the acceptance of that fact goes to the heart of both the narrator's faithfulness to his narrative and the expositor's willingness to set it forth.

I'd like you to note how nicely Augustine sails between the Scylla of literalism and the Charybdis of criticism — the two threats that have dogged you and me all our lives. We've been told that we must either accept every word in the Bible as literally true or cave in to the critics who want us to ignore passages of the Bible they can't accept. But in the process, we've lost the Bible itself — and with it, the *wholeness* of the Holy Spirit's moving picture of history. In fact, we've handed ourselves *two* Bibles: the one, an infallible textbook whose occasional extravagances must be defended as if they were true as turnips (for example, Joshua's command that the sun should stand still upon Gibeon); and the other, a half-Bible in which we mentally skip over passages that don't please the professors (to name only a few: Jesus' bodily resurrection and ascension, Paul's male chauvinism, and almost everything in the Gospel according to John).

But for all the centuries from the day of Pentecost right up to the Enlightenment, that was seldom the case. Everybody had the same, paradoxical Bible, and everyone was free to interpret any part of it in whatever way he or she could manage — even to the point of finding several interpretations in a single passage. Which is why I find Augustine's introductory note on interpretation so comforting. He insists that all we need to accept is the *factuality of the text itself;* everything else is up for grabs. Indeed, I think that for a man who never saw a movie, he comes within a whisker of my "film" approach to the Bible. *Dictum tamen esse dubitari fas non est,* he says: "Still, *that it was said* is not to be doubted."

To give you the overall force of those words, let me make a little tapestry of his remarks in this passage: "Nevertheless, it's not to be doubted that what a writer himself presents as *something done* is meant to be seen [watched!] as *happening* before our very eyes" (or, as I rendered it more strictly in my translation, "by staying as close as possible to the letter of his words"). If that isn't a dead ringer for my insistence that every word in *Genesis, the Movie* — plus all the actions, sequences, camera angles, and incidental music — are the very *history* the Director wants to give us in the context of her film, I'll be a monkey's uncle. In fact, *her movie is the only history we have.* Either we watch the entire picture with an open mind, or we have nothing to watch at all.

Next, though, Augustine takes up the text itself — by going back to the last lines of chapter 2 of Genesis. Here's what he says in section 3:

> 3. *Erant ergo ambo nudi: verum est, omnino nuda erant corpora duorum hominum in paradiso conversantium. Nec pudebat eos: quid enim puderet, quando nullam legem senserant in membris suis repugnantem legi mentis suae?* (Rom. 7:23) *quae illos poena peccati post perpetrationem preavaricationis secuta est, usurpante inobedientia prohibitum, et justitia puniente commissum. Quod antequam fieret, nudi erant et non confundebantur: nullus erat motus in corpore, cui verecundia deberetur; nihil putabant velandum, quia nihil senserant refrenandum. Quemadmodum propagaturi essent filios, jam antea disputandum est* (supra, IX, 3-11): *non tamen eo modo credendum est, quo propagaverunt posteaquam crimen admissum praedicta ultio consecuta est; cum priusquam morerentur, jam in corpore inobedientium hominum justissimo reciprocatu inobedientium membrorum tumultum mors concepta versaret. Nondum erant tales Adam et Eva, cum ambo nudi essent, et non confunderentur.*

Therefore, "they were both naked." That's true: the bodies of the *two men* walking around in the Garden were totally naked. "Nor were they ashamed of themselves." For what was there to be ashamed of when they sensed no "law in their members" that was repugnant to the law of their mind? (Rom. 7:23). The penalty for sin that followed them after their perpetration of the lie, by which their disobedience usurped what was prohibited, brought on them a just punishment for the crime they committed. Before that happened, though, they were naked and not confounded: there was no "motion" in their body to which shame was owed; and there was nothing they thought needed covering, because they felt there was nothing they needed to hold back. Earlier, in Book IX, 3-11, I discussed the question of what influence that freedom might have had on their possible begetting of children [in the state of innocence]. Still, even if they did beget under those conditions, that should not be understood in the same way as their begetting afterward, when their confessed crime was followed by the predicted retribution [namely, death]. Because even before they died, the death that was *conceived* in the body of those disobedient *men* was already causing, by a most just retribution, the tumult of their disobedient members. But when Adam and Eve were both "naked and not ashamed," they were not yet in such a state.

The first thing I want you to note in this passage is its reference to Adam and Eve as "two men" walking around in the Garden of Eden. Augustine has no qualms about calling Eve a *man* because for him, as for almost everyone before our own times, *homo sapiens* included woman: *man*, as created on the sixth day, was made *male and female.* Eve was a guy before she was a doll; and the minute Adam saw her, he recognized that she was "bone of my bones, and flesh of my flesh; she shall be called Woman, because she was taken out of Man." For my money, then, that's good night and sweet dreams to all of the biblical scriptwriters' lapses into male chauvinist piggery — and to all the fuss over "inclusive language."

As I've said, whatever those nodding authors might have *meant,* it's not a sufficient reason for obscuring the concordances of the word *man* in the rest of the scriptural movie — and it's certainly no excuse for invariably using circumlocutions like "the human race" or "humankind." Adam is *man,* Eve is *man,* the Blessed Virgin Mary is *man,* and our Lord Jesus Christ is *man* in whom the Word of God is Incarnate. And when he dies and rises, he saves *man* all at once, by a *cosmic renovation* of human nature, not by running around repairing *men* one by one as if they were piecework. All of *man* is circumcised in his circumcision and baptized in his baptism. All of *man* dies in his death, all of *man* rises in his resurrection, and all of *man* goes to glory in his ascension. And it's all accomplished in the manhood he has restored to his Father's favor by the Mystery of his Incarnation: "I, if I be lifted up from the earth, will draw *all* to myself." Go back and read John, Ephesians, and Colossians one more time.

To be sure, even after that outburst I still understand (and agree with) the feminists' fury at people who justify the subjugation of women by quoting Scripture. But by the same token, it would be nice if they didn't so easily fly off the handle when a sympathizer points out how nicely the Bible exonerates itself of the charge. Look at what Augustine has done here with his second reference to "men" at the end of the quotation. When he expands his earlier discussion of possible procreation in man's first state, he comes up with the brilliant image of the "death" to which Adam and Eve were condemned as something already *conceived* in them but not yet *delivered.* And he picks up on Paul's equally brilliant imagery (in chapters 5–7 of Romans) of *death reigning over us,* even while we are alive in the flesh. "But I see another law in my members, warring against the law of my mind, and bringing me into captivity to the law of sin which is in my members. O wretched man that I am! Who shall deliver me from the body of this death? I thank God through Jesus Christ our Lord. So then with the mind I myself serve the law of God; but with the flesh the law of sin" (Rom. 7:23-25, KJV).

To quote the Book of Common Prayer, "In the midst of life we are in death." Men and women alike, we're all pregnant with death from the moment we're born, and we all suffer its backaches and morning sicknesses as long as we live. But God turns even our impregnation with death into his promise of life. In Baptism, we are buried with Christ in his death; in the Eucharist, we show forth Christ's death till he comes; and at the end, the last enemy he will destroy will be the death that has been gestating in us since the Garden. *He will return us to the condition in which we began.* Naked and unashamed, or wearing robes washed white in the blood of the Lamb, we shall stand before him in the life his Son has re-conceived for us out of the *mors concepta* in our disobedient members. To quote T. S. Eliot's *Little Gidding* once again,

> We shall not cease from exploration
> And the end of all our exploring
> Will be to arrive where we started
> And know the place for the first time.

True enough, Augustine's habit of harping on *disobedience* as the sin of Adam and Eve has led many people (perhaps even Augustine himself in some places) to take an excessively legalistic view of the Fall — and many others, no doubt, to object to it. In fact, when I first began this chapter, that was one of the bones I was going to pick with him. But his imagery here has talked me out of it. I'm not sure whether it was his *two men* that charmed me, or his *mors concepta* — his "*death already conceived* in the body of those disobedient *men*" — that did the trick; but whichever it was, it was another instance of the way his words so frequently lead me to question the bum rap he's gotten for being the granddaddy of everything that went wrong with Western theology. He's first and foremost a commentator on Scripture who can bring *all* of the Bible to bear on any passage he takes up. For me, reading him is like sitting at the feet of Anthony Lane or David Denby, two of the *New Yorker*'s best movie reviewers. Like them, Augustine illuminates earlier episodes of the biblical film with scenes from the rest of the picture — and I always come away from him with a burning desire to see the movie again from start to finish.

On to section 4, to which the Benedictine editors of the Migne Patrology have given the terse caption of *Serpentis sapientia, qualis et unde:* "The wisdom of the serpent, of what sort, and whence." I won't give you Augustine's Latin here; instead, I'll just translate him freely as I go along.

He now takes a look at all the Latin versions he has in hand, and he finds that while the *Itala* describes the serpent as *prudentissimus,* "most clever, most prudent," many other Latin codices have *sapientissimus,* "most wise." He goes on to say,

> [This cannot be taken] in the proper sense (in which "wise" is used only of the wisdom of God, or of the angels, or of rational souls); rather, it must be taken in the sense we use when we call bees and even ants wise: their works, as it were, *imitate wisdom.* But this serpent might be called the "most wise" of all the beasts, not by virtue of his own irrational soul, but now by the influence of an alien spirit — that is, a diabolical one. For however much the lying angels might have deserved to be cast down from their supernal seats because of their perversity and pride, those beings are by nature more excellent than all beasts on account of the pre-eminence of their reason.
>
> For what wonder is it if the devil should now fill the serpent with his own instinctive wisdom, mixing into it his own spirit — in the same way that soothsayers of demons usually fill people — and making the snake the most wise of all the beasts when compared to the living and irrational soul of other living things? Indeed, it's by a fuller use of the word that we speak of this *sapientia,* this "wisdom" in evil, in the same way that we speak of "astuteness" [*astutia*] or "cleverness" in good — especially when the proper and predominant usage in Latin is precisely to call things "wise" as a way of praising them. But calling them "astute" or "clever" can easily apply to evil-hearted things as well. As a result, there are some codices (indeed, we find a number of them) that follow the Latin style and don't use the *literal* word *wise* at all but rather carry over its *sense,* preferring to call this serpent "more astute" than all beasts, rather than "more wise."
>
> But whatever the peculiarity of Hebrew usage might require — whether those beasts might have been spoken of or understood as "wise" not in a deviant sense but in a proper one — the translators will have been looking at a peculiarity they knew perfectly well. In any case, we plainly read in another passage of the Holy Scriptures that "wise" is indeed used in reference to evil, and not to good (Jer. 4:22, KJV: "For my people is foolish, they have not known me; they have none understanding: they are *wise* to do evil, but to do good they have no knowledge"). And the Lord himself says, in Luke 16:8, that "the children of this world are *wiser* than the children of light." He was deliberating with himself, as it were, about the future of those children of the world, albeit concerning their wisdom in *fraud,* not in *law.*

Several things leap out at me from that passage. First, Augustine is fully aware of the problems of translation — and he's far from insisting on merely literal renderings. Indeed, he delights in the *usum latine locutionis,* "the usual way of speaking in Latin," by which, he says, *non verbum, sed potius sententiam transferentes:* "they bring across not the word but rather its sense." But what interests me even more is his introduction of "the peculiarity of Hebrew usage."

Now it's true that Augustine had no Hebrew — so much so, that Jerome (his contemporary, and a whiz at Hebrew) chastised him for his ignorance of it. However, if you take a look at another of Augustine's works (his *In Heptateuchum Locutionum Librii Septem,* his *Seven Books on the Ways of Speaking in the Heptateuch*), you'll have a pleasant surprise in store for yourself. At any rate, he certainly surprised me. (The "Heptateuch," by the way, is the seven books of the Bible from Genesis through Judges.)

I said earlier in this work that because of the KJV's rather literal translations of the Hebrew (and particularly because of its *italicizing* of words not in the original), you could get a fair feel for the Hebrew of the Bible by simply skipping over the italics. Augustine was similarly blessed in his Latin and Greek versions — which were even more literal. And in his "Seven Books of Locutions," he capitalizes on that blessing: in short, he gives himself a mini-course in Hebrew without having seen even a word of the original language. So his allusion here to the "peculiarity of Hebrew usage" shows the fruits of that course. If he lacked a reading knowledge of the language, he nonetheless had a feel for it — a sense of its odor, a *nose* for Hebrew, by which his mind could smell things it couldn't have known. Once again, I commend the KJV to you: you'll find you're not as far from the Hebrew as you may have thought you were.

But before I take you on a hop, skip, and jump through sections 6 through 13, let me finish up on what Augustine has to say about the serpent here. He picks up from where he left off, and he has this to say in section 5:

> Nor do we really have to think that the devil would choose the serpent, all on its own, to be the agent by whom he would tempt and persuade man to sin. Even though that animal might have had a desire to deceive on account of its crooked and invidious will, it was not simply by that will that it could be allowed to do what it did. For while its desire to harm could stem from its own perverse inclination, there is no power except from God, and his power works by a high and hidden justice — because there is no iniquity with God himself.

This, I think, takes us straight back to God's ecology of good and evil — and at the same time, makes a giant leap forward. It takes us far beyond the "natural goods and evils" that God has ordained as the luck of the draw for every creature, and into his acceptance of even the destruction of innocent good by malicious evil. Back in the Garden, God didn't interfere with either the serpent's "crooked and invidious will" or even the devil's "perverse inclination." And throughout the rest of history, God continues that policy. In the book of Job, he positively endorses Satan's murderous plans. When the highjacked planes flew into the World Trade Towers, he didn't prevent the horror of 3,000 innocent deaths. And to cap it all, he himself, in the Person of his only-begotten Word, not only allows the barbarity of the cross but, in his "high and hidden justice," takes it into himself in his beloved Son. GOD IS NOT, NEVER WAS, AND NEVER WILL BE AT WAR WITH EVIL.

You want to remind me, perhaps, that the Bible is filled with the exploits of just such a warrior God. So it is; and there is nothing we can do about that but watch, with perplexed eyes, the Director's horror story of God's shilly-shallying on the subject of evil. He declares the evil world his enemy at the beginning of the Noah story. But then, at the end of the Flood, he renounces (apparently forever) his war against it, only to renew the hostilities, times without number: again and again, he tells his people to take up arms against the enemies of the LORD.

But the movie of Scripture is filled even more with its Star — with the One who humbles himself and becomes obedient unto death (Phil. 2:8), and who, in the fullness of time, said, "You have heard that it has been said, 'You shall love your neighbor and hate your enemy.' But I say to you, Love your enemies, bless those who curse you, and pray for those who persecute you, so that you might be children of your Father who is in heaven, because his sun rises upon the evil and the good, and he sends rain on the just and the unjust" (Matt. 5:43-45, RFC).

This is not pacifism as a non-violent strategy for converting the wicked, or evangelism as a tactic for guiding the righteous to goodness by the example of God's punishment of the wicked. It isn't any kind of plausible "-ism" at all. It's just the way good and evil are held in God — in the high and incomprehensible justice of his divine Complicity in evil. Whatever he may have said about evil as his enemy, and however often he may have said it, he once and forever takes it all back in Jesus. And in its place, he offers us a Mystery that will never — even for a minute — make sense to the prudent: he leaves the deaths of the innocent in the world as the very fingerprints of his hands.

The Holy Innocents die at Jesus' birth, the Innocent One himself dies on the cross, and all the other billions of innocents in our dread-filled history keep right on dying like flies. Could any man in his right mind have a kind word to say for a God who calls such cruelty Good News? Could any sane woman actually *like* the foolishness and weakness of such a God? Of course not. But in the paradoxical Power of God, his foolishness is the only Wisdom there is, and by his incomprehensible Justice, the "bad" news of his weakness is the only Good News the world has ever heard. Thanks be to God for his *unspeakable* gift!

*   *   *

Augustine's wonderfully florid summation of all that will come at the end of this chapter, when we reach section 15. In the meanwhile, here's my promised vault over the intervening sections.

Let me give them to you by simply listing (with one exception) the Benedictine editors' captions. Section 6 is entitled *Tentatio hominis quare permissa:* "Why the temptation of man was allowed." Section 7 has the caption *Homo a tentatore dejectus, quia superbus:* "Man, cast down by the tempter, because he was proud." Section 8 is *Cur Deus permiserat hominem tentari:* "Why God permitted man to be tempted." Section 9 is *Cur homo non talis creatus qui nollet unquam peccare:* "Why man was not created the kind of being who would never want to sin." Section 10 is *Quare creati qui praesciebantur futuri mali:* "Why those who were foreknown to be evil were created." And sections 11 and 12 are jointly captioned *De eadem difficultate:* "On the same difficulty."

In all of these sections, Augustine is preoccupied with those bothersome "others" — with the "they" whose objections to his interpretations of Scripture plague his mind. As always, he tries to explain the errors of their thinking to them. But like all demon explainers, he has only limited patience for the job, and he's not immune to the temptations of grandstanding, sarcasm, and mockery. I find him great fun to read, probably because I have the same inclinations. Still, just as with me, his enthusiasm for the telling word or the killer line sometimes leads him to forget that what he's explaining is fundamentally inexplicable. Not really, of course (either in his case or mine); but born teachers like us should remember to stop hammering at the nail of our point before our hammer does more harm to the woodwork than the nail we've so nicely set.

But because section 10 is Augustine's warmup for the summation of his case in sections 13, 14, and 15, I'll give it to you in full so you can witness both his kill and his overkill (again, no Latin here, just a free translation):

> 10 But who, on sober consideration, would say, "Better that God should not have created someone he foreknew could be corrected by the iniquity of another, than that he should create someone who ought to be damned for his iniquity?" For this would be to say that one who is mercifully

325

crowned by God for making good use of the evil of another is not better off than an evil person who deserves to be justly punished. For when reason certainly demonstrates that these two cases are not equally good, but the one higher and the other lower, those who say "Both cases would be the same" are not just slow-hearted in their understanding; they're saying nothing other than "Only one of them should exist." And so, when they want to equate the two classes, they reduce the number of good people; and if they immoderately augment the class of the good, they take away the other class entirely.

But who would listen to such people if they were to say, "Because the sense of sight is more excellent than the sense of hearing, there should be four eyes and no ears"? Thus, even if that rational creature [Adam] is more excellent (and was subject to God without the offset of any punishment, and without any pride), something has nevertheless been created among men that now makes man unable to acknowledge in himself the beneficence of God, except by seeing the punishment of another's crime. So much so, that they have no sympathy for the predicament of the other, but rather a fear (Rom. 11:20: "Fair enough: they [God's ancient people] were pruned out because of their unfaith, but you [the Gentiles] stand by faith. Don't think highly of yourselves, but rather fear").

What Paul means is that no one should be over-confident about himself, but should rather confide in God. Who in his right mind would say, "This case would be the same as that"; doesn't he see that he's saying nothing other than "This isn't the case; only that is"? But even if it's uneducatedly and foolishly said, "Why then shouldn't God have created even those who he foreknew would be evil?" God's reason is still to show his wrath and to demonstrate his power, and on that account to sustain, with great patience, the "vessels of his wrath" who have their end in perdition. And all of that, so he might make known the riches of his glory in the "vessels of his mercy" that he prepared for glory (Rom. 9:22-23). Thus, then, "Let him who glories glory only in the Lord" (2 Cor. 10:17), since he knows not the things that are his own but the things that are of him by whom he not only exists, but also could not exist well except by that Other from whom he has the power to be.

I give you that passage not only because of the intricacy of its argument but especially because it contains hints of the darker and more problematical side of Augustine's mind. For one thing, there's his misreading of Romans 11. In Romans 9 and 10 Paul has been warming to the climax of his argument that the Jews have *not* been cut off by the New Covenant in Jesus. And he finally reaches it in Romans 11:26-29: "And so all Israel will be saved, as it is written, 'Out of *Zion* will come the rescuer; he will turn away ungodliness from Jacob. And this is my Covenant with them, when I will take away their sins.' According to the Good News, they were enemies for your sakes; but according to God's election, they are beloved on account of the fathers. *For God has no second thoughts about his gifts and his calling*" (RFC, italics mine). But despite Paul's crystal-clear vindication of Judaism, Augustine (and most of the church ever since — including Luther, Calvin, and nearly all of their assigns and devisees) went blithely on perpetuating the sad legacy of anti-Semitism. There's only a whiff of it in Augustine's words here, but a more blatant example will come up shortly.

For another thing, there's also Augustine's almost gleeful harping on God's wrath and his punishments for the wicked — not to mention the fact that he practically casts that old hag, Helen Damnation, as the star of the movie. I have no deep theological objections to what he *says*. After all, I've already given you God's Mercy as a marshmallow with a ball bearing in the middle; and if you like, I might even reverse the image and call it a very hard candy indeed, with a surprisingly soft center. My objection to Augustine, you see, is more a matter of *tone* than of *substance*. In fact, his tone is so severe that I think he ends up doing precisely what he faulted others for — that is, immoderately augmenting one class of divine Activity (damnation) and nearly taking away the other (mercy). True, I can still see God's ecology of good and evil in his words. But it would have been nicer for me if he could have balanced the two with something more palatable than the saints in heaven sending snotty thank-you notes to the damned in hell.

So to complete my hop, skip, and jump, let me tell you what I think Augustine should have done. He should have avoided entirely the temptation to speak of good and evil as if they were two separate, objective realities at war with each other. That was the mistake Adam and Eve made at the tree, and it's the mistake almost all of us have made ever since. It's the error of thinking that because *we've* decided we must choose between them, *God* is obliged to follow suit. But he's not. He sees good and evil not as opposed *states* that his creatures might enter (thus requiring God to like them or hate them) but as *qualities* (happy or unhappy) that might appear in creatures he already — and irrevocably — *loves*.

God is not pissed off at his old creation. His Incarnate Word has once and forever made all things new (Rev. 21:5): new heavens, a new earth — and even a new hell, where even the damned are the objects of his inexhaustible affection and his everlasting goodwill. God loves *things*, not *qualities: Being is good in and of itself.* As Aquinas said, there is no *ontological* evil. By the brooding of God's *Amor Mutuus,* by the Mutual Love of his Holy Spirit — by the Right Hand of the Father — he holds everything in his eternal confidence that all shall be well. And by the mysterious working of his Left Hand — by the Passion and Resurrection of his Incarnate Word — all manner of thing has already been made well.

Whether the damned will wake up someday and realize they're not damned is a question of fact that they will have to decide for themselves. But on God's part, it's not a problem he has to solve because he solved it long ago, from the foundation of the world: "God so loved the world, that he gave his only-begotten Son, that everyone who believes in him may have eternal life" (John 3:16). It's all over but the shouting. How nice it would have been if we could have regaled the ears of the self-condemned with something better than our self-congratulation.

* * *

On at last to section 13, where Augustine, still preoccupied with the cantankerous "they" in his head, now begins to set the nail of his argument. It's for you to decide whether or not he leaves half-moons on the woodwork:

> 13 "But," they say, "God would be able to convert even the will of bad people into good, if he so chose, because he's omnipotent. Clearly, he would be able. Why then didn't he do it? Because he didn't want to. And why didn't he want to? After all, it was in his power." Well, we shouldn't ask such questions. For we ought not to think about more than we ought to think about (Rom. 12:3). But I recall that a little bit earlier I showed quite sufficiently that it was no small good for even this rational creature [Adam] that God should warn him about evil by a comparison with evil people. For the class of "good creature" would be altogether non-existent if God were to convert the evil wills of *everybody* into good — and he would have inflicted due punishment on no iniquity at all. Moreover, there would have been nothing but that class alone, and it could profit by no comparison of evils, since there would be neither sin nor punishment. Because increasing the population of the more excellent class of people in that way decreases [to zero] the number of truly good people in that very class.

This is Augustine, the crafty lawyer for the accused God, proving that his Client actually serves the interests of justice. It seems to me, though, that while his stigmatization of evil people as a group may smack of the *reprobation* of sinners — of God's *predestination* of them to damnation — his final remark in the passage actually supports my notion that he had at least a grip of sorts on God's ecology of good and evil. Not only does he have those opposites co-existing in God; the divine Left Hand that holds evil actually washes the Right Hand that holds good.

Furthermore, Augustine roots his defense in God's bizarre decision to make a world of *free* creatures — and particularly of free *human* creatures. In many other places in his writings, he insists that the distinction between *moral* good and evil can be made only with regard to beings who have a *liberum arbitrium,* a "freedom of rational decision." While he holds that both virtue and vice must be at least *possible,* he refuses to allow God to be seen as making either one of them *necessary.* Sadly, our legal processes sometimes stray from that distinction. Prosecutors and juries may look only at the *facts* of a person's crime and convict on the sole grounds that the accused *knew* at the time that what he was doing was wrong. But at its best, the law itself requires proof that the accused was also *free* enough to choose *not* to commit the crime.

Admittedly, Augustine's defense of his Client's innocence in the passage I just cited is a tricky one. He argues not that God should be acquitted by reason of insanity, but that his accusers are guilty of trying to make themselves better than God by taking away not only God's freedom to do as he pleases but also his creatures' freedom to do the same. To be sure, we might see that as a shameless attempt to enlist the jury's self-interest in not being tarred with a freedom-hating brush. Still, it works, both for the jury and for us, because it's always a comfort of sorts to be told that at our best, we're no worse than God is. Were I ever to need a defense attorney, I would be overjoyed to have Augustine at my side.

In fact, it's precisely his courtroom tone of voice in section 13 (and his even louder tone in sections 14 and 15) that has just now made me think of a different way of presenting those next two sections to you. Rather than just translating his words freely, as I've been doing, I'll go all the way and give you an outright *paraphrase* of them. I'll try to make him sound like an old-fashioned criminal lawyer who's willing to use any weapon in his bag of rhetorical tricks — even an appeal to the jury's prejudices — to make his case.

First, then, my paraphrase of the beginning of his summation to the jury in section 14, captioned *Malorum poenis non indiget Deus, sed ex eis consulit bonorum saluti:* "God does not need the punishments of evil persons; rather, out of them he designs the salvation of the good." I'll print out Augustine's Latin right after the paraphrase, just to keep myself honest:

14 Ladies and Gentlemen of the jury, the prosecution's case is a tissue of irrelevancies. They ask you, "Is there then something in the works of God

that *needs* the evil of another person to promote good?" But I ask you: Are they so deafened and blinded by their passion to prove their case that they neither hear nor see the plain truth that no matter how many people may be punished, many more might be corrected? For what pagan, what Jew, what heretic wouldn't see the truth of this every day in his own house? Indeed, when I listen to the prosecution's fuss and feathers about "the truth," all I hear is people who refuse to pay attention to their own perceptions. For by the working of divine Providence, it's in those very perceptions that they can plainly see the exciting influence of discipline coming straight at them.

So much so, that even if those they punish were not corrected, the rest of mankind would be struck with fear by their example, and the just calamities of the evil ones on whom they inflict punishment would contribute mightily to their own salvation. Does that then make God the author of the malice or wickedness for which he designed a just punishment? Is God guilty of their crimes just because his design made their commission of them *possible*? Not at all, Ladies and Gentlemen. For even though he foreknew that they would be evil by their own vices, he was still kind enough *not* to desist from creating them. He threatened such persons with being cut off because he hoped it would help propel them in the direction of good — unless, of course, their preoccupation with evils made that impossible for them. For if they never existed at all, they couldn't have been propelled toward anything whatsoever. Is it really such a tiny good, then, that those who were left free to behave badly should actually have been propelled into existence? What being of any kind doesn't want to exist? What being is propelled by anything greater than the fear that it should cease to be itself?

Ergo, inquiunt, est aliquid in operibus Dei quod alterius malo indigeat, quo proficiat ad bonum? Itane obsurduerunt et excaecati sunt homines, nescio quo studio contentionis, ut non audiant vel videant, quibusdam punitis, quam plurimi corrigantur? Quis enim paganus, quis Judaeus, quis haeriticus non hoc in domo sua quotidie probet? Verum cum venitur ad disputationem inquisitionemque veritatis nolunt advertere sensus suos homines, ex quo opere divinae providentiae in eos venit imponendae commotio disciplinae; ut si non corriguntur qui puniuntur, eorum tamne exemplo caeteri metuant, valeatque ad eorum salutem justa pernicies malorum. Num enim malitiae vel nequitiae Deus auctor est, de quorum justa poena consulit, quibus hoc modo consulendum esse constituit? Non utique: sed cum eos vitiis propriis malos futuros esse praesciret, non eos tamen creare destitit; utilitati deputans eorum, quos in hoc genere creavit, ut ad bonum proficere, nisi malorum comparatione, non possent. Si enim non essent, nulli rei utique prodessent. Parumne boni est actum ut sint, qui certe illi generi utiles sunt; quod genus quisquis non vult ut sit, nihil aliud agit, nisi ut ipse in eo non sit?

God, Augustine argues, doesn't *need* evil people. In fact, God doesn't need anything: *everything* exists simply because he *likes* it — because, on the sixth day, he pronounced it all *Very Good.* If we prefer to warp his ecology of good and evil into a war between the two rather than allowing them to exist in the fruitful harmony he intended, so much the worse for us. But not for him. He himself goes right on holding all things in being, be they good or bad. The abolition of a wicked world was something he tried only once — and at the end of that once, in Genesis 8:20-22, he put up the Rainbow to remind us that he would never do anything like that again. And at the far end of his irrevocable romance with good and evil — in the death and resurrection of his Incarnate Word — God himself dies for the sins of his creation and rises with his remembrance of evil engraved on the palms of his Hands, in the soles of his Feet, and in the spear wound in his Side.

Admittedly, most of Augustine's interpreters (for example, the Benedictine editors who wrote the captions for these sections) have read him as saying that the *only* thing the wicked are good for is the possible advancement of good people. But he doesn't say that. He says that God likes our *being* no matter what we do with it — and that he will never go back on that preference, not even in hell. Even in our sins, our fondness for our own existence remains a witness to the divine Fondness that holds us *extra nihil* and *extra causas* — outside nothing and outside our causes.

Furthermore, despite the blatant prejudice in Augustine's list of people whom God leaves free to be (pagans, Jews, and heretics — and, by extension, Osama Bin Laden, Saddam Hussein, my in-laws, and your landlord), all he was trying to do was tell the jury that there's no one so far gone as to miss the fact that God *does* put up with people the rest of us would love to get rid of. Once again, it's not that God *needs* the wicked for the sake of the good. Their benefit to the righteous is just a bonus he gets for liking the *being* of everything more than its *behavior.*

But now Augustine is ready for section 15, his florid closing to the jury — under the same caption as section 14. Here's the purple prose with which he addresses them:

15. Ladies and Gentlemen of the jury, let me prove my Client's innocence by quoting Psalm 111:2 for you: "Great are the works of the LORD, sought

out in *all* the purposes of his will." Do you see the force with which that demolishes the prosecution's case? My Client foresees future goods, and he creates. He foresees future evils, and he creates. *For his own satisfaction,* he offers a multitude of gifts to the good — and to the evil as well, by his merciful disregard of their sins. He takes vengeance justly, and by the same token he takes vengeance mercifully. He *fears* nothing from anyone's malice; he *needs* nothing from anyone's righteousness. *Nothing* interferes with his designs. Not his own pleasure in the works of the good, and not his own purposing of good even in his punishments of the evil.

My Client, Ladies and Gentlemen, is guilty of nothing but faithfulness to his own unfathomable ways. You must find him not guilty of the crimes of creating evil and needing evil, because those crimes are due to our ways (and, I might add, the prosecution's ways), not to his. Why then should he not have permitted man to be tested? Why should he not have prepared that test as a way of proving, of convincing — indeed, of punishing — when it was by man's proud lust after his own power that he sinned and would be confounded by his own hatching of evil? And why shouldn't future generations have been deterred by that just punishment for the pride and disobedience of the first man, since it was for their sakes that these things were prepared, written down, and proclaimed?

Ladies and Gentlemen, if God is in the dock for these crimes, we all are. But if he is innocent of them, none of us is guilty. God's forgiveness of sins is conditional on no *works* at all, *not even his own.* He saves us by the Mystery of his own self-emptying on the cross. All we need to do is *trust* that unutterably good gift. I urge you, therefore, to find my Client not guilty by reason of his divine Foolishness and Weakness. Why should you convict yourselves when those two Mysteries have already proved your innocence in his beloved Son?

Magna opera Domini; exquisita in omnes voluntates ejus" (Psa. 111, 2): *praevidet bonos futuros, et creat; praevidet malos futuros, et creat: seipsum ad fruendum praebens bonis, multa munerum largiens et malis, misericorditer ignoscens: juste ulciscens; itemque misericorditer ulciscens: nihil metuens de cujusquam malitia, nihil indigens de cujusquam justitia; nihil sibi consulens nec de operibus bonorum, et bonis consulens de poenis malorum. Cur ergo non permitteret tentari hominem, illa tentatione probandum, convincendum, puniendum, cum superba concupiscentia propriae potestatis quod conceperat pararet, suoque fetu confunderetur, justoque supplicio a superbiae atque inobedientiae malo posteros deterreret, quibus ea conscribenda et annuntianda parabantur?*

As you might realize from Augustine's Latin, the final paragraph of my paraphrase is all mine: Augustine himself doesn't have a word of it. Still, I think it's Augustinian enough to pass muster. So, since I've already worked my slant on his argument into its substance, I think I'll close this chapter and return you to the Garden, where the God of Mercy is cursing everybody in sight. With words that any lover might speak over his beloved's self-destruction, he cries out, "Oh, Damn!"

TWENTY-THREE

The Rest of the Curses:
The First Hint of the Good News

GENESIS 3:16-19

Now for the last two chapters of this long — if not monumental — work. On to what I see as the upbeat ending of *Genesis, the Movie.*

First, though, a little trip through the personal history that led me to the sanguine view of God's curses that I took at the end of the previous chapter. After thirty books, published in some forty editions, I find that there's been a single, sustained bass note — a *pedal point,* as it were — under all the theological chin-music I've written over thirty-seven years.

That note was my constant insistence that in the Bible, and particularly in the Person of God's Messiah, we're dealing not with occasional *insertions* of God's fingers into the pie of history but rather with the Mystery of his *abiding presence* to all of history. Or, to put it in terms I've long used, Holy Scripture gives us a *revelation* of what God has always been doing, not a list of *transactions* he poked into the world as afterthoughts. The events that the movie of the Bible portrays are not improvisations he adds to his divine Bag of tricks for dealing with the world; they're sacraments, real presences, of his *eternal purpose* for creation. In short, "Revelation, Not Transaction" has been the bumper sticker on my authorial car. (If you like, it's been my version of "Honk if You Love Jesus.") And *Anti-Transactionalism* (cumbersome though the abstraction may be) has always been my watchword.

Let me tell you how I arrived at that long-standing antipathy. My first glimpse of the dangers of transactionalism occurred in one of my earliest books, *Hunting the Divine Fox,* where I was trying to reformulate my understanding of *sacramentality.* As a staunch high churchman of the old school,

334

I'd always called the sacrament of the Eucharist "The Holy Mysteries"; but too often I'd ended up thinking of it as a "holy transaction." Quite correctly, I understood that the bread and wine of the Lord's Supper are Jesus himself really present with us. But when I tried to explain that real presence to myself, I talked as if it involved his "showing up" in bread and wine from which he was previously absent: in the Holy Communion, the elements *turned into* a Jesus they hadn't been before. Before the Mass began, they were "plain" bread and wine; but after the transaction of the Eucharistic Prayer, they'd *become* Jesus himself.

One day, though, the theological impossibility of such talk suddenly dawned on me. Jesus, the Word of God by whom all things are made, can't possibly *become* present in anything, because he's already intimately, immediately, and really present to everything and everybody. Therefore, the error in all the transactional doctrines of "Eucharistic change" (and in particular in the doctrine of *transubstantiation*) lay precisely in the *trans-* — in the implication that the Word of God Incarnate is a kind of commuter who makes *transits* to things that didn't previously enjoy his presence.

But the Gospel truth is that he's Incarnate in the world by no "spatial" motion at all. He doesn't have to leave his Father's side to "come down" from heaven: he dies and rises without ceasing for even a second to be the Word in the bosom of the Father. And when he ascends to his Father's right hand, he makes that "trip" without ever leaving the world of time and space. Unmoving in himself, he fills the world of motion. In the Mystery of his Godhead, he's "the still point of the turning world." True enough, Jesus reveals that Mystery in his humanity by making thirty-three years' worth of transits hither and yon. But even in those peregrinations (even in all his words and all his mighty acts), he's not *doing* things he hasn't yet gotten around to; he's *revealing* things he's done from the foundation of the world.

Jesus doesn't *teach* us the way to God; he's always *been* the Way. He doesn't *do* resurrections; he *is* the Resurrection. Lazarus doesn't rise because Jesus waves a resurrection wand over him; he rises because Jesus just has that effect on corpses — on *all* the dead. Admittedly, he raised only three dead people. But even one of them would have been enough, because nothing he does is an insertion of his power into the world. Everything he does — from his crying in the manger, to his drinking with tax collectors and sinners, to his teaching and healing, to his death, resurrection, and ascension, and to his *parousia* at the end — is nothing less than his *drawing of all* to himself.

That's the way it always has been with the Word of God Incarnate. When he makes *man* on the sixth day of creation, he's already raised Lazarus (and you and me) from the dead *in himself*. When he forms Adam from the clay, he's already made the clay with which he opened the eyes of the blind man at the pool. And when he causes the River to flow out of Eden, he's already made the Jordan in which he was baptized. Nothing he does is a transactional afterthought. Every one of his acts is a revelation of the Mystery of Christ — of the *restoration*, the *apokatastasis*, the "standing back on its feet" of the whole creation by the One in whom history has always been whispered into the ear of the Father.

But it was when I came to the sacrament of Baptism that the mischief of transactionalism became plain as day. Our habit of calling it "Christening" has stood Baptism on its head. Instead of seeing it as a real presence of the Incarnate Word who draws the whole world to himself, we've turned it into a transaction by which people who didn't "have" Jesus would be enabled to "get" him. In other words, we marketed it as a salvation-insurance policy for *some* (the "Christian" church) rather than as a sacrament of the Mystery that saves *all* (the "Catholic" expanse of the entire cosmos). In short, we *desacramentalized* Baptism and turned it into a kind of "magic." The church was no longer a fellowship of "believers sent out for the sake of the world"; it was a clique of magicians who could pull the Rabbit of Jesus out of the waters of the font and hand him to prospective members of the church.

The trouble with magic is that it promises something new but ends up with an unchanged world. When the magician is done with his trick, all he has left is the same old rabbit and the same old hat that he had before his *Abracadabra*. But when the Word himself speaks (whether in creation or Baptism), he makes all things new. From the first day to the last day, "New every morning is the Love" that brings us out of nothing into being. The church, therefore, is not a fellowship of people who have something the world lacks; it's the sign to the world that creation, even in its estrangement, is just as renewed as we are in our faith. It's most emphatically not a fellowship of insiders versus outsiders.

God *makes* the whole creation once and for all in his only-begotten Beginning; and he *remakes* all of creation once and for all in his only-begotten Word Incarnate. To his beloved Son, there are no outsiders. So, as I've said many times, the only thing our peddling of old-order magic rather than new-order sacramentality ever did was to turn the Good News of universal grace into the bad news of provincial religion. All it ever gave the peoples of the earth was just one more set of sad divisions to add to their already long list of reasons for hating each other.

And that, at last, opened the floodgates of my anti-transactionalism. I saw that none of the grand abstractions we use to describe the "work" of Jesus should be considered transactions at all: at best, they're only our way of grappling with the Mystery of *Who He Is.* The doctrine of the Atonement, for example, shouldn't be made to rest on his having made a perfect Sacrifice (though indeed he did that). It should be rooted in the Person of the Word who *is* the Sacrifice. Even the doctrine of his Incarnation shouldn't be made to stand or fall on the recorded facts of Jesus' thirty-three years on earth (though they too are part of the story). It should stand only on the Mystery of the Christ who is not only Jesus of Nazareth but also the Messiah of Israel, the Rock in the Wilderness, the Paschal Lamb — and David and all the kings of Israel who were the Lord's Anointed. In fact, to take it all the way back to the beginning, he is not only the Christ who is the second Adam; he is also the Adam who is the first Christ.

But perhaps that's enough of my bumper-sticker theology. I give it to you because it leads me straight to God's curses on Adam and Eve — and especially because I want you to avoid seeing those imprecations as nothing but transactions. It would be far too easy for us to watch God's condemnations and conclude that his disenchantment with the human race has led him to chew us up, spit us out, and tell us to go fly our own wretched kite. But as the title of this chapter has already suggested, I don't see his curses that way at all: they're actually the first hint of the Good News of God's Grace — of the Lover who will not let us go.

Accordingly, let me give you the rest of this chapter in a nutshell. I'll interpret God's *curses* not as declarations of what he himself will do to Adam and Eve for their disobedience, but as warnings of what the *natural world* (in its faithfulness to him and its fickleness to them) will now do to them before their very eyes. His condemnations may be stern; but every one of the hard candies he so liberally passes around will be nothing but sweetness when they dissolve in the mouth of God's Incarnate Word. "Taste and see how gracious the Lord is."

*　　　*　　　*

On, then, to this chapter's texts: the curses on the woman and the man:

| LXX Gen. 3:16 καὶ τῇ γυναικὶ εἶπεν πληθύνων πληθυνῶ τὰς λύπας σου καὶ τὸν στεναγμόν σου ἐν λύπαις τέξῃ τέκνα καὶ πρὸς τὸν ἄνδρα σου ἡ ἀποστροφή σου καὶ αὐτός | אֶל־הָאִשָּׁה אָמַר BHS Gen. 3:16 הַרְבָּה אַרְבֶּה עִצְּבוֹנֵךְ וְהֵרֹנֵךְ בְּעֶצֶב תֵּלְדִי בָנִים וְאֶל־אִישֵׁךְ תְּשׁוּקָתֵךְ וְהוּא יִמְשָׁל־בָּךְ׃ 17 וּלְאָדָם אָמַר כִּי־שָׁמַעְתָּ לְקוֹל אִשְׁתֶּךָ וַתֹּאכַל מִן־הָעֵץ אֲשֶׁר צִוִּיתִיךָ לֵאמֹר לֹא תֹאכַל | VUL Gen. 3:16 mulieri quoque dixit multiplicabo aerumnas tuas et conceptus tuos in dolore paries filios et sub viri potestate eris et ipse dominabitur tui 17 ad Adam vero dixit quia |

337

σου κυριεύσει 17 τῷ δὲ Αδαμ εἶπεν ὅτι ἤκουσας τῆς φωνῆς τῆς γυναικός σου καὶ ἔφαγες ἀπὸ τοῦ ξύλου οὗ ἐνετειλάμην σοι τούτου μόνου μὴ φαγεῖν ἀπ' αὐτοῦ ἐπικατάρατος ἡ γῆ ἐν τοῖς ἔργοις σου ἐν λύπαις φάγη αὐτὴν πάσας τὰς ἡμέρας τῆς ζωῆς σου 18 ἀκάνθας καὶ τριβόλους ἀνατελεῖ σοι καὶ φάγη τὸν χόρτον τοῦ ἀγροῦ 19 ἐν ἱδρῶτι τοῦ προσώπου σου φάγη τὸν ἄρτον σου ἕως τοῦ ἀποστρέψαι σε εἰς τὴν γῆν ἐξ ἧς ἐλήμφθης ὅτι γῆ εἶ καὶ εἰς γῆν ἀπελεύσῃ

מִמֶּנּוּ אֲרוּרָה הָאֲדָמָה בַּעֲבוּרֶךָ
בְּעִצָּבוֹן תֹּאכֲלֶנָּה כֹּל יְמֵי
חַיֶּיךָ: 18 וְקוֹץ וְדַרְדַּר תַּצְמִיחַ
לָךְ וְאָכַלְתָּ אֶת־עֵשֶׂב הַשָּׂדֶה:
19 בְּזֵעַת אַפֶּיךָ תֹּאכַל לֶחֶם עַד
שׁוּבְךָ אֶל־הָאֲדָמָה כִּי מִמֶּנָּה
לֻקָּחְתָּ כִּי־עָפָר אַתָּה וְאֶל־עָפָר
תָּשׁוּב:

audisti vocem uxoris tuae et comedisti de ligno ex quo praeceperam tibi ne comederes maledicta terra in opere tuo in laboribus comedes eam cunctis diebus vitae tuae 18 spinas et tribulos germinabit tibi et comedes herbas terrae 19 in sudore vultus tui vesceris pane donec revertaris in terram de qua sumptus es quia pulvis es et in pulverem reverteris

KJV Gen. 3:16 Unto the woman he said, I will greatly multiply thy sorrow and thy conception; in sorrow thou shalt bring forth children; and thy desire *shall be* to thy husband, and he shall rule over thee. 17 And unto Adam he said, Because thou hast hearkened unto the voice of thy wife, and hast eaten of the tree, of which I commanded thee, saying, Thou shalt not eat of it: cursed *is* the ground for thy sake; in sorrow shalt thou eat *of* it all the days of thy life; 18 Thorns also and thistles shall it bring forth to thee; and thou shalt eat the herb of the field; 19 In the sweat of thy face shalt thou eat bread, till thou return unto the ground; for out of it

RSV Gen. 3:16 To the woman he said, "I will greatly multiply your pain in childbearing; in pain you shall bring forth children, yet your desire shall be for your husband, and he shall rule over you." 17 And to Adam he said, "Because you have listened to the voice of your wife, and have eaten of the tree of which I commanded you, 'You shall not eat of it,' cursed is the ground because of you; in toil you shall eat of it all the days of your life; 18 thorns and thistles it shall bring forth to you; and you shall eat the plants of the field. 19 In the sweat of your face you shall eat bread till you return to the ground, for out of it you were taken; you are dust, and to dust you shall return."

NRSV Gen. 3:16 To the woman he said, "I will greatly increase your pangs in childbearing; in pain you shall bring forth children, yet your desire shall be for your husband, and he shall rule over you." 17 And to the man he said, "Because you have listened to the voice of your wife, and have eaten of the tree about which I commanded you, 'You shall not eat of it,' cursed is the ground because of you; in toil you shall eat of it all the days of your life; 18 thorns and thistles it shall bring forth for you; and you shall eat the plants of the field. 19 By the sweat of your face you shall eat bread until you return to the ground, for out of it you were taken; you are

wast thou taken: for dust
thou *art,* and unto dust
shalt thou return.

dust, and to dust you shall
return."

As you can see, verse 16 is all that the LORD God has to say to the woman at this point — and his entire curse on her has to do with childbirth and marriage. But in keeping with my notion that all of his curses are more about the revenge of the natural order than the revenge of God, let me develop that a bit before we look at the actual words.

The old way of reading this text was to see the human female's unusually difficult labor pains and her subjugation to the "stronger sex" as God's punishment of the woman for being the temptress who led her husband astray. But I think that misses the point of the verse. It's true, of course, that the story of the Fall in the biblical movie has been taken as an instance of male chauvinism — if not in God, then at least on the part of the biblical writers. However, since the entire script for the Fall clearly holds both Adam and Eve responsible for the disaster in Eden, that won't wash. Hence my insistence that God isn't so much threatening Eve with punishments of his own devising as he's telling her the plain truth about what her violation of his ecology of good and evil will mean for her personally.

At this juncture, however, I want to add another off-screen voice for the LORD God — to make one more of my (rare) bows to political correctness. Having already given you God's bass voice with James Earl Jones and the LORD's tenor inflections with Billy Crystal, I'm going to cast a female performer for both parts here. As I listen to this one-sided conversation, I don't hear God's words as man-to-man talk or even as man-to-woman talk. I hear an older woman speaking to an inexperienced girl. I hear the feminine *Wisdom* of God: the *Chokhmah,* the *Sophia,* the *Sapientia* of the second Person of the Trinity; and I hear the feminine *Spirit* of God: the *Rûach Adonai* of the third Person of the Godhead. And for that eminently female role, I can think of no actor more suited to the task than — you guessed it — Whoopi Goldberg, the new God of the Academy Awards.

"Honey," she says, "let me tell you what you've let yourself in for. I still love you like a Mother; but I love Mother Nature too, and I'm not about to punish her for your mistake. She's perfectly capable of punishing you all on her own. If you thought it was unfair of her to give the animals labor pains after the pleasures of sex, just wait and see what she'll give you. Maybe she'll let you conceive, and maybe she won't. But if she does, she'll give you nine months of nausea and lumbago, followed by a delivery that's *un-be-lievable.* Sure, she'll be a kind Mother — kind of. While you're going through all that *tsouris,* she'll make you think you'll never forget it; but when it's over, she'll give you an urge to invite it right back in. As I'll say in my Good Book, 'Thy desire shall be to thy husband.' The old boy — who told you he understood your pain because he remembered a kidney stone he once had — won't remember your delivery much past his first scotch and cigar. Pretty soon he'll be back at you with his old sly line: 'You want to go to sleep, Sweetheart, or what?' Just pray that you're never so fast asleep, or so deaf, that you give him 'What' for an answer."

To be sure, even such a motherly God probably struck Eve as hard to take. However much she may have welcomed her husband's sexual advances before the Fall, that list of the dire consequences of sex after the Fall (and especially the warning about male manipulation) must have given her pause. At any rate, the prospect of risking pregnancy once a month for half a lifetime — and the knowledge that men can convene sexual congresses at the drop of an innuendo — has been with women ever since.

You might rightly argue, of course, that that last bit of risky business is actually a privilege bestowed on humanity by God. I agree wholeheartedly. I too think that our remarkable availability for sexual relations (unlike the animals' more restricted schedule) can be seen as God's suggestion that we lift our copulation to something higher than theirs — that we give it a distinctly human and loving cast. But I don't agree with where I think your argument is going — namely, to the conclusion that the Bible's introduction of curses on our sexuality is the *cause* of our problems with it.

Because it isn't. Ever since the Fall, our sexuality has suffered just as much as anything else about us. Not more, mind you — and certainly not to the point of becoming a promotional line for the movie: SEX SPOILS PARADISE. WATCH IT HAPPEN BEFORE YOUR EYES! The truth is that *all* our faculties have gone awry. Granted, by the mercy of God they're still on the job and can sometimes do great things. But there isn't one of them that can't betray us at a moment's notice. Memory can corrupt the past in the very act of recalling it. Understanding can just as easily become misunderstanding. Will can weaken and choose evil under the guise of good. And even our spirituality (now so often touted as the one dependable faculty we have left) is no less a potential mess. It's certainly not an infallible guide to higher things — any more than our thirst for wine is.

Indeed, had God's curses really been an expression of his own mind and will rather than nature's revenge, I think he would have turned Eve back into Adam's rib, and Adam back into a clay doll, and simply enjoyed the rest of his unfallen creation. He would have cashiered all the faculties in our University of Love — Arts, Sciences, and History; Music, Mathematics, and Medicine;

Physical Education, Theology, and Spiritual Growth — and shut down the whole place. But he didn't. As it turns out, he fired only the Religion faculty. And it took him some four thousand years to do even that.

Once again, though, my checkered career in the Department of Sexuality leads me to write *tacet* against any further remarks on the subject. On to the actual words of verse 16.

God first addresses *the woman*, and he says (KJV), "I will greatly multiply thy sorrow and thy conception." The Hebrew for "greatly multiply" is the now-familiar idiom "multiplying I will multiply," *harbah 'arbeh*. The Septuagint reproduces it exactly: *plēthynōn plēthynō*; but the Vulgate settles for a simple "I will multiply": *multiplicabo*. (You can check the minor variations in the RSV and the NRSV in the quotations I've provided.)

This is Mother Nature's retaliation for the disruption of her ecology. What God tells the woman he will multiply is "thy sorrow and thy conception" (KJV). That follows the Hebrew exactly: *'itsts'bhônekh*, "your pain of travail," and *v'heronekh*, "and your conception [or pregnancy]." The Septuagint fiddles with that a bit: it has *tas lypas sou kai ton stenagmon sou*, "your pains [or griefs] and your groaning"; and the Vulgate has *aerumnas tuas et conceptus tuos*, "your hard labors and your pregnancies." The RSV bunches them together as "your pain in childbearing," which is not bad. But the NRSV (in another instance of "Look, Ma: *Vivid Writing!*") opts for "your *pangs* in childbearing."

God, however, goes right on giving nature her due. "In sorrow thou shalt bring forth children" (KJV). In the Hebrew, that's *b'etsebh tel'dhî bhanîm*: "In pain you will bear sons." The Septuagint has *en lypais texēi tekna*: "In pain [or grief] you will bear children." And the Vulgate has *in dolore paries filios*: "In pain [or sorrow] you will bear sons." (The RSV and the NRSV both echo the KJV.)

But then comes either male chauvinism or the revenge of nature, as you like. "And thy desire *shall be* to thy husband, and he shall rule over thee" (KJV). The Hebrew reads, *v''el-'îshekh t'shûqathekh*, "And to your man [husband] will be your returning," and *v'hû' yimshal bakh*, "and he will rule over you." The Septuagint has *kai pros ton andra sou hē anastrophē sou kai autos sou kyrieusei*: "And to your husband will be your constant turning [or, with your husband will be your dwelling], and he will lord it over you." The Vulgate, however, puts it much more baldly: *et sub viri potestate eris et ipse dominabitur tui*: "And you will be under the power of your husband, and he will rule over [dominate] you." (Again, the RSV and the NRSV follow the KJV.)

Let me give you Whoopi Goldberg's take on all of this:

"Honey," God the Mother says, "I hoped I would never have to tell you this, but you've made yourself a hard bed. You almost make me wish I hadn't invented sexes in the first place. You've taken my monthly gift and turned it into 'the curse.' You've made pregnancy a problem when I wanted it to be a proposal. And you've set yourself up to be pushed around by the man I meant to lift you up. I know, Dear. That last one will be more his fault than yours, and I'll get to him in a minute. For now, I can only tell you I'm sorry, but that's what you get for messing with Mother Nature. The Old Girl will give you a tough time, but she's just making the best of your bad job. If it's any comfort, women will do less damage to her housekeeping than men. However, you're both in the same sinking ship, and it'll be only a matter of time before the whole crew goes down. I'll rescue you all, sure as the rainbow after the rain. But not here, Girl, and not now: while Nature collects her debts, all you'll have will be my Mystery wrapped in your misery. Even the most Blessed Mother in history will get a sword right through her heart."

* * *

Now, though, having given the woman relatively short shrift, the LORD-Mother gives Adam a longer list of the surprises the natural order has in store for him. I say "surprises" because up to this point in the movie, the plants of the ground and the animals of the earth and his own body have been nothing but his friends. If anything grew, it just grew on its own. If any beasts pleased him, they did so simply by pleasing themselves. If he sweated before this, it was the honest sweat of physical exertion, not the sweat of frustration at the soil's refusal to bend to his will. And if he feared anything heretofore, it was not with terror but with the prudent fear of letting an elephant step on his foot, or of putting his head in a saber-toothed tiger's mouth. Otherwise, he'd been as cool as a cucumber and bold as brass.

I know. You want to tell me that in the evolutionary scheme of things, this is highly unlikely. Nature, red in tooth and claw, would have scared the hell out of him from the start. I would have hoped that by now you'd gotten bravely over the bad habit of faulting the film of Scripture for its failure to kowtow to histories other than its own. But since you apparently haven't, let me remind you (after nearly four hundred pages of jaw-boning) that what you may think of as a failure is in fact the secret of the biblical movie's success. To see that, all you have to do is watch what the Director shows you *and nothing else* — for the simple reason that she's the Holy Spirit, and her film, *as it stands,* is the Director's cut.

At the risk of repeating myself ad nauseam, history is not something lying around out there waiting to be discovered. It's not "the facts" — it's what the mind makes of the facts. And the Bible's version of that history is what the Mind of history's God most wants you to see. So take it or leave it as you like. But don't think you can take it and then check it out against "objective" reality. That's just a recipe for not liking movies at all.

If those last two paragraphs didn't apply to you, I not only apologize but congratulate you on getting my point. *Deo gratias.* On to verse 17, where the LORD God has just said to Adam, "Because thou hast hearkened unto the voice of thy wife, and hast eaten of the tree, of which I commanded thee, saying, Thou shalt not eat of it . . ." (KJV).

Let me interrupt the text right there. I refuse to read those words as God's endorsement of male superiority. If we want to see them that way, so much the worse for us — not to mention for our behavior as husbands and wives. But it seems to me that all he's really doing here is pointing out the responsibility of both Adam and Eve for what has happened. The true thrust of the curse God is about to utter is that *all* of mankind has fallen, not just one of the sexes. We're not good guys who have been led astray by naughty girls: men, no less than women, have freely ingested the fallen knowledge of good and evil that upsets the balance of nature. Together, not separately, we've set the world at war with God's mysterious tolerance of a rough-and-tumble creation.

But having repeated his command about the tree of the knowledge of good and evil (and, incidentally, having corrected Eve's misquotation about not *touching* the tree), the LORD God now proceeds to his first curse on the male of the species. "Cursed *is* the ground for thy sake" (KJV). In the Hebrew, that's *'arûrah ha'adhamah ba'abhûrekha*: "Cursed will be the ground in your passing [over it]." The Septuagint has *epikataratos hē gē en tois ergois sou*: "Cursed is the earth in your workings [of it]." And the Vulgate has *maledicta terra in opere tuo*: "Cursed is the earth in your work [on it]."

To me, this says plainly that God himself doesn't have to do anything to punish man's transgression because Adam's own upsetting of the equilibrium of the world will be punishment enough. This perhaps was not obvious in earlier times, when Mother Nature seemed quite able to fend for herself. But now that our presumption has given the human race the upper hand, the vulnerability of the natural order becomes clearer every day. Under our mismanagement, whole species are being wiped out at an alarming rate, global warming may well raise the level of the oceans, there's too much ozone on the ground floor of the atmosphere and too many holes in the ozone layer upstairs — and the Van Allen radiation belt threatens to let go and make our radiation pants fall down around our ankles. Nature, in her traitorous trueness to God, still tries to do her best. But her best is no longer a match for our worst.

Fundamentalists, of course, blame this directly on God's wrath at sin. At most, that's only a half-truth. We may indeed hold him ultimately responsible for making free creatures who could wreck the world (the Bible obviously has no qualms about doing so); and we may justly see it as a punishment. But the "directly" is dead wrong. The world goes sour the way month-old milk goes sour: God is to blame only *indirectly* — only because he made things the way he made them. So it isn't God who punishes you with nasty-tasting milk; it's what you've done to the milk by leaving it in a warm room that causes you to spit it down the drain. There's no doubt, of course, that the taste of us may make him so sick that he feels like vomiting us out of his mouth (Rev. 3:16). But in the long run, he's not the one who throws us up. He's the one who is spat out and spat upon — and when he is, he simply swallows hard and takes it.

Above all, though, he doesn't waste his time by getting angry at us. He's not like me on the morning I smashed my alarm clock against the bedroom wall because it stopped during the night. And he's not like my grandson Alexander, whom, when he was two, I renamed Alexander the Not So Great. Back then, I had a wood-burning stove in my living room, and I'd warned him not to touch it. But he did anyway, and he cried. His solution to the pain, however, was not to run to Mommy for comfort. Instead, he became furious with the stove and punished it by hitting it with both hands — to the accompaniment of still louder wails. Had he been older, he might have hired himself a tort lawyer.

The curses of God the Mother, therefore, are not responses to an injury done to *her*. That's just our tactic for dealing with hurts. She may well be angry with us (angrier than we will ever understand), but she doesn't take up arms against us. Rather, the divine Wisdom lays down her arms and lets them be nailed to the cross. Her anger is a Lover's anger; and in the end, it's directed against her own Person — against the Beloved who is God of God, Light of Light, Very God of Very God. *She herself* bears the punishment for our sins.

In John 3:16, we read, "*Thus* God loved the world: he sent his only-begotten Son so that everyone [and *anyone*] who has faith in him might not perish but might have eternal life." The Mother-God isn't waiting for us to straighten up our act before she'll be nice to us: "*While we were still sinners, Christ died for us*" (Rom. 5:8). And that's always been the way it is with her. It's been her way for all the time I've still been a sinner. It is her way while you're still a sinner. And it was her way when Adam and Eve first became sinners. Her Damns are Lover's Damns, and her Love trumps them all. Go back and read the rest of John 3:17-21. And then read Romans 8:1: "There is therefore now no condemnation for those who are in Christ Jesus" — and then remember that there isn't a scrap of creation that isn't already in the Holy Wisdom by whom all things are made.

Back, though, to the rest of verse 17. The KJV reads, "in sorrow shalt thou eat *of* it all the days of thy life." The Hebrew has just that: *b'itstsabhôn tôkhalennah kol y'mê chayekha.* The Septuagint has *en lypais phagēi autēn pasas tas hēmeras tēs zōēs sou:* "in pains [griefs] you will eat it all the days of your life." And the Vulgate reads, *in laboribus comedes eam cunctis diebus vitae tuae:* "in pains [griefs, toils] you will eat it all the days of your life." (The RSV and the NRSV are similar, but both opt for the singular "toil.") Once again, nature is both loyal to God and deceitful to us; but even in our lapses (*lapsus* is the Latin for *the fall*), God the Mother is true to herself. On to verses 18 and 19, and to more of nature's revenge.

The KJV reads them thus: 18 "Thorns also and thistles shall it bring forth to thee; and thou shalt eat the herb of the field; 19 In the sweat of thy face shalt thou eat bread, till thou return unto the ground; for out of it wast thou taken: for dust thou *art,* and unto dust shalt thou return." Let me give you just the salient words. "Thorns also and thistles" is *v'qôts v'dhardar, akanthas kai tribolous,* and *spinas et tribulos.* "The herb of the field" is an echo of Genesis 2:5: *'esebh hassadheh, ton chorton tou agrou,* and *herbas terrae.* "In the sweat of thy face" is *b'ze'ath 'appekha, en hidrōti prosōpou sou,* and *in sudore vultus tui.* "Dust" is *'aphar, gē* [earth], and *pulvis.* And "bread" (the Bible's first mention of a *human* creation) is *lechem, ton arton,* and *pane.*

Let me make a short digression here. In some circles (among archaeologists and paleontologists, for example), it's often said that the biblical story of the Fall of the human race is actually the beginning of civilization. For them, the Neolithic period some seven or eight millennia ago — and the agricultural "revolution" that accompanied it — are the very things that made *cities* possible. They point out that the concentration of human beings in towns and villages could not have happened until the old hunter-gatherer societies had given way to new associations of human beings: farmers who raised crops, and city dwellers who were dependent on them for their food supply.

Plausible as that may sound, I think it represents a failure to watch what the movie of the Bible in fact shows us. The history that the Director's film gives us points precisely to the opposite conclusion. The City appears *before* the Fall, not after it; and it shows up *flourishing* in the Garden of Eden in the second chapter of Genesis. Therefore, the story of the Fall in chapter 3 is not the *beginning* of civilization but the first intimation of its *downfall.* I won't belabor the point here, because I've already made it previously by quoting Francis Thompson:

> I tempted all His servitors, but to find
> My own betrayal in their constancy,

In faith to Him their fickleness to me,
    Their traitorous trueness, and their loyal deceit.

Accordingly, the "thorns and thistles" of the LORD's curses on Adam, and the warning that he would "eat bread" in the "sweat" of his face, are nothing less than the "traitorous trueness" of God's servitor, Mother Nature — the "loyal deceit" by which she takes her revenge for our tampering with God's ecology of good and evil. They're the *backfire* of the engine of the City that we spoiled by substituting the low-octane gasoline of control for the premium-grade fuel of God's control-free management of creation.

But since I've already commented on this, I'll add just two remarks on the last part of verse 19. For one thing, "dust thou art, and unto dust shalt thou return" is the LORD's first mention of *death* as a punishment for the Fall in chapter 3 of Genesis. These words, to be sure, are familiar to anyone who knows the old burial rites of the church; but they also strike a blow against the mischievous doctrine of the immortality of the soul. They state clearly that when we go, we're *gone*. We may build our cemeteries as *cities* of the dead, but their citizens have no continuing city here.

On balance, then, the Bible never promises us a half-death in which our mortal body goes to corruption in the ground but our imperishable soul floats up to God on its own steam. Instead, it promises us that when we die, both soul and body will go back into the nothing out of which they were made. And when we rise, the Word who brought us out of nothing to begin with will simply do the same trick again — because while we've lost everything, he's never lost us. His new creation is just his old creation, *restored.*

Death may now be our enemy, but it's never been God's. Look at Psalm 116:15: *Pretiosa in conspectu Domini mors sanctorum ejus:* "Precious in the sight of the LORD is the death of all his holy creatures." God loves death because he's made it the engine of all life; *every* new something rises out of the same lovely nothing that's always been his cup of tea. In the Counting-House of the Trinity, the Father gleefully sifts the coins of death through the Fingers of his Two Hands, his Word and his Spirit. He *plays* with them because the money of the world's deaths is as precious to him as the money of its lives. And in the Treasury of the Three-in-One, there's just no counting at all. Even here, where God curses Adam with the common death of all living things, it's not a threat but a promise of life.

And with that, let me conclude this chapter by giving you Whoopi's take on Adam's curse. Speaking as the all-revealing Spirit, the *Rûach Adonai,* she praises Adam with faint damns:

"Okay, Handsome, now it's your turn. I had great hopes for you. I told you to be fruitful and multiply, and I gave you dominion over the fish of the sea, and the birds of the air, and over every living thing that moves upon the earth. But you blew it. You turned dominion into domination, and you made a mess of my lovely world. So now it's time for the world's answer, not mine. Thorns and thistles are coming your way, Charlie, not to mention pushy vegetarians. Salvation by hard work, tofu, wheat germ, and pure thoughts will be the best you'll come up with. None of it will work, of course; but you'll still sweat your way through it, and you'll turn Mother Nature into a real mother. Worse yet, you'll eventually pin the whole rap on me.

"Buster, you are one nasty piece of work. But you underestimate me: I have such good plans for you, they'll take your breath away. Now, you get only a hint; but when I finally do take the rap for you, you'll see. I'll clam up before my accusers. I'll die the death you can only dread. I'll rise with your nature restored. And I'll take you home to Big Daddy. But even now, Bubbuleh, I have you up my sleeve. Just you wait and see."

*   *   *

At last, then, the light at the end of the tunnel — and the end of my labors.

TWENTY-FOUR

The Expulsion:
The First Proclamation of the Gospel

GENESIS 3:20-24

For this final go-around, let's begin directly with the text:

LXX Gen. 3:20 καὶ ἐκάλεσεν Αδαμ τὸ ὄνομα τῆς γυναικὸς αὐτοῦ Ζωή ὅτι αὕτη μήτηρ πάντων τῶν ζώντων 21 καὶ ἐποίησεν κύριος ὁ θεὸς τῷ Αδαμ καὶ τῇ γυναικὶ αὐτοῦ χιτῶνας δερματίνους καὶ ἐνέδυσεν αὐτούς 22 καὶ εἶπεν ὁ θεός ἰδοὺ Αδαμ γέγονεν ὡς εἷς ἐξ ἡμῶν τοῦ γινώσκειν καλὸν καὶ πονηρόν καὶ νῦν μήποτε ἐκτείνῃ τὴν χεῖρα καὶ λάβῃ τοῦ ξύλου τῆς ζωῆς καὶ φάγῃ καὶ ζήσεται εἰς τὸν αἰῶνα 23 καὶ ἐξαπέστειλεν αὐτὸν κύριος ὁ θεὸς ἐκ τοῦ παραδείσου τῆς τρυφῆς ἐργάζεσθαι τὴν γῆν ἐξ ἧς ἐλήμφθη 24 καὶ ἐξέβαλεν τὸν Αδαμ καὶ κατῴκισεν αὐτὸν ἀπέναντι τοῦ πα-ραδείσου τῆς τρυφῆς καὶ

BHS Gen. 3:20 וַיִּקְרָ֧א הָֽאָדָ֛ם שֵׁ֥ם אִשְׁתּ֖וֹ חַוָּ֑ה כִּ֛י הִ֥וא הָֽיְתָ֖ה אֵ֥ם כָּל־חָֽי׃ 21 וַיַּעַשׂ֩ יְהוָ֨ה אֱלֹהִ֜ים לְאָדָ֧ם וּלְאִשְׁתּ֛וֹ כָּתְנ֥וֹת ע֖וֹר וַיַּלְבִּשֵֽׁם׃ 22 וַיֹּ֣אמֶר ׀ יְהוָ֣ה אֱלֹהִ֗ים הֵ֤ן הָֽאָדָם֙ הָיָה֙ כְּאַחַ֣ד מִמֶּ֔נּוּ לָדַ֖עַת ט֣וֹב וָרָ֑ע וְעַתָּ֣ה ׀ פֶּן־יִשְׁלַ֣ח יָד֗וֹ וְלָקַח֙ גַּ֚ם מֵעֵ֣ץ הַֽחַיִּ֔ים וְאָכַ֖ל וָחַ֥י לְעֹלָֽם׃ 23 וַֽיְשַׁלְּחֵ֛הוּ יְהוָ֥ה אֱלֹהִ֖ים מִגַּן־עֵ֑דֶן לַֽעֲבֹד֙ אֶת־הָ֣אֲדָמָ֔ה אֲשֶׁ֥ר לֻקַּ֖ח מִשָּֽׁם׃ 24 וַיְגָ֖רֶשׁ אֶת־הָֽאָדָ֑ם וַיַּשְׁכֵּן֩ מִקֶּ֨דֶם לְגַן־עֵ֜דֶן אֶת־הַכְּרֻבִ֗ים וְאֵ֨ת לַ֤הַט הַחֶ֙רֶב֙ הַמִּתְהַפֶּ֔כֶת לִשְׁמֹ֕ר אֶת־דֶּ֖רֶךְ עֵ֥ץ הַֽחַיִּֽים׃

VUL Gen. 3:20 et vocavit Adam nomen uxoris suae Hava eo quod mater esset cunctorum viventium 21 fecit quoque Dominus Deus Adam et uxori eius tunicas pellicias et induit eos 22 et ait ecce Adam factus est quasi unus ex nobis sciens bonum et malum nunc ergo ne forte mittat manum suam et sumat etiam de ligno vitae et comedat et vivat in aeternum 23 emisit eum Dominus Deus de paradiso voluptatis ut operaretur terram de qua sumptus est 24 eiecitque Adam et conlocavit ante paradisum voluptatis cherubin et flammeum gladium atque versatilem ad custodiendam viam ligni vitae

ἔταξεν τὰ χερουβιμ καὶ τὴν
φλογίνην ῥομφαίαν τὴν
στρεφομένην φυλάσσειν τὴν
ὁδὸν τοῦ ξύλου τῆς ζωῆς

KJV Gen. 3:20 And Adam called his wife's name Eve; because she was the mother of all living. 21 Unto Adam also and to his wife did the LORD God make coats of skins, and clothed them. 22 And the LORD God said, Behold, the man is become as one of us, to know good and evil: and now, lest he put forth his hand, and take also of the tree of life, and eat, and live for ever: 23 Therefore the LORD God sent him forth from the garden of Eden, to till the ground from whence he was taken. 24 So he drove out the man; and he placed at the east of the garden of Eden Cherubims, and a flaming sword which turned every way, to keep the way of the tree of life.	RSV Gen. 3:20 The man called his wife's name Eve, because she was the mother of all living. 21 And the LORD God made for Adam and for his wife garments of skins, and clothed them. 22 Then the LORD God said, "Behold, the man has become like one of us, knowing good and evil; and now, lest he put forth his hand and take also of the tree of life, and eat, and live for ever" — 23 therefore the LORD God sent him forth from the garden of Eden, to till the ground from which he was taken. 24 He drove out the man; and at the east of the garden of Eden he placed the cherubim, and a flaming sword which turned every way, to guard the way to the tree of life.	NRSV Gen. 3:20 The man named his wife Eve, because she was the mother of all living. 21 And the LORD God made garments of skins for the man and for his wife, and clothed them. 22 Then the LORD God said, "See, the man has become like one of us, knowing good and evil; and now, he might reach out his hand and take also from the tree of life, and eat, and live for-ever" — 23 therefore the LORD God sent him forth from the garden of Eden, to till the ground from which he was taken. 24 He drove out the man; and at the east of the garden of Eden he placed the cherubim, and a sword flaming and turning to guard the way to the tree of life.

The KJV has "And Adam called his wife's name Eve; because she was the mother of all living." In spite of the fact that I've used "Eve" for "the woman" for so many chapters, we've only now reached the first point in Genesis at which her name is mentioned. In the Hebrew it's *chavvah;* in the Septuagint, *Zōē;* in the Vulgate, *Hava;* and in all three English versions, "Eve." As you may have noticed, it can be taken as a proper name (like Gertrude), or as a title (like "Actress"), or as both. *Chavvah* leaves all the options open; *Zōē* ("Life") is strictly a title; and *Hava,* like Eve, takes it as a proper name. But just to make sure that no translators will miss the *double entendre,* the Hebrew adds *kî hî' hay'thah 'em' kol-chay,* "because she was the mother of all living [presumably, of all living human beings]." Only the KJV uses "Adam" as a proper name here; the RSV and the NRSV — unnecessarily, I think — switch back to translating *ha'adham* literally as "the man."

In any event, the "mother of all living" brings up not only the subject of human reproduction but also its *sine qua non,* human sexuality. Obviously, Adam and Eve had no children in Eden. But just in case I haven't made myself clear, I don't think sexual intercourse between them *before* the Fall should be ruled out. If they were "naked and not ashamed" at the end of Genesis 2, I would assume that they enjoyed all the prerogatives of such a blissful state — and that they felt no need for a vow of celibacy. But my more practical reason for suggesting that they had conjugal visits in Genesis 2 is that I want to stay miles away from the notion that the *exercise* of their sexuality was a result of the Fall. If the animal and vegetable orders of creation could couple the minute they were made — and above all, if God told the human race, male and female, to "be fruitful and multiply" as soon as he created them — why the rush to deny all that by making their first intercourse lecherous? Why delay their first sex until it could be only naughty sex?

Just a few nights ago, Valerie watched a movie called *Innocence* on the Sundance channel. She told me that it first showed Adam and Eve, both naked, looking at each other with curious, admiring eyes, and touching one another with innocent fascination. But after they ate of the fruit of the tree (*figs,* in fact — many of them), they went into a hiding place, and their eyes burned with lust. *That,* I said, was biblical and theological nonsense. But sadly, it's what almost all people — with a big assist from the church on its worst days — think is the Bible's teaching: namely, that human sexual intercourse was a sin from the start, not a sweet that the first couple soured. They seem to think that it wasn't even invented until it could appear as forbidden.

But enough of my complaining; on to verse 21. "And the LORD God made for Adam and his wife coats of skins, and clothed them" (RFC). "Coats of skins" is *kathnôth 'ôr* in the Hebrew, *chitōnas dermatinous* in the Septuagint, and *tunicas pellicias* in the Vulgate. It appears as "coats of skins" in the KJV, and as "garments" in the RSV and NRSV. Having already given you those coats as God's merciful sense of couture, however — having taken them as his provision of something more elegant than the scratchy fig leaves that now covered the nakedness of Adam and Eve — I'll go right to something I find more central to this chapter's text.

Since skins are taken only from dead animals, the Director would seem to have only two choices for filming this sequence. Either she'll show the LORD God taking them from animals already dead, or she'll show him killing them himself. But whichever she chooses, the LORD's Hands will be wrist-deep in blood and death. And therefore this is more than a hint of the Good

News: it's precisely the first proclamation of the Gospel of death and resurrection. The stylish leather garments God gives them rise out of the animals' hides, which thus become sacraments of his Incarnate Word; and they'll be worn by Adam and Eve, who, without knowing it, are also sacraments of the Word. When they leave the Garden, they'll walk out as real presences of the Christ before Christ.

Moreover, the reverberations of those coats will echo throughout the biblical movie. The "mark" of Cain the murderer (Gen. 4) will be put on him for protection, making him a type of Christ; Joseph's brothers will put the blood of a dead goat on his coat of many colors (Gen. 37), marking him as their unsuspected Savior; the Passover lamb (Exod. 12) will die as a figure of the Paschal Lamb himself; the animal victims of the Temple sacrifices will die as anticipations of him who is both Priest and Victim; Jesus, the ultimate revelation of the Word Incarnate, will die and rise in all four Gospels with the scars of his Passion in the skin of his body. And in the end, the saints — whose death is precious to the Lord — will wash their robes and make them white in the blood of the Lamb (Rev. 7:14).

By now, you may have had enough of my rhapsodies on biblical concordances. But I have no intention of stopping them this late in the game. I've always been fond of making such lists, but you can blame Augustine for my present love affair with them. The writing of this book, as I look over it, has led me to the sincerest form of flattery — to the imitation of his style. I think that comes from the fact that while I've read some of his works in English translations, I've read *De Genesi ad Litteram* only in Latin. Only in the compression of his original tongue do the scriptural passages he quotes sparkle like jewels on the dark velvet of his theologizing. So if all his Latin that I've quoted and translated strikes you as bragging on my part, so be it. The quibbles of better Latinists than I will be quite punishment enough. But as a wise mechanic once said, "If you can do it, it's not bragging." Therefore, thank you, Augustine. You were always one of my favorite fathers; now, you're one of my best friends.

On to verse 22. What begins here is nothing less than the final vectoring of creation onto the landing strip of the City of God. "And the LORD God said, Behold, the man is become as one of us, to know good and evil . . ." (KJV). Once again, the mysterious divine "Us" creeps into the script (as it did in Genesis 1:26); and once again, I have no qualms about seeing it as an intimation of the Trinity. So much so, that I think the Director will now bring on *five* voices for God (her original four-part chorus of soprano, alto, tenor, and bass, plus Whoopi Goldberg) to speak his words. Perhaps she'll make the voice of James Earl Jones predominate in KJV English, with the others chiming along more softly in Hebrew, Greek, and Latin.

Be that as it may, the Hebrew for the start of the LORD's words in this verse is *hen ha'adham hayah k'achad mimmenû:* "Behold, the man has become as one of us." The Septuagint has almost the same thing: *idou Adam gegonen hōs heis ex hēmōn:* "Behold, Adam has become as one of us." And the Vulgate (having omitted the reference to LORD God) has *et ait ecce Adam factus est quasi unus ex nobis:* "and he said, Behold, the man has become like one of us." The "knowing of good and evil," as it appears here, is still a knowledge of them in warfare rather than at peace; but it's presented in the infinitive "to know": *ladha'ath tôbh vara'* in the Hebrew, and in the Septuagint, *tou ginōskein kalon kai ponēron.* The Vulgate, the RSV, and the NRSV all opt for making it a participle: *sciens,* "knowing," and "knowing."

But then, in the rest of verse 22, comes the Mercy of God: "And now, lest he put forth his hand, and take also of the tree of life, and eat, and live forever . . ." (KJV). I'll skip the word lists here and come straight to my point. The Director has kept the Tree of Life in her back pocket ever since Genesis 2. All along, right from the LORD's making of the *'adham* from the clay, it's been the sacrament of man's immortality in God. Now, though, it's about to go into hiding: it will appear mysteriously, under still other signs, until it finally reappears in glory in the New Jerusalem. And the reason for that hiding? Well, you look at the text and tell me if I'm wrong. Isn't it precisely so that Adam's death can excuse him from an unwinnable war — so that he won't live forever as damned by God? Doesn't it have grace and mercy written all over it?

Run your eyes over the words themselves. "Forever" is *l"olam,* "to the age," in the Hebrew; *eis ton aiōna,* "into the age," in the Septuagint; and *in aeternum,* "to eternity [forever]," in the Vulgate. For me, there's no question that the God of Genesis clearly intended the Tree of Life to be the sacrament of eternal life — of a happy eschatological party at which the whole creation would rise in the resurrection of the human race. But the sequestering of the Tree at this point is far from a reneging on that promise. It's still the same promise — but now adapted to the circumstances of our fallen history. Since we have mired ourselves in a condition that, were it to go on forever, would make only an unhappy *eschaton,* God comes up with his saving "lest," his divine *In Order That Not.* The Hebrew is *v"attah pen-yishlach yadhô v'laqach gam me'êts hachayyîm vachay l"olam:* "And now, lest he put forth his hand, and take also of the tree of life, and live forever." The Septuagint has *kai nyn mēpote ekteinēi tēn cheira kai labēi tou xylou tēs zōēs kai zēsetai eis ton aiōna* (the same). And the Vulgate reads, *nunc ergo ne forte mittat manum suam et sumat etiam de ligno vitae et comedat et vivat in aeternum* (the same).

Do you see? God knows that any immortality we could fake out for ourselves in our present state would be only an everlasting disaster. So he won't risk it. He will bar the way of the Tree of Life and send us forth to die in the ship-wreck of our history. *But he will follow us through the rocks and billows, and he will never fail us or forsake us.* On the cross of his beloved Son, he will bring back the Tree of Life and plant it at last in the midst of the world's eternal Home. Even in this forbidding passage, all shall be well, and all manner of thing shall be well. Whether by threats or by promises, God wills us to live forever.

On, then, to verse 23, the expulsion that is itself the promise: "There-fore the Lord God sent him forth from the garden of Eden, to till the ground from whence he was taken" (KJV). The Hebrew for "sent him forth" is *vay'shall'chehû*; the Septuagint has *kai exapesteilen auton,* "and he sent him out"; and the Vulgate has *emisit eum,* "he sent him out." And once again, the place from which he was evicted is named differently in the three ancient texts. The Hebrew makes it *miggan-'edhen,* "from the garden of Eden [or pleasure]"; the Septuagint reads, *ek tou paradeisou tēs tryphēs,* "out of the paradise of pleasure"; and the Vulgate has *de paradiso voluptatis,* "from the paradise of pleasure."

Adam leaves behind him an agreeable life of ease and goes out "to till the ground from whence he was taken." In the Hebrew, that's *la'abhodh 'eth-ha'adhamah 'asher luqach,* "to work the ground he was taken from." In the Septuagint, it's *ergazesthai tēn gēn ex hēs elēmphthē,* "to work the earth out of which he was taken." And in the Vulgate, it's *ut operaretur terram de qua sumptus est,* "that he might work the earth from which he was taken." (All three English versions read "work" as "till" — which has the virtue of speci-ficity but lacks the overtone of penal servitude.)

But even as he's driven out of the Garden, Adam is still a dead ringer for the Christ himself. In Mark 1:12-13, immediately after Jesus' baptism, "the Spirit *drives him out [ekballei auton]* into the desert to be tested by the devil." Just as Jesus the Christ leaves thirty quiet years behind him and goes out to be tested by the devil and to breathe his last for a recalcitrant world, so the same Christ in Adam leaves paradise to work the ground of an uncooperative cre-ation and to die of exhaustion. These two evictions, however, are part and parcel of the single Great Work of the Incarnate Word. Adam's expulsion into the desert of history is the part — indeed, it's the first of many such parts — of the Work that will be repeated again and again (Joseph sold into slavery, Is-rael put into bondage in Egypt, the Jews driven into the wilderness, Jerusalem led away into captivity). But Jesus, despised and rejected, will be the ultimate Parcel in which all those sad parts will be wrapped and delivered to his Father. But for our estrangèd faces, we will have been at home from the beginning.

This text thus becomes the first hint of the *anakephalaiōsis* — of the *re-capitulation,* of the "retelling" of creation's history in the Incarnate Word —

in the very thick of its woes. "While we were still sinners, Christ died for us." Our reconciliation in him has always been the deepest truth about us. It dawned for us on day one of the world, and it will dawn on us the minute we trust it. *He tells our story right, even while we're telling it wrong.* And the New Testament finally spells out that recapitulation in Ephesians 1:6-10.

The writer of this passage says that the Sonship of Jesus has been given to us for the praise of the Father's glorious grace, which he has granted to us *in the Beloved.* But he then goes on to say that *in him* "we have the redemption through his blood, the forgiveness of trespasses according to the richness of his grace, which has abounded for us in all wisdom and understanding. He made known to us the mystery of his will according to his good pleasure, which *he established beforehand in him* as an economy [*oikonomian*] for the fulfillment of the world's seasons, to recapitulate [*anakephalaiōsasthai*] everything [*ta panta*] in the Christ — the things in the heavens and the things on the earth" (RFC).

That *beforehand* mystery of the Father's Will is not an editorial correction he wrote into history at some point prior to its final publication on Jesus' birthday. As the author of Ephesians said almost at the beginning of his letter (Eph. 1:4), the Father "has chosen us in him *pro katabolēs kosmou,* before the foundation of the world." The Incarnation of the Father's Word, therefore, has never not been in the works. In fact, it's the root and ground of the universe. We breathed it in with our first breath; and when we breathe our last, it will still be the Breath of God, the *Rûach Adonai,* the *Creator Spiritus,* the *Amor Mutuus* of the Father and the Son. Even while the Spirit is driving us out into a fallen world, she's moving us on into the reconciled creation.

At long last, we're ready for the expulsion as the first proclamation of the Gospel. The KJV reads, "So he drove out the man; and he placed at the east of the garden of Eden Cherubims, and a flaming sword which turned every way, to keep the way of the tree of life." "He drove" is *vay'gharesh 'eth-ha'adham,* "and he drove out the man," in the Hebrew; *kai exebalen ton Adam* in the Septuagint (the same, except for "Adam" as a proper name); and *eiecitque Adam* in the Vulgate (the same). The RSV and the NRSV follow the KJV, but the NRSV omits the consecutive "and."

The stunning images of the Angel and the Flaming Sword were practically the first things I thought of when I began this book; but alas, they've caught many theologians asleep at the interpretive switch. They see only a forbidding God — and, to be sure, there's no question that they're meant to tell Adam, "You can't go back to paradise; you can only go forward into the mess you've made." But given our inveterate longing to find some unsullied state that will return us to our lost happiness, that warning can never be taken too seriously. We invent unfallen worlds at the drop of a hat, yet all we ever pick up are the same old battered hats. An Atlantis, perhaps, or a Middle Earth, or some unspoiled planet orbiting a distant star. But we put them on as if they were our return ticket to paradise.

At this writing, though, those unfallen worlds have never been found. So we dream up other exercises that will bring us to bliss without having to move an inch. It doesn't matter what they are (sex, drugs, diets, meditation, spirituality). None of them can mend a world that won't listen. And even if some day we do find a perfect planet and go there as settlers, we'll be nothing but the Typhoid Marys of outer space. If its inhabitants were wise, they'd never let us land.

This, I suppose, is what God had in Mind when he stationed the Cherubim at the gate of Eden to protect it from violation. In the Hebrew, those heavenly beings are *hakk'rubhim,* and in the Septuagint and the Vulgate, they're *ta cheroubim* and *cherubin.* And the KEEP OUT sign, the "Flaming Sword turning every way," is *lahat hacherebh hammithhappecheth, tēn phloginēn hromphaian tēn strephomenēn,* and *flammeum gladium atque versatilem.* But both are on guard duty "to keep the way of the tree of life" (KJV). The RSV and NRSV have "guard" the way to the Tree of Life. The Hebrew has *lishmor 'eth-derekh 'ets hachayyîm;* the Septuagint, *phylassein tēn hodon tou xylou tēs zōēs;* and the Vulgate, *ad custodiendam viam ligni vitae —* all meaning the same thing.

But the Angel and the Flaming Sword are not simply *blocking* the way of the Tree of Life. Together, they stand as our perpetual reminder that eternal life has always been God's will for us. If you can accept it, they're the light at the *beginning* of the tunnel of our history; and all through our trip down that dismal cave, they will also stand behind us as the flickering promise that the same Light will be waiting for us at the *end* of the tunnel. We may never try to go back, or even look back. We may only pine for the lost loves that come to us in dreams of sentimental poignancy. But at the beginning and the end of our history stands the iron poignancy of God's irreversible *re-membering* of his lost world.

"If I forget thee, O Jerusalem, let my right hand forget *her cunning.* If I do not remember thee, let my tongue cleave to the roof of my mouth; if I prefer not Jerusalem above my chief joy" (Ps. 137:5-6, KJV). Or, as the second Isaiah puts it in God's own words (Isa. 49:13-16, KJV), "Sing, O heavens; and be joyful, O earth; and break forth into singing, O mountains: for the LORD hath comforted his people, and will have mercy upon his afflicted. But Zion said, The LORD hath forsaken me, and my Lord hath forgotten me. Can a woman forget her sucking child, that she should not have compassion on the son of her womb? yea, they may forget, yet will I not forget thee. Behold, I have graven thee upon the palms of *my* hands; thy walls *are* continually before me."

"Upon the palms of my Hands." In the flesh of the Left Hand of God — on the hands of his Incarnate Word — God the Father has graven the unforgettable "Very Good" he uttered in the Beginning. And by the brooding of the Right Hand of God — of the Spirit who is the *Dextrae Dei Digitus* — he has never ceased to warm the creation he remembers.

Still, there's more. The spear wound in his side, from which the blood of his sacrifice and the water of his grace come forth into the world, is also the opening at the far end of the tunnel of our captivity. The lance that made the wound is none other than the Flaming Sword, now quenched and tempered by the blood and water of the Word. And the Angels who rolled the rock from the mouth of Jesus' tomb are the Cherubim, now relieved of guard duty at the gate of Eden. They proclaim that the way of the Tree of Life has been reopened, because the Way, the Truth, and the Life himself has risen gloriously from the dead.

History is about to come full circle. Nothing has ever seriously gone wrong. He has made all things new.

Amen. Amen. Amen.